ISBN: 9781313987035

Published by:
HardPress Publishing
8345 NW 66TH ST #2561
MIAMI FL 33166-2626

Email: info@hardpress.net
Web: http://www.hardpress.net

LYDGATE'S
FALL OF PRINCES

EDITED BY

HENRY BERGEN

PART III.

(Books VI.–IX.)

The Carnegie Institution of Washington
Washington, 1923

LYDGATE'S FALL OF PRINCES

PART III.

BOOKS VI.-IX.

THE DAUNCE OF MACHABREE

CONTENTS OF PART III.

Book VI 675–773

Book VII 775–821

Book VIII 823–918

Book IX 918–1022

Greneacre's Envoy on Bochas 1023

The Daunce of Machabree 1025–1044

ERRATA

P. 733, line 2172: *read* thassaut.
P. 889, line 2363: *for* epsecial *read* especial.

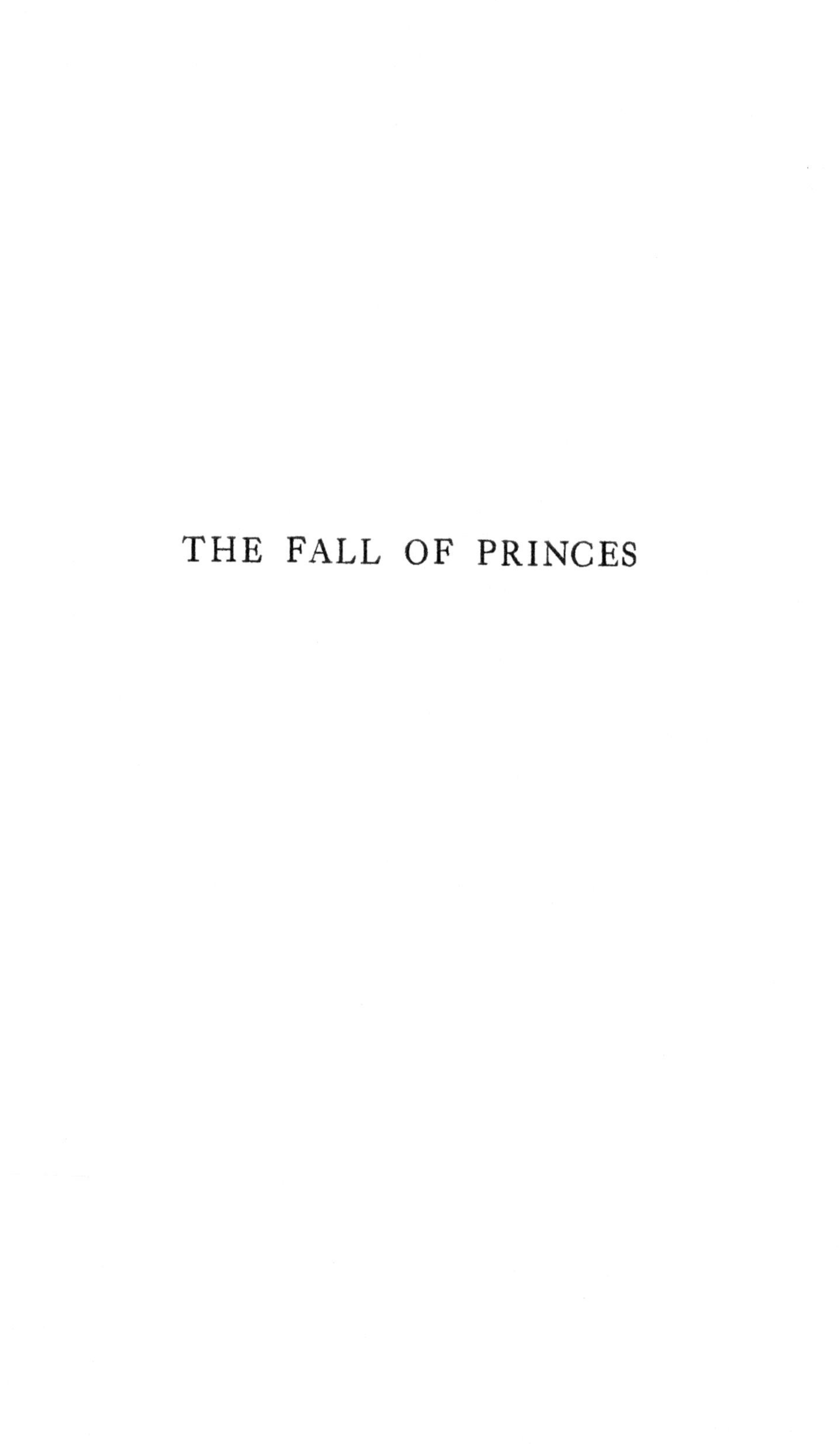

THE FALL OF PRINCES

BOOK VI

[Here Bochas sittyng in his studie allone writeth a grete processe, how Fortune like a monstruous ymage hauyng an hu*n*dred handys appered vn to hi*m* and spak / and Bochas vn to hir makyng betwixt he*m* bothe many grete argume*n*tys & resou*n*s of Fortunys chau*n*c*es*.] [1]

IN his studie allone as Boch*as* stood, [p. 298]
His pen*n*e on honde, of sodey*n* aue*n*ture
To reme*m*bre he thouhte it ded hy*m* good,
How þ*at* no ma*n* may hymsilff assure
In worldli thynges fulli to recure
Grace of Fortune, to make hir to be stable,
Hir dayli chau*n*gis been so variable.

As Bochas stood alone in his study, pen in hand, musing on the vicissitudes of Fortune,

She braideth euer on the chau*n*teplure:
Now song, now wepy*n*g, now wo, now gladnesse,
Now in merthe, now peynis to eendure,
Now liht, now heuy, now bittir, now suetnesse,
Now in trouble, now free, now in distresse,
Shewyng to vs a maner resemblau*n*ce,
How* worldli welthe hath heer non assurau*n*ce.

who turns ever from woe to gladness, and from mirth to trouble, shewing that there is no assurance in worldly wealth,

Whil Bochas pensiff stood sool in his librarie
With cheer oppressid, pale in his visage,
Sumdeel abasshed, alone & solitarie,
To hym appered a monstruous ymage,
Partid on tweyne of colo*u*r & corage,
Hir riht[e] side ful of somer flo*u*rs,
The tothir oppressid with wyntris stormy sho*u*rs.

a marvelous woman appeared to him, her right side decked with summer flowers, her left side beaten by winter storms.

Bochas astonid, feerful for to abraide
Wha*n* he beheeld the wonderful figure
Of Fortune, thus to hymsilff he saide:
"What may this meene? is this a creature
Or a monstre t*r*ansffoormyd agey*n*s nature,
Whos bren*n*yng eyen sparklyng of ther liht
As doon sterris the frosti wyntres niht?"

Bochas was dumbfounded and afraid to speak. He said to himself, "What is this creature or monster, whose eyes burn like the stars on a frosty night?"

2. on] in H. 6. 1st to] *om*. H.
9. song now wepy*n*g] syng now wepe H. 12. 1st in] *om*. H.
14. How] No B, J, H, R 3, H 5, P. 17. abaisshed R.
22. abraide] brayde R.

[1] MS. J. leaf 121 recto.

Her face was cruel and terrible, her hair untressed, her figure loathsome, and she had 100 hands.

And of hir cheer[e] ful good heed he took,
Hir face seemyng cruel & terrible,
And bi disdeyn[e] manacyng of look,
Hir her vntressid, hard, sharp & horrible,
Froward of shappe, lothsum & odible.
An hundred handis she hadde on ech part
In sondri wise hir giftes to depart.

which [illegible] men up to high estate and cast them down into adversity.

Summe off hir handis lefft up men aloffte
To hih estat of worldli dignite,
Anothir hand griped ful vnsoffte,
Which cast another in gret aduersite:
Gaff oon richesse, anothir pouerte,
Gaff summe also bi report a good name,
Noised anothir of sclaundre &* diffame.

Her garment was of many colours, the pale blue of feigned constancy, gold mingled with the green of change, black for mourning, russet brown for labour;

Hir habit was of manyfold colours:
Wachet bleuh of feyned stedfastnesse,
Hir gold allaied like sonne in wattri shours,
Meynt with liht greene for chaung & doubilnesse.
A pretens red: dreed meynt with hardynesse;
Whiht for clennesse, lik soone for to faille;
Feynt blak for moornyng, russet for trauaille.

all in harmony with her changeable nature.

Hir colours meynt of wollis mo than oon;
Sumwhile eclipsed, sumwhile she shon briht.
Dulle as an asse whan men hadde haste to gon,
And as a swalwe gerissh of hir fliht,
Tween slouh & swifft; now crokid & now vpriht,
Now as a crepil lowe coorbid doun,
Now a duery and now a champioun.

Sometimes she is a coward, sometimes as bold as a lion; sometimes Croesus, sometimes Agamemnon; to-day a man, to-morrow a woman.

Now a coward, durst nat come in pres,
And* sumwhile hardi as leoun;
Now lik Ector, now dreedful Thersites,
Now was she Cresus, now Agamenoun,
Sardanapallus off condicioun;
Now was she mannyssh, now was she femynyne,
Now coude she reyne, now koude she falsli shyne.

34. hundrith H. 42. &] & off B, R.
44. stedfastnesse] stablenesse H, stabilnesse R 3.
45. sonne] golde H. 48. Whiht] which R.
49. 2nd for] off R. 50. meynt] ment H. 53. Swalouh H.
56. and] an R.
58. And] Now B, R, J — as] as a P.
60. 2nd now] now was she H.

Now a mermaide angelik off face,
A tail behynde verray serpentyne,
Now debonaire, now froward to do grace,
Now as a lamb tretable & benigne,
Now lik a wolff of nature to maligne,
Now Sirenes to synge folk a-slepe
Til Karibdis drowne hem in the deepe.

Now a mermaid with angelic face and the tail of a serpent; now a lamb and again a wolf.

Thus Iohn Bochas consideryng hir figure,
Al hir fetures in ordre he gan beholde,
Hir breede, hir heihte, hir shap & hir stature,
An hu*n*drid handis & armys ther he tolde:
Wheroff astonid, his herte gan to colde;
And among alle hir membris euerichon,
He sempte she hadde no feet upon to gon.

John Bochas looked at her well, and after observing her features one after another, his heart grew cold. It seemed to him that she had no feet to walk upon;

And whil that he considered al this thyng,
Atween[e] tweyne, as it wer in a trau*n*ce,
She sodenli toward hym lookyng,
He conceyued be hir contenau*n*ce, —
Wer it for ire, wer it for plesau*n*ce,
Outher for fauour, outher for disdeyn, —
Bi the maner she wolde su*m*what seyn.

and while he stood as in a trance, she turned to him and said,

Lookyng a-scoign as she had had disdeyn, [p. 299]
"Bochas," quod she, "I knowe al thyn entent,
How thou trauailest, besiest the in veyn,
In thi studie euer dilligent,
Now in the west, now in the orient
To serche stories, north & meredien,
Of worthi p*r*incis that heer-toforn ha been.

"Bochas, I know what you are about, searching out stories of worthy princes,

Sum*m*e duellid vndir the pool Artyk,
Be my fauour vpreised to the sterris;
Othir vndir the pool Antartik,
Which in contrarye from vs so ferr is.
Sum*m*e encresid & set up bi the werris,
Lik as me list ther tryu*m*phes to auau*n*ce;*
Frownyng on othir, I brouht hem to myschau*n*ce.

upon whom I have smiled or frowned.

I see the besi remembryng be scriptures
Stories of pryncis in eueri man*er* age,
As my fauour folwed ther auentures,

"I have seen you describing their deeds in plain unadorned language,

73. heihte] length R.
77. He] Hym H.
97. to auaunce] tauau*n*ce B.

Be humble stile set in pley*n* langage, —
Nat maad corious be non auau*n*tage
Of rethoriques, with musis for to stryue,
But in pleyn foorme ther deedis to descryue.

diligently giving them praise or blame, as they deserve.
"Some were extolled to Jupiter with a trumpet of gold.

In which processe thou dost gret dilligence,
As thei disserue to yiue hem thank or blame:
Settest up oon in roiall excellence
Withyn*ne* myn hous callid the Hous of Fame, —
The goldene tru*m*pet *with* blastis off good name
Enhau*n*ceth oon to ful hih[e] parties,
Wher Iubiter sit among the heuenli skies.

while others, with the blast of a sable trumpet, were plunged down from their royal estate.

Anothir tru*m*pet, of sownis ful vengable,
Which bloweth up at feestis funerall,
Nothyng briht[e], but of colo*u*r sable,
Fer fro my fauo*u*r, dedli & mortall,
To plonge pryncis from ther estat roiall,
Whan I am wroth, to make hem loute lowe,
Than of malis I do that tru*m*pet blowe.

"You have concealed nothing, spared neither their crowns nor their purple robes, but given them their deserts.

Thou hast writyn & set togidre in gros,
Lik ther desert worldli men*n*ys deedis,
Nothyng conceled nor vndr[e] couert cloos,
Spared [not] ther crownys nor ther purpil weedis,
Ther goldene sceptris; but youe to them ther meedis:
Crownid oon with laureer hih on his hed vpset,
Other with peruynke maad for the gibet.

"Thus I distribute my gifts, sometimes to one, sometimes to another, as in a game of chance.

Thus dyuersli my gifftes I* departe,
Oon acceptid, a-nothir is refusid;
Lik hasardours my dees I [do] iuparte,
Oon weel foorthrid, anothir is accusid.
My play is double, my trust is euer abusid,
Thouh oon to-day hath my fauour won*ne*,
To-morwe ageyn I can eclipse his son*ne*.

"And now I have come to shew you what my disposition is like: to-day I may flatter, and frown to-morrow.

Cause of my comy*ng*, pleynli to declare
Bi good auis, vnto thi presence,
Is to shewe my maneres & nat spare,
And my condiciou*ns*, breeffli in sentence,
Preued of old & newe experience,
Pleynli to shewe, me list nat for to rowne,
To-day I flatre, to-morwe I can weel frowne.

106. gret] þi H.
113. sownis] sown H. 120. &] an R. 123. not] *om.* R.
127. I] I gan B. 131. euer] ay H.
132. my fauour*e* hath I-wonne J. 138. newe] nex H.

"I am as fickle as the wind or a weathercock, and my ways are marvelous.

This hour I can shewe me merciable,
And sodenli I can be despitous:
Now weelwillid, hastili vengable,
Now sobre of cheer, now wood &* furious.
My play vnkouth, my maners merueilous
Braid on the wynd; now glad & now I mo*u*rne;
Lik a wedircok* my face ech day I to*u*rne.

"It is foolish of you, Bochas, to try to change my habits and nature.

Wheryn Bochas, I telle the yit ageyn,
Thou dost folie thi wittis for to plie;
All* thi labour thou spillest in veyn,
Geyn my maneres so felli to replie, —
Bi thi writyng to fynde a remedie,
To interupte in thi laste dawes
My statutis [and] my custumable lawes.

"All the labour of old philosophers was of no avail against me: when I desire it they must descend.

Al the labour off philisophres olde,
Trauaile off poetis my maner to depraue,
Hath* been of yore to seyn lik as thei wolde
Ouer my fredam the souereynte to haue.
But of my lawes the libertes to saue,
Vpon my wheel thei shal hem nat diffende,
But whan me list[e] that thei shal dessende.

"Why should men blame me? Is it not the same with the changing seasons

Whi sholde men putte me in blame,
To folwe the nature of my double play?
With newe buddis doth nat ver the same,
Wha*n* premeroles appeere fressh & gay? —
To-day thei shewe, to-morwe thei gon away;
Somer afftir of flouris hath foisou*n*,
Til Iun with ȝithes aftir mowe he*m* dou*n*.

and the sea, now calm, now stormy? Why should I not have my will?

Now is the se calm and blandisshyng; [p. 300]
Now ar the wyndis confortable & still;
Now is Boreas sturdi in blowyng,
Which yong[e] sheep & blosmys greueth ille.
Whi also shold I nat haue my wille,
To shewe my-silf now smothe and aftir trouble,
Sith to my kynde it longeth to be double?

144. &] now B.
147. wedircok] woodcok B (wedircok R, wedirkok H, wethircok J, wedircoke R 3, wedyrcok H 5, wedrecok P).
150. All] And B.
155. labours H, R 3, laboures P.
157. Hath] Haue B.
165. p*r*imerolis R, p*r*imrollis H, p*re*merollis R 3, Prymerolis J.
170. comfortable H.

"No man is so miserable but he hopes that some day I may relieve him.

No man so ferre is falle in wrechidnesse
But that he stant in trust to rise ageyn;
Nor non so deepe plungid in distresse,
Nor with dispeir nor wanhope ouerleyn,
But that ther is sum hope lefft certeyn
To yiue hym cou*n*forte, seruyng his entente,
To be releued whan me list assente.

"The flowers and green of spring disappear in August,

The erthe is clad in motles whiht & rede;
Wha*n* Estas entrith with violettis soote,
The greuis greene, & in euery meede
The bawme fleteth, which doth to hertis boote.
August passid, ageyn into* the roote
Be cours of nature the vertu doth resorte
Be reuoluciou*n* to Kynde, I me reporte.

and only fools blame me for my inconstancy.

Who sholde thanne debarre me to be double,
Sith doubilnesse longeth to me of riht?
Now fressh with somer, now *with* wyntir trouble,
Now blynd of look, dirk as the cloudi niht;
Now glad of cheer, of herte murie & liht:
Thei ar but foolis ageyn my myht that muse
Or me atwite; thouh I my poweer vse.

"Men must take me as they find me; and they have no right to complain of my doubleness,

Seelde or neuer I bide nat in o poynt:
Men must at lepis take me as thei fynde;
And whan I stonde ferthest out of ioynt
To sette folk[es] bakward ferre behynde,
Than worldli men with ther eyen blynde
Sore compleyne upon my doubilnesse,
Calle me thanne the froward fals goddesse.

because it is my nature to be double. "It is no slander to me, for I am the lady and princess of change."

Thus bi yo*ur* writyng & m*er*ueilous langage
I am disclau*n*drid of mutabilite,
Wheroff be riht I cach gret* auau*n*tage,
Sith dubilnesse no sclau*n*dre is to me,
Which is a parcel of my liberte,
To be callid, be title off rihtwisnesse,
Off chau*n*gis newe ladi & pryncesse."

John Bochas heard with a frightened face all that Fortune said, and then replied meekly:

Thus whan Fortune hadde said hir will,
Parcel declared of hir gouernau*n*ce,
Made a stynt & sobirli stood still.
Iohn Bochas sat & herd al hir daliau*n*ce,

181. comforte H. 187. into] vnto B.
194. of herte] sadde H.
198. lepis] lopis R, loopis H, J, lopis R 3, lepys H 5, loupes P.
203. the] a H. 206. gret] a gret B, H, R, J, P, R 3, H 5.

Feerful of cheer[e], pale of contenau*n*ce,
In ordre enpreentid ech thyng that she saide,
Ful demurli thus he dede abraide.

He took onto hym vertu & corage
Vpon a poynt for to abide* stable:
"Certis," quod he, "lik to thi visage,
Al worldli thyngis be double & chau*n*gable;
Yit for my part bi reme*m*brau*n*ce notable*
I shal parfourme, sothli yif I con*n*e,
This litil book that I ha[ue] begon*n*e.

"Certainly all worldly things are changeable, nevertheless I am going to finish my little book if I can.

And lest my labo*u*r deie nat nor [a]palle,
Of this book the title for to saue,
Among myn othir litil werkis alle,
W*ith* lettres large aboue vpon my graue
This bookis name shal in ston be graue,
How I, Iohn Bochas, in especiall
Of worldli p*r*incis writyn haue the fall.

"And lest the memory of my labour die, there shall be engraved in large letters above my tomb, how I, John Bochas, have written the Fall of Princes.

Off which emprise the cause to descryue, —
This was first grou*n*d, I wil it nat denye,
Teschewe slouhthe & vices al my lyue,
And specialli the vice of glotenye,
Which is norice vnto lecherie:
This was cheeff cause whi I vndirtook
The compilaciou*n* off this litil book.

"I undertook to write it, that I might avoid idleness and vice, and especially gluttony, the nurse of lust.

Yit bi thi talkyng, as I vndirstonde,
Ech thyng heer of nature is chau*n*gable,
Afftir thi sentence, bothe on se & londe;
Yit koude I rekne thynges that be stable:
As vertuous [lyf] abidyng vnmutable,
Set hool to Godward of herte, will & thouht,
Maugre thi poweer, & ne chau*n*gith nouht.

"You say that everything here is changeable of nature: yet certain things, such as virtuous life, are stable in spite of your power.

Thou maist eek callyn [vn]to reme*m*brau*n*ce
Thynges maad stable bi grace which is dyuyne, —
Hastow nat herd[e] the perseuerau*n*ce
Of hooli martirs, which list nat to declyne
Fro Cristis feith til thei dide fyne?
Thi wheel in hem hadde no*n* interesse,
To make hem varie fro ther stabilnesse.

"Have you not heard of the holy martyrs? "The turning of your wheel had no power over them.

219. to abide] tabide B, H, R. 222. ful notable B.
228. large] long H. 239. thi] the R. 250. thei] he R, J.

[p. 301]

"A man armed with virtue, who trusts in Christ Iesu, is proof against your variance!

A man that is enarmed in vertu
Ageyn thi myht to make resistence,
And set his trust be grace in Crist *Iesu*,
And hath al hool his hertli aduertence
On rihtwisnesse, force & on prudence,
With ther suster callid attemperau*n*ce,
Hath a saufconduit ageyn thi variau*n*ce!

"Such men pay no attention to your wheel, their trust stands on faith, hope and charity, which are called theologic virtues.

The[i] sette no stoor be thi double wheele,*
With supportaciou*n* of other ladies thre;
Ther trust stant nat in mail[e], plate or stel,
But in thes vertues: feith, hope & charite,
Callid vertues theologice,
Which with foure afforn heer specefied,
Thi wheel & the han vttirli defied.

"If I had wings to fly to heaven, I should see that you had nothing to do with the seven planets: it is only worldly fools who call you a goddess.

Yiff I with wyngis myhte fleen to heuene,
Ther sholde I see thou hast nothyng to doone
With Iubiter nor the planetis seuene,
With Phebus, Mars, Mercurie nor the moone.
But woorldli foolis, erly, late and soone,
Such as be blent & dirkid with leudnesse,
Bi fals oppynyou*n* calle the a goddesse.

"The virtues are far removed from your domain.

Giftes of grace nor gifftes of nature,
Almessede[de] doon with humylite,
Loue and compassiou*n*, been ferr out of thi cure, —
Semlynesse, strengthe, bou*n*te nor beute
Vertuousli vsid in ther degre, —
Geyn non of these thi poweer may nat strechche;
For who is vertuous lite of the doth rechche.

"And fools blame you in their adversity only to excuse themselves.

Off* thi condiciou*n*s to sette a-nother preeff,
Which foolis vsen in ther aduersite
For excusaciou*n*, as su*m*tyme seith a theeff,
Wha*n* he is hangid: 'it was his destyne' —
Atwitith Fortune his iniquite,
As thouh she hadde domynaciou*n*
To reule man bi will ageyn resou*n*.

"But I, who am unable to solve the problems of existence, leave them to those who are scholars by profession.

For which I, Bochas, in parti desolat
To determyne such heuenli hid secrees,
To them that been dyuynes of estat
I remitte such vnkouth pryuites;
And with poetis that been off low degrees

253–3268 *are omitted in* R. 260. wheele] variau*n*ce B.
262. or] nor H. 277. nor] or H.
281. Off] Aff B — condiciou*n* H.

I eschewe to clymbe to hih alofte,
List for presu*m*pciou*n* I shold nat fall[e] softe.

But yif I had hid in my corage
Such mysteries of dyuyn prouidence,
Withoute envie I wolde in pleyn langage
Vttre hem be writyng with humble reuerence, —
Predestynaciou*n* nouther prescience
Nat apperteene, Fortune, vnto the;
And for my part I wil excuse me,

"At any rate, I am sure that neither predestination nor prescience appertain to you, Fortune.

And proceede lik as I vndirtook,
Aftir that I haue told my mateer,
Of Fall of P*r*incis for to write a book.
But yit afforn[e], yif thou woldest heere,
I desire of hool hert & enteer
To haue a copee of p*r*incis namys all,
Which fro thi wheel[e] thou hast maad to fall.

"And so I will go on with my book; yet I should be very grateful for a list of the names of all the princes who have fallen from your wheel.

Thi secre bosum is ful of stories
Of sondry p*r*incis, how thei ther liff haue lad,
Of ther triu*m*phes & ther victories,
Which olde poetis & philisophres sad
In meetre & prose compiled han & rad,
Sunge ther laudis, ther fatis eek reserued
Bi rememb*r*ance, as thei haue disserued.

"Your secret bosom is full of the stories of princes whose praises have been sung by the old poets.

Of which I haue put sum*m*e in memorie,
Theron sette my studie & my labour,
So as I coude, to ther encres of glorie,
Thouh of langage I hadde but smal fauo*u*r,
Cause Caliope dede me no socour.
For which thou hast duryng al this while
Rebuked me of my rud[e] stile.

"Some of them I have myself put in remembrance, although I am a poor hand at writing, and Calliope has given me no help.

Men wolde acou*n*te it wer a gret dulnesse,
But yiff langage conveied be bi prudence,
Out declared bi sobre auysynesse,
Vndir support fauoured be diffence
Of Tullius, cheef p*r*ince of elloquence, —
Sholde mor proffite, shortli to conclude,
Than my stile, spoke in termys rude.

" Language favoured by the eloquence of Tully is very superior to my rude style.

294. for] of H.
308. fro] frome H.

yet it often happens that good grain is found growing under husks, and good counsel spoken in blunt terms sometimes succeeds where rhetoric fails.

Yit ofte tyme it hath be felt & seyn,
Vnder huskes growyng on lond* arable,
Hath be fou*n*de & tried out good greyn;
Vndir rude leuys, shakyng & vnstable,
Pullid fair frut, holsum & delectable.
And semblably, wher rethorik hath failed,
In blunt termys good cou*n*seil hath auailed.

"It was through music and philosophy that the commons first became civilized;

Philisophres of the goldene ages [p. 302]
And poetes that fond out fressh ditees,
As kyng Amphiou*n* with his fair langages
And with his harpyng made folk of louh degrees,
As laborers, tenhabite first cites; —
And so bi musik and philosophie
Gan first of comou*n*s noble policie.

for music is harmony, and philosophy sprang from prudence, and upon concord and wise policy were built the walls of Thebes.

The cheeff of musik is mellodie & accord;
Welle of philosophie sprang out of prudence,
Bi which too menys gan vnite & concord
With politik vertu to haue ther assistence:
Wise men to regne, subiectis do reuerence.
And bi this grou*n*d, in stories men may see,
Wer bilt the wallis of Thebes the cite.

"Discord goes hand in hand with diversity, peace with prudent policy, and quarrels were first brought in by you, Lady of Contest and Strife —

Accord in musik causith the mellodie;
Wher is discord, ther is dyuersite,
And wher is pes is prudent policie
In ech kyngdam and euery gret contre.
Striff first inducid bi thi duplicite;
For which thou maist, as clerkis the descryues,
Be callid ladi of contekis & of stryues.

slaughter, debate, froward dissensions and the desolation of towns and countries.

First wer fou*n*de out hatful dyuysiou*n*s
Be thi contreued fals mutabilites, —
Slauhtre, debat, froward discenciou*n*s
In regiou*n*s, prouynces and cites,
Desolaciou*n* off townis & contrees,
Wheroff men hadde first experience
Bi thi chau*n*gable geri violence.

"It is you who first got men into trouble with your uncouth snares, and made them hate one another;

Thus bi thoppynyou*n* of thi wheel most double,
As ferr be nature as it was possible,
Ouerthwertli thou brouhtest men in trouble,
Madest ech to other froward & odible
Bi thi treynys vnkouth & terrible,

331. land] grou*n*d B. 334. delitable H.
339. kyng] *om.* H. 346. concord] accorde H. 349. story H.

Lik a corsour makth coltis that be wilde
With spore & whippe to be tame & mylde,

Thus bi the tempest off thyn aduersites,
To make men mor tame of ther corage.
In [ther] discordes tween kyngdames & cites,
Afftir the sharp*e*[nesse] of thi cruel rage*
Onli bi mene of speche & fair langage,
Folk be thi fraude fro grace ferr exilid,
Wer be fair speche to vnite reconcilid.

and then you would tame them with adversity, and afterwards it was fair speech that reconciled them to unity.

Peeplis of Grece, of Roome & off Cartage,
Next in Itaille, with many a regeou*n*,
Wer inducid bi swetnesse* of langage
To haue togidre ther conuersaciou*n*,
To beelde castellis & many roial tou*n*.
What caused this? — to telle in breeff the foorme,
But eloquence rud peeplis to reffoorme.

"Sweetness of language induced them to consort together and build castles and cities.

Affor tyme thei wer but bestiall,
Till thei to resou*n* be lawes wer constreyned,
Vndir discreciou*n* bi statutis naturall
Fro wilful lustis be prudence wer restreyned.
Bassent maad oon, & togidre [en]cheynyd
In goldene cheynys of pes and vnite;
Thus gan the beeldyng of eueri gret cite.

"At first they were ignorant, until laws constrained them to reason, and prudence checked their wilfulness.

But whan thou medlist to haue an interesse,
Thei that wer oon to brynge hem at discord,
To interupte with thi doubilnesse
Cites, regiou*n*s, that wer of oon accord, —
Lik as this book can ber [me] weel record,
Fro the tyme that thou first began
Thi mutabilite hath stroied many a man.

"But you interfere to bring them into discord, and many a man has been destroyed by your mutability.

Thou causest men to been obstynat
In ther corages & incorrigible,
Wilful, froward, causeles at debat,
Ech to other contrarious & odible,
Them to refourme almost impossible, —
Til fair[e] speche, voidyng dyuisiou*n*,
Pes reconcilid tween many a regeou*n*.

"You make men obstinate and wilful, froward and hateful to one another; but fair speech has reconciled many a region.

375. sharp*e*nesse] sharp J, R 3, H 5, R 2, H 3, H 4 — rage] outrage B, H, H 5, rages J, P.
381. bi] *with* H — swetnesse] Record B, swifftnesse H — of] of fair J.
383. roial tou*n*] regiou*n* H. 387. to] bi H — be] to H.
401. corage H.

"No outrage is so terrible, nothing so wrong but it may be reformed by gracious language.

For ther is non so furious outrage,
Nor no mateer so ferr out of the weie,
But that be mene of gracious language
And faire speche may a man conveie
To al resou*n* meekli for to obeie, —
Bi an exau*m*ple which I reherse shall
Weel to purpos and is historiall.

"When Achilles was in his wrath nothing served to still the tempest of his rage but the sweet sound of a harp.

¶ The hardi kniht, [the] cruel Achilles,
Whan hatful ire assailed his corage,
Ther was no mene with hym to trete of pes,
To stille the tempest of his doolful rage,
Sauff onli this, which dede his ire asswage
Bi attemprau*n*ce tobeien to resou*n*,
When of an harpe he herde the sueete sou*n*.

"And in like manner gentle language can bring men to peace who were parted by division."

Which instrument bi his gret suet[e]nesse [p. 303]
Put al rancour out of his reme*m*brau*n*ce,
Wrestid hym ageyn to al gladnesse,
From hym auoidyng al ranco*ur* & greuau*n*ce.
Semblabli, faire speche and daliau*n*ce
Set men in reste in rewmys heer & yonder
Bi good langage that wer ferr assonder."

With these words Bochas became more affable and spoke pleasantly about his work, and besought Fortune to help him on with his book,

With these woordes Bochas wex debonaire,
Toward Fortune as he cast his look,
Withdrouh his rancour & ga*n* speke faire
Touchyng his labour which he upon hy*m* took,
Besechyng hir for to forthre his book,
That his name, which was litil knowe,
Be good report myhte be ferther blowe.

so that his fame, as yet shrouded in darkness, might shine forth to all people.

That his fame myhte ferther spreede,
Which stood as yit shroudid in dirknesse,
Bi hir fauour his name forth to leede,
His book to foorthre doon hir bysynesse
Bi good report to yiue it a brihtnesse,
With laureat stremys shad foorth to peeplis all,
Bi foryetilnesse that it neuer appall.

This was the request that he made to Fortune, who after a little while began to smile and answered:

This was the bille which that Iohn Bochas
Made vnto Fortune with ful humble stile.
Whan Fortune hadde conceyuyd al his* caas,
Sobirli stood and gan [to] stynte a while,

421. sootnesse H. 430. to speke H.
444. his] this B. 445. to] *om.* J.

And glad of cheer[e] aftir she gan smyle
On myn aucto*u*r, & with a fressh visage
In sentence spak to hym this language:

[Hic loquitur Fortuna.] [1]

¶ "Soothli," quod she, "I see thi besynesse,
Of mortal men, how corious that thei bee,
How thei studie bi gret auisynesse
Off my secretes for to been preue,
To knowe the conceitis hid withyn*n*e me
And my cou*n*sailles, ye men doon al yo*u*r peyne,
Al-be nat lihtly* ye may therto atteyne.

"Truly, I see how curious you men are to learn my secrets, although you do not come by them easily.

In this mateer your witt doth neuer feynte,
Ymagynyng liknessis in yo*u*r mynde,
Lik your conceitis ye forge me & peynte,
Sumtyme a woman with wenges set behynde,
And portreye me with eien that be blynde.
Cause off al this, breeffli to expresse,
Is your owne coueitous blyndnesse!

"You imagine me in all forms: sometimes a woman with wings, sometimes blind; but the cause of all this is your own covetousness.

Your appetitis most strau*n*ge & most dyuers,
And euir ful of chau*n*g & doubilnesse,
Froward also, malicious & peruers,
Be hasti clymbyng to worshepis & richesse,
Alway void of trouthe & stabilnesse,
Most presumptuous, serche out in al degrees,
Falsli tatteyne to worldli dignites.

"You have strange desires, and you are always full of deceit, malicious and perverse, and ever seeking worldly dignity.

Bochas, Bochas, I parceyue eueri thyng
And knowe ful weel the grete difference
Hid in thi-silff of woordes & thynkyng,
Atween hem bothe the disconvenience.
Hastow nat write many gret sentence
In thi book to sclau*n*dre with my name,
Off hool entent my maneres to diffame?

"Bochas, I understand and know very well the great difference between your words and thought.
"Have you not written many a slanderous sentence about me,

Thou callest me stepmooder most vnkynde,
And sumtyme a fals enchau*n*teresse,
A mermaide with a tail behynde,
Off scorn sumwhile me namy*n*g a goddesse,
Sumtyme a wich, sumtyme a sorceresse,
Fyndere off moordre & of deceitis alle;
Thus of malis mortel men me calle!

calling me an unkind stepmother, a false enchantress, a mermaid with a tail behind, an instigator of murder?

455. lihtly] likli B — nat] that J, P — may] maynat J, P.
481. wich] wrechch H.

[1] MS. J. leaf 124 verso.

"All this in despite of me: accusing my mutability when I refuse your covetous requests.

Al this is doon in despiht of mee;
Bi accusaciou*n* in many sondri wise
Ye offte appeche my mutabilite,
Namli whan I your requestis do despise,
For tacomplisshe yo*u*r gredi couetise:
Whan ye faille ye leyn on me the wite,
Off yo*u*r aduersites me falsli tatwite.

"And only to slander me you wrote an unpleasant story of how I wrestled with Glad Poverty, whom you favoured, and now you beg me to help you!

And thou of purpos for tesclau*n*dre me
Hast writt vngoodli a contrarious fable,
How I wrastled with Glad Pouerte,
To whos parti thou wer fauourable,
Settest me abak, geyn me thou wer vengable,—
Now of newe requerist my fauour
The for to helpe & foorthre thi labour!

"As if I were changeable as a woman or the wind! Yet that is your doctrine.

As-scau*n*s I am off maneres most chau*n*gable,
Off condiciou*n*s verray femynyne;
Now heer, now ther, as the wynd vnstable,
Be thi descripciou*n* and be thi doctryne,
To eueri chau*n*g[e] reedi to enclyne,
As women be & maidnes tendre of age,
Which of nature be dyuers of corage.

"However, I am willing to help you,

But for to forthre in parti thyn entent, [p. 304]
That of thi book the processe may proceede,
Be my fauour to the accomplishment
I am weelwillid to helpe the in thi neede.
Lik thi desir the bettir thou shalt* speede,
Whan I am toward with a benigne face
To speede thy iourne bi support of my g*r*ace,

so that both your name and your surname may flourish. "I will have you begin with Saturninus.

That thi name and also thi surname,
With poetis & notable old auctours,
May be registrid in the Hous off Fame
Bi supportaciou*n* of my sodeyn fauours,
Bi assistence also of my socours
Thi werk texpleite the laurer for to wyn*n*e,
At Saturninus I will that thou begyn*n*e.

484. is] *om.* J.
491. tesclau*n*dre] to sclau*n*dre H.
495. ageyn H.
509. the bettir thou shalt] thou shalt the bettir B.

[Here reherceth Fortune hir co*n*diciou*n*s vnto Bochas shewyng how many oon she enhau*n*ced for a tyme/ and anoon aft*er* hem sodenly ouerthroweth.] [1]

¶ Among Romey*n*s this said[e] Saturnyne
Was outraious off condiciou*n*s,
Caused in Roome whan he ga*n* maligne
Gret debatis and gret sediciou*n*s.
And bi his froward conspiraciou*n*s
He was sharp enmy ageyn the prudent iuge
Callid Metellus,* deuoid of al refuge.

"This said Saturnine was an outrageous person, who caused great trouble in Rome.

Fro the Capitoille fette with myhti hond,
Fond no socour Metellus in the tou*n*, —
The same tyme, thou shalt vndirstond,
How be my*n* helpe and supportaciou*n*
Oon that was smal of reputaciou*n*
Callid Glaueya, in pouert brouht up lowe,
Maad consuleer, the stori is weel knowe.

"He was an enemy of Metellus at the time Glaucia became consul.

A seruau*n*t first & almost set at nouht;
And afftirward I made hym fortunat,
Lefte neuere til I hadde hym brouht
Bi a prerogatiff chose of the senat
To been a pretour, an offise of estat.
Which also wrouhte be conspiraciou*n*
To brynge Metellus to destrucciou*n*.

"I made, Glaucia fortunate; he was at first nothing but a servant.

Off whos assent ther was also another
Callid Marius, beyng the same yeer,
Texpleite this*tresou*n* beyng ther [own]sworn brother,
Which was also that tyme a consuleer.
I, Fortune, made hem ful good cheer,
Lik ther desirs gaff hem liberte
To banshe Metellus out of ther cite.

"He, Marius, and Saturnine conspired to banish Metellus,

Of the[s] [thre] Romeyns, the first[e] Saturnyne,
And Glaueya was callid the secou*n*de,
And Marius, leid out hook & lyne,
As I haue told, Metellus to confou*n*de.

and I shewed them my favour, that they might later on themselves come to mischief.

525, 27, 39. Metellius B.
531. Glaueya] Glabeya H, Glabeia J, Glaucia P.
532. the] this H.
542. this] ther B.
548. Glaueya] Glabeya H, Glaucia J, P.

[1] MS. J. leaf 124 verso.

To ther purpos I was also founde
Fauourable to brynge hem to myscheeff,
As ther stori sheweth an open preeff.

"They banished Metellus, and Saturninus presumed to be called lord and king of Rome:

Thei ban[y]shid hym out of Roome toun;
And Saturnynus bi his subtil werkyng
Clamb up faste, of hih presumpcioun,
To be callid of Roome lord & kyng.
I gaff hym fauour bamaner fals smylyng,
Til at the laste, pleynli to declare,
Off his destruccioun I brouht hym in the snare.

but all the while I was deceiving him.

The senatours knowyng the malis
Of Saturnyn, which made a gret gadryng
Of sondry folk, castyng in his auys
Bi ther fauour he myhte be callid kyng.
Al this while off his vpclymbyng
I shewed hym duryng a long[e] space
Hym to deceyue a benigne face.

"Finally Marius arose and drove him into the Capitol for refuge.

Til Marius, a myhti consuleer,
To withstonde his presumpcioun
Ros with strong hand, & with a knihtli cheer
Besette his paleis abouten enviroun,
Brak his gatis amyddis of the toun;
And Saturnynus, void of al fauour,
To the Capitoille fledde for socour.

"Marius then besieged the Capitol, and Saturninus, brought to great distress, lost all his riches.

He was forbarrid be Marrius of vitaille,
The Capitoille beseged round aboute;
At the entryng was a strong bataille,
On outher parti slay[e]n a gret route.
Thus of my fauour he gan stonde in doute,
This Saturnynus brouht in gret distresse,
His good achetid, lost al his richesse.

"Experience teaches that those who ascend highest on my wheel shall descend when they least expect it; and then I laugh at them.

Experience ful openli men lereth,
Such as hiest therupon ascende,
Lik as the tourn of my wheel requereth,
Whan thei lest weene doun thei shal descende.
Thei haue no poweer themsiluen to diffende
Ageyn my myht, whan thei been ouerthrowe:
What do I than, but lauhe & make a mowe!

556. hih] *om.* H, J, R 3, H 5, P.
575. forbarrid] so barrid H.

¶ Drusus also born of gret lynage [p. 305]
And descendid of ful hih noblesse,
Vnto vertu contraire of his corage,
Froward fou*n*de to al gentilesse;
Yit chose he was, the stori doth expresse,
Questour of Asia, an offis of degree,
For his berthe to gouerne that contre.

"Drusus, born of high lineage and contrary to all virtue was chosen quaestor of Asia.

But ofte tyme vertu nor gentilesse
Come nat to heires bi successiou*n*, —
Exau*m*ple in Drusus, the stori berth witnesse,
Which bothe of corage and disposiciou*n*
Was euere froward off condiciou*n*.
For which lat men deeme as thei mut needis,
Nat afftir berthe but afftir the deedis.

"But it often happens that neither virtue nor gentility are inherited by heirs: we must judge men by their actions rather than their birth.

Vertues alle in hym wer set aside:
Slouh to been armyd, hatid cheualrie,
Most coueitous, deyncus, ful of pride,
His deedis froward, ful of trecherie.
To hih estat I dede hym magnefie,
Yit al my gifftes in hym ne myhte strechche,
For heer tofor the, he kometh lik a wrechche.

"Drusus was lazy, covetous, disdainful and full of treachery. "I could not help him. "Here he comes before you like a wretch,

He dar for shame nat shewen his visage,
So ferr disclau*n*drid is his wrechidnesse,
Whos couetise and vicious outrage
Falsli causid bi his doubilnesse,
Maguldusa, a prince of gret noblesse,
Betrasshed was for meede to the kyng
Callid Boccus bi Drusus fals werkyng.

and dares not shew his face for shame. He betrayed Magulsa to Bocchus.

What maner torment or what greuous peyne
Wer compotent, couenable or condigne
To hym that can outward flatre &* feyne,
And in his herte couertli maligne,
As Drusus dede, which shewed many a signe
To Maguldusa of loue and freendliheede;
Vndirnethe fals tresou*n* hid in deede.

"And what torment were appropriate to him who can outwardly flatter and inwardly hate, as Drusus did?

But Maguldusa, lik a manli kniht,
Geyn kyng Boccus hath hymsilff socourid,
Whan he bi doom was iugid agey*n* riht
Of an olifau*n*t for to be deuourid.
Scapid freeli, & aftir that labourid

"But Magulsa, sentenced to be devoured by an elephant, escaped and afterwards slew Drusus in Rome.

595. that] þe H. 596. gentilnesse H. 597. Come] cam H.
614. Magulsa P.
618. competent H, J, R 3, H 5, P. 619. &] or B.

Taquite hymsilff[e] throuh his hih renoun,
Slouh fals Drusus myd of Roome toun.

"Bochas, men blame me for being the cause of the destruction of Scipio,

¶ Bochas, also, men put the lak in mee,
That I was cause of the destruccioun
Be my contrarious mutabilite
Off the notable famous Scipioun,
Which in the tyme of Sensoryn Catoun
Gat the tryumphe for many gret victorie
To putte his name perpetuel[ly] in memorie.

consul and chief bishop of Rome at the time of the wars between Cæsar and Pompey.

For his meritis chose a consuleer
And cheeff bisshop to gouerne ther cite,
To al the senat patroun most enteer,
Most famous off name and dignite,
Saued Romeyns from al aduersite,
Tyme whan the werre dreedful & despitous
Gan atween Pompeie & Cesar Iulius.

"When he stood highest in my favour he was suddenly cast down from my wheel; but it was by the malice of the Romans.

Thus whan the said[e] famous Scipioun
Was thoruh my fauour acountid most notable,
He fro my wheel was sodenli cast doun,
Which neuer in woord nor deede was coupable.
But the Romeyns malicious & vnstable, —
Bi ther hangman first cheynid in prisoun,
Afftir rakked, ther geyned no raunsoun.

"They hung his body high aloft for a spectacle, although he had saved them from all adversity.

Thus he that hadde auailed hem so ofte,
To saue hymsilff fond socour on no side;
His dede bodi thei heeng it hih aloffte
For a spectacle longe ther tabide.
Thus gerisshli my giftes I deuide,
Stound[e]meel, now freend, now aduersarie,
Rewarde goode with guerdouns ful contrarie.

"My fickleness was well shewn in the fate of Scipio.
"I also made Fanaticus, born a churl, ascend to high degree, for my amusement.

This was expert ful weel in Scipioun:
Gan with ioie, endid in wrechidnesse.
Bochas, remembre, mak heeroff mencioun,
And off Fanaticus, how I off gentilesse
Made hym ascende to notable hih prowesse;
Yit bookis sey[e]n touchyng his kynreede,
Manli of persone, born a cherl* in deede.

"He rose to royal estate by sleight,

For my disport[e] with a glad visage
I sette hym up ful hih upon my wheel,
Gaff hym lordship, out of louh seruage;

631. in] on H. 662. gentilnesse H, R 3, H 5.
665. born a cherl] a cherl born B, J, P.

To doon hym fauour it liked me ful weel.
Wherfor Bochas, his stori euerideel,
Note it weel, & in especiall
How he be sleihte cam to estat roiall.

Be sleihti feynyng to dyuers folk he tolde, [p. 306]
How that he spak with Cirra the goddesse
At eueri hour pleynli whan he wolde,
Of presumpciou*n* descryued hir liknesse,
Seide also how that she of hir goodnesse
Hadde grau*n*tid hym, his staat to magnefie,
Duryng his lyff a sperit off prophecie.

telling people how he could converse at will with a goddess, and how she had given him a spirit of prophecy.

And ferthermore the peeple for to blynde
He fantasied bi a crafft vnkouth,
Withyn*ne* a scale, the stori maketh my*n*de,
Of a note to haue fyr in his mouth.
Blewe it out sparklyng north & south,
Affermede, wherwith folk wer blent,
It was a sperit to hym fro heuene sent.

"He blew fire from a nutshell in his mouth, and said it was a spirit sent to him from heaven.

Bi which he wrouhte many gret vertu,
Gadred peeple til he hadde in deede
Two thousand cherlis at his retenu,
Which aftirward, his purpos for to speede,
To sixti thousand encreced, as I reede.
I suffrid al; seruid hym at the tide
Til al the contre gruchchede at his pride.

"Finally he had 60,000 followers; and I permitted all, until the country grumbled at his pride.

Thouh of berthe he was but a vileyn,
Roos up of nouht bi sodeyn auenture,
My geri fauour made hym to be seyn
Roial of port, dede his besi cure
To reise his baner, wered a cote-armure,
And be my gracious supportaciou*n*
Brouht gret peeple to his subiecciou*n*.

Born a serf, he rose from nothing;

At the laste my lust gan to appall,*
Towardis hym nat beyng fauourable;
Dou*n* fro my wheel anon I made hy*m* fall,
For bi Romeyns was sent a gret constable
Callid Porpen*na*, a prynce ful notable,
Which fill on hym, venquisshid hym anon,
Slouh and outraied his cherlis euerichon.

but at last I wearied of him and made him fall from my wheel.
"He was defeated by Perpenna and hanged, and his churls were scattered and slain.

682. scale] shale J, P. 691. encreced] *om.* H.
701. to] *om.* J, P, H 5 — tappall B, H, R 3.

"I remain with no man always.

Hymsilff was hangid on an hih gibet;
Sum*me* of his meyne wer cast in prisou*n*.
Thus to his pride I gaff a gret tripet
And fro my wheel I caste hym lowe dou*n*
In his most hiest domynaciou*n*, —
Took non heed wher he dede lauhe or mo*u*rne,
For with no man I do alway soio*u*rne.

"Bochas, I can both further and injure: see how Athenion, once a shepherd, became a robber.

¶ Bochas," quod Fortune, "tak good heed also
How I can bothe foorthre & disauaile:
For exau*m*ple see houh Athenyo,
That whilom was a shepperde in Ytaille,
A brigau*n*t aftir, marchau*n*tis to assaille,
Lay in a-wait beside a gret mou*n*teyn,
Off fugityues he was made a capteyn.

"He slew his lord and broke out of many prisons, and for a time I helped him gather churls together and make war on Rome.

Slouh first his lord, a riche senatour,
Bi violence brak many strong *pri*sou*n*;
And for a tyme I gaff hym gret fauour
To gadre robbours aboute hy*m* envirou*n*, —
Alle the cherlis of that regeou*n*
He assemblede thoruh his iniquite,
To holde a werre with Roome the cite.

"He besieged castles and slew and robbed throughout the country and wore purple like a king,

Beseged castellis, brak dou*n* myhti to*u*rs,
Slouh & robbede aboute in ech contre,
Spoiled paleis of worthi senato*u*rs, —
Title hadde he non sauff title of volunte, —
Took upon hym of pride & cruelte
For to be clad in purpre lik a kyng,
Bar a sceptre among his men ridyng.

and a coif embroidered with rich stones on his head. "I laughed to think of him, a false robber, upheld by my favour.

Vpon his hed ordeyned for the nonys
His gold her tressid lik an empero*u*r,
A coiffe enbroudid al of riche* stonis —
Me list to lauhhe, that a fals robbour
Be supportaciou*n* of my geri fauour,
Which last nat longe, — for aftir in short while
As is my custum I dede hym begile.

"Finally a consul came down from Rome and hanged him.

I suffred hym, made hym feyned cheer,
As I haue do to othir mo ful ofte,
Till dou*n* fro Roome was sent a consuleer,
Which took hym proudli & heeng hym hih alofte,

709. *is replaced by* 702 *in* H.
734. purple H. 737. goldher B.
738. coiffe] corff H, coive R 3 — of riche] riche off B.

His cherlis slayn; & sum*me* of hem nat softe
In cheynys bou*n*de, for short conclusiou*n*,
Wer dempt be lawe to deien in prisou*n*.

¶ Bi which[e] stori[es], Bochas, thou maist lere
A gret parti of my condiciou*n*.
But now in haste a stori thou shalt heere,
How in the yeer fro the fundaciou*n*
Mor than sixe hundred — I meene of Roome tou*n* —
Was a gadryng & a gret cu*m*panye
Togidre sworn bi fals conspiracye,

"From these stories, Bochas, you may learn to know me. "Now I will tell you how there was a conspiracy about the year 600 of Rome,

Them to withdrawe fro the obeisau*n*ce* [p. 307]
Of a tribun callid Lodonee,
Which for knihthod hadde gouernau*n*ce,
And was sent dou*n* fro Roome [the] cite
With myhti hand to reule a gret contre
Callid Chau*m*payne; & pleynli for to seie,
The peeple ther list hym nat obeie.

when the people of Campania would not obey the tribune.

Thre score & foure wer of hem in nou*m*bre
That named wer[e] cheeff conspirato*u*rs,
Which that caste hem ther captey*n* to encou*m*bre
With multitude of theuis & robbours,
Which ches among hem to been ther supporto*u*rs
Thre myhti capteyns, off which ther was oon
Callid Spartharchus, cheuest of echon.

"There were three score and four chief conspirators, and Spartacus was their captain.

Gadred cherlis, made hemsiluen strong,
On an hih hill took ther duellyng place,
Hauyng no reward, wer it riht or wrong,
To spoille the contre, bestis to enchace.
I cherisshed hem with a benigne face
For a sesou*n*, & gaff hem liberte
Bi fals rauyne to robbe the contre.

"They gathered churls together, and, sallying forth from a hill stronghold, ravaged the country.

What thyng mor cruel in comparisou*n*
Or mor vengable of will & nat off riht,
Than whan a cherl hath domynaciou*n*!
Lak of discreciou*n* bleendith so the siht
Of comouneres, for diffaute of liht,

"For a time I helped them; but what is more cruel than a knave who has power to rule!

750. stories] stori J, P.
755. &] *om.* J, P — gret] *om.* H.
757. obeisau*n*ce] presence B, J. 759. hadde] & H.
760. the] *om.* J, H.
770. Spartharchus] Spartachus R 3, Spartacus P (*throughout*) — cheuest] cheff H.
771. hy*m* silf H. 781. siht] liht H. 782. liht] siht H.

Whan thei haue poweer contrees to gouerne
Fare lik a beeste [that] can nothyng disserne.

"They were called gladiators, who fought wild animals; and they encamped on Mt. Vesuvius

Gladiatores folkes dede hem calle;
For ther suerdis wer with steel maad fyn
For to fihte geyn wylde beestis alle,
As leou*n*s, beres, bores, wilde swyn.
And the mou*n*teyn wher thei dede lyn
Callid Venuse, and thoruh ther cruelte
Slouh & robbede aboute in ech contre.

"Spartacus was of low birth and came of nothing; and Claudius, who was sent down from Rome to protect the country, was driven away,

Spartharchus was ther cheeff capteyn,
Brouht up of nouht & born of louh degre;
But Claudius, a myhti, strong Romayn,
Was sent with poweer fro Roome the cite
For to diffende & saue that contre,
The hill besegyng afforn hem as he lay:
He was rebukid, bete & dryue away.

although many of Spartacus' men were slain.

Many of them that kepte the mou*n*tey*n*
Wer hurt that day, the stori tellith thus,
Amongis which was slayn a gret captey*n*
That was felawe vnto Spartharchus.
As I fynde, he hihte Ynomaus;
For whos deth was take so gret vengau*n*ce,
That al the contre felte therof greuau*n*ce.

"Two consuls were then sent against him, and both were put to flight, to the shame and fear of the Senate.

Thei of the mou*n*teyn, alle off oon assent,
Withoute merci or remyssiou*n*,
Most vengable, haue robbed & Ibrent
Al the contre aboute hem envirou*n*,
Til too consuleris cam fro Roome dou*n*:
The firste off hem callid Lentulus,
Bothe put to fliht be said[e] Spartarchus.

"Finally, Crassus came down with a legion and slew 36,000 of Spartacus' followers;

Wherof the Romeyns gretli wer dismaied.
The senatours off indignaciou*n*,
Bothe ashamed and in hemsilff affraied,
Sente oon Crassus, a gret lord of the tou*n*,
With the nou*m*bre off a legiou*n*.
And whan that he on Spartarchus first sette,
Slouh of his men six* thousand whan thei mette.

792. Spartacus H, Spartachus R 3. 798. dryue] dreven H.
802. Spartachus H, R 3, Spargachus H 5.
803. Oenomaus P. 808. vengeably H — brent P, H 5.
812. be] the J — Spartachus H, R 3.
818, 22, 34. Spartachus H, R 3. 819. six] vj B.

And aftirward beside a gret ryueer
Callid Salaire thei hadde a gret bataile,
Wher Spartarchus stood in gret dau*n*geer;
For his cheer and contenau*n*ce gan faille.
Thretti thousand clad in plate & maille
Wer slayn that day, ther geyned no rau*n*sou*n*,
Al ther capteyns assigned to p*r*isou*n*.

Withoute al this, as maad is menciou*n*,
Sixti thousand in the feeld lay ded,
And six thousand wer sent to p*r*isou*n*,
The feeld with blood[e] steyned & maad red.
And foure thousand, quakyng in ther dreed,
Wer thilke day, aftir the Romeyn gise,
Take to merci, resceyued to f*r*anchise,

"6000 were put in prison and 4000 taken to mercy.

And Spartarchus at mischeeff put to fliht.
Whan I from hym turnyd my visage,
He loste his cheer; he loste also his myht
Whan I appalled the fyn of his passage.
And for he was a cherl off his lynage,
Off his encres I likid nothyng weel,
Therfor vnwarli I cast hym fro my wheel.

"Spartacus fled; and I cast him from my wheel, for he was but a churl.

Off [my] maneres to make a gretter preeff, [p. 308]
Ther was another famous gret robbour,
Which thoruh Spaigne was a disclau*n*drid theeff.
And for he dradde of iustise the rigour,
Trustyng he sholde fynde in me socour,
Callid Viriatus,* he Spaigne anon forsook
And to Roome the riht[e] weie he took.

"There was another robber called Viriathus, who lived in Spain,

Gadred meyne of his condiciou*n*
Of eueri sect to make hymseluen strong,
Theuys, robbours of eueri regiou*n*,
Many a cherl was medlid hem among.
His name tencrece, wer it riht or wrong,
What-euer he gat in cite or village,
With his soudiours he partede the pillage.

and gathering men set out to attack Rome;

Thus be myn helpe he cam to gret richesse,
Which brouhte in pride & presumpciou*n*;
He nat prouided, of my doubilnesse,
Gan to maligne ageyn[e]s Rome tou*n*;

for through my aid he had become rich and proud. But he was slain by Scipio, son of Lepidus.

845. fynde in me] in me fynde H, P.
846. Viriatus] Vriatus H, R 3, J, Vrinatus B, J, Vyratus H 5.
854. the] his H. 858. ageynes] geyn H.

But bi the prudence of laste Scipiou*n*,
Sone of Lepidus, makyng therof no bost,
He slay[e]n was bi them he trustede most.

"Thus, Bochas, you may see my power and my mutability.

Bi which exau*m*ple[s] notable of reme*m*brau*n*ce
Shewed heer-toforn, Iohn Bochas, vnto the,
Thow maist knowe in parti my puissau*n*ce,
Mi sodeyn chau*n*gis, my mutabilite.
And for tauoide al ambiguite,
To declare the som*m*e of myn entent,
Grete Marrius to the I do presente.

"And now I present to you great Marius, clad in black, with downcast look and tangled grey hair.

Blak his weede & his habite also,
His hed vnkempt, his lokkis hor & gray,
His look dou*n* cast in tokne of sorwe & wo,
On his cheekis the salt[e] teris lay,
Which bar record off his dedli affray, —
Wherfor, Bochas, do thi pen*n*e dresse
To descryue his mortal heuynesse.

"His robe was stained with Roman blood, and all his delight lay in slaughter.

His robe steyned was with Romey*n* blood,
His suerd ay redi whet to do vengau*n*ce,
Lik a tirau*n*t most furious & wood,
In slauhtre & moordre set al his plesau*n*ce.
Yit nat for thi I gaff hym gouernau*n*ce
Ouer the peeple, ros on my wheel up faste,
But as vnwarli dou*n* I dede hym caste.

"Great strife arose between him and Sulla; but I made them both end in mischief.

Tween hym & Scilla the woful dedli stryues
At large heerafftir, Bochas, thou shalt write, —
How many Romeyns lost bi them ther lyues,
I will also in ordre that thou endite.
And yiff I shall rebuke hem & atwite,
As I fro nouht made hem in hono*u*r shyne,
So I ageynward made he*m* in myscheef fyne.

"I give you in charge to write, when you have leisure, about Mithridates,

Forget nat also the dedli pitous fate
Off hym that was so notable in his lyff, —
I meene the grete famous Mitridate,
Whos name yit is ful kouth and ryff,
To whom I gaff a gret prerogatiff,
Fourti wyntir, the deede was weel seene,
Ageyn Romeyns the werr*e* to susteene.

862. which] whos H — exau*m*ple J.
896. werr*e*] werris H.

For which heer-aftir I gyue it the in charge
Of Mitridate the stori set along;
Whan thou hast leiseer & a space large,
Remembre his conquest & his deedis strong,
And how that I medlid me among,
For al his noblesse and felicite,
To yiue hym part of gret aduersite."

whom I helped make war against Rome for forty years."

¶ Next in ordre, aftir hir owne chois,
Fortune, vntrusti vpon ech partie,
To Iohn Bochas hath conveied fro Parthois
Strong Herodes regnyng in Parthie.
"Loo, Iohn," quod she, "tak heed of this storie, —
Al his kynreede, yiff it be weel out souht,
Wer be Sithiens chacid & brouht to nouht.

Next in order came Orodes of Parthia. And Fortune said, "Lo, John, all his kindred were defeated by the Scythians, although some were restored to their dignity."

And yit, for al my mutabilite,
Som*m*e of hem which stood[e] disespeired
I restored to ther dignite,
Vnto which whan thei wer repeired,
This Herodes was hyndred & appeired
Bi my chau*n*ges for his hatful pride,
Whan he lest wende, vnwarli set aside."

¶ Suyng aftir withyn*n*e a litil while,
This gerissh ladi of condiciou*n*
Gan an illouh falsli for to smyle,
Lookyng on Boch*as*, brouhte with hir dou*n*
A myhti p*r*ince, which in Rome tou*n*
Hadde in his daies notable pris & fame,
Al-be that she expressed nat his name.

Soon afterwards Fortune began to smile falsely, and caused a mighty Roman prince to appear.

Bochas than*n*e his hed gan dou*n* declyne, [p. 309]
Seyng that p*r*ince, of face disfigured,
Of suspeciou*n* gan to ymagyne,
Whan he his mynde fulli hath recurid,
Be certeyn toknis & signes weel assured
It was Pompeie, surquedous of estat,
Which with Cesar so longe was at debat.

And Bochas, looking closely at his disfigured countenance, saw that it was Pompey, who was so long at war with Cæsar.

Disconsolat thoruh his vnhappi caas,
His face soiled with water of the se,
Tyme whan Fotynus & cruel Achillas
Drowned his bodi of furious enmyte.
His face disfigured at the solempnite

Disconsolate, his face was soiled with smoke and by the water of the sea;

911. yit] þat H. 916. Bi] to H.
920. illouh] alouh R 3, yll laughyng P.

With smokes blake, dedli & mortall,
Callid of clerkis the feeste funerall.

for Codrus had caused his corpse to be burnt. Fortune then said in scorn:

Codrus caused that the corps was brent
And consumed into asshes dede;
To Cesar aftir his hed was born & sent
Vpon a pole, his stori who list reede.
Afftir al this, Bochas took good heede,
How Fortune bamaner mokerie,
In scorn of hym gan thus to specefie:

"I raised his glory to the heavens and enabled him to give battle to Cæsar,

"Vp to the heuene aftir his deuys
I gan enhau*n*ce & encrece his glorie.
Bi my fauour I gaff hym many a pris,
Cònquest of kynges with many gret victorie;
And mor to putte his noblesse in memorie,
Bi my support thoruh his cheualrie,
With Cesar Iulius to holde chau*m*partie.

and while I shewed him my favour his fame arose until I withdrew it again.

And whil that I my fauour did applie
Toward hym his victories to assure,
His fame aros, til that in Thesalie
I gan withdrawe his parti to socoure,
Suffryng his enmyes make disconfiture
Vpon this Pompeie, hyndred in my siht,
Whan he to Lesbos at myscheeff took his fliht.

"Finally he was taken and slain: I gave him up, and he lost his head. "Yet no man takes heed of my changes, except that you are busy to set them in your book.

Bi the seruau*n*tis of yonge Tholome,
Regnyng in Egipt, Pompeie in his dreed
Was take & slayn; he fond no* help in mee:
I gaf hym vp; & so he lost his hed.
Yit of my chau*n*ges no man taketh heed,
Nor how vnseurli I cast my dreedful look,
Sauf thou art besi to sette hem in thi book."

Bochas astoned, parcel of hir presence,
Bothe of cheer[e], face and contenau*n*ce,
And in this while hauyng his aduertence,
Thouhte he sauh a maneer resemblau*n*ce
Of a persone, which stood in gret greuau*n*ce;
Til at the laste Fortune caste hir sihte
Toward Bochas, & told[e] what he hihte:

947. I] *om.* H.
957. make] maky*n*g a H, make a P, R 3, H 5.
962. no] non B.
965. vnseurli] vnseemly H, vnsemly R 3, H 5.
969. his] this H. 971. which] which þat H, R 3.

"This is," quod she, "pleynli to termyne,
The famous man, [the] prynce of elloquence
That gaf to Latynes the scole & the doctrine
Of rethorik, as welle of that science.
For which I will thou do thi dilligence
To write with othir of this Tullius
Al hool the caas, & gynne at Marrius."

"This is Tullius," said she, "the famous man who taught the Romans the arts of rhetoric and oratory."

¶ These woordes saide, Fortune made an eende;
She beet hir wynges & took hir to the fliht:
I cannat seie what weie she dede weende,
Sauf Bochas tellith, lich an aungel briht
At hir partyng she shewed a gret liht.
But as soone as she gan disapeere,
He took his penne [&] wrot as ye shal heere.

Telling Bochas to begin with Marius, Fortune flapped her wings and flew away in a great light.

[How Gayus Marrius, of low birthe born/ cam to high estat whiche blent with couetise after many grete batailes deied att mischeef.] [1]

HEER Bochas gynneth to tellen of þe man
Callid in his tyme Gayus Marius,
Born at Aprina[s], a castel of Tuscan,
Sone of a carpenteer, the stori tellith thus,
Pursued armys, manli & vertuous;
Thoruh al Rome nor in that contre
Was ther no man hold so strong as he.

Gaius Marius was born at Arpinum in Tuscany. He was the son of a carpenter,

Disciplyne and gret subtilite
He hadde also, as bookis specefie,
Prudence, manhod and habilite
Bothe in armys and in cheualrie,
Most famous holde toward that partie,
Withynne a while, myn auctour seith certeyn,
Chose a tribun & a gret capteyn.

strong and well disciplined, prudent and able in arms.

But fro the gynyng of his tendre age,
As histories put in remembraunce,
He was priked so sore in his corage
Bagredi fret of long contynuaunce,
Neuer to staunch[e] with non habundaunce; —

Chosen first a tribune, he later became a great captain, but was always covetous.

975. 2nd the] *om.* J. 977. that] þe H.
987. &] *om.* H, J, R 3.
988. tellen] writen H.
990. Aprina J, Arpynas H 5, Arpinas P.
1003. histories] stories H. 1005. by a gredy H.

[1] MS. J. leaf 126 recto.

The world nor Fortune, with al ther gret richesse,
Suffised nat tappese his gredynesse.

A diviner counselled him to go to Rome, where he should not fail to rise to high office

Entryng a temple he fond a dyuynour, [p. 310]
Cou*n*sailed [him] ther bi his dyuynaille
Tentre Rome & holde ther soiour,
Bi good auys and knihtli apparaille;
Made hym promys that he shal nat faille
Tatteyne be fauour of the comou*n*te
To gret offis & staat in the cite.

He became a consul, although the Senate scorned his low birth.

Fauour of comou*n*s brouht hy*m* to hih estat,
Bi them resceyued vnto the dignite
Of consuleer, al-be that the senat
Hadde disdeyn off his felicite,
Because he was born of louh degre.
Grau*n*tid to hym after be the tou*n*
To conquere rewmys a com*m*yssiou*n*.

Granted a commission to lead the Roman legions, he conquered Numidia and captured Jugurtha, for which he was given a triumph.

He gat the prouynce thoruh his hih renou*n*
Of Numedie, as he dede hem assaile,
And took the kyng of that regiou*n*
Callid Iugurta proudli in bataile.
For which emprise bi marcial apparaille
He gat the tryu*m*phe, thoruh the tou*n* ridyng,
Because onli for taky*n*g of that kyng.

The commons believed that all their prosperity lay in his hand;

And for he was a persone so notable
For many famous sodeyn gret victorie,
Namli in conquest preued proffitable,
To al the comou*n*, as put is in memorie;
And for thencres of his renou*n* & glorie,
Bi thoppynyou*n* hool of the cite,
In his hand lay al ther prosperite.

for he brought many nations into subjection to Rome, and overcame the Cimbri and the Tigurini, who presumptuously took upon themselves to pass the mountains of Italy.

Ageyn a peeple that callid was Tymbrois,
Them to conquere fro Rome he was sent dou*n*,
Also ageyn the boistous Tigurnois,
Gadred togidre of many naciou*n*.
Alle them he brouhte to subiecciou*n*,
Lik as Romeyns hadde afforn desired,
Because thei hadde ageyn ther tou*n* conspired.

1010. him] *om.* J. 1012. good] goodly H. 1016. hih] gret H.
1031. gret] *om.* H. 1032. Namli] manly H.
1033. comou*n*] comons H.
1036. ther] þe H.

Thei took upon hem of fals presu*m*pciou*n*
To passen alle the mou*n*teyns of Itaille,
First discou*n*fited, as maad is menciou*n*,
Thre Romeyn dukis felli in bataille,
Four scorre thousand clad in plate & maile
Slay*n* of Romeyns, the stori is weel knowe,
Vnder Thalpies at myscheef ouerthrowe.

He also put the Teutones to flight and took their leader prisoner.

This Marrius of marcial auenture
In Germanye hadde a gret bataille
With Tewtobochus, a geau*n*t of stature,
Put first to fliht with al his apparaille;
For Marrius dide hym so sore assaille,
At the chas[e] proudli born to grou*n*de,
Maugre his miht, tak & in cheynis bou*n*de.

Afterwards he slew 200,000 of the Cimbri and captured 8000.

Marrius aftir with his host hym drouh
Toward the peeple off Cymbrois for to fiht:
Too hundred thousand*, I fynde, of hem he slouh,
Eihte thousand take, thre thousand put to fliht;
Kyng Bolerus, a ful famous kniht,
Slayn in the feelde, for al his gret[e] pride,
Ageyn Marrius as he dide ride.

They were all slain, even the women, who would gladly have served in the Temple of Vesta.

That day of Cymbrois was al the peeple slay*n*,
The women afftir he list nat to reserue;
Yit thei proffered & wolde haue be ful fayn
Ther chastite deuoutli to obserue,
In the temple of Vesta for to serue.
But ther request[e] for he list nat heere,
With hym thei fauht; echon slay*n* ifeere.

Some slew one another and the rest hanged themselves.

Except that sum*m*e, wha*n* thei sauh non othir
Remedi, of purpos thei wer set,
Euerich of them to slen & moordren othir;
And som*m*e thouhte also that it was bet
To hang hemsilff vpon an hih gibet,
Than tabide of Marius the outrage,
Perpetueli to lyuen in seruage.

Thus Marius conquered three nations. He was chosen consul six times.

Thus Marius of thre naciou*n*s
Thoruh his conquest co*m*plisshed the victorie.
With p*r*isoneres of sondri regiou*n*s

1047. Thre] þe H. 1050. Vnder] ovir H.
1060. thousand] peeple B, J.
1062. Bolerus] Borelus H 5, Beleus P.
1080. co*m*plisshed] acco*m*plisshid H, R 3.

Entred Roome to his eneres of glorie,
With special laudes notable of memorie:
First the tryu*m*phe, a guerdou*n* synguleer,
He tymes sexe chose a consuleer.

Fortune was favourable to him at first, but later on she became adverse.

Thus Fortune was to hym fauourable,
To sette hym up in worldli dignites
For a sesou*n*; but for she was chau*n*gable,
Among hir gifftes & gret prosperites
She gaf hym part of gret aduersites:
And specialli the tyme acou*n*tid than,
Tween hym & Scilla wha*n* the werris ga*n*.

Lucius Sulla, Marius's great enemy.

Lucyus Scilla abidyng in Chau*m*payne, [p. 311]
Marrius at Roome tho present,
Whan the diuysiou*n* gan atween hem tweyne,
Ech to other contrarie of entent,
Malencolius and inpacient,
Which of bothe, the stori weel co*n*ceyued,
To gouerne sholde son*n*est be receyued.

marched on Rome against him.

Al sodenli, wher it wer riht or wrong,
Toward Roome takyng his passage,
Ageyn Marrius to make hy*m*seluen strong,
Gan slen & bren*n*e, & of gret outrage,
Wilful, hasti, furious of corage,
For sodeyn komyng & vnwar violence
Ageyn[e]s hym fond[e] no resistence.

and entering the city took the Capitol.

Too myhti batailles he dede with hym leede,
Entryng the cite, gan thoruh the wal[le] myne;
With o bataille faste ga*n* hym speede
To passe the gate callid Aquilyne
(The tothir gat[e] namyd was Colyne),
At whos entryng, bi record of the book,
Scilla be strengthe the Capitoile took.

Marius, who fled with his people into a marsh, was captured and sent to prison.

But whan Marrius hadde knowlechyng
That Scilla hadde so gret poweer & myht,
Withoute arest or lenger abidyng,
Into a maris Gayus anon riht
With al his peeple took sodenli his fliht.
Fet out be strengthe, koude hym nat diffende,
Scilla aftir to p*r*isou*n* dede hym sende.

1089. hir] his H. 1097. Impacient H. 1098. stori] tothir H. 1099. sonnest shulde H, sonest shold R 3. 1117. Marish P. 1119. be] wit*h* H.

Thus the prowesse for a while slepte
Of Marrius liggyng in prisoun.
Scilla that tyme the Capitoille kepte,
Wherbi al Roome stood in subieccioun.
And of hatrede in haste he sente doun
A sturdi cherl to Marius in his dreed,
Whil he lay bounde to smyten of his hed.

Sulla kept Rome under his subjection and sent a sturdy knave to smite off Marius's head while he lay bound.

This cherl weel compact of braun & of bonys,
Sent of purpos Marrius for toppresse,*
For his strengthe ordeyned for the nonys, —
To the prisoun the cherl gan faste hym dresse,
Wher Marrius was fetrid in distresse,
Fulli in purpos, withoute mor delay,
To heuedyn hym in prisoun ther he lay.

Losed hym first, liggyng on his couche;
And Marius [a]roos up lik a man,
The cherl feerful to smyte or to touche.
And Marius ful proudli tho began
To entre a place beside of a woman,
Fond an asse ther of auenture,
Vpon whos bak the se he gan recure.

After he had loosened his bonds the churl was afraid to strike, and Marius escaped on an ass

Toward Affrik ther he fond passage,
Bi enprisownyng thouh he wer wex[e] feynt;
Yit ther abood, stille in his corage,
Hih worthynesse with prudence meynt,
Which in his persone wer* nat [fully] queynt,
Ageyn the malis to make a countirtaille,
Off proude Scilla the malis eft tassaile.

to the sea and thence to Africa, where he dwelt until he was able to give battle to Sulla again.

Of Itaille rood thoruh the contre,
Took his viage towarde* Roome toun,
With foure batailes entreth the cite,
Sixe hundrid knihtis be computacioun
Slayn in the feeld, as maad is mencioun.
Wher men may seen, who list looke a-ferre,
What damage diuysioun doth in werre.

Returning to Rome, he entered the city, with four battalions; and 600 knights were slain,

1123 *is misplaced at end of stanza and marked* a, 1124 *is marked* b, H.
1128. 2nd of] *om.* H.
1129. to oppresse B.
1146. wer] was B, H — fully] *om.* J, P.
1150. towarde] thoruh B.

including the great consul Octavius, whose head was set on a pole.

First bi the manhod off this Marius,
In this dyuisiou*n*, the stori who list reede,
The grete consul callid Octauyus
Lost his hed[e] & his lyff in deede; —
Vpon a pole whil it dede bleede
Was cruelli presentid of entent
Tofor the iuges sittyng in iugement.

Merula, priest of the Temple of Jupiter, was also slain, and Crassus and Catulus.

Of whos deth[e] sum*me* of hem wer fayn,
Sum*me* sori, of loue as thei wer bou*n*de.
And in this werre Merula was slay*n*,
Preest in the temple, lik as it is fou*n*de,
Of Iubiter, with many mortal wou*n*de.
The Romey*n* slayn that callid was Crassus;
With fyr consumyd was proude Catulus.

Marius held his own against his enemies

Alle his enmyes Marius dede encou*m*bre,
Which ageyn hym be conspiraciou*n*
Wer assentid with a ful gret nou*m*bre
In ther auys for to haue put hym dou*n*,
Take from hym his domynaciou*n*.
But he abood the torment & the shours,
Strong to co*n*dempne alle his conspirato*ur*s.

and was chosen consul six times. Finally, Fortune turned away from him.

Sixe tymes, afforn rehersed heer, [p. 312]
Of condiciou*n* thouh he wer despitous,
He was chose so ofte consuleer;
Til Fortune gan wexen envious
Ageyn this saide cruel Marius,
Which made the senat with al the cheualrie
To gruchche ageyn his hatful tiran*n*ye.

At this time Damasippus sent four Romans,

In this tyme, the stori maketh mynde,
Damasippus, a pretour of the tou*n*,
Freendli to Marius & helpyng, as I fynde,
Vnder a shadwe of decepciou*n*
Vnto ther cite for to do tresou*n*,
Causyng foure Romey*n*s come I-feere
Toffor Marrius a certey*n* day tappeere.

Scævola, Cotta, Domitius and Antistius to Marius, whom he slew unlawfully.

And ther namys to putte in memorie,
Sceuola, Carbo and Domycius,
The fourthe off them, as seith the stori,
Callid in Roome the wise Antistius.

1173. ther] þat H.
1179. offten H. 1186. helpyng] helpely H, helply R 3.
1188. do] *om.* H. 1192. Sevola H — Carbo] Cotta P.

Togidre assemblid tofor Marrius,
He of rancour, geyn iugement or lawe,
Made hem be slayn & thoruh the cite drawe.

Ther bodies aftir wern in Tibre cast
Bi cruelte of saide Marius.
Alle this while the cruel werre last
Tween hy*m* & Scilla, til duk Campanyus
Cam on the parti, hard[y] & despitous,
To helpe Scilla ther baneres first displaied,
Wherof al Roome was sodenli affraied.

Their bodies were thrown into the Tiber. Duke Campanus aided Sulla,

At the gate that callid was Colyne
Marrie & Scille hadde a gret bataille, —
Foure score thousand, the nou*m*bre to termyne
On Marrius side slayn, it is no faille;
Scilla victorious, with marcial apparaille
Entryng the tou*n*, ageyn his oth, parde,
Thre thousand citeseyns slouh of the cite.

and Marius was defeated in a great battle, losing four score thousand of his men.

Of folk disarmyd & naked in the tou*n*,
Thei nouther spared old nor yong of age,
The cruel moordrers walkyng up nor dou*n*
Be Scilla sent in that mortal rage,
Till Catullus, a p*r*ince fall in age,
Saide vnto Scilla, "we can no difference
Atween rebelliou*n* nor atween in*n*ocence;

Sulla massacred the people until an old prince named Catullus

We moordre & slen withoute excepciou*n*
Both hih & louh, holdyng no maneere;
Ageyn al knihthod, to myn oppynyou*n*,
We do proceede in our conquest heere, —
Our title is lost the tryu*m*phe to requere
Of hih prowesse, wh*a*n we canat obserue
No difference to slen nor [to] reserue."

remonstrated with him, saying that if they continued thus to slaughter they would have no title of triumph.

And in this while, of hatful cruelte
Scilla contreued lettres diffamable,
Wherbi fyue hu*n*dred out of that cite
Wer falsli banshed, citeseyns notable, —
Ageyn[e]s hem he was so vntretable, —
Alle ther goodes achetid in that rage
Of auarice and of fals pillage.

Sulla also banished 500 notables and confiscated their goods out of avarice.

1195. afforn H. 1202. on] vnto J, to P, on in H 5.
1204. was] wer H.
1216. Catallus H.

A brother of Marius hid in a goat-house but was dragged to Catulus's grave,

Another Romeyn namyd Marrius,
Brother to Marrius, of who*m* tofor I tolde,
For dreed of Scilla fledde & took an hous
Which vnto goot was set up for a foolde;
Fou*n*d & rent out in his daies olde,
With cordes drawe (no rescus myhte hy*m* saue)
Of cruel vengau*n*ce to Catullus graue,

where Sulla commanded his eyes to be torn out, his hands smitten off, and his head to be set on a pole and sent to Marius.

Wher Scilla made bi cruel* iugement,
With a sharp suerd[e], forgid for to bite,
Aftir tyme his eien wer out rent,
Bothe attonys his handis of to smyte.
His hed smet of, no rau*n*sou*n* myhte hy*m* quite,
Set on a pole, it wolde be non othir,
And off despiht[e] sent vnto his brothir,

Marius himself was in great danger;

To grete Marius, of whom I spak now riht, —
The grete duk, so mihti & so huge,
Which hadde afforn[e] tak hy*m* to the fliht
For feer of Scilla in that mortal deluge,
Into a cite to fynde ther refuge,
Callid Preueste, ther stondyng in gret dreed,
Namli whan he beheeld his brothris hed.

and when he saw his brother's head he despaired, and drawing a sword bade his servant kill him.

For-asmoche as he no soco*u*r fond,
Disespeired, this was his purpos:
To slen hymsilff[e] with his owne hond
In thilke place wher he was kept[e] cloos.
Drouh out a suerd, up anon he roos,
Constreyned his seruaunt in that sodey*n* affray
Smyte off his hed, the silue same day.

Men may see that death is the end of all trouble and adversity. Fortune once more shewed in the case of Marius how she can vary her course.

¶ Men seen how deth is fyn of al myscheeff, [p. 313]
Eende off aduersite that doth wrechchis tarie.
Fortune heer maketh another preeff
In Marrius, how she hir cours can varie,
Bi an euidence hatful and contrarie
To shewe hir malis and vngoodliheed
Ageyn this duk, alas, whan he was ded.

This frowarde* ladi, of malis most vengable,
Whan hir list furiousli to raue
And shewe hirsilff[e] cruel & vnstable,

1239. Catallus H. 1240. cruel] gret B.
1268. frowarde] frowardli B.
1269. H *repeats here the 2nd line of preceding stanza, but alters last word to* rave.

To non estat she list no reward haue.
Causede Marius be take out of his graue
Bi cruel Scilla, in stori it is fou*n*de,
His ougli carey*n* smet on pecis rou*n*de.

And aftir, mor to shewe his cruelte, —
Marrius sholde haue no burying place, —
Caste his careyn, of kankrid enmyte,
Into Tibre, ther was non othir grace.
Loo, thus can Fortune for hir folk purchace!
Bi which exau*m*ple touchyng Marrius,
Off worldli chau*n*ges Bochas writeth thus,

After his burial, Sulla had his body dug up again, and his ugly corpse cut into round pieces and cast into the Tiber. Thus Fortune rewards her folk!

Maketh in this chapitle a descripsiou*n*,
First what thyng is verray gentilesse,
To sette a preeff & a probaciou*n*,
No thyng atteyneth vnto hih noblesse
But the cleer shyny*n*g of vertuous clennesse,
Which may nat shewe, in louh nor hih* parage,
But wher it groweth out of a peur corage.

Bochas says that nothing attains to high noblesse except the clear shining of virtue, that can spring only from a pure heart.

Worldli poweer, oppressiou*n*, tiran*n*ye,
Erthli tresour, gold, stonis nor richesse
Be no menys vnto gent[e]rie,
But-yif vertu reule ther hih prowesse:
For wher vices haue any interesse
In hih[e] berthe, mene, or louh kynreede,
Deeme no man gentil, but onli bi his deede.

Worldly power, tyranny, and wealth are no means to gentility unless they are ruled by virtue.

In roial paleisis of ston & metal wrouht,
With galleries or statli cloistres rou*n*de,
Gentilesse or noblesse is nat souht,
Nor in cileris nor in voutis rou*n*de;
But onli ther wher vertu doth habou*n*de:
Corious clothes nor gret pocessiou*n*s
Maketh nat men gentil but co*n*dic[i]ou*n*s.

No man is gentle except by his deeds;

Philisophres conclude* in ther entent
And alle thes worthi famous old aucto*u*rs,
No man may quethe in his testament
Gentilesse vnto his successours;
Of wikked weed[e] come non holsum flours.
Concludyng thus: of good[e] men & shrewes,
Calle ech man gentil aftir his good[e] thewes.

and gentility cannot be devised by testament to our successors. Wholesome flowers do not grow on weeds.

1274. on] in H. 1282. chapiter H 5, Chapter P.
1283. ge*n*tilnesse H. 1287. hih nor louh B, P.
1292. hih] his H. 1293. haue] hath H. 1299. Sileer*e*s H.
1303. concluden B. 1305. questh H.

Duke Marius, born of poor parents, was a man of courageous nobility, but his heart was cankered by the worm of avarice.

Duk Marrius, of whom I spak toforn,
Of nature, the stori berth witnesse,
As* he discent [both] poore and nedi born,
Bi disposicioun of coraious noblesse,
Hadde in his persoone wit, strengthe [&] hardynesse;
Vndir al this, ther dide his herte myne
A werm of auarice his worshep to declyne.

What avails plenty that can never suffice? The river of Tantalus cannot assuage the thirst of greed.

What uaileth plente, that neuer may suffise?
Or what the flood, that staunche may no thrust?
Or what an appetit, that euer doth arise,
Alwey to ete, and euer to ete hath lust?
Of kankrid hunger so fretyng is the rust,
That the ryueer of Tantalus in his rage
Of gredi etikes the fret may nat asswage.

You have heard the end of Marius. Three Cleopatras next appeared before Bochas, with woeful downcast looks.

¶ Of Marrius ye han herd the eende,
His woful fall & his vnhappi caas,
Into fate how he dede weende.
Now wil I folwe myn auctour Iohn Bochas,
How onto hym thre Cleopatras,
With look[e] doun cast, woful face & cheere,
Alle attonys to hym dide appeere.

The first of them had had three husbands, of whom the last was Antiochus;

The firste of hem, bi processe of writyng,
Hadde thre husbondis, Bochas doth expresse:
Weddid in youthe to Alisaundre the kyng
Callid Zebenna, a prince* of gret noblesse;
Aftir that for hir gret fairnesse
She weddid was vnto Demetrius,
And laste of all to kyng Anthiochus.

and as Bochas has already written their unfortunate fate and her son's great unkindness, it were idle to rehearse it all again.

Of hir thre husbondis woful auenture
And of hir sonis gret vnkyndenesse,
Bochas afforn hath doon his besi cure
Ceriousli the maner to expresse,
Which to reherse ageyn wer idilnesse,
Sith al the processe heer-toforn is founde
Of the firste & eek of the secounde,

The second Cleopatra was wedded to Ptolemy Euergetes, who served her son up to her at table.

Which weddid was to kyng Tholome, [p. 314]
Lik as toforn is maad eek mencioun
Bothe of ther ioie & ther aduersite.
The firste slayn be drynkyng of poisoun,

1312. As] Al B, & H, And R 3 — both] *om.* J, H 5.
1317. availith H. 1319. which nevir doth rise H.
1334. prince] princesse B.

And the secou*n*de, to hir confusiou*n*,
Bi Euergetes, wher she wer wo or fayn,
Was with hir child[e] seruid, that was slayn.

The thridde weddid was to kyng Grispus,
Slayn in a temple bi ful gret outrage,
For dreed & shame gan wexe furious,
To saue hirsilff[e] knew non auau*n*tage,
Saue she enbracid of Iubiter an image,
In the stori as heer-tofforn is fou*n*de,
Or she was ded suffred many a wou*n*de.

The third married King Grypus; and she was slain in a temple.

[How kyng Mitridate bood vij. yere *in* wildernesse had grete torme*n*tys bothe *in* see & londe, by his blood brouht to vttrau*n*ce slouh hi*m*silf *with* a swerde.] [1]

I WIL passe ouer thes Cleopatras thre,
Foorth proceede to the hasti fate
Soone execut bi Parchas cruelte
Vpon the duk callid Mitridate.
First reherse the grete vnky*n*dli hate
Of them that wern his tuto*u*rs, as I reede,
Hym to destroie bassent of his kynreede.

Duke Mithridates was in his young days nearly destroyed by his tutors, who, seeking his death,

Which of purpos dide his deth p*ro*uide
Bi many vnkouth strau*n*ge occasiou*n*:
In tendre youth[e] first thei made hy*m* ride
Vpon an hors wildere than [a] leou*n*,
Off purpos onli for his destrucciou*n*.
But al-be-so that he was yong of age,
The hors he reuled in al his moste rage.

made him ride a wild horse.

Nat of doctryne, but onli of nature
He was disposid kon[n]y*n*gli to ride,
Ouer hym the maistri to recure,
Maugre the hors, of wit he was his guide.
What weye he took[e], froward or a-side,
He dau*n*tede hym, that wher-so-euer he rood
Bridled hym & on his bak abood.

But he was so skilled a horseman that he escaped all danger.

His owne kyn & his next allies
Most laboured to brynge hy*m* to myscheeff,
With venymous drynk set on hym espies

His own kin tried to poison him,

1362. duke] king P. 1369. a] *om.* H.

[1] MS. J. leaf 128 recto.

At good leiseer, as dooth a couert theeff,
Of ther fell poisou*n* for to make a preeff,
In ther entent, the stori is weel kouth,
Hym to moordre in his tendre youth.

and for self-protection he provided himself with all manner of notable antidotes.

But whan that he appareeyued ther tresou*n*,
To saue hymsilff[e] made gret ordenau*n*ce;
Anon as he gan haue suspeciou*n*
Of the[r] vnkyndli hatful purueyau*n*ce,
For remedies made cheuisau*n*ce:
Was prouided ther malis to declyne,
Be many notable preeued medecyne.

To avoid his enemies he withdrew from his country and hunted wild beasts

And ther malis prudentli teschewe,
Is reme*m*bred, whil he was yong of age,
With certey*n* freendes, which that dede hy*m* sue,
He disposed of custum his corage
To hunte & chase beestis most sauage;
Vndir that colour he dede it for a wile,
Ferr from his contre absente hy*m* for a while.

and lodged in caves and hollow trees among high hills in the wilderness for seven years.

Of o corage, of oon hert & o cheer
Suffred man̄li, took non heuynesse,
In desertis space of seuene yeer,
Among hih hilles abood in wildirnesse.
Set in Asia, the stori berth witnesse,
Fond no loggyng, tracyng the contres,
Saue in kauernys & in holwe trees.

He lived on the beasts he slew, slept little and avoided idleness,

The book reme*m*breth how that his diete
Wer beestis wilde enchacid *with* gret miht,
Fledde idilnesse, eschewed al quiete,
And litil sleep suffised hy*m* at niht;
Bexercise his bodi was maad liht:
Ther was nouther, wha*n* hym list pursue,
Hert nor hynde that miht his ha*n*d eschewe.

and was so swift and strong that no animal could escape him.

He nouther dradde tigres nor leou*n*s;
He was so swifft, thouh thei dede hy*m* assaile, —
Lik of strengthe to olde champiou*n*s,
No wilde beeste of gret nor smal entaille
Tescape his hand[e] myht nat cou*n*tiruaille
Yif he wer war[e], erli outher late,
So gret[e] swifftnesse hadde Mitridate.

1407. 2nd in] gret H. 1411. at] at þe H.

Among he hadde in armys excersise,
Among to tourneye & ren*n*e on hors[e]bak;
Al delicat fare he dede also despise,
Of gredi excesse; in hy*m* ther was no lak:
A-nihter-tyme his slep ful ofte he brak,
Sto*u*ndemeel the hour[e]s for to marke;
In the dawenyng roos up or the larke.

He was a good jouster and rider and despised luxury.

The space accomplisshid fulli of seuene yeer, [p. 315]
He is repeired hom to his contre;
Shewed hymsilf of manhod and of cheer
Ful lik a kniht, his stori who list see.
Wherof his enmyes sore astoned bee;
Kauhte of his comyng in herte a maner dreed,
Supposyng afforn that he was ded.

At the end of the seven years he went home and was feared by all his enemies.

In whos absence his wiff Leodices
Conceyued a childe, as maad is me*n*ciou*n*.
For the diffame sholde nat kome in pres,
Hym for to moordre she souhte occasiou*n*,
Fulli in purpos to slen hym be poisou*n*.
Of which diffautis hir lord was nothy*n*g fayn,
Knowyng the trouthe, made hir to be slayn.

During his absence his wife had a child, and to hide her shame sought to poison him, for which he caused her to be slain.

Took on hym aftir many knihtli deede:
First to conquere al Pafflagonye
Bi the helpe of worthi Nychomeede,
That tyme callid kyng of Bithynye,
Togidre assurid to been of allie
In losse or lucre, Fortune to be ther guide,
And therto swor[e]n neuer to deuyde.

He conquered Paphlagonia with the help of Nicomedes,

To Mitridate legat*es* wer dou*n* sent
From the Romeyns, hym lowli requeryng,
That he wolde, lik to ther entent,
Pafflagonie restore vnto ther kyng,
Which he hadde won*n*e, the cite assailyng.
But he list nat aduertise ther praieere,
Nor on no parti ther requestis heere.

and afterwards was required by the Romans to restore the kingdom. This he refused to do.

He dradde nat ther thretis nor manacis,
Gat proudli after the lond of Galathie,
In his conquest*es* wan* many othir placis,
Capadoce took to his partie,

He had no fear of them, and soon conquered Galatia and Cappadocia.

1426. full offt his sleep H.
1435. that] trowid þ*at* H.
1459. wan] gat B.

Slouh ther kyng, of hatrede & envie,
Ariaractes, a ful manli man;
And in this wise his co*n*quest he began.

He then fell out with Nicomedes, who took the crown of Cappadocia without Mithridates' consent.

Ageyn thassuraunce tween hy*m* & Nichomeede,
Alle sodenli he gan falle at debat;
Thouhte he wolde werreie hy*m* in deede,
Because that he, pompous & elat,
In Capadoce took on hym the estat
To regne as kyng, ageyn[e]s his entent,
He nouther beyng of cou*n*sail nor assent.

although he had married his sister.

Yit Nichomeede, or thei ga*n* debate,
Hadde long afforn[e] to his owne encres
The sustir weddid of this Mitridate,
Whan thei as brethre lived in rest and pes.*
And she was also callid Leodices,
Hauyng too sonys born for to succeede
Afftir disses of seid[e] Nichomeede.

After Nicomedes' death he deprived his two sons of the kingdom

But bi processe thes said[e] childre tweyne
In Capadoce, bi help of Mitridate,
Cleymed a title, iustli for tatteyne
Vnto the crowne, ther fadir ded but late.
For which thei gan felli to debate,
Til Mitridate falsli ga*n* co*n*tryue
His too neuews vngoodli to depryue.

and had his own son crowned there. The Romans sent down Ariobazarnes to chase him out, but Mithridates allied himself with Tigranes and was victorious,

Al Capadoce he took into his hand,
His owne sone he hath ther crowned ky*n*g.
Capadociens, bassent of al the lond,
Gan disobeie of purpos his werkyng.
Whan the Romeyns co*n*sidred al thys thi*n*g,
Ariobarzanes in haste thei sente dou*n*
Geyn Mitridate to keep that regiou*n*.

The sone of whom fro them thei ha[n] refusid,
Out of ther kyngdam ga*n* hy*m* to enchase;
For thei sempte ther franchise was abusid,
To seen a foreyn occupie that place.
Mitridate gan newli hem manace,
And took with hym to susteene his partie
Tigranes the kyng of Armenye.

1462. Arriarattes H, Ariarectes J, Ariarathes P.
1474. lived in rest and pes] list to leue in pes B.
1493. hy*m* to] them H.

Ariobarzanes, that was fro Roome sent
To Capadoce to helpe hem & cou*n*saille,
Of Mitridate knowyng the entent,
How he cam dou*n* proudli hym tassaille
With Tigranes set in the ferst bataille,
Of Capadoce that al the regiou*n*
Was brouht that day to ther subiecciou*n*.

Thus Mitridate hauyng his entent,
In short tyme co*n*trees co*n*queryng,
Was myhtiest p*r*ince of al the orient,
And in tho daies oon the grettest kyng.
And as it is reme*m*bred be writy*n*g,
He delitid most in astronomye,
In sortilege & in sorcerye.

and soon became the most powerful prince in the East. He delighted in astronomy and divination and sorcery,

And with al these, he dede his besi cure [p. 316]
For to lerne vnkouth conclusiou*n*s
And secretes souht out bi nature,
Knew the langage of dyuers regiou*n*s,
Of too and tuenty sondri naciou*n*s,
And heeld[e] women many mo than oon,
Loued Hipsicrata aboue hem euerichon.

and in abstruse problems, and knew 22 different languages. He had many wives, but loved Hypsicratia best.

To the Romeyns this manli Mitridate,
As bookis olde recorde of hy*m* & seyn,
Vpon a day, of verray cruel hate
Thoruh al Asie he bad that ech Romeyn
Sholde of his men merciles be slayn:
Twenti thousand he slouh eek on o day
Of Romey*n* marchau*n*t*es*, ther durst no ma*n* sei nay.

He hated the Romans and slew 20,000 of their merchants in one day,

To hym he drouh dyuers naciou*n*s
To encrece* his parti bi puissau*n*ce,
Kymbrois, Gallois, with othir regiou*n*s,
Bastornois took to his alliau*n*ce;
With strau*n*ge peeple made his aqueyntau*n*ce
Wher that euer he rood nyh or ferre,
With them of Roome for to holde werre.*

and allied himself with various strange peoples against Rome.

In Grece also he gat many an ile,
Al Ciclades to his subieccioun;
Conquered so, that withyn*ne* a while
Of Athenes he gat the famous tou*n*.
But whan Romeyns knew his ente*n*ciou*n*,
Thei sente Scilla in a furious heete
With Mitridate in Grece for to meete.

In Greece he conquered the Cyclades and Athens. Sulla was sent against him,

1525. o] a H. 1528. Tencrece B. 1533. a werre B.

and, defeating his general Archelaus,

Archelaus, which that was constable,
Leedyng the host of kyng Mitridate,
Gan ageyn Scilla, trusty*ng* he was able,
Maugre Romeynes* with hy*m* to debate.
As thei mette in ther furious hate,
Beside Ortonia of Grece a gret[e] tou*n*,
Of Archelaus the parti was born dou*n*.

conquered Ephesus, Cappadocia and Bithynia.

Ther gan Scilla to been victorious
Geyn Mitridate, & be gret violence
Gat al Ephese, a kyngdam ful famous,
Rood thoruh Asie, fond no resistence;
Bi his knihthod & manli prouidence
Capadoce, Bithynye eek also
To Romeyn handis he gat hem bothe too.

At this, Mithridates hastened to make peace, hoping to succeed better later.

Whan Mitridate parceyued hath this thy*n*g,
How the conquest of Scilla took encrees,
Anon he caste withoute long tarieng,
For a tyme with hym to haue a pes.
Of hih[e] wisdam he was nat rek[e]les
To dissymule til* he fond tyme & space
In Fortune to fynde bettre grace.

On Sulla's return to Rome,

Abood his tyme, kept hymsilue cloos
Til he fond leiseer lik his oppynyou*n*.
In this while of auenture aroos
Withyn*n*e Roome a gret discenciou*n*
Tween too consuleris beyng in that tou*n*,
Which tappese bi his auctorite
Scilla cam up ageyn to the cite.

Mithridates collected an army and laid siege to Cyzicus, the greatest city of Asia,

Whan Mitridate his absence dede espie,
To his purpos fond oportunyte,
Gadred peeple, & with his cheualrie
A siege leid to Cizite the cite,
Of al Asie most off auctorite.
Til Lucullus, a myhti consuleer,
To breke the seege aproche ga*n* ful neer.

but was attacked by Lucullus, who

Mitridate hadde on fyue capteyns
Tofor the tou*n* made a disconfiture,
Of hih despiht he hadde to Romey*n*s.
But Lucullus the damage to recure,

1544. Romeynes] with Romey*n*s B. 1552. &] of H.
1555. hath] *om.* H. 1557. long] *om.* H.
1560. til] whan B. 1566. that] þe H, R 3.

Tenclose ther enmyes dide his* besi cure:
To his mynours gaf anon in charge
Aboute the siege to make a dich ful large.

Thei withyn*ne* hadde knowlechyng
Be certeyn toknys of al þ*er* gouernau*n*ce;
Wherupon thei made no taryeng
To caste a weie for ther deliuerau*n*ce.
Mitridates seyng ther ordenau*n*ce,
Of hih prudence scaped awey beside,
And at the seege no lenger list abide.

dug a ditch about the besieging army and drove Mithridates away.

Lucullus than, the myhti consuleer,
Pursued aftir, slouh of his meyne
Swich multitude, that Asapus the ryueer
Was maad with blood[e] lik the Rede Se.
With wynd & tempest fordryue also was he,
And whan he sauh no soco*u*r on the lond,
To shipp he wente with strong & myhti hond.

and, pursuing him, slew so many of his men that the river Asopus became like the Red Sea.

He fond Fortune cruel aduersarie [p. 317]
On lond & se, this worthi Mitridate;
And Neptunus made the se co*n*trarie,
Ageyn[e]s hym his puissau*n*ce to abate.
What shal men calle it? — influence or fate? —
So sodenli a p*r*ince of hih renou*n*
From hih noblesse to be plongid dou*n*.

Fortune was contrary to Mithridates and threw him down from his high estate.

For any myscheeff he kept ay o visage,
This Mitridate, & loth was for to plie
Or for to bowe, so strong was his corage,
But efft ageyn goth with his cheualrie
Toward Adrastus, an hill of Armenye,
Where-as Pompeie besette hym enviro*u*n,
Sent fro Roome to his destrucciou*n*.

Nevertheless he did not lose courage, and once more gave battle to his enemies in Armenia.

Mitridate makyng his loggyng place
Vndir that hill, whan it drouh to niht,
The troubli heuene with thundryng ga*n* manace;
The firy leuene dirkid hath his siht;
The cloudi moone clipsed of hir liht,
Astoned hym bi vnwar violence,
That he stood confus of al prouidence.

The sky was troubled with thunder and fiery lightning, and the moon eclipsed.

1580. his] ther B. 1582. the] his H. 1587. Mitridate H.
1592. Asopus H, J, P, R 3.
1608. Armonye H.

He grew almost weary of life; but his faithful wife never once left him and followed him wherever he went, disguised as a page.

He was be tempest & vnwar dirknesse
Almost maad wery of his woful liff;
Yit I fynde, of verray kyndenesse,
Hipsicrata, which that was his wiff,
Nouther for werre nor no mortal stryff
Left hym neuere: disgised of visage
Folwed hym arraied as a page.

Yet even when Fortune was most menacing, his courage did not fail him.

Yit in his moste mortal heuynesse,
Wha*n* cloudi Fortune ga*n* hy*m* most manace,
Of his corage the naturel quiknesse
Appalled nat nor remeued fro*m* his place,
So hih prowesse dide his hert enbrace.
Nat disespeired for no sodeyn fall,
Of condiciou*n*s he was so marciall.

He shewed no sign of weakness, although there was the greatest occasion for despair.

In tokne wherof, he stondyng at myscheeff,
Chau*n*ged nouther cheer nor co*n*tenau*n*ce:
An euidence & a ful gret preeff
Of manli force and hertli assurau*n*ce.
Deffying Fortune, with al hir variau*n*ce,
Whan that he fond to his destrucciou*n*
Of disespeir grettest occasiou*n*.

With him was a bailiff named Castor, who traitorously sent his master's children as hostages to Rome,

With hym he hadde a bailiff, as I fynde,
Callid Castor, which of condiciou*n*
Was to his lord[e] fals & eek vnkynde,
And conspired ageyn hym fals tresou*n*.
In tokne wherof, up to Roome tou*n*
His lordis childre, yong & tendre of age,
Lik a fals theeff he sent hem in hostage.

and murdered one of his sons. Another son, Pharnaces, was ungrateful

Oon of his sones he moordred be tresou*n*,
Which Mitridate took ful sore at herte.
Another sone, as maad is menciou*n*,
Fals to his fader, which wha*n* he dide adu*er*te,
The vnkyndnesse made hym sore smerte;
For of al vicis, shortli to conclude,
Werst of alle is ingratitude.

and disloyal, and, taking possession of the army,

This same child, of whom I make mynde,
Callid Pharnax, which ageyn nature
To his fadir tretour & vnkynde, —
And his purpos ageyn hym to recure
In al hast[e] dede his besi cure;
For tacomplisshe his purpos in partie,
Took to hym hool his fadris cheualrie.

1622. no] for H. 1635. Of] & H.

Be sleihte & meede whan he was maad[e] stro*n*g,
He beseged his fadir rou*n*d aboute, —
Vnto nature, me seemeth, he dide wro*n*g
To putte his fadir in so gret a doute.
Kyndenesse was ferr shet withoute,
Wha*n* the sone, with hate set affire,
Ageyns his fadir list falsli to co*n*spire.

laid siege to his father (which, it seems to me, was wrong),

With multitude his fadir was co*n*streyned,
Maugre his myht, into a to*ur* to flee,
His sone vnkynde hath at hym disdeyned;
And yit for al his strau*n*ge aduersite,
Of his corage the magnanymyte
In his persone stood hool, list nat varie,
Thouh Fortune was to hym co*n*trarie.

and compelled him to seek refuge in a tower.

Yit myn aucto*ur* Bochas berth record,
That Mitridate, yif it wolde haue bee,
Requered his sone to been at accord
And set aside al old contrariouste.
But he vnkynde, was indurat parde,
Euere froward, malicious of corage,
So disposed from his tendre age.

Although he bade his son make peace with him, the son was obdurate;

So that the kyng Mitridate, alas, [p. 318]
Was ouercome be vnkyndenesse,
That neuer afforn[e] in no man*er* caas
Stood disamaied, but of hih prowesse
Kept ay o face al passiou*n*s to represse.
This vertu force, bi marcial doctryne,
For non aduersite suffrid* hy*m* declyne.

and Mithridates, who never before had lost heart, was overcome by unkindness.

Eende of his werris & his mortal stryues,
Of his debatis and discenciou*n*s,
His co*n*cubynes, his douhtres & his wyues,
Be mene onli of certeyn pociou*n*s,
Slouh hem alle be drynkyng of poisou*n*s;
For he nat wolde, the cause to descryue,
Aftir his deth thei sholde abide alyue.

He slew his wives and daughters and concubines by giving them poison,

His owne deth, of mortal fel rigour
Compassed afforn[e], thus he ga*n* deuise:
Made a Frensh kniht that was a soudio*ur*,
With a sharp suerd in ful cruel wise
To ren*n*e hym thoruh; wherbi the frau*n*chise
Conserued was his purpos to fulfill,
He shold nat deie but bi his owne will.

and made a Gallic knight run him through with a sharp sword.

1687. suffrid] listnat B. 1694. on live H. 1697. Franch H.

This was the end of Mithridates. Let all princes take heed of his death.

Loo, heer the eende of kyng Mitridate!
Lat p*r*incis alle of his deth take heede,
How reklesli he passed into fate
And bi assent made his herte bleede.
And Bochas heer, who list his book to reede,
Pleynli rehersyng but in woordes fewe,
To worldli p*r*incis doth his conceit shewe.

Lenvoye.

Mighty Princes, compare in your minds the concord and gladness of heaven and the worldly changes of Fortune.

MYHTI P*r*incis, lefft up yo*u*r corages,
Toward heuene doth yo*u*r hert*es* dr*e*sse,
Of yo*u*r memorie* to*u*rne up þe visages,
Wher ioie is euere, co*n*cord and gladnesse,
Trewe armonye, celestial suetnesse, —
Cou*n*tirpeiseth in yo*u*r remembrau*n*ce
Worldli chau*n*gis, Fortunys variau*n*ce.

Think of the outrage of war, slaughter, murder, division, deceit, brought about through a sudden change of worldly variance.

Aduertiseth the mortal fel out*r*ages
Of blodi werris impossible to represse,
Whil fals envie with his furious rages
In sondry rewmys hath so gret interesse, —
Slauhtre, moordre, deuisiou*n*, falsnesse,
Which conscience haue brouht[e] to vttrau*n*ce
Thoruh sodeyn chau*n*g of worldli variau*n*ce.

Reckon up the princes, who sat on high thrones, and their end, and the bloody wages of tyrants.

Rekne up p*r*incis that sat on hih[e] stages:
What was the fyn of ther roial noblesse?
Or of tirau*n*tis rekne up the bloodi wages:
Sodey*n* slauhtre guerdouned ther woodnesse.
Mitridate can bern herof witnesse,
Bi blood vnkynde brouht vnto vttrau*n*ce,
Thoruh sodeyn chau*n*g of worldli variau*n*ce.

Remember the Golden Age, when Saturn ruled, and the silver world of Jupiter, and the fierce world made steel by Mars.

P*r*incis remembreth vpon the goldene ages,
Wha*n* Satourn reuled the world in rihtwisnesse;
Next Iubiter, for peeplis auau*n*tages,
In silueren world co*n*serued in clen*n*esse,
Which Mars hath now to*u*rnid to felnesse,
Made it stelene, with suerd, dagger & lau*n*ce,
Thoruh sodeyn chau*n*g of worldli variau*n*ce.

1711. memorie] memoire B, J.
1716. the] their H — out*r*ages] Coragis H.

Of Mitridate registreth the viages,
Conspired poisou*n*s taffraie his hih prowesse,
On lond and se tempestuous passages,
Bi constrey*n*t bood seuene yeer in wildirnesse.
Of his wandryng peiseth thu*n*sekirnesse,
His eende in myscheef, knew non auoidau*n*ce
Geyn worldli chau*n*g nor Fortunys variau*n*ce.

Remember the warlike enterprises and insecure life of Mithridates, who could not avoid the variance of Fortune.

Yif neccligence haue brouht you in rerages
Towardis God, or he rekne in streihtnesse,
Lat resou*n* medle for you to ley*n* hostages, —
Compassiou*n*, merci, party*n*g of almesse,
Toward heuene to supporte yo*u*r feeblesse,
Wha*n* yo*u*r meritis shal peisen in ballau*n*ce
Of worldli chau*n*gis & Fortunys variau*n*ce.

If you have been negligent towards God, let reason help you to lay compassion, charity and mercy as hostages in heaven.

Deth spareth* nouther hih blood nor hih lynages,
Hath mynde heeron for any reklesnesse;
Transitoire been heer yo*u*r pilgrymages,
Set with brigau*n*tis vnwarli you toppresse,
But-yif prudence bi gret auysenesse
With prouidence preserue yo*u*r puissau*n*ce
Geyn worldli chau*n*g & Fortunys variau*n*ce.

Death spares no man, but prudence may preserve you against worldly change.

[How Eucratides kyng of Sithie was slayn bi Demetrius, and aft*er* his careyn cast to houndys.] [1]

NEXT in ordr*e* to Boch*as* dide appeere
A woful prince, which put hi*m*silf i*n* pres,
Regny*n*g in Sithia, his stori doþ us ler*e*,
The name of whom was Eucratides.
But to disturbe his quiete & his pes,
Ageyn[e]s hy*m*, pleynli, as I fynde,
Ca*m* Demetrius the myhti* ky*n*g of Ynde.

A woeful prince, Eucratides of Scythia, next appeared before Bochas.

Of whom the poweer & the violence [p. 319]
To Eucratides was verray importabl*e*:
Beseegid first, and for lak of diffence
Take at myscheef, his foon nat merciable;
For Demetrius was on hy*m* so vengable,
Whan he was slayn withyn*n*e his owne bou*n*dis,
Made the careyn [to] be caste out to* hou*n*dis.

He was besieged by Demetrius, king of India, and finally captured and slain,

1738. hih] *om.* H. 1751. spareth] spared B — lynage J.
1760. Sithia] Bactris P. 1764. myhti] worthy B.
1771. to] *om.* J, H 5 — out to] vnto B, out to the J.

[1] MS. J. leaf 131 recto.

and his body thrown to the dogs, although he was a worthy king. I will not dwell any longer on such a hateful story.

Natwithstondyng he was a worthi kyng,
Born of hih blood, swich was his auenture.
Demetrius sone aboue al erthli thyng
Hatede hym, bi record of scripture,
Of rancour denied his sepulture.
And for the mateer is hatful & contrarie,
On his stori I wil no lenger tarie.

[How herodes kyng of Parthos, werred with Romayns whiche aftir his sone & heir was slayn / made his bastard son kyng þat anon aftir slouh his fadir.] [1]

Artabanus, king of Parthia, had two sons, Mithridates and Orodes,

TO Arthabanus whilom of Parthos king
I purpose my stile to transporte,
A ful olde prince, had in his lyuyng
Sonys tweyne, bookis so reporte,
Which in his age dide hym most counfort:
Mitridate was the elder* brothir,
And Herodes callid was the tothir.

and when he died was succeeded by Mithridates, the elder, who was a tyrant and, banished, fled to Babylon.

Mitridate, be resoun of his age,
His fadir ded, dide aftir hym succeede,
Which banshed was for tirannye & outrage.
Aftirward for myscheeff & for neede
Into Babiloun he took his fliht for dreede.
The peeple anon, after his partyng,
Of indignacioun made his brothir kyng.

Orodes then became king, and, taking Babylon, caused his brother's head to be cut off.

Thus kam Herodes to estat roiall,
Pursuede his brothir into Babiloun,
Leide a seege round aboute the wall;
Thei to hym yold[e] up the toun.
Thus was his brothir brouht to confusioun, —
Afforn the castel, withoute lenger date,
Made smyte of the hed of Mitridate.

Afterwards he made war on Rome. Crassus, who came down against him,

In Parthos aftir he took pocessioun,
This yonge Herodes, of volunte & pride
Gan a werre geyn* hem of Roome toun,
Whom to withstonde thei list nat longe abide.

1784. elder] eldest B.
1785. Herodes] Orodes P.
1802. geyn] ageyn B, H, J, R 3, H 5, P.

[1] MS. J. leaf 131 recto.

The consul Crassus kam doun on ther side,
Comaundid was short processe to make,
Toward Parthos his viage for to take.

Crassus list nat tentren in that rewm,
Lefte Parthos, the stori doth deuise, —
Took his weie toward Iherusalem
To take ther a solempne enprise,
In the temple, onli of couetise,
Took ther, ageyn the title of rihtwisnesse,
Vp al ther tresour & ther gret richesse.

first went to Jerusalem to rob the temple,

Bi which he gat in dyuers regiouns
Gret multitude to holde up his partie,
Ladde with hym elleuene legiouns,
Toward Parthos faste gan hym hie,
Bi his lettres proudli gan defie
The said Herodes, and with gret apparaille
Mid his contre proffred hym bataille.

and then gave battle to Orodes with eleven legions.

The nexte morwe whan Crassus took þe feeld,
To hym was brouht of blak a cotearmure,
Which whan his knihtes auysili beheeld,
Dempte it a tokne of disconfiture;
For in contrarie* Romeyns do ther cure,
Whan ther capteyn shal fihten, or ther hed,
His cotearmure is owther whit or red.

He wore a suit of black armour, which his knights considered bad luck;

A-nother tokne froward to beholde,
The firste egle bete in his baneer,
Also soone as men it dide vnfolde
Contrariousli he tournid look & cheer,
The bak to Crassus, folk sauh that stood[e] neer:
A pronostik to Romeyns ful certeyn,
How Fortune that day was hem ageyn.

and when one of his banners was unfolded, the eagle turned his back on him.

Bi the flood passyng of Eufrates,
With vnwar tempest his standardis euerichon
Into the ryuer wer cast among the pres,
To rekne hem all, vpriht stood nat oon.
Wherof astoned, thei wolde no ferther gon,
Thes pronostiques made hem so affraied,
Lik men in herte dispeired & dismaied.

His standards were blown into the Euphrates by a sudden tempest, and the army was dismayed and refused to advance.

1806. Parthia P.
1810. emprise J, H, P. 1817. Parthia P.
1823. beheeld] tooke heede H. 1825. contraire B, J.
1836. tempestis H.

But Crassus was heedless of these tokens and crossed the Euphrates out of covetousness, so that he might despoil Parthia.

Of thes toknys Crassus was rek[e]les,
The pronostikes he dede also despise,
Took upon [hym] to passen Eufrates,
Tentre Parthos onli for couetise.
To whom Herodes sendith in this wise,
That his comy*n*g was mor for pillage
Than for knihthod, ma*n*hod or corage.

All the power of the country came down against him; his son was slain and he himself taken prisoner.

Al the poweer of Parthos tho ka*m* dou*n* [p. 320]
With many prefect in that mortal rage
Ageyn Crassus and them of Roome tou*n*,
Which, as I tolde, abood on ther pillage,
That turnid aftir to ther gret damage:
The sone of Crassus slayn in that affray,
His fadir take, & al upon o day.

His head was cut off; and Orodes commanded it to be poured full of molten gold.

His hed smet of, in whom was no diffence,
And discou*n*fited with many legiou*n*,
The hed of Crassus brouht to the p*re*sence
Of Herodes withyn*n*e his roial tou*n*,
Which hath comau*n*did gold to be brouht dou*n*,
To be molte ther as he lay ded,
And to poure therof ful his hed.

This was done because no amount of gold or treasure could staunch his thirst of covetousness.

This thyng was doon for a moquerye,
In signe onli, the stori doth deuise,
That gold nor tresour, upon no partie,
Stau*n*che myht his thrust of couetise.
Such gredynesse ech man owith despise;
For auarice of custum in ech place
Of hih prowesse doth the p*r*is difface.

Orodes then took all of Crassus' pennons and standards and hung them up in his temples as trophies of victory.

Herodes aftir did serche al the wardis
Thoruh al the feeld[e] upon Crassus side,
Took the penou*n*s, baneres & sta*n*dardis,
And in his templis, large, longe & wide
Leet hang hem up of surquedie & p*r*ide,
In signe onli, and eek for a memorie,
He of Romeyns hath get[e] the victorie.

1849. Parthia P.
1850. in that mortal rage] & mych gret Costage H, & many gret costage R 3, & much great costage P, and many gret constable J, H 5.
1852. as] *om.* H — ther] þe H. 1865. tresour] siluer H.
1867. owith] doth H, should P.
1870. serche] sechen H.

With whiche he list nat onli be co*n*tent,
Weenyng his fortune sholde abide stable,
Into Surrye he hath his sone sent,
Callid Pachorus, made hym a co*n*stable,
Of that regiou*n* with hym to be partable
Of al tresours & meobles that he fond,
Wher-euer he rood thoruhout al the* lond.

Not content with all this, and believing that his fortune would continue stable, he sent his son Pacorus to Syria and made him constable there.

Thus Pachorus bi his cheualrie
Encrese gan in his tendre age,
Wherof Herodes, his fader, had envye,
Feerful it sholde turne to his damage,
List he wolde be title of heritage,
Maugre hym, at his ageyn komy*n*g
Take upon hym in Parthos to be kyng.

Afterwards, fearing that he should become too powerful, he recalled him.

Than Pachorus was callid hom agey*n*,
And of Surrie, wher in conclusiou*n*,
Al that he had wrouht[e] was in veyn,
Because oon Cassius fro Roome was come dou*n*, —
Slouh al the peeple in that regeou*n*
Which apartened to Pachorus, as I fynde,
Withoute capteyn for thei wer lefft behy*n*de.

During Pacorus' absence Cassius came down from Rome and slew all the people in Syria,

To withstonde this Romeyn Cassius
Herodes hath his sone sent ageyn,
Which anon aftir, the stori tellith thus,
Amyd the feeld vnhappili was slayn.
To truste Fortune it is a thy*n*g but vay*n*,
Which of custum to-day is fauourable,
And to-morwe gerisshli chau*n*gable.

and so Orodes sent him back again to defend his country; but he was slain.

Of Pachorus deth whan the noise aroos
A*n*d the distrussyng of his cheualrie,
And to Herodes abidyng in Parthos
Tidyng was brouht, ferde as he wolde die,
Of hertli sorwe fill into frenesie:
Heir was non left of the roial lynes,
Sauf thretti bastardis born of concubynes.

When Orodes heard of Pacorus' death, he acted as if he were going to die and nearly went mad; for he had no sons left except 30 bastards.

Thus Herodes was cast in gret seeknesse,
His sonis deth was to hym importable,
His worldli ioie was gon and his gladnesse,
Fortune contrarie, which neuer can be stable;

He was a very sick man; his worldly joy gone, old in years, Fortune contrary.

1882. meobles] richesse H, mouables P. 1883. the] that B.
1884. Pacorus P.
1889. at his agey*n*] ageynst his geyn H.
1894. Cassus H. 1895. that] þe H.

> Finally he gave the crown to one of his bastards named Phraates and soon after was slain by him.

Age fill on; his liff was nat durable:
And of o thyng most he dede hy*m* dreede,
Cause he hadde non heir to succeede,
Which wold[e] nat suffre hym lyue in pes.
Til at the laste he cauhte a fantasie,
Ches a bastard callid Pharactes,
Because he was famous in cheualrie,
Gaf hym the crowne & the regalie,
Which anon aftir, breefli to co*n*clude,
Slouh Herodes of ingratitude.

[How Fymbria a consul of Rome slouh himsilf.] [1]

> Four mighty princes cast their look on Bochas, like unfortunate folk who had fallen from Fortune's wheel.

AFFTIR to Boch*as*, bi p*ro*cesse of the book,
Foure mihti p*r*incis notabl*e* of estat,
Towardis hy*m* thei caste cheer & look,
Lik vnto folk that wer infortunat,
With who*m* Fortune had been at debat;
For be ther maner, as it sempte weel,
Thei wer at mischeeff fallyn fro*m* hir wheel.

> The first of them, Fimbria, a Roman consul sent to help Flaccus, whom he found slain, presumptuously took command of the army and made himself be called emperor.

First Fymbria, a Romey*n* consuleer, [p. 321]
Sent bi the Romey*ns* to a gret cite
Callid Nichomeed[y]e, cam* as a massageer
To helpe Flaccus, & entryng that contre,
Fond Flaccus slayn bi gret aduersite.
Aftir whos deth, his parti to auau*n*ce,
Of Flaccus meyne took the gou*er*nau*n*ce.

Of presumpciou*n*, withoute auctori[t]e,
This Fymbria bi dilligent labour,
Ful ferr abouen his staat & his degre,
Took upon hym bi Fortunys fals fauo*u*r
To be callid capteyn and empero*u*r
Thoruh al that cuntre, bokis specefie;
Of whos presu*m*pciou*n* Scilla had envie.

> The result was that Sulla compelled him to take refuge in a castle, where he slew himself.

Pursued hym thoruh many gret cite,
To a castel made hym take his fliht,
Wher Fymbria of gret necessite
Constreyned was, maugre al his myht,
Disespeired, forsake of eueri wiht,
To slen hymsilf, the stori tellith thus,
Withyn*ne* the temple of Esculapius.

1935. cam] sent B. 1953. the] a H.

[1] MS. J. leaf 131 recto.

[Of Albynius that was slayn with stonys.] [1]

ANOþ*ER* consul stood in cas se*m*blabl*e*,
In his tyme callid Albynyus,
Whos hatful pride was abho*min*abl*e*,
To alle folkis lothsum and odious;
Which lik a rebel, wood & furious
Agey*n* Romeyn[e]s oft[e]nere than onys, —
Whan he lest wende slay[e]*n* was wi*th* stonys.

Another consul, Albinus, abominably proud, and odious to all men, rebelled against Rome and was stoned to death.

[How Adriane of low degre falsly vsurped to be kyng of Rome whiche wi*th* his cherlys was aftir bre*nt*.] [2]

NEXT Adrian, which ros to hih estat:
First in Roome bor*n* of louh degr*e*,
Chose a pretour, sent bi þe senat
To gouerne of Affrik the contre,
Wher of his owne pompous auctorite
Took upon hym bi sotil fals werkyng,
Maugre Romey*n*s, ther to be crowned ky*n*g.

Adrian, born of low degree, became a praetor, and was sent to govern Africa, where he took upon himself to be crowned king.

Whom to supporte, shortli to conclude,
Was a gret nou*m*bre of the comou*n*te,
Of cherlis gadred a confus multitude,
Title was non nor grou*n*d but volunte.
Gentil-men than beyng in that contre,
Alle off assent and oon oppynyou*n*,
Assemble[d] hem to his destrucciou*n*.

He was upheld by churls and had no title except his own will.

At Vtices, a large gret cite,
Hym and his cherlis besette rou*n*d aboute,
Of wode & faget with large qua*n*tite
In compas-wise closed hy*m* withoute,
Gadred with hym of viley*n*s a gret route,
Leide on fyr, that with flawmes rede
Echon consumyd into asshes dede.

The gentlemen of the country laid siege to him in Utica, and, piling up wood and faggots, burnt him into ashes together with a large number of his oafs.

1955. Albinus P.
1961. *This stanza is as follows in* P:
Next came Adrianus which to estate full hye
Rose in his time (and that ful sodeynlye)
First in Rome borne but of lowe degre
toke upon him to gouerne the countre
Off Affrike through hys great auctorite,
and by hys slye, subtel, and false werking,
Mauger Romains ther to be crouned king.
1975. Vtices] Stites H, Utica P.

[1] MS. J. leaf 131 recto. [2] MS. J. leaf 131 recto.

[How Synthonyus kyng of Trace þat moche coueted affor went and deied in pouerte.] [1]

Sothimus, king of Thrace, came tearfully to Bochas; for he was suddenly cast from his royal estate

NEXT Adrian cam Syntonyvs
Tofor Bochas, with teris spreynt his face;
As the stori rehersith vnto us,
In his tyme he was kyng of Trace,
Falle sodenli fro Fortunis grace,
Cast doun lowe from his estat roiall,
Which kam to Bochas to compleyne his fall.

because he tried to conquer seven realms in Greece that were subject to Rome.
He who covets all loses all.

Whos purpos was, yiff it wolde haue be,
Seuene rewmys taue conquered with his hond,
That were soget to Roome the cite;
And alle seuene wer of Grekis lond.
Who al coueiteth, ye shal vndirstond,
He al forgoth, ful weel afferme I dar,
At vnset hour, wheroff ech man be war.

He was conquered by Sentius and died in poverty.

Longe or his conquest was brouht to a preeff,
From hir wheel Fortune cast hym doun.
The pretour Sencyus brouht hym to myscheef,
Deide in pouert, as maad is mencioun.
And Bochas heer maketh a digressioun,
Compendiousli withynne a litil space
To descryue the regioun of Trace.

[Here Bochas in party makith a descripcioun of the kyngdam of Trace and passith over lightly to the accomplisshment of his book.] [2]

¶ The discripsion of þe same.

Thrace, once a very famous country, was named after Tiras, son of Japhet. It lies towards the north beside the Danube,

TRACE, whilom a contre of gret fame,
And conteneth a ful large space;
And of Tiras it took[e] first þe name,
Sone of Iaphet, & so was callid Trace.
Which many a day duelled in that place,
Toward Septemptrion, plenteuous of good,
Beside Dynoe, the large famous flood.

1982. Next to Adrian P — Sothimus P.
1998. Sentius P.
2009. Dynoe] Danubie P.

[1] MS. J. leaf 131 recto. [2] MS. J. leaf 131 recto.

Southward Trace ren*n*eth the flood Egee, [p. 322]
Macedoyne stant in the occident,
And the kyngdam callid Perpontide
Stant in Trace toward the orient,
Wher gret plente of blood was shad & spe*n*t,
Wha*n* Sencyus thoruh his hih prowesse
Kyng Adrian ther manli dede oppresse.

and the Aegean Sea is to the southward.

Ebrus in Trace is the cheeff ryueer,
As my*n* aucto*u*r maketh menciou*n*; —
I caste nat to tarie in this mateer,
To make of Trace a descripciou*n*,
But to proceede in my *tra*nslaciou*n*,
Folwe my*n* aucto*u*r, which writ a long p*ro*cesse
Of gret Po*m*peye & of his worthynesse.

The Hebrus is its chief river; but I shan't write any more about it, as I want to go on with my translation and tell about Pompey the Great.

[How aftir many grete conquest*es* of Duk Pompeye/ bega*n* grete werre betwixt him and Iulyus iij^c^ M^l^ were slayn/ and at last the heed of Pompeye smyten of.] [1]

THIS Po*m*peius, of who*m* þe name is kouþ,
Wis & worþi & famous of prowesse,
Took upo*n* hy*m* i*n* his te*n*dre youth, —
Afftir his fadir bi fortunat duresse,
Callid Po*m*peye, the stori berth witnesse,
Distrussid was bi sodey*n* deth komy*n*g,
The stori seith, thoruh thundry*n*g & lihtny*n*g,

Pompey was named after his father, whose army he once led

His host destroied be the violence
Of vnwar tempest, lik as seith the book,
Fourti thousand slayn in that pestile*n*ce;
For feer the re*m*nant anon þe feeld forsook, —
Til yonge Po*m*peie of corage o*n* hym took
In his begyn*n*y*n*g proudli to proceede
Ful lik a kniht his fadris host to leede.

when it had been nearly destroyed by a sudden tempest.

Roome that tyme bi ther discenciou*n*s
Amo*n*g hemsilf nih brouht[e] to ruyne,
Bi the froward fals dyuysiou*n*s
Tween Marie & Scilla, breefli to t*er*myne,
Till that a newe son*n*e ga*n* to shyne
Of worthynesse, which that shadde his liht,
In ma*n*li Pompeie the noble famous kniht.

Rome was at that time almost brought to ruin by the wars of Marius and Sulla, and it was then that the sun of Pompey began to shine.

2012. Propontidiee P. 2015. Sencyus] Sothimus P. 2016. dede] to H. 2017. Hebrus P. 2022. long] gret H.

[1] MS. J. leaf 131 verso.

He slew Brutus, one of Marius' captains, in Lombardy

This said Pompeie, this noble knihtli ma*n*,
At his begyn*n*y*n*g, thoruh his cheualrie,
The proude capteyn slouh wha*n* he bega*n*,
Which of Marrius heeld up the partie,
Callid Brutus, which in Lombardie
Was be Po*m*peye thoruh kniyhtli gou*er*nau*n*ce
With al his host[e] brouht vnto myschau*n*ce.

and also Gneus Carbo in Sicily to bring peace to Rome.

In his begyn*n*yng Po*m*peie eek also,
To sette Romey*n*s in reste & in quiete,
Oon that was callid Gnevs Carbo,
He slouh hym knihtli wha*n* he dede hy*m* meete,
Which in Sicile proudli heeld his seete.
And alle the contres aboute hy*m* envirou*n*
Pompeie made hem soget to Roome tou*n*.

Afterwards he reconquered Africa, defeating Domitius.

Aftir al this Pompeius on the se
With many a shipp*e* stuffid with vitaille
Toward Affrik made a gret arme,
And ther in haste aftir his aryuaille
With Domicius hadde a gret bataille,
Brouhte the contre thoruh his hih renou*n*
To be to Róome vndir subieccio*un*.

He pursued Hiarbas, king of Numidia, Marius's ally,

He pursued the grete myhti kyng
Callid Iertha, to Marrius fauourabl*e*,
And hadde also his roial abidyng
In Numedie, a contre ful notable.
Ageyn Po*m*peie his poweer was nat habl*e*;
For at a castell as thei mette in fiht,
He slouh kyng Iertha, ful lik a ma*n*li kniht.

and in a short time brought the whole country to subjection.

Thus in breef tyme, holdyng his passage
For comou*n* proffit, as maad is menciou*n*,
Bi his wisdam & knihtli hih corage
Brouht al Affrik to subieccio*u**n*,
Which stood affor[e]n in rebelliou*n*
To the Romey*n*s; but al ther sturdynesse
The said[e] Po*m*peie dede in haste redresse.

In those days one Sertorius was Rome's greatest enemy, and he was slain by his own men.

The grettest enmy ageyns Roome tou*n*
Thilke daies was oon Sertorius;
And of fortune, which is now up now dou*n*,
On Pompeie onys was victorious.

2062. rivaile H, ryuaile R 3, ryuaille H 5.
2067, 72. Iertha] Iercha H, Hiarbas P. 2077. afforn stoode H.

But aftir soone of hy*m* it happid thus:
Amo*n*g his meyne fallyng at debat,
He slay[e]n was in his most hih estat.

Aftir the deth of this Sertorivs
Ca*m* Porpen*n*a Po*m*peie for tassaile;
And as thei mette anon[e] Po*m*peius
Ful lik a kniht slouh hym in bataile,
Which victorie gretli dide auaile
To the Romey*n*s. Aftir bi gou*er*nau*n*ce
He brouht al Spayne to ther obeissau*n*ce.

Perpenna also attacked Pompey, but was killed by him in battle.

Bi auctorite youe bi the Senat, [p. 323]
This noble Pompeie, for vail of the cite,
Vpon the se wolde suffre no pirat;
Wher-euer he cam from hy*m* thei dede flee:
For with his shippis he scoured so the se
And bar hym ther so manli with his hond,
That maugre them he brouht hem to the lond.

By the authority of the Senate, Pompey scoured the sea for pirates,

Al the piratis and thes fals robbo*u*rs
Igadred wern out of the regiou*n*
Callid Silice*, which lik to rauyno*u*rs
Made ageyn Roome a conspiraciou*n*,
Robbede, spoillede, seillyng up & dou*n*,
Romeyn marchau*n*tis & peeple of ech contre,
That non was hardi to passe bi the se.

who gathered together out of Cilicia, robbing Roman merchants.

Afftir Pompeie hath maad the se tobeie,
That pirat non durst[e] theron abide,
He bi the Senat was sent out to werreye
Toward thorient, his knihtis be his side.
And wher-so-euer that he dide ride,
Myn auctour writ, bynfluence of heuene
His co*n*quest was swifft as wynd or leuene.

After he had made the seas safe, he was sent to the East,

And to encres of his eternal glorie,
Perpetueli to geten hym a name,
His laude & renou*n* to putte in memorie
He bilt a cite in Asia of gret fame,
Callid Nichopoli, Bochas seith the same,
Tween too floodis, the ton Araxzases,
And the tothir was callid Eufrates.

where he made swift conquests and built the city of Nicopolis, between the Euphrates and the Araxes,

2088. Perpenna P — for] *om.* H.
2100. brouht] brouh H. 2101. the] this H.
2103. Silice] Sicile B, J.
2120. Artaxerses H, Araxases J, Araxzases R 3, Araxes P.

as a home for knights grown old and poor in the service of Rome.

He bilte this cite onli of entent
That Romey*n* knihtis, which wer falle in age,
And such as wer[e]n in the werris spent,
Sike, wou*n*did, in pouert or in rage,
Sholde of custum haue ther herbergage
In that cite alway, & nat faille
Beddyng, clothes, spendyng & vitaille.

He next rode into Armenia and defeated Tigranes, who had rebelled,

Pompeye aftir rood into Armenye,
Rebel to Roome, wher Tigranes was ky*n*g.
Fauht with hym the*r*, & thoruh his cheualrie
Discou*n*fited hy*m*, ther was non abidyng.
Wher Tigranes hymsilue submyttyng
Vnto Po*m*peie with eueri circu*m*stau*n*ce,
Euer tabide vndir his obeissau*n*ce.

and then marched in all haste to Asia and won the kingdom of Albania, where all the people are

Than in al haste Pompeie ga*n* hy*m* hie
To ride in Asia, wher lik a manli kniht
He gat the kyngdam callid Albanye,
Which took his name, who-so looke ariht,
Of whiht[e]nesse; for eueri maner wiht
That ther is born, be record of writyng,
Whiht as snouh[e] hath his her shynyng.

born with white hair, and there are dogs that can overcome all manner of wild beasts.

Ther been hou*n*dis merueilous of nature,
For tassaile bolis and leou*n*s;
No wilde beeste ageyn hem may endure.
So Po*m*peye, bi many regiou*n*s
Rood thoruh Armenye with his champiou*n*s,
Wher growen herbes that may neuer fey*n*te,
What-euer colour men list with hem pey*n*te.

He conquered Iberia, Syria and Phoenice, the city named after Phoenix,

Conquered rewmys aboute in eueri cost:
Of Hiberie he gat the regeou*n*,
And Artaces the kyng with al his host
Discou*n*fited, as maad is menciou*n*.
With his poweer to Surrie he ca*m* dou*n*,
Than to Fenise, a cite of gret fame,
Which of Fenix whilom took his name.

and took possession of Sidon and Ituraea, and passed the mountains of Lebanon into Judaea.

Brouhte al thes contres to subiecciou*n*:
Of Sydonye, the myhti strong cite
Of Iturye, he took pocessiou*n*;
Thoruh Arabie he ca*m* dou*n* to Iudee,

2122. this] a H. 2139. ariht] riht H. 2149. to peynt H. 2155. Phenice P. 2156. Phenix P — his] þe H. 2158. Sidon P.

Which of Iewes was su*m*tyme the contre.
Of Libanus he passed the mou*n*teyn*n*,
Wher cedris growe[n], as auctour[e]s seyn.

Sent [to]forn hym, entryng in that reum,
Oon Gabynus, a myhti stro*n*g constable;
Regnyng that tyme in Iherusalem
Aristobolus, a p*r*ince ful notable.
And for the temple was stro*n*g & nat p*er*miable,
Leide a siege aboute in breede & lengthe
Space of thre monethes, & gat it so bi strengthe.

Jerusalem was besieged by Gabinus for three months, Aristobolus then reigning,

Thre thousand Iewes vndir the wal wer fou*n*de,
Ded at thassat, which made resistence;
The wal aftir doun beten to the* grou*n*de.
Pompeye afftir bi sturdi violence
Is entrid in withoute reuerence,
Sancta sancto*rum* men that place call,
Made Hircanius hiest preest of all,

and 3000 Jews died at the assault.

The grete bisshop Aristobolus, [p. 324]
Sent to Roome in myhti cheynis bou*n*de.
Toward Septemptrion, I fy*n*de write thus,
Gat seuene kyngdames with citees wallid rou*n*de,
Rebel to Roome, he dide hem co*n*fou*n*de;
With mihti suerd[e] gat al the contre
Fro Caucasus dou*n* to the Red[e] Se.

Aristobolus was sent to Rome in chains, and Pompey subdued seven rebel countries, conquering from the Caucasus to the Red Sea.

In his conquest, it sempte v*er*raily
As the goddis hadde doon ther cure,
And that Fortune was with hem eek besi,
This myhti Po*m*peye p*r*ince to assure,
What-euer hym list be conquest to recure:
In Spaigne he gat, whan thei wer rebell,
Thre hundred citees & sixty* stro*n*g castell.

It seemed as if the gods and Fortune had united to assure him in his conquests,

Hard to remembre his conquestis eu*er*ichon,
Alle the prowessis of this knihtli ma*n*:
Toward the parti of Septemptriou*n*
A thousand castell I fynde that he wan,
Sixe hu*n*dred mo, fro tyme that he gan,
Eihte & thretti cites, out of doute,
With myhti wallis closed rou*n*d aboute.

which were so many that it is hard to remember them all.

2164. toforn] frome H.
2168. nat] *om.* J — p*er*miable] pregnable P. 2170. thre] iij B.
2173. doun beten to the] beten dou*n* to B, J, H, R 3, P.
2191. sixty] thretti B. 2195. castellys J.

He was chosen consul three times; and if you read, you will find that he was the peer of Alexander and Hercules.

Peise his deedis, his conquestis marciall:
Thries consul chose for his eneres;
Reed, ye shal fynde how he was egall
To Alisandre or to Hercules.
Wher that euere he put hy*m*silff in pres,
Al cam to hand, concludyng, ye may see,
To comou*n* proffit of Roome the cite.

Tryphanes, famous of eloquence, was chosen to put his conquests in writing at the public expense.

His marciall deedis to putte in reme*m*braun*c*e,
Oon was chose to do his dilligence
To enacte* his conquest in substaun*c*e
And his knihthod of synguler excellence;
And Triffanes, famous of elloque*n*ce,
Assigned was onto that labour,
Took his guerdou*n* of ther comou*n* tr*e*so*ur*.

Pompey became chief governor of Rome, Cæsar then absent in Gaul,

Pompeye of Roome was cheef gouerno*ur*,
Cesar absent in Gaule, a ferre* contre,
Which tyme Pompeie stood in gret fauo*ur*
Bothe of Fortune and Roome the cite,
Sumwhat maad blynd of his prosperite,
Purposyng, in his clymbyng nat stabl*e*,
He wolde haue non that wer to hy*m* semblabl*e*.

but, as neither love nor high worship will have fellowship, he desired to be alone in power,

Vnto purpos was saide ful yore agon,
How that loue nouther hih lordshippe, —
Preeff hath be maad in many mo tha*n* oon, —
Nouther of hem wolde haue no felashipe;
Ech bi his oon wolde his parti keepe:
In thes too caas, brothir onto brothir
Failleth at a poynt; ech wil put out othir.

and made all the laws himself.

To Pompeye resorty*n*g now ageyn, —
He took on hym al the gouernaille
Of the Romeyns, as ye haue herd me sey*n*,
Bothe of estatis, comou*n*s & poraille,
And for his part al that myhte [a]vaille
In makyng lawes, statut or decre,
Al up engrosed bi his auctorite.

The enemies of Cæsar conspired against him and enacted a statute forbidding men to hold office while absent from Rome.

Folk this while which that had envie
Toward Cesar in his longe absence,
Leet make a lawe bi conspiracye
And a statut, concludyng in sentence,
Withoute excepciou*n*, fauour or* reu*er*ence,

2208. enacte] encrece B, J. 2214. ferre] gret B.
2225. caas] cases P, casys H 5. 2230. comou*n* H.
2238. or] of B.

No man sholde, be wil of the Senat,
In his absence be chose to non estat,

Nor been admittid be no procutour
Taue auctorite of dignite [n]or offis,
In court of tribun nor off senatour
To be promotid; this was ther auys,
Wer he neuer so manli nor so wis.
This lawe ordeyned be folk envious,
For hyndryng onli of Cesar Iulius.

Whan Iulius knew al ther fals werki*n*g,
Fro Gaule sente up to the cite,
Al the Senat requery*n*g be writyng
To grau*n*te hym bi ther auctorite
Of tryu*m*phe the notable dignite,
To haue also thoffis and thestat
Callid in Roome the seconde consulat,

When Julius heard of this he demanded the triumph and the estate of second consul,

For hym aleggyng many gret victorie
In dyuers contres doon for the cite,
Many conquest notable of memorie
Wrouht bi his knihthod; for which of equite
Requeryng them guerdoned for to bee.
But contrarie vnto his entent
Denied hym al bi oon assent,

alleging his conquests as his right to reward. The Senate, however,

Which was cheeff grou*n*d, roote & occasiou*n* [p. 325]
That brouht in first the contrauersie,
Cyuile discordes, froward dyuysiou*n*,
Whan eueri man drouh to his partie
Of old hatreede to kyndle newe envie,
Causyng p*r*incis Iulius & Pompeie
To ther confusiou*n* ech othir to werreye.

denied his request, and that was the chief cause of the civil war.

The tryumphe denyed to Cesar, —
Fraude of Po*m*peie made hy*m* therof faile,
Of whos deceit Iulius was war,—
Made hym redi with many strong bataille,
Passed ouer the Alpies of Itaille,
Fulli in purpos, pleynli, yiff he myhte,
With the Romey*n*s and Pompeie for to fihte.

Cæsar knew the fraud of Pompey and, crossing the Alps,

Thus gan the werre atween thes p*r*incis tweyne.
Pompeye chose for parti of the tou*n*
To been ther duk & captey*n* souereyne
Ageyn Cesar, as maad is menciou*n*.

prepared to fight the Romans; and thus the wars between these two princes began.

2242. auctorite] Auctours H. 2258. of equite] of riht & equyte H.

And thus alas the desolaciou*n*
Suede of the cite, be many strau*n*ge signe,
With vnkouth toknis, wha*n* thei ga*n* maligne.

At their beginning strange comets and uncouth stars were seen in the sky, burning like lamps all night long, and spears and darts flew about in the air.

At the gyn*n*yng of thes woful werris,
In the heuene wer seyn dreedful siht*es* —
Sparklyng brondis, cometis, vnkouth sterris,
With flawme of fyr many feerful liht*es*
Lik lau*m*pis bren*n*y*n*g al the longe niht*es*,
Castyng of speres, dartis in the hair,
Wherbi Romey*n*s fill in gret dispair.

Great flashes of lightning came from the north, and stars were visible at noon. The sun shone like blood; the moon eclipsed; and Mt. Ætna cast red flames towards Italy from his caverns.

From the parti of Septemptrion
Toward Roome cam ful gret lihtny*n*g;
At non seyn sterris; lik blood the sun*n*e shon;
The moone eclipsed, terrible in shewy*n*g;
The mou*n*t[e] Ethna, feerfulli bren*n*yng,
From his cauernis cast up flawmys rede
Toward Itaille, which set hem in gret dreede.

Terrible waves boiled up at Charybdis; and from the rocks of Sicily was heard the howling of mad hounds.

Out of Karibdis, a dau*n*ger of the se,
Wawes terrible boiled up lik blood;
From the rokkes that in Cecile bee
Was herd howlyng of hou*n*dis that wer wood.
Vesta the goddesse, in Roome ther she stood,
Mid hir temple was al with teres sprey*n*t,
Wha*n* the heuenli fyris wern afforn hir quey*n*t.

The statue of Vesta was sprinkled with tears; the perpetual fire that burned before her parted in twain.

Afforn this goddesse, at the aulter p*r*incepall
Was fyr perpetuel bren*n*yng day & niht,
Til werris cyuyle, hatful & mortal,
Gan* among Romeyns, & the co*n*tagious fiht.
Tha*n* of vengau*n*ce anon was quey*n*t the liht
Tofor Vesta, the fire partyng on tweyne,
Of dyuisiou*n* a tokne ful certeyne.

Castles were overturned by sudden earthquakes; there were tidal waves, drowning villages and upsetting the golden vessels in the temples.

Erthe-quaues sodeyn & terrible
Ouertournede castellis vp-so-dou*n*;
With rage floodis hidous & horrible
Neptunvs dide gret destrucciou*n*,
Drowned villages & many a ma*n*siou*n*,
Reuersed in templis of gold al ther vessellis,
Threw dou*n* baners, standardis & penselis.

2292. noon H, J. 2302. hir] his H.
2304. aulter] Aucteer H. 2307. Gan] Gat B.

Geyn these signes was fou*n*de non arest,
The vnwar myscheeff koude no ma*n* declyne.
Leou*n*s, wolues kam dou*n* fro the forest
With many othir beestis sauagyne;
Wilde beris & serpentis of rauyne
Kam to the cite; & sum*m*e ageyn[e]s ky*n*de
Spak as do men, in Bochas thus I fynde.

No man could turn away the mischief. Lions and wolves came down from the forests to Rome, wild bears and ferocious serpents speaking the language of men.

Dyuers foulis,* which of ther nature
Haue in custum to fleen but a-niht,
Affor thes werris dede he*m*silf assure
Euene at mydday, wha*n* Phebus is most briht,
Thoruh the cite for to take her fliht.
Wom*m*en with childre — the stori list nat feyne —
Brouht foorth sum*m*e that hadde hedis tweyne.

Night birds were seen flying at midday: and some women brought forth children with two heads.

Tofor thes werris, that callid wer cyuile,
Senatours beyng in Roome tou*n*
Cam to the woman that callid was Cybile,
Vnto hire made this questiou*n*:
To declare bi short conclusiou*n*,
Among ther other questiou*n*[e]s all,
Of ther cite what fortune sholde fall?

Before the wars the senators went to Sibylla and inquired the fate of the city.

To whom she gaff an ansuere ful obscure,
Wherupon she made hem sore muse:
Took hem sixe lettres set in pley*n* scripture,
Which in no wise thei myhte nat refuse,
For false rihtis that thei dede vse;
Lik the thre lettres twies set in nou*m*bre,
Who vndirstondeth, thei shal the tou*n* encou*m*bre.

She set six letters in a row,

Thre R. R. R. first[e] she set on a rowe [p. 326]
And thre F. F. F. in ordre faste bi, —
Long tyme aftir or thei koude knowe
Thexposiciou*n* therof openly,
Til ther dyuynours gan serche sotilly
To fynde[n] out, lik to ther entente,
Be the sexe lettres what Cibile mente.

three R's and three F's; and it was long before the diviners could find out that the letters meant,

Off this woord Regnu*m* the first lettre is R,
So is the capital off Roome the cite;
Who looke ariht, the thridde is nat ferr*e*, —

Regnum Romae Ruet;

2318. fou*n*de] doon H. 2324. thus] as H.
2325. foulis] folkis B, folkys J. 2326. on niht H.
2340. sore] full sore H. 2341. sixe] vj B — pley*n*] *om.* H.
2351. lik] firste lik H. 2352. the] thes H.
2354. 1st the] *om.* H.

This woord Ruet gynneth with R, parde.
Of which[e] woordes whan thei ioyned be,
The sentence concludeth in meenyng,
Off ther cite the ruynous fallyng.

Ferro, Flamma, Fames.

Touchyng thre F. F. F., who can aduertise,
Of this woord Ferro, F go[e]th toforn;
And the cheeff lettre off Fames to deuyse
Is F also, the processe weel forth born.
The same of Flamma, bi which þe toun was lorn,
Off which resouns make a coniunccioun,
Causyng of Roome fynal destruccioun.

Fire, sword and hunger, froward ambition, the shewing of comets and strange stars and wilful division accomplished the ruin of Rome.

Fyr, swerd & hunger caused be the werris,
Desyr of clymbyng, froward ambicioun,
Shewyng of cometis & of vnkouth sterris,
With pronostikes off [ther] deserciou*n*,
Werst of alle, wilful dyuysioun
Among hemsilff bi vnwar violence,
Off lettres sexe accomplisshid the sentence.

The wars between Cæsar and Pompey lasted long and caused the death of many a Roman, as Lucan testified.

The suerd of Cesar, werris of Pompeye,
Tween thès tweyne lastyng a long[e] while,
Made many Romeyn & Italien to deie,
Bi the batailes that callid wer cyuile,
With prophecies remembred of Cebile,
As the writyng ful weel reherse can,
Of the old poete that callid was Lucan.

In the temple of Mars the priests offered up their blood with lamentations; for the gods were contrary to Rome.

In Martes temple on heihte wher he stood,
And Bellona, the goddesse despitous,
The preestes cried & offred up ther blood
With lamentaciouns, lik folkis furious,
Cause off toknys fell and contrarious
Which that wer shewed in that seyntuarie,
How ther goddis to Romeyns wer contrarie.

The voices of madmen were heard among the dead bones in their graves, and the cry of ghosts in field and cavern, terrifying the agriculturists.

Mong dede bonys that leyen in ther grauis
Wer voises herd lik wood men in ther rages,
Cry of goostis in cauernys & cauys,
Herd in feeldis, paththis & passages;
Laboureres fledde hom to ther villages.
Serpentis, adderes, scaled siluer* briht,
Wer ouer Roome seyn fleeyng al the niht.

2373. sexe] vj B.
2375. attween H — longe] gret H, J, great P. 2378. of] by H.
2387. ther] þat H. 2390. &] & in H.
2393. siluer] *wonder B.

Another tokne, pitous for to heere,
Which astoned many proud Romey*n*,
Dede bodies* dide in the feeld appeer*e*,
Which in bataille hadde afforn be slayn,
Fro*m* ther tombis arisyng wher thei lay*n*,
Which in the werris, woful & despitous,
Wer slay*n* be Scilla & proude Marrius.

Serpents with scales of silver flew over the city all the night, and corpses of men slain before in the wars of Marius and Sulla arose from their tombs.

It was eek tolde bi ther dyuynours,
How Po*m*peyus was lik to haue a fall,
And how thestat of Romey*n* empero*urs*
With ther tryu*m*phes that been imperial
At Iulius first ther begyn*ne** shal;
And afftir hym thestat shal foort[h] p*ro*ceede
Be eleccíou*n* or lyneal kynreede.

Pompey's fall was foretold by diviners, who said also that the estate of Roman emperor would begin with Cæsar.

To withstonde the poweer of Cesar,
Which toward Roome took his weie riht,
Po*m*peye was sent, wis, ma*n*li & riht war;
But whan he herd[e] tellyn of the myht
Of Iulius, he took hym to the fliht;
Eek alle the senato*urs* with hy*m* dede flee
Toward Epire, in Grece a strong cite.

Pompey was sent out to withstand the power of Cæsar, but fled together with the senators to Epirus,

Pompeye was old, famous in cheualrie,
Cesar but yong [&] hardi for tassaille.
Vppon the pleyns of Grece & Thesalie
Pompeye & he hadde a gret bataille:
Geyn Iulius suerd no Romey*n* mihte auaile;
Constreyned of force the feeld[e] to forsake,
Toward Egipt thei haue the weie take.

where there was a great battle on the plains of Thessaly. Pompey lost and sought refuge in Egypt,

Pompeye thoruh Cipre cam to Tholome,
Bi a gret watir at Paphus dede aryue;
On the stronde ther he dide see
A statli place, & up he wente blyue,
The name of which, pleynli to descryue,
Cacabosile the contre dede it call,
Of which[e] name the fortune is thus fall:

journeying by way of Cyprus and landing first at Catobasilea, which means "unfortunate arrival."

2397. bodies] bonys B.
2406. ther] *om.* J — begyn*n*yng B.
2417. &] *om.* J, R 3.
2418. playn H.
2424. Paphos P.
2426. & ther he went vp blive H.
2428. Cacobasile P.

At this he fell in despair, and, sailing on, came to Egypt.

The name tokne of froward arryuaill, [p. 327]
Sownyng in Greek vnhappi auenture.
Be which the trust of Po*m*peie did[e] faille, —
Fill in dispeir, myht it nat recure, —
Forsook that ile, dede his besi cure
To take a shipp, so bi the se saillyng
Toward Egipt, wher Tholome was ky*n*g.

He hoped to be helped by Ptolemy; but Ptolemy, pretending friendship, told his men to murder him,

Of trust he fledde to this Tholome,
In hope he sholde fynde in hym socour:
Fair cheer shewed vndir duplicite,
Failled at the poynt, gaf hym feynt fauo*ur*,
Al-be Po*m*peye bi his freendli labour
Crownid hym kyng in Egipt, as I fynde,
To whom ageyn he was fals & vnkynde.

To meete Po*m*peye he leet stuffe a barge
Be a maner pretence of freendliheede,
Gaff his meynẹ that wer ther in charge
To moordre Po*m*peie, behiht hem a gr*e*t meede.
Tweyne ther wern, which to hy*m* bar hatreede;
And in the vessel, wi*th* sharp suerdis whette,
Or he was war[e], of his hed thei smette.

and Achillas and Photinus smote off his head. Born of gentle stock, he was one of the best knights of his time;

The ton of hem was callid Achillas,
And his felawe namyd was Fotyne.
Took up the hed[e] of that p*r*ince, alas,
Famous in knihthod, born of gentil lyne,
Among Romey*n*s, as aucto*ur*s determyne,
Holde in his tyme, yiff men doon hy*m* riht,
Thoruh al the world[e] oon the beste kniht.

but earthly princes, for all their pompous fame, first took their title by murder and extortion; and by the burning of countries and conquest by violence rose to dominion.

Thus erthli p*r*incis, wi*th* al ther pompous fame,
Which thoruh the* world yiueþ so gr*e*t a sou*n*,
Of slauhtre & moordre thei took[e] first þ*er* name,
Bi fals rauyne and extorsiou*n*
Clamb up so first to domynaciou*n*.
Bren*n*yng of contres, co*n*quest bi violence
Sette hem in chaieres of worldli excellence.

300,000 men, not counting kings and praetors, consuls and centurions, were slain.

In this bataile, which callid was cyuyle,
Hold atween Po*m*peye & Cesar Iulius,
Thre hundred thousand slay[e]n in a while,
Thre thousand take, the stori tellith thus,

2440. Failled] faily*n*g H. 2448. bar] born H.
2459. the] al the B, H, J, R 3, H 5, P.

Withoute princis notable & glorious,
As kyngis, pretours, reknid all attonys,
Tribunys, consulis & centuryonys.

Phebus on the soil myht nat his bemys spreede,
Nor on the ground shewe out his cleer[e] liht;
Men that wer slay[e]n lay so thikke on breede,
That of the erthe no man hadde a siht.
Wolues, beres, rauynous foul off fliht,
Kam gret plente to feede hem ther ech day
Beside the ryueer of Nile wher thei lay.

The rays of the sun could not strike the ground for the dead, which were eaten by wolves and bears and ravenous fowls.

Gobetis of flessh, which foulis dede arace
Fro dede bodies, born up in the hair,
Fill from ther clees vpon Iulius face,
Amyd the feeld wher he had his repair.
Made his visage bloodi & nat fair,
Al-be that he to his encres of glorie
Hadde thilke day of Romeyns the victorie.

Gobbets of flesh fell from the claws of birds upon Julius' face, soiling it with blood.

The hed of Pompeye, brouht with his statli ring,
Offrid up to Iulius hih presence,
He be compassioun, the moordre aduertisyng,
Of his innat imperial excellence
Brast out to weepe, & in his aduertense
Thouhte gret pite, a prince of so gret myht
Sholde so be slayn, that* was so good a knyht.

The head of Pompey and his ring of state were brought to Cæsar, who burst into tears of pity.

The corps abood withoute sepulture,
Til oon Coodrus of compassioun
Aftir the bataille & disconfiture
Besouht[e] hym, of gret affeccioun,
To hide the trunke lowe in the sondis doun.
Souhte tymbir, and ther he fond but smal,
To doon exequies with fires* funeral.

His body was buried by Codrus in the sand, and there was but little wood for a funeral pyre.

Now, sithe this prince kam to such myscheeff,
Moordred and slayn bi Tholome the kyng:
Heer of hir poweer Fortune hath maad a preeff,
What trust ther is in any worldli thyng.
Aftir his deth wantid he nat buriyng? —
This proude Pompeie, so famous of his hond,
Of fissh deuoured, as he lay on quik sond!

What trust is there in any worldly thing? Think of this proud Pompey devoured by fishes, as he lay in quicksand.

2482. had] made H — his] *om.* J.
2489. Iunat B. 2492. that] & B. 2499. fires] feestis B.

What store should men set by transitory things and worldly glory?

What shal men sette bi poweer or noblesse
Of* slidyng goodis or any worldli glorie,
Which to restreyne may be no sekirnesse?
Fortune and the world is transitorye;
Thouh Mars to-day yiue a ma*n* victorie,
Parcas to-morwe vnwarli he shal deie, —
I take record of Cesar and Pompeie.

Since all stands under the control of Fortune, look, worldly men, to that place where the Blind Lady has no power.

Sith al stant vndir dau*n*ger of Fortune, [p. 328]
Ye worldli men doth your look up-dresse
To thilke place wher ioie doth ay contune;
The Blynde Ladi hath ther non interesse.
Set pride aside, tak you to meeknesse,
To sue vertu doth treuli your labour,
Gey*n* worldli pompe mak Pompeie yo*u*r mero*u*r!

Lenvoye.

This tragedy of Duke Pompey declares that vain ambition to have lordship was the chief cause of the war between him and Cæsar.

THIS tragedie of the duk Po*m*peie
Declareth in gros þe cheef occasiou*n*
Whi he and Cesar ga*n* first to werreie,
Ech ageyn othir, thoruh veyn ambiciou*n*
To haue lordshipe and domynaciou*n*
Ouer the Romeyns, bi fauour, fraude or myht, —
Pocessiou*n* take no fors of wrong or riht.

Pride is unwilling to obey truth; wise policy, prudent counsel and discretion are far away. Possession cares not for wrong or right.

To trouthis parti p*r*ide is loth tobeie;
Extort poweer doth gret destrucciou*n*;
Wis policie al out of the weie,
Prudent cou*n*sail, age with discreciou*n*
Loste ther liberte of free ecciou*n*.
Who was most strong, wit*h* hym heeld eu*er*y wiht, —
Pocessiou*n* take no fors of wrong nor riht.

Finally Fortune cast them both down from her wheel; for their eyes were made blind by subtile deceit, fraud and collusion.

Swich dyuysiou*n* made many ma*n* to deie,
Brouhte the cite to desolaciou*n*.
With these too p*r*incis Fortune list to pleie,
Til from hir wheel she cast hem bothe dou*n*.
Sotil deceit, fraude & collusiou*n*
Ba*m*bicious clymbyng blente ther bothe liht, —
Pocessiou*n* take no fors of wrong nor riht.

2508. Of] Or B.

Noble p*r*incis, reme*m*breth what I seie,
Peiseth this stori withyne in yo*u*r resou*n*,
Of fals surmou*n*ty*n*g auarice berth þe keie,
Record of Cesar, Pompeye of Roome tou*n*,
Whos wilful werris, hatful discenciou*n*
Yiueth cleer warnyng to you & eueri wiht,
No cleym is worth withoute title of riht.

Noble Princes, remember Cæsar and Pompey of Rome. No claim is valid without title of right.

[How victorious Iulius Cesar brent the vessels of Tholome slouh Achillas that wolde ha moordred hi*m* & aft*er* grete victories hi*m*silf was mordred wi*th* boidekens bi brutus Cassius.] [1]

AFFTIR the woful co*m*pleint lame*n*tabl*e*
Of Po*m*peis deth*e*, pitous for to heer*e*,
Werris reme*m*brid, wi*th* tr*e*sou*n*s importabl*e*,
Compassid fraudis farcid wi*th* fair cheer*e*,
Conspired moordre, rehersid the maneer*e*
How kyng Tholome, fraudulent of corage,
The deth conspired of Po*m*peie fall in age.

After the woeful complaint of Pompey's death and the manner of King Ptolemy's conspiring it,

The processe tolde, I holde it wer but vey*n*
Therof to write a newe tragedie;
Thyng onys said, it to reherse ageyn,
It wer but idil, as for that partie.
But how Cesar went out of Thessalie,
Kam Talisau*n*dre to logge hy*m* in that place,
I wil remembre with support of yo*u*r grace.

I hold it vain to write thereof a new tragedy; but I will tell how Cæsar went to Alexandria

He logged was in his paleis roiall,
Wher he was besi, be diligent labour
Thoruh that regiou*n* in templis ouerall
To spoile goddis and haue al ther treso*u*r,
Wher he was mokkid, fond ther no fauo*u*r;
For Achillas, which that slouh Pompeie,
Cast hym with Cesar proudli to werreie.

and busied himself in spoiling temples, finding little encouragement, for Achillas, who slew Pompey,

His purpos was to falle upon Cesar,
As of nature was his condiciou*n*
Falsli to moordre men or thei wer war,—
Bi sum sleihte to fynde occasiou*n*
To destroye Iulius be tresou*n*,
And taco*m*plisshe his purpos in partie
Hadde twenti thousand in his cu*m*panye.

withstood him with 20,000 men, hoping to fall upon and destroy him.

[1] MS. J. leaf 134 recto.

2561. Alexandry P.

Achillas, who was leader and constable of the Egyptians, intended to give battle to the Romans, but Cæsar burnt Ptolemy's navy

This Achillas, fals, cruel, deceyuable,
Cast hym deceyue Cesar yif he myhte,
Of Thegipciens leder and constable
With the Romeyns purposeth for to fihte.
But whan Cesar therof hadde a sihte,
He is descendid, & faste bi the se
Brent al the naue of kyng Tholome.

together with a great part of the city and the famous library of 40 000 volumes.

Alle the vesselis wer dryue up with a flood
To gret damage of seide Tholome;
Iulius brente hem euene ther thei stood,
And a gret part beside of the cite.
And ther was brent, which was ful gret pite,
The famous librarie in Egipt of the kyng,
Ful fourti thousande volumys ther liggyng.

Bochas says that it was highly commendable of Ptolemy to gather together such a notable collection of books for the use of scholars.

In which thyng Bochas reherseth in sentence,
How Tholome was gretli comendable,
That thoruh his besi roial prouydence
Made hymsilff a librarie so notable;
For to al clerkis in studie that wer hable,
Of seuene sciences, the stori maketh mynde,
Lik ther desire myhte bookis fynde.

After this fire, there was a battle, and Cæsar, near defeat, took a barge from Egypt

Afftir this fyr, in Farus the contre, [p. 329]
The Egipciens hadde a gret bataille,
Wher Cesar was of gret necessite
That day constreyned, whan the feeld gan faille,
Take a barge from Egipt for to saille,
But so gret pres[e] folwed at his bak,
Almost the vessel was lik to go to wrak.

and narrowly escaped being wrecked. He was forced to swim 200 paces to land in his heavy armour.

Cesar armyd, with lettres in his hond,
Put his persone that day in auenture;
Two hundred pas manly swam to lond,
And kunnyngli to lond he doth recure,
Natwithstondyng his heuy strong armure.
But yit toforn or Cesar took the se,
He in the feeld hadde take Tholome.

He then took Ptolemy prisoner and slew Achillas and all his fellows.

And Achillas, the moordrere of Pompeie,
With alle his felawes that wer of assent
Wer slayn that day; ther went[e] non aweye:
Many Egipcien the same tyme brent.
Cesar of mercy for Tholome hath sent,

2582. the] *om.* H. 2590. thousande] M B.
2598. Pharos P. 2604. to wrak] awrak H.

To Alisau*n*dre sent hym hom of newe,
Chargyng he sholde to Romeyns forth be trewe.

But whan he was delyuered fro p*ri*sou*n*,
Of Egipciens in Alisau*n*dre the cite,
From eueri coost he gadred gret foisou*n*,
Ageyn Iulius kam dou*n* with his meyne;
But yit for al his hasti cruelte,
Swich resistence Cesar gan to make,
That* twenti thousand that day wer slay*n* & take.

Ptolemy was taken to mercy and sent home with the bidding to be loyal to Rome; but as soon as he was set free he came down against Cæsar with an army and lost 20,000 of his men,

Sixti galeis nat ferr fro the lond,
Tuelue thousand men komyng to Tholome, —
Echon wer yolde and brouht onto the hond
Of Iulius his prisoneres to bee.
Than Tholomeus besied hy*m* to flee
Toward the watir, wher maugre al his myht,
He drowned was in his gret hasti fliht.

60 galleys and 12,000 more men, who were on their way to aid him.

He knowen was bi his riche haberiou*n*,
Of gold and steel[e] it was entermaylid,
Bi Cesar sent onto the roial tou*n*,
Which for diffence was strongli enbatailed, —
Bokelis of gold richeli enamailed,
Which[e] toknis anon as thei haue sey*n*,
Disespeired to Cesar sente ageyn.

Ptolemy fled towards the sea and was drowned. His body was recognized by its rich armour with golden buckles.

Of them to Cesar was maad feith & homage;
The rewm of Egipt brouht to subiecciou*n*,
Til he of grace and merciful corage*
To Cleopatra gaff al that regiou*n*,
Longyng to hire be successiou*n*,
Be title of riht that tyme & non othir,
Because only Tholome was hir brothir.

The Egyptians submitted to Cæsar, and he made Cleopatra, Ptolemy's sister, queen.

Kyng Lagus whilom in his testament,
Fadir to Cleopatra & to Tholome,
Toforn his deth bi gr*e*t auisement
Cleerli enacted his laste volunte,
That his kyngdam departid sholde be,
Half to Tholome, as his bequethe was,
The tothir halff to queen Cleopatras.

Their father had devised the kingdom to both of them, each to rule one half;

2620. Alisaundry P. 2625. That] Than B.
2632. his] þe H.
2634. entirmailed J, entirmailled R 3, entyrmaylled H 5, entermayled P.
2642. corage] werkyng B. 2646. only] only þat H.

but Ptolemy had kept his sister in prison to deprive her of her share.

She bi hir brothir was holde in prisou*n*
To keepe hir wrongli fro*m* hir heritage,
Wheroff Cesar hadde compassiou*n*,
Purposed hy*m* to refourme hir damage.
And whil that he heeld ther his hostage,
Of equite, of lawe and of resou*n*,
Of al Egipt gaff hir pocessiou*n*.

Then came Juba, king of Lybia, a proud and cruel man, who hated the last Scipio because he succeeded Pompey as consul and wore purple, which Juba claimed was fitting only for himself as king.

¶ Than kam Iuba, of Libie lord & kyng,
Sowere of stryues and discenciou*n*,
Proud, hih of port, cruel in werkyng,
Which in especial hadde indignaciou*n*
Vnto the worthi laste Scipiou*n*,
Cause he was chose, lik as bookis seie,
To succeede next consul to Pompeie.

This Iuba eek bar to hy*m* gret hatreede,
Souht a quarel agey*n* hy*m* for o thyng,
Cause that he was clad in purpil weede,
For hym aleggyng, how onli that clothy*n*g
No maner estat sholde vse but a kyng:
Mente for hymsilff, sittyng in roial throne,
He wold as kyng that colour were* allone.

Bochas makes a digression here and says that no nation is so wasteful of clothing as the people of Almayne.

Heer my*n* auctour maketh a digressiou*n*,
Puttyng exau*m*ple of Almayne the co*n*tre;
Seith that ther is non othir naciou*n*
Touchyng array that is so disgise
In wast of cloth and superfluite,
Rehersyng her* in ful pleyn langage,
In many wise such wast doth gret damage.

Such superfluity in attire causes pride and gives occasion for lust and brings people to poverty and makes the rich disdainful of the poor.

It causeth pride and ambiciou*n*, [p. 330]
Ageyn the vertu of humylite;
To lecherie it yiveth occasiou*n*,
Which is contrarie* vnto chastite.
Wast of array sett folk in pouerte,
Causeth also such costage spent in vey*n*
Off othir porere to haue ful gret disdeyn.

2658. that] *om.* H.
2662. dissenciou*n*s H.
2674. that colour were] vse that colour B.
2680. her] ther B.
2685. contraire B, J.

Wher superfluite is vsid of aray,
Riot folweth, proud port & idilnesse;
With wast of tyme dryue forth the day,
Late drynkyng, wach, surfet, dronkenesse,
Engendreth feueres & many gret axcesse.
Thus eueri surfet englued is to othir,
And o mysreule bryngeth in anothir.

Riot, proud behaviour, idleness and drunkenness follow, engendering fevers and agues: each surfeit gives rise to another, and all move in a vicious circle.

God suffreth weel ther be a difference
Touchyng array, as men been of degre:
Hih estatis, that stonde in excellence,
Mut be preferrid, of resoun men may see;
As cloth of gold, stonis & perre
Was for princis, with othir fressh clothynges,
But specialli purpil was for kyngis.

God permits a difference in clothing: high estates must be well dressed and wear cloth of gold and jewels; and purple is the colour for kings.

Thus was ther set, of hih discrecioun,
Array accordyng to princis hih noblesse;
And for othir estatis lower doun,
Lik ther degrees tween pouert & richesse,
An ordre kept from scarsete & excesse,
A mene prouided atween hih & lowe,
Lich to hymsilff[e] ech man may be knowe.

Other estates lower down should array themselves according to their degrees.

But kyng Iuba, insolent & mad,
Of surquedie kauht [an] oppynyoun
That non but he in purpil shal* be clad,
Causyng debat tween hym & Scipioun.
Yit wer thei parti bothe with Roome toun
Ageyn Cesar, and drouh toward Pompeie,
For which at myscheef bothe thei dide deie.

King Juba, insolent and mad, thought that he alone was entitled to wear purple, and quarrelled with Scipio, although both were against Cæsar.

Whan Iuba felte hymsilf of noun poweer
Ageyn Cesar to holde chaumpartie,
For sorwe he loste contenaunce & cheer;
Of hih disdeyn[e] and malencolie
Callid on Pectryn, a kniht off his allie,
Made hym bassent that thei wer bothe fayn
Felli to fihte til oon off hem was slayn.

When he saw that he was too weak to fight Cæsar, he lost heart, and in a rage challenged Petreus, a knight of his acquaintance, to mortal combat.

Ageyn nature was this straunge fiht,
Ech to slen othir, & knew no cause whi, —
But for kyng Iuba was an hardi kniht,
He slouh his felawe and abood proudli,

Juba killed his friend Petreus, and then chose to die himself rather than live in bondage.

2693. excesse H, J, R 3, P, H 5. 2708. providyng H.
2712. but he non shal in purpil B.
2721. peyntryn H, Peitryn J, Peytryn R 3, H 5, Petreus P.

And rather ches to deien wilfulli,
Of hih despiht[e] & of proud corage,
Than vndir Cesar to lyuen in seruage.

So he summoned another friend, and, giving him a large reward, bade him smite off his head.

Maad calle a man who*m* he loued weel,
Gaff vnto hym gret gold & gret guerdou*n*
To take a suerd[e] forgid of fyn steel,
And make theroff no long dilaciou*n*,
But bad he sholde, for short conclusiou*n*,
Take upon hy*m*, & haue no feer nor dreed,
Withoute tarieng to smyten of his hed.

Aristobolus, who had been sent prisoner to Rome by Pompey, was released by Cæsar, and hoped to regain his kingdom.

Thus kyng Iuba rather ches to deie
Than lenger lyue in subiecciou*n*
Vndir Cesar; he loued so weel Pompeye.
¶ Tha*n* next to Bochas, as maad is menciou*n*,
Cam Aristobolus, with face & look cast dou*n*,
Which was to* Roome, afforn as I haue told,
Sent bi Po*m*peye to* be kept in hold.

[Aristobolus.]

Which aftir was delyuered fro prisou*n*
Bi help of Cesar in ful hasti wise,
Stondyng in hope of his regiou*n*
To be restored vnto the frau*n*chise,
Wher Hircanus, as ye haue herd the guise,*
Preferred was, to his gret foorth[er]yng,
Bi Po*m*peie of Iewes crowned kyng.

Unfortunately he fell into the hands of a captain who had been in Pompey's service and who killed him by poisoning.

Which Aristobolus hopeth to recure,
Caste menys ther to regne ageyn,
Wrouhte theron, dide his besi cure,
Whos hasti labour was but spent in veyn.
Fill in the handis of a proud capteyn
Which that whilom was longyng to Po*m*peie;
And he with poisou*n* vnwarli made hy*m* deye.

[How the last Scipiou*n* Consuler*e* of Rome for he not list to lyue in seruage of Iulyus roff hi*m*silf to þe hert.] [1]

Next appeared the last of the Scipios, who was defeated together with Juba by Cæsar.

NEXT ca*m* the laste worthi Scipiou*n*,
Which aftir Po*m*peie was maad consuleer,
Wit*h* whom Iuba was at discenciou*n*
For weryng purpre, as it was told wol er,

2743. to] in B. 2744. to] for to B. 2748. the] his H.
2749. the guise] deuise B. 2750. to] in H. 2762. purpull H.

[1] MS. J. leaf 135 recto.

And aftirward fill in ful gret[e] feer,
Whan Cesar hadde withyn*n*e Libie-lond
Outraied [hem] bothe with strong & myhti hond.

Wherbi Sipiou*n* gan fallen in despair, [p. 331]
Loste his cheer, as man disconsolat,
With thre Romeyns gan make his repair, —
Damasippus, Plectorie and Torquat, —
Goyng to shipe, the tyme infortunat,
Toward Spayne; but tempest ga*n* he*m* dryue,
That thei in Affrik vnwarli dede aryue.

Despairing, he took ship to Spain, but was driven back to Africa,

Scipiou*n* seeyng this woful caas sodeyne,
How he was brouht vnwarli to myscheeff;
For Scicius, a myhti strong capteyn,
Beyng a pirat and off the se a theeff,
Which is a name of ful gret repreeff, —
The same pirat, longyng to Cesar,
Fill on Scipiou*n* or that he was war,

where Sicius, a pirate friendly to Cæsar, fell on him,

Beyng in purpos take hym p*r*isoneer
Withyn*n*e his shipp toforn his arryuaill;
For which, alas, dulle gan his cheer,
His contenau*n*ce appallen & eek faille.
To fynde cou*n*fort no man coude hy*m* cou*n*saille,
Pullid out a suerd, whan he myht nat a-sterte,
And roof hymsilff[e] euene to* the herte.

intending to take him prisoner. In his extremity he pulled out a sword and thrust it into his heart.

This was the eende of laste Scipiou*n*:
Leuere he hadde at myscheef for to deie
Than vndir Cesar lyn fetrid in p*r*isou*n*
Or to his lordshipe in any wise obeye.
¶ To Bochas next hym cam Pompeye,
Sone and heir to gret[e] Pompeius,
Contraire also to Cesar Iulius,

He, too, died rather than be a captive of Cæsar. After him, Pompey, son and heir of Pompey the Great, appeared before Bochas.

Hadde brethren & sistren mo than oon,
And many another of ther alliau*n*ce.
And of assent thei cast hem euerichon,
Ther fadris deth hauyng in reme*m*brau*n*ce,
Vpon Cesar to take therof vengau*n*ce,
Eek upon Tholomee, which bi collusiou*n*
Slouh ther fadir bi ful fals tresou*n*.

He and his brothers and sisters determined to be revenged on Cæsar and Ptolemy.

2775. Sicyus H, Sicius R 3, P.
2783. H *inserts the word* purpose *before* contenau*n*ce.
2786. to] thoruh B, H 5.

Pompey fought with Cæsar in Spain, and, put to flight,

The eldest brothir callid eek Po*m*peye,
Beyng in Spaigne with ful gret apparaill,
Cast hym of newe Cesar to werreye
And his peeple proudli to assaille.*
And, as I fynde, ther was a gret bataille,
In which Pompeie, the eldest sone of thre,
Bi Iulius men constreyned was to flee.

and not knowing what to do, hid in a cave and was slain.

He fond no socour nor receit hy*m* to saue,
Off his lyff, he, stondyng in gret dreed,
Knowyng no reffut, fledde into a caue,
Tescape* awey knew no bettir reed,
Wher he was slayn; to Cesar brouht his hed,
Sent foorth in scorn anon to Hispalee,
Which in Spaigne is a ful gret cite.

Finally, all of Pompey's kindred were brought to destruction by Cæsar, whose renown increased.

Thus bi processe al hooli the kynreede
Of Pompeius, for short conclusiou*n*,
Bi Cesar wern & bi his men in deede
Withoute mercy brouht to destrucciou*n*.
Thus gan encrece the fame & the renou*n*
Of Iulius conquest on se & eek on londe,
Whos mortal suerd ther myht[e] non wit*h*stonde.

His power had been proved in Lybia, Spain, Italy, Germany, Lombardy and France.

First in Libie, Spaigne and eek Itaille*
Thexperience of his roial puissau*n*ce,
In Germanye bi many strong bataille,
His poweer preved, in Lumbardie & in Frau*n*ce.
Brouhte alle thes kyngdames vndir thobeissau*n*ce
Of [the] Romeyns: peised al this thy*n*g & seyn
Touchyng his guerdou*n*, his labour was i*n* veyn.

Returning to Rome, he put an end to the civil war and received the triumph,

Toward Roome makyng his repair,
Of hym appesed cyuyl discenciou*n*s,
Of throne imperial cly*m*byng on the stair;
For the conquest of threttene regiou*n*s,
Of the tryu*m*phe requered the guerdou*n*s,
Which to recure his force [he] hath applied,
Al-be the Senat his request hath denied.

2804. tassaille B. 2811. To scape B.
2822. in Itaille B.
2825. Lumbardie] Germanye H, R 3, H 5 — in Lumbardie &] ful often tyme J, ful oft times P.
2827. al] as H. 2832. xiije B.
2834. recure] replye H.
2835. request] conquest H.

And his name mor to magnefie,
To shewe the glorie* of his hih noblesse,
To the Capitoile faste he ga*n* hy*m* hie,
As emperour his doomys ther to dresse.
That day began with ioie & gret gladnesse;
The eue nothyng accordyng* with the morwe:
The entre glad; the eende trouble & sorwe.

and, hastening to the Capitol, issued his decrees as emperor. That day began with joy but ended in sorrow.

Calipurnia, which that was his wiff,
Hadde a drem the same niht afforn,
Toknis shewed of the funeral striff,
How that hir lord was likli to be lorn
Be conspiracy co*m*passed & Isworn,
Yiff he that day, withoute auisement,
In the Capitoile sat in iugement.

One night Calpurnia dreamt that her lord would die if he went to the Capitol the next day.

She drempte, alas, as she lay & sleep[te], [p. 332]
That hir lord, thoruh girt wit*h* many a wou*n*de,
Lay in hir lappe, & she the bodi kepte
Of woma*n*heed, lik as she was bou*n*de.
But, o alas, to soth hir drem was fou*n*de!
The nexte morwe, no lenger maad delay,
Of his parodie was the fatal day.

She dreamt that her lord, pierced with many wounds, lay in her lap. Alas, her dream came true!

A poore man callid Tongilius,
Which secreli the tresou*n* dede espie,
Leet write a lettre, took it Iulius,
The caas declaryng of the co*n*spiracie,
Which to reede Cesar list nat applie.
But, o alas! ambicious necligence
Caused his mordre bi vnwar violence.

A poor man named Tongilius knew the treason, but Cæsar neglected his warning,

Cesar sittyng myd the consistorie,
In his estat[e] most imperiall,
Aftir many conquest & victorie,
Fortune awaityng to yiuen hy*m* a fall,
With boidekenys, percyng as an all,
He moordred was, with many mortal wou*n*de.
Loo, how fals trust in worldli pompe is fou*n*de!

and, sitting in the midst of the consistory, was murdered with bodkins.

2837. gloire B, J.
2841. accordyng nothyng B.
2844. toforn H, R 3, beforn J.
2868. bodkyns H, bodkynes R 3, boidekynes J, Boydkynnys H 5, Bodkins P.
2869. many a H.

Lenvoye.

No tragedy is more woeful than the fall of Cæsar.

THORUH al this book[e] rad ech tragedie,
Afforn rehersid & put in remembrance,
Is non mor woful to my fantasie,
Than is the fall of Cesar in substaunce,
Which in his hiest imperial puissaunce
Was, whil he wende haue be most glorious,
Moordred at Roome of Brutus Cassius.

He brought all countries to subjection, and yet he was murdered at Rome by Brutus Cassius.

This marcial prince ridyng thoruh Lumbardie,
Ech contre yolde & brouht to obeissaunce;
Passyng the Alpies rood thoruh Germanye,
To subieccioun brouht the rewm of Fraunce,
Gat Brutis Albioun bi long contynuaunce:
To lustris passed, this manli Iulius
Moordred at Roome bi Brutus Cassius.

The conspiracy was hatched by the Senators, in spite of whom he had celebrated his triumph.

Among the Senat was the conspiracye
Alle of assent & of oon accordaunce, —
Whos tryumphe thei proudli gan denye;
But maugre them was kept thobseruaunce,
His chaar of gold with steedis of plesaunce
Conveied thoruh Roome, this prince [most] pompous,
The moordre folwyng bi Brutus Cassius.

Reckon up his conquests and his chivalry, and compare them with worldly variance!

Rekne his conquest, rekne up his cheualrie
With a countirpeis of worldli variaunce:
Fortunys chaungis for his purpartie; —
Weie al to-gidre, cast hem in ballaunce,
Set to of Cesar the myscheeuable chaunce,
With his parodie sodeyn & envious, —
Moordred at Roome bi Brutus Cassius.

Mars and Jupiter united to enhance his noblesse, yet he was murdered at Rome by Brutus Cassius.

Bookis alle and cronicles specefie,
Bi influence of heuenli purueiaunce,
Mars and Iubiter ther fauour did applie
With glade aspectis his noblesse to enhaunce:*
Mars gaf hym knihthod, Iubiter gouernaunce,
Among princis hold oon the moste famous, —
Moordred at Roome bi Brutus Cassius.

2896. myschevous H.
2902. tenhaunce B, J, R 3.

Behold of Alisaundre the grete monarchie,
Which al the world had vndir obeissaunce,
Prowesse of Ector medlid with gentrie,
Of Achilles malencolik vengaunce, —
Rekne of echon the quaueryng assuraunce,
Among remembring the fyn of Iulius,
Moordred at Roome bi Brutus Cassius.

Behold the monarchy of Alexander, the chivalry of Hector, Achilles' vengeance, and the end of Cæsar! Consider of each one the trembling security!

Princis considreth, in marcial policie
Is nouther trust[e], feith nor assuraunce:
Al stant in chaung with twynclyng of an eye.
Vp toward heuene set your attendaunce,
The world vnseur & al worldli plesaunce;
Lordship abit nat, record on Iulius
Moordred at Roome bi Brutus Cassius.

Princes, there is no trust in martial policy: all may change in the twinkling of an eye; record on Julius, who was murdered at Rome by Brutus Cassius.

[How Octavian / succeded next and how the mordres of Iulius / deied at mischeff.] [1]

AFFTIR the moordre of þis manli man,
This noble prince, this famous* emperour,
His worthi nevew callid Octouyan
To regne in Roome was next his successour.
Which dide his deueer bi dilligent labour
To punshe all tho, of nature as he ouhte,
Bi rihtful doom, that the moordre wrouhte.

After Cæsar's death, his nephew Octavian succeeded to the empire, and his endeavour was to punish all those who had been guilty of the murder.

Cheeff conspiratour was Brutus Cassius,
Which of this moordre made [al] the ordynaunce.
Anothir Brut, surnamyd Decius,
Was oon also conspiryng the vengaunce
Wrouht on Cesar; he aftir slayn in Fraunce.
Heer men may seen, what coostis that men weende,
How moordre alwey requereth an euel eende.

Brutus Cassius was chief conspirator, Decius another, slain afterwards in France. Murder always demands an evil end.

Withyne the space almost of thre yeer [p. 333]
Destroied wern al the conspiratours
Be sodeyn deth; & summe stood in daungeer
To be banshed or exiled as tretours.
And as it is cronicled bi auctours,
Space of thre yeer, reknid oon bi oon,
Deide at myscheeff the moorderis euerichon.

Within three years all the conspirators were either destroyed or exiled.

2921. famous] manli B.
2922. Octauian P. 2926. the] he H.
2937. banyssh H.

[1] MS. J. leaf 136 recto.

It is a sad thing to murder a prince. God will take vengeance. Yet there is but little security in high estate.

To moordre a prince, it is a pitous thyng.
God of his riht wil take therof vengaunce;
Namli an emperour, so famous in ech thing,
Which al the world[e] hadde in gouernaunce.
Rekne his conquest digne off remembraunce,
Al peised in oon, Bochas ber[e]th witnesse,
In hih estat is litil sekirnesse.

[How Tullius was too tymes exiled and atte last/ slayn by Pompylyus.] [1]

My author next made ready to write about Tullius, complaining that his barren style was inadequate to describe the life of so noble a rhetorician.

MYN auctour heer writ no long processe,
Of Iulius deth compleynyng but a while;
To write of Tullie in hast he gan hym dresse,
Compendiousli his liff for to compile,
Compleynyng first, seith his bareyn stile
Is insufficient to write, as men may seen,
Of so notable a rethoricien.

Prince of eloquence, he gathered up the flowers on Mt. Parnassus and was crowned with laurel by the nine Muses.

Laumpe and lanterne of Romeyn oratours,
Among hem callid prince of elloquence,
On Pernaso he gadred up the flours,
This rethoricien most of excellence.
Whos meritis treuli to recompence,
The Muses nyne, me thouhte, as I took heed,
A crowne of laureer set upon his hed.

Bochas hung his head and thought he had so little skill and language, that if he laboured all his life he could not properly describe Tully's merits.

Bochas astoned, gan of hymsilff conclude,
His look abasshed, dul of his corage,
Thouhte his termys & resouns wer to rude,
That he lakked kunnyng & langage,
Wherebi he sholde to his auauntage,
Thouh he laboured writyng al his lyue,
Of Tullius the meritis to descryue.

But he remembered that although sometimes the wind drives a cloud across the sun, it does not lessen its light, and that his dull writing would not eclipse the brightness of Tullius.

Wherof supprised, he kauhte a fantasie,
Withynne hymsilf remembryng anon riht,
Thouh it so falle sumtyme a cloudi skie
Be chacid with wynd affor the sunne briht,
Yit in effect it lasseth nat his liht;
So Bochas dempte that his dul writyng
Eclipsed nat of Tullius the shynyng.

2953. sufficient H. 2958. excellence] Elloquence H.
2960. me] *om.* H.

[1] MS. J. leaf 136 recto.

With rud language a ma*n* may weel r*e*porte
The laude off tryu*m*phes & conquestis m*er*ueilous,
Which thyng remembryng gretli gan co*m*forte
The herte of Bochas; & to hymsilf spak thus:
"Too colours seyn that be contrarious,
As whiht and blak; it may bee non othir,
Ech in his kynde sheweth mor for othir.

It comforted him to think that all manner of things can be told in unadorned language, and that colours shew best by contrast.

In Phebus presence sterris lese her liht;
Cleer at mydday appeereth nat Lucyne;
The fame of Tullye whilom shon so briht,
P*r*ince of fair speche, fadir of that doct*r*ine,
Whos brihte bemys into this hour doth shyne:
Sothli," quod Bochas, "of who*m* wha*n* I endite
Myn hand I feele quakyng wha*n* I write.

Nevertheless he said, "I feel my hand tremble when I write about him.

But for to yiue folk occasiou*n*,
Which in rethorik haue mor* experience
Than haue I, & mor inspecciou*n*
In the colo*u*rs and craff[t] of elloquence,—
Them texcite to do ther dilligence,
Onto my writyng wha*n* thei may attende,
Of compassiou*n* my rudnesse to amende."

"However, people who are more skilled than I will have opportunity to amend my rudeness out of compassion."

Vnto hymsilff[e] hauyng this langage,
Bochas to write gan his pen*n*e dresse,
Vndir support afforced his corage
To remembre thexcellent noblesse
Of this orato*u*r, which wi*th* the suetnesse
Of his ditees, abrod as thei haue shyned,
Hath al this world most cleerli enlumyned.

After he had said this to himself he began to write.

This Tullius, this singuler famous* ma*n*,
First to reme*m*bre of his natyuyte,
Born at Aprinas, a cite of Tuscan,
Of blood roial descendid, who list see.
Grekissh bookis of old antiquite,
Maad of rethorik and in ther vulgar songe,
He translatid into Latyn tunge.

Tullius was born at Arpinum in Tuscany. He was of royal descent, and at first translated old Greek books into Latin.

In tendre youthe his contre he forsook
And fro Tuscan his passage he ga*n* dresse;
Toward Roome the riht[e] weie he took,
Entry*ng* þe cite, the renom*m*ed noblesse

In his youth he went to Rome; and his fame spread abroad like a sun.

2983. liht] siht H.
2991. mor] no*n* B. 3004. famous singuler B.
3005. of his] his famous H.

Hid in his persone shewed the brihtnesse
Of dyuers vertues, tyme whil he abood,
That lik a son*n*e his fame spradde abrod.

He was made a citizen for his virtues and chosen consul in the time of Catiline.

For his vertues made a citeseyn, [p. 334]
The goode report of hym shon so cleer,
Lik as he hadde be born a Romeyn,
In ther fauour his name was so enticer.
Among hem chose for a consuleer, —
Ageyn the cite, tyme of his consulat,
Whan Catalyne was with hem at debat.

Catiline, cruel and full of wrath, was always busy to injure Rome;

Bi the prudence of this Tullius
And his manhod, reknid bothe Ifeere, —
Catelyna, most cruel and irous,
Froward of port & froward of his cheer*e*,
Besi euere to fynde out the maneer*e*,
How he myhte be any tokne or signe
Ageyn the cite couertli maligne.

and 689 years after the foundation of the city he conspired with others against its franchises and freedoms,

Sixe hundrid yeer, fourscore told & nyne,
Reknid of Roome fro the fundaciou*n*,
This cruel tirau*n*t, this proude Catalyne,
Made with othir a coniuraciou*n*
Ageyn frau*n*chises & fredam of the tou*n*.
First discurid, as bookis telle can,
In the parties & bou*n*des of Tuscan.

purposing to bring Rome to ruin.

The purpos hooly of this Catalyne,
Imagyned on fals[e] couetise,
Was to brynge Roome vnto ruyne.
And therupon in many sondri wise
Fond out weies, menys gan deuise,
To his entent bi dilligent labo*u*r
In the cite ga*n* gete hym gret fauo*u*r.

Tully was told about the conspiracy, and by his prudence and the help of Antony it was broken and withdrawn.

But fynali his coniuraciou*n*
Discured was bi oon Quintius,
Which was afforn[e] fals vnto the tou*n*.
Tolde al the caas vnto Tullius,
Bi whos prudence & werkyng m*er*veilous,
Bi help of Antoyne, that was his felawe,
The coniuraciou*n* was broken & withdrawe.

3016. whil] whan H.
3027. Catilina P — most Irous H.
3036. Ageyn] geyn H.

Bi witt of Tullie al the coniuratours
Espied wern and brouht onto myschaunce,
Ther namys rad tofor the senatours,
Of ther falsheed told al the gouernaunce,
Manli ordeyned thoruh his purueiaunce.
With al his peeple, as maad is menciouin,
Catilyna departid fro the toun.

Through his ability all the conspirators were punished. Catiline left Rome

With Antonye* the said[e] Catalyne
Beside Pistoie hadde a gret bataile.
Slayn in the feeld; he myht[e] nat declyne,
For he abood whan the feeld gan faille.
Poweer of oon litil may auaile,
Namli whan falsheed, of malis & of pride
Ageyn[es] trouthe dar the bront abide.

and was slain in a battle with Antony near Pistoia.

Ther was another callid Lentulus
Of his felawes, that namyd was Fabyne;
The thridde of hem eek callid Cetegus, —
Alle assentid & sworn to Catallyne,
Stranglid in prisoun, at myscheef dide fyne.
Cause Tullius dide execucioun,
Tullyane was callid the prisoun.

Three of his companions were strangled in prison; and the prison was afterwards called Tullian, after Tully, who had defeated the plot.

Thus koude he punshe tretours of the toun,
Outraie ther enmyes, of manhod & prudence;
Callid of ther cite gouernour & patroun,
Sent from aboue to been ther diffence,
Ther championn, most digne of reuerence,
Chose of ther goddis ther cite for to guie
Bi too prerogatyues: knihthod & polycie.*

Thus he punished traitors to Rome. He was called patron and governor of the city.

Lik a sunne he dide hem enlumyne
Bi hih prowesse of knihtli excellence;
And thoruh the world his bemys dede shyne
Of his rethorik & his elloquence,
In which he hadde so gret experience.
Bi circumstaunces that nothyng dede lakke,
He transcendid Polityus & Grakke.

He illumined the Romans like a sun; and the beams of his rhetoric and eloquence shone through the world.

Of oratours it is put in memorie,
This Tullius, thoruh his hih renoun,
Of all echon the honour & the glorie
Was youe to hym, as maad is mencioun:

He surpassed all orators and won the golden triumph of the House of Fame.

3060. Antoyne B. 3063. faille] falle H. 3073. Tullianum P.
3076. ther] þe H, the R 3. 3080. polycie] clergie B, J.
3087. Plotyus H, R 3, Plocius J, Plotius P.

Surmountid all; & in conclusioun,
The goldene trumphe of the Hous of Fame
Thoruh al the world[e] bleuh abrod his name.

He knew the secrets of philosophy and studied in Athens, where he profited in all sciences.

He knew secretis of philosophie,
Cam to Athenys* to scoole for doctryne,
Wher he profited so gretli in clergie
In al sciences heuenli and dyuyne,
That he was callid, as auctours determyne,
Among Romeyns, of verray dieu[e] riht,
Of elloquence the lanterne & the liht.

He pleaded two great causes in Rome before the senators,

It is remembred among oratours, [p. 335]
How Tullius pleted causes tweyne
In the Romeyn court affor the senatours,
The cause defendyng be langage souereyne
Of too accusid geyn hem that dede pleyne
On ther defautis, them sauyng fro myscheef,
The court escapyng fro daunger & repreeff.

saving two accused, and spoke such beautiful Latin and dealt so wisely with his material that no man could deny what he said.

Thes causes tweyne he pleted in Latyn,
With so excellent flouryng fair langage,
With suich resouns concluded at the fyn,
That he be wisdam kauhte the auauntage
In his mateeres with al the surplusage
That myhte auaile onto his partie:
What he saide ther koude no man denie.

In Greece his reputation and authority were so great that he was compared to Plato, upon whose infant lips bees laid honey, a sign that he would be the source and well of rhetoric. Yet Tully was his equal.

Among Grekis [at] Athenys the cite
He was so gret of reputacioun,
So famous holde of auctori[t]e,
To be comparid bi ther oppynyoun
To the philisophre that callid was Platoun,
To whos cradel bees dede abraide
And hony soote thei on his lippes laide.

A pronostik[e], lik as bookis tell,
Plato sholde bi famous excellence,
Of rethorik be verray sours & well,
For his langage, merour off elloquence.
Yit the Grekis recorden in sentence,
How Tullius in parti and in all
Was onto Plato in rethorik egall.

3096. to Athenys] Tathenys B, H 5.
3107. them] *om.* H. 3109. Thes] The H. 3116. at] *om.* H.

Thoruh his langage this saide Tullius
Reconsilede bi his soote orisou*n*s
To the lordshipe & grace of Iulius,
P*r*inces, kynges of dyuers regiou*n*s,
That suspect stood bi accusaciou*n*s,
Because thei dide Iulius disobeie,
Wer enclyned with Romey*n*s to Po*m*peie.

Through his orations he reconciled the princes and kings of many regions to the lordship of Julius.

He coude appese bi his p*r*udent langage
Folkis that stoode at discenciou*n*;
Bi crafft he hadde a special auau*n*tage,
Fauour synguleer in pronu*n*ciaciou*n*,
In his demenyng gret prudence & resou*n*:
For the p*ro*nou*n*cyng of maters in substau*n*ce,
His thank resceyueth bi cheer & contenau*n*ce.

He could soften people who were at enmity with one another,

To a glad mateer longeth a glad cheer,
Men trete of wisdam with woordes of sadnesse,
Pleyntes requeere, aftir the mateer,
Greuous or mortal, a cheer of heuynesse,
Lik as the cause outher the processe
Yiueth occasiou*n* to hyndren or to speede, —
The doctryne in Tullius men may reede.

and knew well how to adapt his expression to the matter of which he treated.

The name of Tulie was kouth in many place;
His elloquence in eueri lond was ryff;
His langage made hy*m* stonde in grace
And be preferrid duryng al his lyff.
Maried he was, and hadde a riht fair wiff,
Childre manye, seruau*n*tis yonge & old;
And, as I fynde, he heeld a good houshold.

His reputation was known in every land.
He had a wife, who was right fair, and many children and servants.

De Officijs he wrot bookis thre,
De Amicitia, I fy*n*de how he wrot oon,
Of Age another, notable for to see;
Of moral vertu thei tretede eu*er*ichon.
[And] as Vincent wrot ful yore agon
In his Merour callid Historiall,
Nou*m*bre of his bookis be ther remembrid all.

He wrote three books *de Officiis*, *Cato Major* (Vincent described all his writings in his *Speculum Historiale*),

3150. in] of H.
3151. Tullyus H.
3154. be] he H.

the Dream of Scipio, two books of divination, on agriculture, vainglory, *de Republica*, twelve books of orations and many moral sayings.

He wrot also the Drem of Scipiou*n*,
Of Rethoriques co*m*piled bookis tweyne,
And tweyne he wrot of dyuynaciou*n*;
Of tilthe of lond to write he dede his peyne,
A large book of glorie that is veyne,
De Re publica; & as he seith hymselue,
Of his Orisou*n*s he wrot bookis tuelue.

But in spite of all, he was banished from Rome

And of his dictes that callid be morall
Is remembred notabli in deede
In the said Merour Historiall.
And yit this saide Tullius, as I reede,
Mid his worshepes stood alwey in dreede
Of Fortune; for in conclusiou*n*,
He be envie was ban[y]shed Roome tou*n*.

to Campania; and there, at the house of a friend,

Beyng in exil, this famous Tullius,
In Campanya at Atyne the cite
Resceyued he was of oon Plancius,
A man that tyme of gret auctorite.
And whil that he abood in that contre,
Slepyng aniht, the book makþ menciou*n*,
How that he hadde a wonder visiou*n*.

he had a wonderful dream of how he met Gaius Marius in a desert. Marius inquired the cause of his trouble, and on learning what it was

He thouhte thus, as he lay slepyng: [p. 336]
In a desert and a gret wildirnesse
Fyndyng no path, but to & fro erryng,
How he mette, clad in gret richesse,
Gaius Marrius, a p*r*ince of hih* noblesse,
Axyng Tulli with sad contenau*n*ce,
What was cheef grou*n*d & cause of his gr*e*uau*n*ce.

assigned a sergeant to convey him in all haste to his sepulture, where Tullius should receive tidings of his recall to Rome.

Whan Tullius hadde hy*m* the cause told
Of his disese & his mortal wo,
Marrius with his hand set on hy*m* hold,
To a sergau*n*t assigned hym riht tho,
And in al haste bad he sholde go,
To conveie hym doon his besi cure
In al haste possible to his sepulture,

3171. Orisouns] Oracions P.
3172. dictes] ditees H, dictes H, dities P, dites R 3, H 5.
3175. this] þe H.
3176. worshipp H. 3180. Ative H.
3181. Plantius P.
3190. hih] gret B, J, H 5, R 3, great P — Cayus P.
3198. doon his besi] dou*n* bi his H.

Wher he sholde haue tidyngis of plesau*n*ce
Of his repeir into Roome tou*n*,
Been aleggid off his old gr*e*uau*n*ce.
This was the eende of his auiseou*n*.
The nexte morwe, as maad is menciou*n*,
Ther was holde, to Tullius gret auail,
Tofor Iubiter in Roome a gret cou*n*sail

Withyne the temple bilt bi Marrius:
The senatours accorded wer certey*n*
To reconcile this prudent Tullius,
Out of his exil to calle hy*m* hom agey*n*.
Aftir resceyued as lord & souereyn
Of elloquence, bassent of the Senat,
Fulli restored vnto his first estat.

The next day a council was held in Rome in the temple built by Marius, and shortly afterwards Tully was restored to his former estate.

This thi*n*g was doon wha*n* that in Roome tou*n*
The striff was gr*e*ttest tween Cesar & Po*m*peie;
And for Tullius drouh hym to Catou*n*,
With Pompeius Cesar to werreie
And of Iulius the parti disobeie,
Out of Roome Tullius dide hy*m* hie,
Fledde with Po*m*peie into Thesalie.

This was done during the struggle between Cæsar and Pompey; and although Tullius had fled with Pompey to Thessaly,

Cesar aftir of his fre mociou*n*,
Wha*n* that he stood hiest in his glorie,
Hym reconciled agey*n* to* Roome tou*n*,
Vpon Po*m*peie accomplisshed the victorie.
But Iulius slayn in the co*n*sistorie
Bi sexti senatours beyng of assent,
Tullius ageyn was into exil sent.

Cæsar became reconciled with him.

And in a cite callid Faryman
Tullius his exil dide endure;
For Antonyus was to hym enmy than,
Because that he, parcas of auenture,
Compiled hadde an invectiff scripture
Ageyn Antoyne, rehersyng al the cas
Of his defautis & of Cleopatras.

After Cæsar's death he was again exiled; and Antony hated him and compassed his murder because he had exposed his relations, with Cleopatra.

Thus of envie and [of] mortal hatreede,
His deth compassed bi Antonyus,
And aftirward execut in deede
Bi procuryng of oon Po*m*pillius; —

Finally one Popilius went to Campania on the authority of Antony

3201. into] vn to H.
3223. to] into B. 2224, 25 *are transposed, but corrected* H.
3232. invectiff] Inuentive H, Inuentif J.

Gat a commyssioun, the stori tellith thus,
Of fals malice, & foorth anon wente he
Into Gayete of Campaigne* a cite.

and slew Tullius, although he had once saved him from the gallows.

And bi the vertu of his commyssioun,
Takyng of Antoyne licence & liberte,
Cheeff rethoricien that euer was in the toun,
Among Romeyns to worshep the cite,
Was slayn, alas, of hate and enmyte
Bi Pompilius, roote of al falsheed, —
Proffryng hymsilff to smyten of his hed.

Whoever saves a thief, when the rope is tied about his neck, will have an evil reward.

Tullius afforn[e] hadde been his diffence
Fro the galwes, & his deth eek let,
Which hadde disserued for his gret offence
To haue been hangid upon an hih gibet.
Who saueth a theef whan the rop is knet
Aboute his nekke, as olde clerkis write,
With sum fals tourn the bribour wil hym quite.

Experience shews that a thief will always be ungrateful.

Loo, heer the vice of ingratitude,
Bexperience brouht fulli to a preeff,
Who in his herte tresoun doth include,
Cast for good wil to do a man repreeff.
What is the guerdoun for to saue a theeff?
Whan he is scapid, looke, ye shal fynde
Of his nature euere to be vnkynde.

This odious traitor Popilius smote off Tully's right hand after he was dead;

This Popilius, tretour most odible,
To shewe hymsilff fals, cruel and vengable,
Toward Tullie dide a thyng horrible:
Whan he was ded, this bribour most coupable,
Smet of his riht hand, to heere abhomynable,
With which[e] hond, he lyuyng, on hym took
To write of vertues many [a] famous book.

and his hand and head were afterwards set up on a stake, until the wind and weather wasted them.

The hand, the hed of noble Tullius,— [p. 337]
Which eueri man ouht of riht compleyne, —
Wer take and brouht[e] bi Popilius,
Vpon a stake set up bothe tweyne,
Ther tabide, wher it dide shyne or reyne,
With wynd & wedir, til thei wer deffied,
In tokne al fauour was to hym denied.

3239. a] *om.* H.
3241. Gayete] Gaire J, Caiatte P — Compaigne B, J, compaygne H 5, Campaygne H, Campaynge R 3, Champayne P.
3255. bribour] labour H.
3263. Popilius] Pompelyne H, Pompilyn R 3.
3270. R *begins again with this line.*

¶ A chapitle ageyn [Iangelers and][1] diffamers of Rethorique.

BOCHAS compleynyng in his studie allone
The deth of Tullie and the woful fall,
Gruchching in herte made a pitous mone,
The folk rebukyng in especial,
Which of nature be boistous & rurall,
And hardi been (for thei no kunnyng haue)
Craft of rethorik to hyndren and depraue.

> Bochas, complaining the death of Tully, rebuked those people who are rude and tumultuous by nature and bold (for they have no skill themselves) to decry the art of rhetoric.

Clerkis olde dide gretli magnefie
This noble science, that wer expert & wis,
Callid it part of philosophie,
And saide also in ther prudent auys,
Ther be thre partes, as tresours of gret pris,
Compiled in bookis & of old prouided,
Into which philosophie is deuyded.

> In the old days scholars called it a branch of philosophy.
>
> There are three branches of philosophy:

The firste of hem callid is morall,
Which directeth a man to goode thewes;
And the secounde, callid naturall,
Tellith the kynde of goode men & shrewes;
And the thridde, rac[i]ounal, weel shewes
What men shal uoide & what thing vndirfonge,
And to that parti rethorik doth longe.

> moral, natural and rational, and to rational rhetoric belongs.

Bi Tullius, as auctours determyne,
Of his persone rehersyng in substaunce,
Translatid was fro Greek into Latyne
Crafft of rethorik; and for the habundaunce
Of elloquence stuffed with plesaunce,
All oratours remembrid, hym to-fore
Was ther non lik, nor aftir hym yit bore.

> The art of rhetoric was transferred from Greece to Rome by Tullius. No orator like him was ever born.

Bochas also seith in his writingis
And preueth weel be resoun in sentence,
To an oratour longeth foure thingis:
First naturel wit, practik with science,
Vertuous lyff, cheef ground of elloquence,
Of port and maner that he be tretable;
Thes menys had, myn auctour halt hym able.

> Bochas says that an orator must have natural wit, broad knowledge, a virtuous life and affability.

3280. The] tho H. 3283. and] or H.
3288. gret] *om.* H. 3290. deuyded] prouyded R.
3307. longeth] longe R.

[1] *Supplied from* MS. J. leaf 139 recto.

Bochas also demonstrates that every notable rhetorician must have five armours, which he calls the five banners of eloquence.

In his writyng and in his scriptures
Bochas weel preueth, if mut needis been,
How that of riht ther longe fyue armures
To eueri notable rethoricien,
Set heer in ordre, who that list hem seen,
Which he callith, rehersyng in sentence,
The fyue baneeres longyng to elloquence.

The first is Invention,

The firste off hem callid Inuenciou*n*,
Bi which a man doth in his herte fynde
A sikir grou*n*de fou*n*did on resou*n*,
With circu*m*stau*n*ces, that nouht be left behy*n*de,
Fro poynt to poynt enprentid in his my*n*de
Touchyng the mateer, the substau*n*ce & þe grete,
Of which he caste notabli tentrete.

the second Disposition, which helps us avoid digressions;

Another armure, in ordre the secou*n*de,
Of riht is callid Disposiou*n*,
As of a mateer whan the grou*n*d is fou*n*de,
That eueri thyng bi iust dyuysiou*n*
Be void of al foreyn digressiou*n*,
So disposid touchyng tyme & space,
Fro superfluite keepe his dewe place.

the third is Elocution, the art of effective expression;

The thridde armure namyd in sentence
Is Ellocuciou*n*, with woordes many or fewe,
Materes conceyued bi iust co*n*uenyence,
Disposid in ordre couenably* to shewe, —
Lik a keruer that first doth tymbir hewe,
Squier* & compas cast fetures & visage,
With keruyng tool makth [up] a fair image.

the fourth is Pronunciation, which is joined to execution,

Pronu*n*ciaciou*n* is the fourth armure,
Necessarie to eueri oratour,
In such caas wha*n* craft onto nature
Iioyned is bi dilligent labour
With execuciou*n*, and that ther be fauour
In declaryng, with eueri circu*m*stau*n*ce,
Folwyng the mateer in cheer & contenau*n*ce.

whereby the orator conforms his mien and gestures to his matter;

An heuy mateer requereth an heuy cheer; [p. 338]
To a glad mateer longeth weel gladnesse;
Men in pronou*n*cyng mut folwe the mateer, —
Old oratours kan bern herof witnesse, —

3336. couenable B, R 3.
3338. Squiers B.
3339. toolis H.
3342. craft *is repeated* R.
3350. herof] ther off R.

A furious compleynt vttrid in distresse:
This was the maner, as poetis do descryue,
In his tragedies whan Senec was alyue.

The fiffte armure callid Reme*m*brau*n*ce,
With quik memorie* be prouidence to see,
So auisili to grose up in substau*n*ce
Hooli his mateeris, that nouht forgetyn be,
Liste foryetilnesse dirke nat the liberte
Of cleer report, ech thing hadde in my*n*de,
That in pronou*n*cyng nothi*n*g be left behy*n*de.

the fifth is Memory, that nothing may be forgotten;

Afforn prouided, so that foryetilnesse
Be non hyndrere to inuenciou*n*,
And in proceedyng no forey*n* reklesnesse
Trouble nat the ordre of disposiciou*n*.
And for tacomplisshe al up with resou*n*,
That pronou*n*cyng be cleer[e] reme*m*brau*n*ce
Be weel fauoured with cheer & contenau*n*ce.

for forgetfulness should not hinder invention or trouble the order of disposition.

Thes said[e] thynges be inli necessarie
To euery prudent notable orato*u*r,
Nat to hasti nor ouer long to tarie,
But to conveie his processe be meso*u*r;
In cheer accordyng stant al the fauo*u*r:
For in pronou*n*cyng, who lakketh cheer or* face,
Of Tullius scoole stant ferr out of grace.

These things are necessary to every able orator.

¶ Al erthli beestis be muet of nature,
Sauf onli man, which haueth auau*n*tage
Bi a prerogatiff aboue ech creature
To vttre his conceit onli be langage.
The soule be grace r*e*pressith al outrage,
Namli wha*n* resou*n* hath the souereynte
To bridle passiou*n*s of sensualite.

All earthly creatures are dumb by nature; only man has the power of speech.

Kynde onto man hath youen elloquence,
A thyng couenable in especiall
Whan that it is conveied bi prudence,
To talke of mateeris that be natural
And secrees hid aboue celestial, —
Doth entrete of sun*n*e, moone & sterris
Thynfluent poweer dou*n* sent of pes & werris.

Nature has given him eloquence, a convenient thing when it is prudently managed.

3352. maner] mateer H.
3355. memoire B. 3366. be] wit*h* H.
3373. For] & H — or] & B. 3374. ferr] full H.
3376. haueth] hath H. 3386. secretis H.
3388. Thynfluence R.

Man only can talk about the universe and express his thoughts in words.

God of al this hath grau*n*ted knowleching
Onli to man bi wisdam and resou*n*,
And thoruh langage youe to hy*m* shewy*n*g,
Outward to make declaraciou*n*
Of the heuenli cours & sondri mociou*n*,
Diuers chau*n*ges, &, pleynli to diffyne,
The reuoluciou*n* of the speeris nyne.

He can discuss the moving and mutations, accord and discord of the four elements, the coming and departing of earthly things;

Men bi langage shewe out ther ententis,
The naturall meeuyng & mutaciou*n*s,
Accord & discord of the foure elementis,
Kyndli variau*n*ce of foure co*m*pleccciou*n*s,
The generaciou*n** & the corupciou*n*s
Of erthli thynges, co*n*trarie ech to other,
Corrupciou*n* of oon engendryng to another.

and he is taught by language to be steadfast in virtue.

This the poweer & the p*re*cellence
Youe vnto man, which is resonabl*e*,
That bi langage and bi elloquence
A man is tauht in vertu to be stable, —
Of soule eternal, of bodi coru*m*pable,
Tauht w*ith* his tunge whil he is alyue
Of his defautis how he shal hym shryue.

Bochas tells us that there is natural rhetoric learned in youth, and the art of eloquence to which we come only by great diligence.

Bochas eek tellith, touchyng rethorik,
Ther been too maneres: oon is of nature,
Lernyd in youthe, which doth oon spek[e] lik
As he heereth & lerneth bi scripture; —
Crafft of rethorik youe to no creature
Sauff to man, which bi gret dilligence
Be studie kometh to crafft of elloquence.

Language enables preachers to teach the people virtuously, and instils in folk the respect of holy church.

Crafft of langage and of prudent speche
Causeth prechours bi spiritual doctryne
Vertuousli the peeple for to teche,
How thei shal lyue bi moral disciplyne.
Langage techeth men to plau*n*te vyne,
Enfourmeth folk to worshepe hooli cherche,
The artificeer treuli for to werche.

But there are some who say that God has more regard to our hearts than to our language.

Yit ther be sum*m*e that pleynli preche and teche,
Haue of langage this oppynyou*n*:
God ha[th] nat most reward onto speche,
But to the herte & to thaffecciou*n*;

3400. generaciou*n*s B.
3413. &] or R. 3416. to] bi R.
3426. nat] *om.* H — reward] rewardid H.

Best can guerdone the inward entencioun
Of eueri man, nat after the visage,
But lik the menyng of ther inward corage.

To vttre langage is gret dyuersite [p. 339]
Whan that men shewe theffect of ther menyng,
Be it of ioie or off aduersite,
Cheer for taccord therwith* in vtt[e]ryng,
Now debonaire, sumwhile rebukyng,
And in rehersyng, lik cheer alwei tapplie,
Be it of rudnesse, be it of curteisie.

There is great variety in our means of expression, depending upon our feelings

Of discreciour sette a difference
In his pronouncyng to perce or vndirmyne,
To drawe the iuge vnto his sentence
Or to his purpos to make hym to enclyne,
Seen wher he be malencolik or benigne, —
Or his mateer be vttrid or vnclosid,*
Considre afforn how that he is disposid.

and according with our intentions, as, for example, when we try to win over a judge.

Peised al this thyng, the rethoricien,
With other thynges which appertene of riht
To crafft of speche, he mut conueye & seen
Mateeris of substaunce & mateeris that be liht,
Dispose hymsilf tentretyn euery wiht
Lik to purpos & fyn of his mateere,
As for the tyme rethorik doth requeere.

Thus the rhetorician must prepare himself to treat all manner of subjects and in many different ways.

As bexaumple, myn auctour* doth record,
Men sette at werre, in herte ferr* assonder,
The rethoricien to make hem for taccord
Mut seeke weies & menys heer & yonder,
Of old rancour tappese the boistous thonder,
Be wise exaumplis & prouerbis pertynent
Tenduce the parties to been of oon assent.

He must bring warring men to concord and allay the thunder of old rancour,

A man also that stant in heuynesse,
Disespeired and disconsolat,
The rethoricien mut doon his besynesse,
The ground considred & felt of his estat,
The cause serchid whi he stant desolat,
Which to reffourme be dilligent labour
Is the trewe offis of eueri oratour.

and he must also aid and comfort those who are despaired and disconsolate.

3434. for taccord therwith] of accord therof B.
3443. vnclosid] enclosid B. 3444. that] *om.* H.
3445. the] bi R, J. 3446. apperteneth R.
3449. tentretyn] tentren H, tentrete J, P.
3452. As] A H — myn auctour] Rethorik B.
3453. werre] a werre R — ferr] be ferr B.

In old days the virtuous words of orators appeased the wrath of tyrants,

Of rethoriciens whilom that wer old
The sugrid langage & vertuous daliaunce
Be goode exaumples & prouerbes that thei tolde,
Woordes pesible enbelisshed with plesaunce,
Appesid of tirauntes the rigerous vengaunce,
Sette aside ther furious sentence
Bi vertu onli of prudent elloquence.

but on the other hand men may often see fools and brainless people talking at random.

And in contrarie,* pleynli to conclude,
Men seen alday bi cleer experience
Folk vnauised, & hasti foolis rude,
And braynles peeple, of wilful necligence,
Because thei wern bareyn of elloquence,
Vttringe* ther speche as nakid folk & bare,
For lak of rethorik ther mateer to declare.

Just as purple belongs to kings and rich garments fret with precious stones, pleasant objects to the sight,

¶ Bi cleer exaumple, as purpil, who takþ heede,
Longeth to kynges, in stori men may fynde,
With clothes of gold & riche velwet weede
Fret with rubies and othir stonis Ynde,
Saphirs, emeraudis, perlis of ther kynde, —
As alle thes thynges aproprid been of riht,
Plesaunt obiectis to a mannys siht,

so is the speech of rhetoricians, like the song of musicians, a glad object to the hearing.

So the langage of rethoriciens
Is a glad obiect to mannys audience,
With song mellodious of musiciens,*
Which doth gret counfort to euery hih presence.
Bexaumple as* Amphioun, with song & elloquence
Bilte the wallis of Thebes the cite,
He hadde of rethorik so gret subtilite.

Amphion built the walls of Thebes with his eloquence and song, for men were so attracted that all the country came to help him.

In his langage ther was so gret plesaunce,
Fyndyng therbi so inli gret proffit,
That al the contre kam to his obeissaunce,
To heere hym speke thei hadde so gret delit;
The peeple enviroun hadde such an appetit
In his persone, in pes & in bataille:
Heer men may seen what rethorik doth auaille!

3472. vertu onli] þe vertu H.
3473 contraire B.
3478. Vttrid B.
3485. As] *om.* H.
3489. Musciciens B.
3491. as] of B.

[How Sextus werreide Tryumvir, and of the deth of grete Antonye and Cleopatras.] [1]

FOLWYNG the ordre Boch*as* of his book,
With penne in hond[e], castyng up his eye,
Tofor hym ca*m* pale of cheer & look
A myhti p*r*ince, sone onto Pompeye,
Callid Sextus, which as bookis seye,
Delited hym, with a gret naue
Lik a pirat to robben on the se.

Bochas, looking up, saw before him a mighty prince, Sextus, son of Pompey, who robbed on the sea like a pirate.

To his fadir contrarie in such caas, —
For eueri pirat of custum he dede hate,
Vpon the se whos vsage alwey was
Ageyn[es] hem proudli to debate,
Pursued hem erli and eek late, —
Wher this Sextus, to his gret repreeff,
Was of* the se a robbour and a theeff.

He was very different from his father, who hated pirates;

The sclau*n*dre of hym* gan to spreede ferre, [p. 340]
Reportid was to many ferr contre;
With Tryu*m*vir* this Sextus gan a werre, —
Which is an offis and a dignite
Bi the Romeyns co*m*myttid onto thre
Notable estatis, chose for* cheualrie,
Thempire al hool to gouerne & to guie.

and his ill fame was widespread. He began a war with the Triumvirate,

The firste of hem namyd Lepidus,
And the secou*n*de callid Octouyan,
The thridde in nou*m*bre was Antonyus,
Ageyn[s] which thre Sextus, this proude ma*n*,
Of surquedie a newe werre gan,
Afforn bi Iulius for his rebelliou*n*
Banisshed for euere out of Roome tou*n*.

Lepidus, Octavian and Mark Antony.

Triu*m*vir of politik gouernau*n*ce,
Weel auised afforn in ther resou*n*s,
Tretyng for pes bi notable purueyau*n*ce
With proude Sextus vndir condiciou*n*s
Write & enact in ther conuenciou*n*s, —
But anon afftir, list no while tarie,
He to his promys was froward & co*ntr*arie.

The Triumvirs first made peace with him under conditions, but Sextus was perverse

3514. of] on B. 3515. hym] hem B.
3517. Tryumvir] tryu*m*phir B — this] *with* H. 3520. for] of B.
3521. 2nd to] *om.* H. 3523. Octauian P (*throughout*).
3525. this] the R. 3527. bi] *om.* H. 3535. his] *om.* R.

[1] MS. J. leaf 139 recto.

and broke his agreement. Bochas, disgusted with his lack of virtue, did not care to magnify his name by writing about him.

For his convict outraious falsnesse,
And on the se for his robberye,
Bochas of hym writ no long processe,
Hauyng disdeyn his name to magnefie;
For he to vertu list nothi*n*g applie, —
The difference cause which [is] in thestat
Atwixe knihthod & liff of a pirat.

He associated with fugitives and men of evil life, and made one Moena captain of 40 of his ships.

With fugityues, theuys and robbo*u*rs
And men exiled out of Roome tou*n*,
Banissched peeple, fals conspirato*u*rs,
With othir convict of moordre & tresou*n*, —
He took al such vndir proteccio*un*;
And oon Moena, a cherl of his certey*n*,
Of fourti shippes he made hy*m* a captey*n*.

This churl allied himself with Octavian and came down against his lord;

The said[e] cherl vnwarli tho began
Folwe the nature of his condicio*un*,
Allied hymsilff[e] with Octauyan
Ageyn his lord[e], bi ful fals tresou*n*;
W*ith* al his naue and shippes he ca*m* dou*n*,
Spared nat to meete of verray p*r*ide
With Menecrates, that was on Sextus side.

but as soon as the battle began, Octavius' ships were sunk by a storm, and Sextus fled in disaster.

But also soone as the bataile gan
And the parties togidre sholde gon,
Alle the vessellis of Octauyan
With sodeyn tempest wer drownid eu*er*ichon
Beside a castell bilt of lym & ston
Callid Nauletu*m*, wher yit to gret repreeff
Sextus fledde & was brouht to myscheeff.

He then went to Greece to fight Antony, but was taken and slain.

Wente into Grece to make hy*m* stronge ageyn
To holde a bataile with Antonyus,
Take in his komyng bi strengthe of a captey*n*
Longyng to Antoyne, callid Furnyus,
Whilom neuew to Cesar Iulius:
And or duk Sextus myhte ferþ*er* weende,
He slay[e]n was & made ther an eende.

One of the Triumvirs was Lepidus, who reconciled Antony with Octavian;

Of Tryu*m*vir in thempire, as I tolde,
Ther was a capteyn callid Lepidus,
Which bi his offis lik as he was holde,
Riht besi was, the book rehersith thus,

3546. &] & of R, J. 3549. a] *om.* H, P. 3553. bi] w*ith* R, J.
3556. Menecratus P — on Sextus side] an homy side H.
3562. repreeff] preeff R. 3563. was brouht] brouht was H.
3568. Cesar] *om.* R. 3570. an] his R, P, H 5.

To reconcile the proude Antonyus
To the grace of gret Octouyan,
Ech thyng forgete wherof the werre gan.

And to conclude shortli, who list see,
Fortune a while was to hym gracious,
Thempire al hool gouernid bi thes thre:
Lordship of Affrik hadde Lepidus,
Bi which he wex proud & contrarious,
To hym assigned vndir commissiouns
Fulli the noumbre of tuenti legiouns.

and for a time the three governed the empire in peace.

Wherof in herte he kauhte such a pride,
Causyng be processe his destruccioun.
Surquedie a while was his guide,
From his estat til he was falle doun;
Namli whan he, of fals presumpcioun,
Took upon hym of malis to werreye
The said Octouyan, & gan hym disobeie.

Finally Lepidus, who was lord of Africa, maliciously disobeyed Octavian,

Whan Octouyan his malis dide see,
That he gan wexe sodenli contrarie,
He threw hym doun from his dignite,
Cast hym in exil, list no lenger tarie.
Loo, how Fortune sodeynli can varie,
To maken hym that hadde gouernaunce
Off al Affrik to comen to myschaunce!

who exiled him. Lo, how Fortune can vary!

Another prince, Cesar Lucyus, [p. 341]
Exiled was fro Roome the cite
Bi his vncle, the saide Antonyus,
Of wilfulnesse & hasti cruelte;
For in that tyme, as men may reede & see,
Contreued causes wer founde up* of malis
Texile princis notable holde & wis.

Another prince, Cæsar Lucius, was exiled from Rome by his uncle Antony out of wilfulness. Many notable princes were then exiled on contrived causes:

Summe because thei heeld[e] with Cesar,
Other for Pompeie that heeld on that partie,
Summe for ther good, afforn or thei wer war,
Summe for suspecioun, summe for envie,
Summe for thei koude nat flatre nouther lie,
Summe for vertues, which was gret[e] routhe,
Because thei wern so stable in ther trouthe.

some for siding with Cæsar or Pompey, others for their wealth or out of hatred, or because they were honest and could not flatter and lie.

3576. gret] *om.* R. 3579. gracious] contraryvs H.
3600. from R. 3603. For in] fro H. 3604. up] out B.
3610. nouther] nor H, J.

Paulus Lucius was exiled for malice after the death of Antony and Cleopatra.

In this trouble dreedful & odious,
As is rehersid in ordre ye may reede,
The noble kniht, Paulus Lucyus,
Exilid was of malis & hatreede,
Folwyng upon the grete horrible deede,
The pitous deth & the hatful caas
Of gret Antonye and Cleopatras.

I shall not write their tragedy because Chaucer has already done so in his *Legende of Cupide*.

The tragedie of these ilke tweyne
For me as now shal be set aside,
Cause Chauceer, cheef poete of Breteyne,
Seyng ther hertis koude nat deuyde,
In his book, the Legende of Cupide,
Remembryng ther, as oon thei dide endure,
So wer thei buryed in oon sepulture.

It were presumption for me to write again a thing once said by Chaucer.

Thyng onys said be labour of Chauceer
Wer presu*m*pciou*n* me to make* ageyn,
Whos makyng was so notable & enteer,
Riht co*m*pendious and notable in certey*n*.
Which to reherse the labour wer but vey*n*,*
Bochas reme*m*bryng how Cleopatras
Caused Antonye* that he destroied was.

As Bochas says, Cleopatra caused Antony's destruction. He fell in love with her, and as she desired to be empress, he made war on Octavian.

Hir auarice was so importable,
He supprised with hir gret fairnesse,
Folwyng ther lustis foul & abho*m*inable,
She desiryng to haue be emperesse;
And he, alas, of froward wilfulnesse,
To plesen hire, vnhappily began
To werreye the grete Octouyan.

Froward ambition made him wish to reign alone in Rome.

Froward ambiciou*n* sette his herte affire
To clymben up to the imperial see,
To haue pocessiou*n* of the hool empire,
Took upon hym, yiff it wolde haue be,
To regne allone in Roome the cite,
Cleopatras to fostren in hir pride,
Title of Octauyan for to sette aside.

First he fought on the sea and was put to flight. Despairing, he went home,

With multitude of many legiou*n*s,
As I haue told, ageyn Octauyan,
To hym acrochid of dyuers regiou*n*s
Gret multitude of many ma*n*li ma*n*;

3613. dreedful] hatful R.
3628. make] take B, H.
3631. Which] wher H — veyn] in veyn B, R, J.
3633. Antoine B.

First on the se to werreye he bega*n*,
Wher he was first, maugre al his miht,
To his confusiou*n* vnwarli put to fliht.

Disespeired, fledde hom to his contre,
Knowyng no* helpe nor mene to recure,
But to encres of his aduersite,
Wha*n* that he sauh this woful auenture,
Geyn Octouyan he myhte nat endure,
With a sharp suerd his dau*n*geer to dyuerte
Hymsilff he rooff vnwarli to the herte.

and, knowing no help, pierced himself to the heart with a sword,

Of whos deth the queen Cleopatras
Took a sorwe verray importable;
Because ther was no recure in the caas,
Thouhte of his wo she wolde be partable,
Whos fatal eende pitous & lame*n*tabl*e*:
Slouh eek hirsilf[e], loue so did hir raue;
Afftir thei bothe buryed in o graue.

whereupon Cleopatra slew herself for sorrow, and afterwards both were buried in one grave.

3655. Disepeired R. 3656. no] non B.
3657. encres] thencres H.

¶ Finis libri Sexti.

¶ Incipit liber septim*us*.

BOOK VII

[Off Antonye son and heire to grete Antonye, and of Cesarius, Iulia, Agrippa, Cassius, and Galbus.] [1]

THIS stori eendid, last of þe sixte book, [p. 343]
Boch*as* weri, thouhte for the beste,
Of gret *tr*auaile oppr*e*ssid i*n* his look,
Fill in a slombre lenyng on a cheste,
Fulli in purpos to haue* take his reste.
But euene as he sholde his reste haue take,
Cam a gret pres & made hy*m* to a-wake.

This story, the last of the sixth book, ended, Bochas leaned on a chest and fell asleep. But just as he began to take his rest, a great number of people appeared to him,

¶ First of that felashipe ca*m* the sone & heir
Of Antonye, with blood spreynt al his weede,
Callid eek Antonye,* falle in gret dispeir
Cause Octoyuan bar to hym hatreede,
Whos suerde he fledde, quakyng in his dreede,
To an old temple socour for to haue,
Trustyng fro deth the* place sholde hy*m* saue.

of whom Antony, son of great Antony, was the first. Octavian had caused him to be slain in the temple

In that temple Cesar was deified,
Of whom be Romeyns set up a gret image;
But whan he sauh [that] he was espied,
He ran to Iulius hih upon the stage,
Gan hym tenbrace in his pitous rage, —
He, rent awey be sodeyn violence,
Vnwarli slayn; ther geyned no diffence.

where Cæsar was deified, as he embraced Cæsar's image.

¶ Next in ordre cam Cesarius,
Of who*m* ther fill a wonder pitous caas,
Whilom begete of Cesar Iulius
Vpon the yonge faire Cleopatras,
Slay*n* in his youthe, thus writeth Bochas,
As Octouyan dide hymsilff assigne,
For he gey*n* Romeyns sholde nat maligne.

Next came Cæsarius, son of Julius Cæsar and Cleopatra. He too was slain in his youth by Octavian.

1. vj^te B. 4. in] on H — a] his R, P.
5. to haue] taue B — to haue take his] for to take a H.
7. &] *om.* H. 8. Phelishipp*e* R.
10. Antonye] Antoyne B — disespeir R. 11. to] vn to H.
14. the] that B. 23. pitous] *om.* H.
28. gey*n* Romeyns sholde] ageyn Romayns did H.

[1] MS. J. leaf 140 recto.

Julia, Octavian's daughter, began, howling and crying, to tell Bochas her grievous complaint; for she was exiled by her father in punishment of her lechery, and she died in poverty.

¶ Folwyng in ordre, Iulia began
Hir greuous co*m*pleynt to Bochas specefie,
Whilom douhtir to grete Octouyan,
With weepyng eyen ga*n* to houle & crie,
Which bi hir fadir to pu*n*she hir lecherie
Exilid was out of hir contre,
For lak of socour deide in pouerte.

Her son Agrippa, who spent his time in slumber and idleness, was allowed to die in mischief by Octavian.

¶ Hir sone Agrippa, yong & tendre of age,
Born off hih blood[e], Bochas doth expresse,
Cam next in ordre, pale of his visage,
Which spent his tyme in slombre & idilnesse,
Froward to vertu; & for his wrechidnesse
Octovyan, which was gret[e] routhe,
Suffrid hym deie at myscheeff for his slouthe.

After Agrippa came Cassius of Parma, a manly knight, a poet and friend of Mark Antony.

¶ Afftir Agrippa cam forth ano*n* riht
Cassius of Parme, a famous gret co*n*tre,
Which in Itaille was holde a ma*n*li knyht,
With Marc Antonye* weel cherisshed & secre,
Bood in his court, & therwithal parde
Gretli allowed, first for his cheualrie,
And for his notable famous poisye.

He was accused to Octavian for having assented to the death of Cæsar,

And therwithal he hadde in existence
A riht gret name & stood in gret fauo*u*r
For his knihthod & for his hih prudence.
Afftir accusid vnto the empero*u*r
Octouyan for a coniurato*u*r,
He sholde haue bee of froward fals entent
To Iulius deth fulli of* assent.

for which Octavian had him taken and offered up in sacrifice to Julius' image.

For which be biddyng of Octouyan
Take he was, beyng but yong of age;
And as myn auctour weel remembre* can,
Brouht tofor Iulius hih upon a stage,
Ther offrid up onto his ymage
Be cruel deth, the stori tellith thus,
For the fals moordre of Cesar Iulius.

32. eyen] *om.* R, J.
33. hir] his H.
44. Parma P.
46. Antoyne B.
59. remembre] reherse B.

¶ Aftir the deth of saide Cassius,
Another ca*m* of Roome the cite,
Which, as I reede, callid was Galbus,
Of a pretour hauyng the dignite;
And for suspeciou*n* slay[e]n eek was he,
His eyen first out of his hed wer rent,
For Iulius deth than into exil sent.

Galbus, a prætor, was slain by brigands after his eyes had been torn out. He was exiled on suspicion of aiding in Cæsar's death.

Toward his exil bi brigau*ntes* he was slay*n*.
And aftir that, withyne a litil while,
Of his labour nouther glad nor fayn,
Boch*as* began to direct his stile
To gret Herodes, breeffli to co*m*pile
His greuous fall & hooli the maneer*e*
To sette in ordre heer next, as ye shal heer*e*.

Bochas next turned to Herod the Great.

[How the tirau*n*t herodes slouh wiff and children and deied atte mischeff.] [1]

REMEMBRYNG first in Iurie he was ky*n*g,
Antipater his fadir, who list see,
In Arabia myhtili regnyng
Ouir the prouynce callid Ydumee.
This same Herodes, gard[e]yn of Gallile,
Ordeyned was, [first] for his hih prudence,
And for his notable knihtli excellence.

He was king in Jewry, son of Antipater, and for his knighthood made guardian of Gallilee.

Famous in ma*n*hod, famous of* his lyne, [p. 344]
Famous also bi p*ro*creaciou*n*,
I reede also he hadde wyues nyne;
And among alle, as maad is menciou*n*,
To his plesau*n*ce and his oppynyou*n*,
Maister of stories reherseth ther was oon
Marian*n*es, fairest of euerichon.

A famous man, he had nine wives. Mariannes was fairest of them all.

Bi whom she hadde worthi sones tweyne,
Alisau*n*dre and Aristobolus.
But for his sustir* dide at hir disdeyne,
Callid Saloma, the stori tellith thus,
He vnto hir wex suspecious,
Because she was accusid of envie
Bi Saloma touchyng auoutrie.

She had two sons by him, Alexander and Aristobolus; but because his sister Saloma disdained at her and accused her of adultery, Herod became suspicious and slew her.

64. saide] the sayde R.
66. reede] tolde H. 74. began] gan H. 82. garden H.
85. of] i*n* B, H. 88. among] mong R.
93. Aristobolus] Aristobus R, Aristolus J, Aristobolus H.
94. his sustir] hir stustir B.

[1] MS. J. leaf 140 verso.

Afterwards he greatly regretted her death.

Ageyn[e]s hire of rancour sodenli
He gan of herte greuousli disdeyne;
With rigerous suerd he slouh hir furiousli.
But as the stori doth vs acerteyne,
He for hir deth felt aftirward gret peyne,
Euere whan it cam to his remembraunce,
Hir port, hir cheer, hir womanli plesaunce.

That is what follows when a prince is hasty to believe every tale he hears.
For sorrow Herod fell into melancholia

Loo, what it is a prince to be hasti,
To eueri tale of rancour to assente,
And, counsailles, proceede wilfulli
To execucioun, of froward fals entente;
For Herodes so sore dede hym* repente
That he for thouht[e] fill into anoye
Of hertli sorwe & malencolie.

and, troubled with fits of fury and bad dreams, was lunatic once a month.

Reste hadde he non novther day nor niht,
Troublid with furye that he wex frentik,
With dremys vexid & many an vnkouth siht;
Of cheer nor colour to no man he was lik,
And eueri moneth onys lunatik.
A gret[e] while he hadde this woful lyff
For sorwe onli he hadde slayn his wiff.

But he was made king of Judæa by Antony and Octavian,

And as the stori weel reherse can,
In the Capitoile mid Roome the cite,
Bi Antonye and bi Octouyan
He crownid was & maad kyng of Iude,
Bi the Senat maad theron a decre,
And registred that he and his kynreede
Sholde in that lond lynealli proceede.

although a foreigner and a usurper.
This was at the time of the birth of Christ Jesus.

In Roome was maad the* confirmacioun
To this Herodes, bookis specefie,
Beyng a foreyn the translacioun
Was maad of Iuda & of Iuerye,
Sceptre, crowne, with al the regalie
Bi hym vsurpid, as ye haue herd toforn,
Vpon the tyme whan Crist Iesus was born.

103. aftirward] *om.* R.
109. entente] *om.* R.
110. so sore dede hym] dede hym so sore B — dede hym] he did R, J, he dyd P.
113. nor] ne H, J. 116. no] *om.* H. 117. onys] he wex R.
119. he] þat he H.
127. the] a B. 133. Crist] cast R.

This same Herodes bi procuraciou*n*
Of Antonye did also occupie,
Bi Augustus plener com*m*yssiou*n*
The grete estat[e] callid Tetrarchie
In too kyngdames, *with* al the regalie:
Of Traconytides, Iturye eek also,
Bi the Romeyns maad lord of bothe too.

Herod also occupied the estate of Tetrarch.

Maister of stories r*e*herseth of hy*m* thus:
For comendaciou*n* in especiall
In Ascalon he bilt a statli hous
Of riht gret cost, a paleis ful roiall,
Was non so riche, for to reknyn all.
Aftir which, myn auctour doth so write,
He callid was Herode Ascolonyte.

He built a stately palace in Ascalon, which Bochas thought was to his credit.

This same Herodes, cruel of nature,
Of cheer & port passyng ambicious,
Ay to be uengid dide his besi cure
On al that wern to hym co*n*trarious.
His wyues brothir Aristobolus,
In Iherusalem cheeff bisshop, as I reede,
Falsli he slouh of malis & hatreede.

But he was cruel and ambitious, and slew his wife's brother Aristobolus, Bishop of Jerusalem, out of hatred.

Vniustli regnid, born heuy thoruh his reum,
His herte fret & kankrid with envie.
Another bisshop in Iherusalem,
Callid Hircanvs, myn auct*our* list nat lie,
This same Herodes in his malencolie
Slouh hym vnwarli be ra*n*c*our* ful vengable,
Sittyng at dyneer at his owne table.

He reigned unjustly and killed another bishop named Hyrcanus as he sat at dinner at his own table.

Ther was no ma*n* of corage mor cruell
Nor mor desirous to be magnefied;
To make his name also perpetuell
Foure statli cites he hath edefied,
Of which the names been heer specefied:
Cesaria, Sebasten, cites souereyne,
Antipadra, Cipre, the othir tweyne.

No man was ever more desirous of fame. To perpetuate his name he built four stately cities.

He hadde also a fals condiciou*n*: [p. 345]
He truste[d] non that was of his kynreede,
His sonis tweyne hadde in suspeciou*n*,
Ther purpos was to slen hym of hatreede,
Wha*n* he wer ded[e] hopyng to succeede.

He also had the evil habit of not trusting his own family, and suspecting his two sons made them to be slain without cause.

149. port & cheer R. 156. kankrid] cancrik H.
158. Hircamvs H. 168. Antipătra and Cipre P.

And causeles, as fadir most vnkynde,
Made hem be slayn, in stori thus I fynde.

He was deceitful and a tyrant; and when the three magi came to Jerusalem to worship Jesus, whom they called king.

In al his werkyng he was fou*n*de double,
A gret[e] tirau*n*t holde thoruh his rewm,
Neuer thyng so gretli dede him* trouble,
As whan thre kynges ka*m* to Iherusalem,
I*esus* to seeke, that was [born] in Bethlem,
Boldli affermy*n*g, cause of ther komy*n*g
Was to worshepe that blissid yonge ki*n*g.

he imagined that a child had been born to deprive him of his realm,

The which[e] thyng whan he did aduertise,
Prophecies reme*m*bry*n*g & writyngis,
Withyn*n*e hymsilff a mene he ga*n* deuise
First to destroye thes hooli famous kynges;
Namli, wha*n* he knew of ther offrynges,
Imagynyng, ga*n* suppose blyue
The child was born that sholde hy*m* depryue,

and, falling into a rage, slew all the infants of Bethlehem.

Newli descendid from Dauid dou*n* be lyne, —
Cast almost Herodes in a rage;
Of cursid herte gan frowardli maligne,
Lik a tirau*n*t of venymous outrage
Slouh al the childre *with*yn*n*e too yeer age
Aboute Bethlem a ful large space;
He spared non for fauo*ur* nor for grace.

One of his own children, out at nurse, was slain by his knights with the others, probably out of vengeance.

On of his childre beyng at norcerye,
As the stori put in remembrau*n*ce,
Of auenture or thei koude it espie
His kniht*es* slouh; I trowe it was vengau*n*ce.
Ech tirau*n*t gladli eendith *with* myschau*n*ce,
And so must he that wex agey*n* Crist wood,
Which for his sake shadde innocent*es* blood.

Altogether 144,000 children were put to death for Christ's sake.

The nou*m*bre of childre that wer slay*n* in deede
Aboute Bethlem & in tho parties,
An hundrid fourti four thousa*n*d, as I reede,
Too yeer of age souht out be espies*
Of Herodes; & for the prophecies
Of Cristes berthe menciou*n* did[e] make,
Thei wer echon slay[e]n for his sake.

176. werkyng] werk*es* H. 178. him] hem B.
180. Bethlem] bedlem R, Bedleme H, Betheleme J.
195. Bethleem R, P, Bedlem H, R 3, Bethelem J.
198. stori] *om.* R. 206. fourti] fourty & H. 207. bespies B.

Fro that day forth, as maad is menciou*n*,
He fill in many vnkouth malladie;
His flessh ga*n* turne to corrupciou*n*,
Fret with wermys upon ech partie,
Which hym assailed bi gret tormentrie:
His leggis suell[e], corbid blak ga*n* shyne;
Wher vengau*n*ce werkith, a-dieu al medecyne.

From that day Herod fell into a strange illness; his flesh corrupted and was tormented with worms; his legs swelled and bent and turned black.

Of his seeknesse the stench was so horrible,
Tawaite on hym no man myhte abide;
Vnto hymsilff his careyn wex odible,
So sore he was troublid on ech side.
Lechis for hym did a bath prouyde,
But al for nouht; in such myscheeff he stood,
Of greuous constreynt he sodenli wex wood.

His odour was so awful that no man could wait on him, and a bath prepared by his physicians did him no good.

In tokne he was weri of his liff,
So importable was his mortal peyne,
To pare an appil he axed a sharp knyff, —
His malladie did hym so constreyne, —
Fulli in purpos to kutte his herte in tweyne.
The knyff he rauhte, leiser wha*n* he fond; —
Oon stood beside,* bakward drouh his hond.

Unable to stand it any longer, he went mad, and asking for a knife to pare an apple tried to kill himself.

For peyne vn*n*ethe his wynd he myhte drawe,
Gaff al his freendis in comau*n*deme*n*t
Bi a decre & a furious lawe,
That al the worthi of parties adiacent,
Which that wer fayn or glad in ther entent
Of his deth, he, void of al pite,
The same day thei sholde slay[e]n bee.

He could hardly draw in his breath for pain, and in his fury ordered all the worthies of the country, who were glad of his sickness, to be slain on the day of his death.

This cursid wrech, this odious caitiff,
I reede of non stood ferther out of grace,
In sorwe & myscheeff eendid hath his liff.
Ech man was glad[e] wha*n* he shold[e] pace.
And for his stori doth this book difface
With woful clauses of hym wha*n* I write,
Therfor I caste no mor of hym* tendite.

Finally this cursed wretch came to an end. No one ever stood farther out of grace. His story disfigures this book.

¶ Explicit.

215. Which] with R. 216. blak] bak R.
219. Tawaite] to waite H, to wait R 3.
225. was] wex H. 226. inportable R. 229. 2nd in] on H.
231. beside] behynde B.
245. no mor of hym] of hym no mor B.

[Lenvoye.]

Herod, who slew his wife and children and the infants of Bethlehem and frowardly shewed malice to Jesus, ended miserably.

OFF Herodes the vnwar cursid fall, [p. 346]
The lyff vng*r*acious of hy*m* & his ki*n*reede,
Euere vengable in his estat roiall,
His wiff, his childre slouh of old hatreede;
In*n*ocentis he made in Bethlem bleede,
Regnyng in Iuda, born of a foreyn lyne,
The firste tirau*n*t (ye may the Bible reede)
Which ageyn Crist gan frowardli maligne.

His sword of vengeance was always ready whet to shed innocent blood.

His suerd of rigour, cruell & mortall,
Ay reedi whet to do vengau*n*ce in deede,
Hasti, fumous with furies infernall
Of wilful malis in*n*ocent blood to sheede.
Dide execuciou*n* also in woma*n*heede,
Slouh his allies, which was a cursid signe, —
Was the firste cause he stode in dreede, —
Which ageyn Crist ga*n* frowardli maligne.

He would have no one his equal to succeed him, and as he was but an alien, he especially dreaded Jesus, who was of the line of Jesse.

He wolde that non wer to hym egall
That day alyue in Israel to succeede;
The berthe of Crist dradde in especiall,
Cause fro Iesse his lyne ga*n* floure & seede.
He but a foreyn, cam in be fraude & meede,
Withoute title, to that estat vndigne,
The firste also, who list take heede,
Which ageyn Crist ga*n* frowardli maligne.

Noble Princes, do not oppress your people; remember the end of Herod, who maligned against Christ.

Noble Pryncis, that gouerne all
This large world[e] bothe in lengthe & breede,
Wha*n* ye sit hiest in yo*u*r roial stall,
Doth nat the peeple oppresse nor ouerleede.
Vpon Herodes remembreth, as ye reede,
In what myscheeff that tirau*n*t dide fyne,
To shewe that non shal in his purpos speede,
Which ageyn Crist doth frowardli maligne.

[Off Antipas exilid bi Octavian and of Achelaus son of herodes the secounde.] [1]

Herod Antipas succeeded Herod the Great; but as he was exiled by Octavian

COMPE*N*DIOUSLI as ye haue herd þe fall
Of Herodes remembrid be Bochas,
How bi his testame*n*t set i*n* especiall
To succeede was Herode Antipas;

246. cursid vnwar H. 255. whet] wher R.
256. fumous] furious H. 265. ga*n*] did H.

[1] MS. J. leaf 141 verso.

In hast exilid, of hym this was the caas,
Bi Octovian to Vyenne, as I reede,
Archelaus ordeyned to succeede,

Sone of Herodes callid the secounde,
Which in effect took pocessioun,
In Iherusalem regned, as it is founde,
Of whom myn auctour, for short conclusioun,
Maketh in his book but smal mencioun:
Hym and his brothir set sodenli aside;—
Of them to write no lenger list abide.

and set aside, together with his brother, in favour of Archelaus,

Sauff that he writ how forseid Antipas
At Vyenne, a myhti gret cite,
In [his] exil soone aftir slay[e]n was.
Archelaus, succeedyng in Iudee,
With Herodias, the stori who list see,
Bi Agrippa to Tiberie accusid,
Of certeyn crymes koude nat been excusid.

my author says little about him, except that he was slain during his exile. Archelaus, accused by Agrippa to Tiberius,

A certeyn tyme comaundid to prisoun,
Of themperour koude neuer gete grace;
Ban[y]shed hym [ferr] from his regeoun
Into Spayne for a certeyn space.
And his worshepe breeffli to difface,
Fortune causid to his fynal repreff,
He deide ther in pouert & myscheeff.

was sent to prison and died in poverty in Spain.

The fatal eende rehersid of thes tweyne,
In what distresse that thei dide fyne,
Myn auctour aftir gan his penne ordeyne
To write the caas be many a woful lyne,
Vpon the striff atween[e] Messalyne
And othir tweyne stondyng bi hir side,
Tofor Iohn Bochas how thei dide chide.

Bochas next turned his pen to the unseemly quarrel between Messalina, wife of Claudius,

Tofor Bochas thei cam al thre to pleyne,
Messalyne, wiff onto Claudius,
Ageyn[e]s whom ther wer othir tweyne,
Calligula and Tiberius,
In whos tyme was slay[e]n Crist Ihesus.
Touchyng debat that was among thes thre,
Suende the processe, heer folwyng ye shal see.

and Caligula and Tiberius, who upbraided one another in his presence.

282. this] thus H. 285. secounde] secounde in deede H, R 3.
287. regned] regnyng H—it is founde] I reede H, R 3, R, J, H 5, I rede P.
296. who list the story R, J.
311. hir] his H. 319. Suende] sueng H, Suyd H 5, Suinge P.

[Off the striff / betwene, Calligula, Tiberius & messalyne.] [1]

> Tiberius and Caligula stood angrily before Bochas, with Messalina between them.

THIS emperesse namyd Messalyne,
As I haue told, was wif to Claudius,
Successour, as bookis determyne,
To Calligula callid Gayus.
And, as I fynde, that Tiberius
With Calligula, bothe wood for teene,
Stood affor Bochas, & Messalyne atweene,

> Caligula first spoke, and he said to Messalina, without respect or shame,

Meetyng al thre *with* furious look & cheere. [p. 347]
Gayus Calligula, callid be his name,
Gan first reherse, anon as ye shal heere,
Withoute reuerence or any maner shame,
With an exordie to diffame,
Bochas present, felli ga*n* abraide
To Messalyna, & euene thus he saide:

> "You defamed, adulterous woman, what are you doing here in your mourning garments? I suppose you have come to visit the five most infamous women who ever lived.

¶ "Thou sclau*n*drid woman, noised in lecherie
Thoruh al the world, as folk thi name atwite,
And reportid for thyn auoutrie,
What dost thou heer in thi murny*n*g habite?
I trowe thou komest of purpos to visite
In this place thunhappi women fyve,
Touchyng disclau*n*dre that eu*er* wern alyue.

> "As a token, one of them, Æmilia, was taken in adultery and divorced by her husband.

The firste of hem callid Amylia,
And Lepida was named* the secou*n*de,
Lyuia, Plaucia, & the fifte Elia,
Diffamed echon in deede, as it was fou*n*de.
In tokne wheroff the lecherye to co*n*fou*n*de
Off Emylia, in auoutry take,
Was bi the lawe of hir lord forsake.

> "It is well known that you murdered Drusus; nor are you any better than Claudia, who also was thrown out by her lord for adultery.

Bi the whilom was knowe that Drusus
Istranglid was and moordred be poisou*n*;
Lik to Claudia, douhtir of Claudius,
Which bi hir lord, the book makth me*n*ciou*n*,
Was throwen out, to hir confusiou*n*,
For hir defautis fou*n*de in auoutrie
Sclau*n*drid for euere; ther was no remedie.

328. Gayus] geyn H. 331. exordie] Exody H.
333. Messaline P. 334. noised in] namyd *with* H.
341. Emilia R, P, Emylia H. 343. Elia] Helya H.

[1] MS. J. leaf 142 recto.

Thou koudest whilom mak thi lord to slepe,
W*ith* certeyn drynkis to cast hym i*n* a r*er*age,
Bi which he was maad his bed to keepe,
To gete leiseer in thi flour*y*ng age,
For to mysuse of fals lust thyn out*r*age,
Anihter tyme took upon a weede,
At the bordel dist amys for meede.

"You knew how to drug your husband and make him sleep; while you went to the brothel and debauched yourself for money.

Thyn appetit was verray vnstau*n*chable;
It is a shame to write it or expresse.
Thyn hatful lyff was so abho*m*inable, —
Tiberi and I can bern heerof witnesse."
And with that woord anon she ga*n* hir dresse,
Whan she had herd[e] al ther fel langage,
Gaff hem this ansuere w*ith* a sad visage:

"It is shameful to write about your insatiable lust and your hateful, abominable life. Tibery and I can bear witness to it."

¶ "Certis," quod she, "I koude neu*er* keepe
To saue my-silff, a woful creature, —
I haue gret cause to co*m*pleyne & weepe
My sclau*n*drous lyff, which I may nat r*e*cure.
But I suppose I hadde it of nature
To be such oon; for be daies olde
An astronomyen so my fadir tolde,

"It is true," she replied, "I have good reason to weep over my scandalous life, but it was nature's fault; for when I was born an astronomer

At my berthe takyng the ascendent,
Tolde longe afforn of my mysgou*er*nau*n*ce:
The sun*ne*, the moone toward thorient
Wer in the signe that bereth the ballau*n*ce; —
And saide also, mor for assurau*n*ce,
The same signe hadde be descripciou*n*
His* foot in Virgyne, armys in the Scorpiou*n*.

told my father that the sun and moon were in Libra, and that Libra's foot was in the Virgin and his arms in Scorpio.

Amyd the heuene was Venus exaltat,
W*ith* Mars conioyned, þe book makth me*n*ciou*n*;
And Iubiter was also infortunat
To my saide disposiciou*n*,
W*ith*ynne the Fissh heeld tho his ma*n*siou*n*:
Thus be the lordship pleynli of Venvs
I was disposed for to be lecherous."

Venus was in a position of greatest influence, and, as the book says, in conjunction with Mars; and Jupiter too, was unfavourable to my disposition, and had his mansion in the Fish. Thus it is plain that Venus disposed me to be wanton."

In hir excus the saide Messalyne
Gan alegge hir constellaciou*n*;
But prudent clerkis pley*n*li determyne,
Of the heuenly cours the disposiciou*n*

365. Tiberius P. 382. His] The B.

In this manner Messalina pleaded her constellation in excuse; but clerks say that no well behaved person is constrained to do wrong by force. Nor is there any necessity for living a vicious life. There is no sin that is not voluntary.

Is obeissau*n*t & soget to resou*n*,
That eueri man which weel gou*er*nid is,
Is nat constreyned of force to doon amys, —
Nor bynt no man of necessite
Vicious lustis frowardli to sue.
A vertuous man stant at liberte
Fals inclynaciou*n*s be p*r*udence to r*e*mewe;
Euery man be grace may eschewe
All thyng to vertu that fou*n*de is cont*r*arie:
For ther is no syn*n*e but it be volu*n*tarie.

Yet Messalina would not leave off excusing herself. "Hercules once bore up the heavens, yet for all his chivalry he never could overcome the vice of lechery.

Yit for al this, the saide Messalyne
In hire excus[e] wolde nat been in pes:
"The heuene," quod she, "as poetis det*er*myne,
Was born up whilom be myhti Hercules,
Yit coude he neuere of nature ha[ue] reles,
For al his knihthod & his* cheualrie,
To ouercome the vice of lecherie.

"And as for you, Caligula and Tiberius, I shall not heed what either of you say. You, Gaius Caligula, are yourself besmirched, and should know better than rebuke others.

But thou Calligula and thou Tiberius, [p. 348]
What-euer ye seyn I take therof non heede;
For thou Calligula, callid eek Gayus,
Thi-silff diffoulid with lecherie in deede,
To rebuke othir thou sholdest stonde in dr*e*ede,
But thi rebukis in parti for to quyte;
Who is diffoulid non othir sholde atwite.

"Your scandalous behaviour is reported through all the world: you seduced your three sisters, and may well blush for shame. Don't blame me again as long as you live!

Bi Fames tru*m*pet thi sclau*n*dre is out blowe,
Thoruh al the world reportid shamfullie,
Thi thre sustren fleshli thou dest he*m* knowe, —
Wex red for shame; and for thi partie,
For the vice of hatful lecherie
Duryng thi liff put me no mor in blame,
Which art thi-silff diffoulid in the same.

"It is not fitting that a thief should sit in judgment on theft, nor should one profligate chastise others.

It sittith nat in no man*er* wise
A theef for theffte to sitte in iugement;
A lecherous man a lechour to chastise,
Nor he that hath al his lyff Ispent
In wast & riot, forfetid & myswent,
To been a iuge othr*e* to redresse,
Nor leprous lechis to cure men of seeknesse.

409. his] al his B.
411. 1st thou] *om.* H, R 3.
418. Fames] famous H — out] vp H. 420. dest] didst H.
423. thi] the R. 430. to] for to R.

I wolde ha suffrid and take [in] pacience
Yiff of Affrik the chast[e] Scipiou*n*
Hadde me rebukid for* my gr*e*t offence:
I wolde haue suffrid his yerde of iust resou*n*.
Or yif the famous prudent old Catou*n*
Hadde ageyn me in swich cas maad abraid,
I wolde haue suffrid what-euere he hadde said.

"If chaste Scipio of Africa had rebuked me, or prudent old Cato, I should have accepted it with submission.

Or yif Lucrese for my correcciou*n*
Hadde seid to me, for vertuous doct*r*ine,
Alle my surfetis myd of Roome tou*n*,
I wolde haue bowed [bothe] bak & chyne,
To have obeied onto hir disciplyne.
Shame for* a crepil, to stonde that hath no miht,
To rebuke othir for thei go nat vpriht!

"Or if Lucrece had held up to me my excesses I should have bowed down to her discipline.

Ageyn[e]s the also I may replie,
Many another fals conspiraciou*n*
Touchyng mateeres of nigroma*n*cie,
And many another co*n*treued fals poisou*n*
Fou*n*de in too bookis, Bochas makth me*n*ciou*n*,
Oon callid Pugio, most supersticious,
And the secou*n*de Inamyd Gladius,

"I may also say that you dabbled in necromancy, and, as Bochas mentions, concocted poisons with the help of two books, and

Hable al this world tenvenyme & encloie;
Ageyn thre statis duellyng in Roome tou*n*,
Ther namys write of them thou cast destroie,
Which to reme*m*bre is gret abusiou*n*.
A chest also fulfilled of poisou*n*,
Aftir thi deth cast in the se, I reede,
Bi which an hu*n*dred thousa*n*d fisshes wer dede" . . .

kept a list of the people you wished to destroy. After your death your poison chest, cast into the sea, killed 100,000 fishes.

¶ (On this mateer is tedious for tabide,
Namli to p*r*incis* born of hih estat;
It sittith nat gentil blood to chide,
Bi furious ranco*u*r to stonde at debat.
And for thes mateeres been infortunat,
I wil passe ouer & no mor of hem write,
Sauff of ther eende co*m*pendiousli tendite.)

(This subject is so unpleasant, especially to princes, with its ill-bred quarreling, that I will pass over to the last part of it.)

432. in] *om.* R. 434. for] bi B.
444. for] to B, H, R 3, H 5.
446. I may also R.
453. this] þe H.
461. p*r*incis] princis princessis B, H, R 3, R, J, P, R 2, H 3, H 4, Sl, Add, H 5.

"I have also something to say to you, Tiberius: the people of Campania scorned you for your unnatural vices,

"To the Tiberye I haue sumwhat to seyn:
Knowe and reportid be many a creature,
How in Chau*m*payne folk hadde of the disdey*n*
For thi most hatful lecherous ordure,
In thilke vice which is ageyn nature,
Which tacomplissh, void of al hap & grace,
Thyn abidyng was in suspecious place.

and even when you grew old you would not forbear, and used restoratives, so infatuated you were in your debauchery. "What right have you to scold me?

To swich fals lustis duryng al thi lyff,
List nat forber[e]n in thi latter age,
Thou vsist many riche restoratiff
In suiche vnthrifft tencrece thi corage,
Of ribaudi thou fill in such dotage, —
How maist thou than*n*e rebuke me? For shame!
Which in such caas art blottid with* diffame.

"I did wrong when I was young, as Gaius has just said, but you were outrageous all your life; and both of you became froward gluttons to enforce your excesses.

I dide amys, but it was in my youthe,
Horrible thynges, which Gayus heer hath told,
But thyn outrage, the* report is yit kouthe,
Thou dist hem vse bothe yong & old.
And for tafforce your vices manyfold,
Thou & Calligula, in al swich ribaudie,
Dide grettest surfet in froward glotonie.

"Moreover, Tibery, when you were emperor, you murdered Asinius, the famous orator,

Also Tiberye, thou beyng empero*u*r,
Cruel causeles, & most malicious,
Dist moordre in Roome the famous orato*u*r
Callid in his tyme prudent Asynyus,
Which thoruh thempire, Romeyns tolde thus,
Was liht & lanterne fou*n*de at al assaies,
Of rethorik[e] callid in his daies.

and you exiled the king of Parthia out of covetousness, for you wanted his wealth; and he died in distress.

Thou wer eek cause that worthy* Nonomus, [p. 349]
Kyng of Parthois, thoruh thi cruelte
Exilid was, thou wer so coueitous
To haue pocessiou*n* of his tresour, parde, —
Deide in myscheeff and in pouerte.
Be sham[e]fast any wiht taccuse,
Which in such caas thi-silf ca*n*st nat excuse!

"You let Agrippina starve to death, although she ran to the image of Octavian in the temple for aid.

¶ To Agripyne thou dist ful gr*e*t outrage,
As Romeyn stories weel reherse can,
Wha*n* she for soco*u*r to the gret image
Ran to be sauyd of Octouyan,
Mid the temple a place callid tha*n*,

480. with] for B. 483. outrage the] outrages be B.
495. worthy] werri B, werrey H, werry R, R 3, H 5, H 4, werrei R 2, wery H 3, werreie Add, verry Sl, wourthy H 2.

Which halp hir nat þat she list thidir weende:
Put out be force; for hunger made an eende.

Thyn owyn brothir callid Germanicus,
Which in his tyme was so good a kniht, —
¶ Thi brothir also named eek* Drusus, —
Bothe wer poisowned & slayn ageyn[es] riht
Bi fals conspiryng of thyn imperial* myht.
Texcuse the moordre, thi-siluen at the leste
Wer clad in blak, at ther funeral feeste.

"You had your brothers Germanicus and Drusus poisoned, and then wore black at their funerals to excuse the murder.

I haue no kunnyng, speche nor langage
To reherse nor make mencioun
Specialli of the gret outrage
And sacrilege thou dist in Roome toun,
Be violence whan thou drouh[e] doun
The image of Ianus, & aftir in al hast
Into Tibre madest hym to be cast.

"I have neither art nor language to tell the outrage and sacrilege you did when you pulled down Janus and threw him into the Tiber.

And thou Calligula, among thi vices all,
Of surquedie and fals presumpcioun
Woldest that men a god the sholde call,
Tueen Pollux Castor to haue thi mansioun.
Fro whiche place* thou art now throwe doun,
Which heeld thi-silff among the goddis seuene
Egal with Iubiter for to sitte in heuene.

"And you, Caligula, wanted men to call you a god and to have your mansion between Castor and Pollux!

Ansuere to me, heer beyng in presence,
Which of thes foure, Mars, Ianus, Mynerue,
Or Mercurie, god of elloquence,
Hath rent the doun, as thou dist disserue,
Fro Iubiter in myscheef for to sterue?
That thou heer-aftir, wher-so thou lauh or frowne,
Shalt haue no fauour mor with hym to rowne.

"Inasmuch as you thought yourself equal to Jupiter, tell me now which god, Mars, Janus, Minerva or Mercury, cast you down?

With these defautis & many another
Affor[n] rehersid in hyndryng of thi name —
How thou ordeynest first to slen thi brothir
With men of armes, which was to the gret shame;
¶ To Tholome thou dist also the same,
Sone & heir to kyng Iubatoun;
And many a senatour thou slouh in Roome toun.

"You slew your brother with men-at-arms, and Ptolemy and many a senator.

511. also named eek] also callid B, eke namyd also H.
513. imperial] owen B. 521. al] al þe H.
526. Castor] & Castor H, P.
527. Fro whiche place] For which B.

"You shut up the granaries and starved the people of Rome, so that, dreadful to say, they ate their own members.

Shettist up myd Roome the cite
Ther gerneris, which neuer afforn was* seyn;
Wherbi enfamyned was the comounte, —
Pite to heere; this [is] plat & pleyn, —
Of necessite constreyned in certeyn
(Shame to reherse or put [it] in scripture)
Eet ther membris, a thyng ageyn nature.

"I don't suppose that Jupiter or Juno told you to do this: very likely it was Venus, who wanted to flatter you, or Mars. Soon afterwards you yourself were murdered by your own servants.

Iubiter nor Iuno the goddesse
Gaff no such counsail, I suppose, onto the;
But it was Venus, to flatre thyn hihnesse,
And furious Mars, bi froward cruelte
To slen senatours grettest of that cite;
Thi-silff soone aftir, wherof the toun was fayn,
Bi thi seruauntes moordrid were & slayn.

"Look to your left; is that not Cæsonia, your wife, whom you afterwards slew, and your daughter Drusilla?

And for tabate thyn outrage & [thi] pride,
Which[e] thou hast vsid al thi liff,
Lefft up thyn hed, looke on thi lefft[e] side,
Thou fyndere up of moordre & of striff!
¶ Slouh thou nat Cesonia thi wiff? —
Thi douhtir aftir, that callid was Drusill,
Of cursid entent thi malis to fulfill?

"I am astonished that neither of you is ashamed to blame me for a small mote like lechery, and cannot see the beam in your own eye.

I haue merueile how any of you tweyne,
Thou Calligula or thou Tiberius,
Be nat ashamed any thyng to seyne
Ageyn[e]s me, with visage despitous
Me for tatwite that I was lecherous!
Of a smal mote ye can abraide me,
But in your eye a beem ye cannat see.

"Where do your souls dwell? I suppose Charon landed you on the strand of Styx in hell,

Wher haue your soules take þer herbergage,
That been contrarie with me for to stryue?
I trowe that Caron hath maad your passage
Vp at the stronde in helle for taryue,
Ther ye abide, thus I [can] descryue,
Wher dredful Stix, callid þe infernal flood,
Of custum renneth with furious wawes wood.

544. Shettist] Settist R, H 5 — myd] amyd H.
545. was] wer B. 547. is] *om.* R, J, P, H 5.
549. it] *om.* R, J, R 3.
558. thi] *om.* H, R 3, H 5.
560. looke on thi] take on þe H.
576. can] *om.* R, J, H, R 3, H 5, P, Sl, H 4, H 3, R 2.

Radamantus, oon of the iuges tweyne, [p. 350]
With kyng Mynos hath youe a iugement,
Perpetueli ye shal abide in peyne;
And Eacus hath ordeyned your torment:
In Flegeton,* the flood most violent,
Ye shal be drowned & an eende make,
Euere for tabide among the stremys blake.

where Rhadamanthus, Minos, and Æacus have ordained that you shall be forever drowned in Phlegethon.

I may you calle of emperours the refus,
Ye sholde be shamfast to shewe out your visages,
Verray astoned, dreedful and confus
To haue to me so vncurteis langage!"
Thus Messalyne daunted ther corage
With hir femynyn crabbid elloquence.
Thei durste no lenger abide in hir presence.

"You are the refuse of emperors, and ought to be ashamed to speak so discourteously to me." At this they lost countenance and no longer dared remain in her presence.

[Off the most vicious tiraunt Nero that slouh Petir and Paule and atte laste himself.] [1]

THIS hatful stori with many a woful lyne
Of Calligula and Tiberius,
Touching þe strif tueen* hem & Messalyne,
Shamful rebukis, froward & odious,
Bi them rehersed with cheer most furious,
As ye haue herd, heer eendeth ther chidyng;
Nero the tirant kometh next onto þe ryng.

After this hateful quarrel, with its odious and shameful rebukes, Nero appeared on the ring.

Oon most cursid in comparisoun
That euer was, of hih or louh degre,
Most disnaturel of condicioun
Bi gret outrages of cursid cruelte,
That euere regned in Roome the cite.
His fadir callid, bookis determyne,
Domycius, his moodir Agripyne.

He was one of the most cursed men who ever lived or reigned in Rome. His father was Domitius and his mother Agrippina.

This Agripyna bi hir subtilite, —
And blynde Fortune beyng fauourable,
That set up tirauntes of froward volunte
(Be ther demeritis thouh thei be nat hable)

She was subtile, and Fortune favourable; but what thing is more dreadful than cruel tyrants!

582. Eacus] Gacus R, J, Cacus P, H 5, Carus H, R 3.
583. Flageton B. 587. visage H. 589. languages R 3.
590. corages R 3.
595. atueen B.
599. onto] on H. 600. Oon] This Nero H.
607. hir] his H.

[1] MS. J. leaf 143 verso.

To estat imperial, famous & notable.
What thi*n*g mor dr*e*dful, who ca*n* vnd*er*stonde,
Tha*n* cruel tirau*n*t*es* w*it*h bloodi suerd on honde!

When Nero was twelve years old and had learned his grammar and the seven liberal arts, he was put in the hands of Seneca,

Whan this Nero of age was twelue yeer
He was ordeyned in especiall,
Afftir he hadde lernid his grameer
And the seuene artis callid liberall,
Vnto a maister in al vertu morall,
Callid moral Senec, which did al his peyne
From all vices his youthe to restreyne.

who kept him from all vices, knowing that his natural inclination was towards evil.

He kepte hym euere, this Senec, as I reede,
Maugre his fatal disposiciou*n*,
Bi a constreynt & a maner dreede
From al outrage and dissoluciou*n*.
Conseyued weel his inclynaciou*n*
To be vicious as of his nature,
Which to restreyne he dede his besi cure.

When he was twenty-one years of age he married Octavia, daughter of Claudius and Messalina.

At oon & tuenti wyntir of his age,
Cronicleers rehersen of hym thus:
How he that tyme took in mariage
Octovia, douhtir off Claudius, —
Al this while beyng vertuous,
Whil Senec hadde hym vndir disciplyne, —
His moodir-in-lawe callid Messalyne.

All this while Seneca kept him on the path of virtue; and when he was first crowned emperor he won the favour of the Senate.

The saide Senec made hym to desire
To pursue kun*n*yng bi dillige*n*t labo*ur*;
At entryng in first of his empire, —
I meene wha*n* he was crownid empero*ur*, —
Of alle the Senat hadde gret fauo*ur*;
And be report, as clerkis of hym write,
In prose and metre he koude riht weel endite.

He wrote very well in both prose and verse, and made a notable book of poetry called Lusce.

In Iohn Boch*as* as it is maad[e] my*n*de,
He dide excelle gretli in poetrye,
Made in tho daies also, as I fynde,
A book notable of strau*n*ge poisie,
Lik as myn aucto*ur* of hy*m* doth specefie,
The title therof callid[e] Lusce,
Ageyn a preto*ur* Clodius Polle.

614. twelue] xij B.
618. vertu] werkes H. 629. Cronyclis H, Cronycles R 3.
637. in] *om.* R. 647. Luscio P. 648. Pollio P.

Excelled in musik & in armonye,
Crownid with laureer for the beste harpo*ur*
That was that tyme; & he did edefie
In Roome a paleis, wit*h* many a riche to*ur*,
Which in beeldyng coste gret tresour,
The circuit beyng thre thousand pas;
And T*r*ansitorie that paleis callid was.

He was also an excellent musician and the best harper of his time. He built a palace called Transitory

For this cause, as put is in memorie,
The said[e] paleis aftirward was brent,
Therfor it was callid T*r*ansitorie; —
But aftir that, Nero in his entent
Leet beelde an hous, bi gret auisement,
To reco*m*pence the tothir that was old,
And callid it the riche hous of gold.

because it burnt down soon afterwards, and a rich house of gold,

In al this world[e] was non to it liche, [p. 351]
Wher that euer men did ride or gon,
Tables of iuor fret with perre riche,
Pileres of cristal garnished wit*h* many a ston,
Saphirs, rubies & topazion,
Crisolitis & emeraudis greene,
With plate of gold tiled that shon ful sheene.

to which none other was comparable, with its ivory tables, crystal pillars ornamented with precious stones, and gold-tiled roof.

To bodili lust* and delectaciou*n*
This said[e] Nero set al his desires;
Gardyns, conduitis for recreaciou*n*
He dide ordeyne tendure many yeeris.
Wit*h* nettis of gold fisshed in his ryueeris,
His garnementis of golde & Ynde stonis,
And neuer he wolde haue hem on but onys.

All his inclination turned to sensuality. He built gardens and artificial streams in which he fished with golden nets.

In his begyn*n*yng, the stori doth deuise,
Lord & emperour in Roome the cite,
To senatours he gaf ful gret frau*n*chise,
Grau*n*ted comou*n*s many gret liberte;
But in his most imperial dignite,
Of froward wil lefft al good policie,
And al attonis gaf hym to ribaudie.

His clothes were of gold and jewels, and he would never wear them but once.

670. lust] lustis B.
672. conductes R, J.
674. *is misplaced at end of stanza, but correction indicated* R.
678. in] in the R.
679. To] þe H.

At first virtuous and liberal, he suddenly turned to ribaldry, left the company of old senators, and harped and sang among vagabonds and openly danced with common women at the brothel.

Of Grece a*nd* Egipt wit*h* dyuers io[n]glo*u*rs,
And among vileyns hymsilf[e] disporti*n*g,*
Lefte the presence of olde senatours
And among ribaudis he wold harp & sy*n*ge,
Made comedies dishonestli sownyng,
At the bordel dide hy*m*silf auau*n*ce
Wit*h* comou*n* women openli to dau*n*ce.

In the course of time he fell into gluttony and incontinence, for one vice leads to another; but idleness was the cause of all.

Thus be processe, to al vertu co*n*trarie,
Be gret excesse he fill in glotonye,
And aftir that list no lenger tarye, —
As euery vice to othir doth applie, —
Surfet & riot brouht in lecherie;
And grou*n*d of al, as cheef[e] porteresse,
Texile vertu was froward idilnesse.

At Ostia he ordained tents for debauchery, housing cooks and taverners at great expense. Ladies who took part in these revels were not well spoken of afterwards.

Aboute the cite callid Hostience,
Beside Tibre & othir fressh ryuers
Dide ordeyne bexcessiff expence
Tentis for riot, kookis, tauerneeris,
And al the niht reuel aboute the feeris.
Ladies komen, that wer afforn weel namyd,
Bi suich fals riot wer aftirward diffamed.

It is also said that this same Nero violated the priestesses of Vesta, who were vowed to chastity.

The same Nero be fals abusiou*n*,
It is reportid, his* stori who list see,
Bi violence from ther religiou*n*,
Suich as hadde auowed chastite
And wer professid to virgynyte
In the temple of Vesta the goddesse, —
Of froward lust he dide hem oppresse.

One of them, Rubria, he dragged out of the temple and put in a bordel-house in spite of her being a nun.

Amongis which Rubria was oon:
Maugre hir wil, she durste [it] nat denye,
From the temple bilt of lym & ston
Sacrid to Vesta, my*n* aucto*u*r list nat lie,
He rente hir out to vse his lecherie;
Natwit*h*sta*n*dyng she was religious,
Made hir tabide at the bordel-hous.

Men shall never read any writing of mine about his foul and outrageous deeds with Sporus and Ompharus,

Be my writyng men shal neuer reede,
The mateer is so foul & outragous
To be rehersed, & the horrible deede
Which Nero vsid whilom on Sporus
And on another callid Ompharus:

684. Ioglers P. 685. dispart*ing* B, dispartynge R.
698. Aboute] Aboue R. 706. his] the B. 707. ther] the R.
723. Ompharus] Doriphorus P.

Bothe male childre, as bookis telle ca*n*,
Them to transffoorme to liknesse of [wo]man.

Som*me* bookis of hym determyne,
Lik a ribaude horrible & detestable,
He mysusid his moodir Agripyne,
And lik a tirau*n*t cruel & vengable, —
Which to reme*m*bre it is abho*min*able, —
He made hir wombe be korue upon a day
To seen the place nyne monethes wher he lay.

and some books say of him, that like a detestable ribald, he had his mother's womb carved open to see where he had lain for nine months.

Of disnaturel hatful cruelte,
To God nor vertu hauyng no reward,
And of the vice of prodigalite
He was accusid, in knihthod a coward,
And to al vertu contrarie & froward, —
Of whos woodnesse good heed wha*n* I took,
I was ashamed to sette hym in this book.

He was accused of unnatural, hateful cruelty, a prodigal and a coward; and when I took heed of his madness I felt ashamed to put him in this book.

He hated alle that wer vertuous
And to hem hadde specialli envie;
His brethre, his wiff, this tirau*n*t despitous,
He falsli slouh in his malencolie;
His maister Senec, auctours specefie,
Ay wha*n* he sauh hy*m*, hauy*n*g a maner dreede,
In an hot bath to deth he made hy*m* bleede.

He hated all virtuous people, and slew his brother and his wife and Seneca, his master.

Cristis feith[e] first he ga*n* werreye, [p. 352]
Of emperou*r*s, in his froward ente*n*t;
Petir & Poule in Roome he made deie
Vpon a day; ther legende doth assente.
Half the cite of Roome, I fynde, he brente;
And senato*ur*[e]s wol nih euerichon
This Nero slouh; spared almost neu*er*oon.

The first emperor to persecute the Christians, he martyred Peter and Paul, killed almost all the senators, and burnt up the half of Rome.

To Pollifagus, a wood ma*n* most sauage,*
Which that fedde hym most wit*h* flessh of ma*n*,
Nero took men, olde & yong of age ,
To fynde hy*m* vitaille in streetis wher he ca*m*.
Cursid at his eende, cursid wha*n* he ga*n*,
Whan he did offre in*n*ocent*es* blood
To be deuoured of hym that ra*n* so wood.

He fed Polyphagus, a savage madman, with human flesh.

725. woman] man H, R, R 3, H 5, a man J, woman P.
749. in] & H.
752. wol nih] volneth R.
753. neu*er*oon] noon H, R 3, none P.
754. *This stanza is transposed with the next in* P *and MSS. except* H.
760. ran] was H.

His mules were shod with silver for pride; and after he burnt Rome the people chased him from his suburban palace

Made his mules be shod with siluer shoone
Of surquedie, whan he shold[e] ride;
The cite brent. Romeyns aftir soone
Pursued hym upon eueri side;
And from a subarbe wher he dide abide,
Tween Salaria & Numentana riht,
Ther stant a path whidir he took his fliht.

to a deep marsh, and there, seeing himself trapped, he pierced his heart with a dagger. A cursed end!

Bi a deep maris as* Nero took his fliht,
Whan he sauh he myht[e] nat asterte, —
He was [so] pursued bi a Romeyn kniht
To fynde socour he myht[e] nat dyuerte, —
Rooff hymsilff anon [un]to the herte
With a sharp dagger, a cursid eende, loo!
Of the fals tiraunt that callid was Nero.

Lenvoye.[1]

No prince should take pleasure in reading the story of Nero; it has to do only with murder, treason, adultery, excess, poison, riot, gluttony, lechery, vengeance, and suicide.

OFF this Nero to write[n] a Lenvoye,
Nor of his deedis to make mencioun,
To reede þe processe no prince shold haue ioye,
For al concludeth on moordre and on tresoun,
On auoutrye, excesse & poisoun,
Riot, glotonye, lecherie, vengaunce,
Slauhtre of hymsilff[e]; eendid with myschaunce.

If I could, I would scratch his name out of my book. Let no one remember anything more about him than this: that every tyrant ends in misfortune.

Yif that I myhte, I wolde race* his name
Out of this book, that no man sholde reede
His vicious lyf, cheef merour of diffame.
Set hym aside; let no wiht take[n] heede
For to remembre so many a cruel deede,
Sauf onli this, to thynken* in substaunce,
How eueri tiraunt eendith with mischaunce.

What I say of him is said only in reproof.

Of hym I caste to write now* no more,
And what I seie is* seid but in repreeff
Of the vices that he wrouht of yore
Duryng his empire, concludyng for a theeff.
Al tirannye shal eende with myscheeff,
Record on Nero, which for mysgouernaunce,
As ye haue herd[e], eendid with myschaunce.

768. as] whan B. 772. unto] even to H.
782. racen B, R, J.
783. reede] it reede R, J, P. 787. thynken] maken B.
789. to write now] now to write B. 790. is] I B.
794. on] of R.

[1] "In stede off a Lenuoie," R.

[How Eleazerus a Iewe born / for extorciou*n* and robbery / was brouht in prisou*n* and there ended.] [1]

AFFTIR Nero ca*m* Eleazarus,
A Iew of berthe, a p*r*ince of robberie,
An extursioneer cruel & despitous;
For his outrages doon in that partie,
To redresse his hatful tiran*n*ye,
A myhti preto*ur* sent fro Roome dou*n*,
Callid Phelix, into that regeou*n*.

Eleazar, a Jew, came after Nero. He was a prince of robbery and a cruel extortioner, but Felix came down from Rome

Be force of Phelix take he was & bou*n*de,
Maugre his myht[e], onto Roome sent,
Stro*n*gli fetrid with massif cheynis rou*n*de,
Suffred in p*r*isou*n* many gret torme*n*t.
At the laste, this was his iugeme*n*t,
Ther tabide because he was a theeff;
For euermore eendid in myscheeff.

and captured him and sent him to prison for life.

[How the hede of Galba was smyten of filled full of gold / and offred atte the Sepulcre of Nero.] [2]

¶ Tofor Boch*as* next ca*m* Galba dou*n*,
Which in Spayne did many knihtli deede.
Afftir the deth rehersed of Nero*u*n
He stode in hope, this Galba, as I reede,
In thempire iustli to succeede,
Parcel for knihthod, he hath hy*m* so weel born,
And* for gr*e*t mariage which he had had beforn.

Galba, who had done many a knightly deed in Spain, usurped the throne after Nero.

I fynde in Boch*as* rehersed in sentence,
He was disclau*n*drid of hatful vices thre;
He was cruel, co*n*trarye to clemence,
Streiht in keepyng, geyn liberalite,
Vengable of herte, geyn mercy & pite, —
A thyng nat sittyng onto cheualrie, —
Of custom youe to slouthe & slogardie.

He was a cruel, avaricious, revengeful and lazy man.

798. extorsioner R, R 3, extorcioner H, H 5, P.
802, 3. Felix R, H, J, R 3, H 5, P.
809. For euermore] For euer for eu*er* more R.
816. And] As B, H.

[1] MS. J. leaf 144 verso. [2] MS. J. leaf 144 verso.

He claimed title to the empire by his adopted son, but not long afterwards his head was smitten off by Otho

To occupie thempire he began,
Among[es] Romey*n*s took pocessiou*n*,
Cleymyng a title bi oon Licynyan
That was his sone bi adopciou*n*.
But [anone] aftir for his presu*m*pciou*n*,
Oon callid Oththo, a ful ma*n*li kniht,
Smet of his hed, wher it wer wro*n*g or riht.

and filled with gold by Patrabolus and offered up to the gods of the lower regions at the sepulchre of Nero.

This said[e] Galba, my*n* aucto*u*r writeth thus, [p. 353]
From his empire vnwarli pullid dou*n*,
Hadde an emny callid Patrabolus,
The hed of Galba took in pocessiou*n*,
Filde it *with* golde, made an oblaciou*n*
At the sepulchre of Nero therwithal
To alle the goddis & goddessis infernal.

[How Ottho and Vitellius / for glotony lechery ribaudrie and cruelte / ended in mischeef.] [1]

After this sacrifice, Piso came to make his complaint to Bochas. Surnamed Licinian and adopted son of Galba, he was slain by Otho.

¶ And after that this offry*n*g was ful do,
As ye haue herd[e], to Iohn Bochas than
To make his co*m*pleynt in ordre ca*m* Piso,
Affor surnamyd iustli Licynyan,
Sone adoptiff, to telle as I began,
Of saide Galba, cleymy*n*g to succeede,
Slayn anon aftir bi Ottho, as I reede.

The empire was then divided into three and governed by Otho, Vitellius, and Vespasian.

Than was themp[i]re partid into thre:
Ottho took Roome vnto his partye;
And Vitellius to regne in the contre,
Ouer the bou*n*dis of al Germanye;
And Vespasian regned in Surrye.
But first this Ottho, surnamyd Siluyus,
Cam to co*m*pleyne, cruel and despitous.

Otho, whose family name was Silvius, usurped the empire by murder and outrage, and began a war against Vitellius.

Of al thempire this same* Siluyus
Be slauhtre, rauyne & extorsiou*n*,
Bi moordre, deth & deedis outraious
With myhti hond took ther pocessiou*n*.
And ther began a gret deuysiou*n*,

829. *The name* Otho *is spelled variously with* c's *and* t's *in the MSS.; it is probable however that* the c's *are usually meant for* t's (Occho R, R 3, Octho J, Ochcho B, H, Otho P).
833. Hadde] And R — Patrobolus R, H, J, R 3, H 5, Patrobius P.
836. sepultur*e* H. 841. lycyvian H. 845. into] in R.
852. this same] surnamyd B.

[1] MS. J. leaf 144 verso.

Which was occasiou*n* of gret sorwe & wo,
Atween Vitellius and this seid Ottho.

It is rehersed, that in Germanye
In sondri placis thei hadde batailes thre,
In the which Ottho w*ith* his partie
Venquisshed the feeld & maad his foon to flee.
But thoruh Fortunys mutabilite,
The fourte tyme, pley*n*li this the caas,
Maugr*e* his myht discou*n*fited þ*er* he was.

He won three battles in Germany, but was defeated in a fourth battle,

Tofor Bedrye, a myhti stro*n*g cite
Of Germanye was this disconfiture.
Aftir which of froward cruelte
The said[e] Ottho, seeyng his auenture,
With wo supprised miht[e] nat endure
Of his co*n*streynt thymportable peyne;
Took a sharp suerd & roof his herte o*n* tweyne.

and, overcome with despair, killed himself.

Vitellius hauyng the victorye,
With his poweer, as maad is me*n*ciou*n*,
Of surquedie & fals[e] veynglorie,
Ca*m* with his host[e] into Roome tou*n*.
But Bochas heer maketh a descripciou*n*,
Rehersyng shortli his berthe & eek his lyne,
And how that he of blood was Saturnyne.

Vitellius came vaingloriously into Rome with his army;

This to seyne, Saturnyus, kyng of Crete,
Chacid bi Iubiter out of his regiou*n*, —
And Ianus hadde in Itaille take his seete
Vpon a mou*n*t callid Ianiculu*n*,
Wher now of Roome is bilt the large tou*n*, —
Ianus resceyuyng of liberalite
Wha*n* Saturn fledde, into his cite.

and Bochas says that he was descended from Saturn, whom Jupiter expelled from his kingdom. Saturn was received in Rome by Janus,

Toforn the komyng of Satvrn, this no faille,
Rud & boistous, & bestial of resou*n*
Was al the peeple abidyng in Itaille;
Lond was non sowe nor turnid up-so-dou*n*,
Nor marchau*n*dise vsid in no tou*n*
Til Saturn tauhte the man*er* of lyuyng,
Of tilthe & labour to Ianus that was ky*n*g.

and before his coming the people were rude and unlettered and did not even know how to till the soil or chaffer in merchandise,

869. The] This R.
880. Saturnus P.
893. & labour] of londe H — to Ianus] *om.* R.

and were like beasts until Saturn taught Janus the art of living.

Afforn whos comyng, tofor as I you told,
Craft was non vsid be no creature,
Nor no beeldyng of housis newe [n]or old,
But lyued as beestis the[r] lyflode to recure,
Lik as thei wern Ilernid of Nature.
Thei koude tho daies make no cloth nor shape,
Off* frosti wedris the greuous cold tescape.

They could not make cloth, and were very poor cooks, and had no markets in their towns.

Thei wer nat besi be costful apparaille
Of sondry metis and confecciou*ns*,
Off dyuers drynkes & manyfold vitaille
To be corious to ther refecciou*ns*.
Marketis wer none in cites nor in tou*ns*;
No man with othir bouhte nouther solde
Til Saturn ca*m* & them the man*er* tolde.

But after Saturn had taught them how to be civilized, these simple folk worshipped him as the mightiest of their gods.

And wha*n* he hadde tauhte them þe maneer*e*
And set an ordre of ther gouernau*n*ce,
The symple peeple, as bookis doth vs lere,
Lich as to God dide ther attendau*n*ce,
With certeyn riht*es* to doon þ*er* obs*er*uau*n*ce,
Worsheped hym, & aftir dide hy*m* calle
Saturn, most myhti of ther goddis all.

Latinus was a descendant of Saturn and so was Lavinia, his daughter, ancestress of Vitellius.

[Aftyr this Saturne was made a pe-degre,
To sett an ordre conveied from his lyne
Descendyng dou*n*, the maneer who list see,
To oon Latynus and so foorth to Lavyne,
Which was his douhtir, as poetis determyne.
Thus bi discent from* Saturne and Funus,
Born off ther bloode cam Vitellius,]

The first knight of the lineage was Vitellius Publius; and his descendant, Vitellius Lucius, was father of the emperor.

The firste kniht bor[e]n of that lynage. [p. 354]
Because he was ma*n*li & riht famous,
Hadde in armys prowesse & gret corage,
He callid was Vitill[i]us Publius;
And of hym ca*m* Vitell[i]us Lucius,
Fadir to hym, my*n* aucto*ur* doth expresse,
Of whom that I haue gun*ne* this p*ro*cesse.

900. Off] The B.
903. Off] to H.
910. The] Thei R, Ther J — doth] don R, J.
914. of] to H.
915. *This stanza is supplied from* R.
920. from] to R.

DYUERS stories remembre & pleynli tell,
Dvryng his youthe & stood at liberte,
How þis forseid, that callid was Vitell,
Was the most vicious that owher myhte be,
Youe to ribaudie & al dishoneste,
Because of which chaungid was his name,
Callid Spyntoire, a name of gret diffame.

It is said that this Vitell was one of the most vicious youths that ever lived, given to all dishonesty and called Spintor, an infamous name.

I fynde that he was an hazardour,
In al his werkis passyng riotous,
For his surfetis gret with the emperour
That whilom was callid Claudius.
And for his deedis & maneeres outraious,
For his gret wast and prodigalite
Of gret dispence he fill in pouerte.

He was a gambler and a prodigal, and fell into poverty because of his excesses.

Among his riotis [&] surfetis mo than oon
Which he dide in contres heer & ther,
I fynde that he for neede solde a ston
Which his mooder bar whilom* at hir ere.
For be old tyme was vsid, who list lere,
Women that wern that tyme of hih degre
Bar at ther eris stonis & perre.

Finally he sold a stone his mother had worn at her ear (for in olden times women of high station wore jewelry in their ears),

And bi the sellyng of that riche ston,
For which that he resceyued gret tresour,
Be sotil werkyng & sleihtis mo than oon
He gat hym freendis & was maad emperour.
And therwithal he dide eek his labour
To resceyue another dignite,
To be cheef bisshop in* Roome the cite.

and through the proceeds and his cunning he got himself friends and was made emperor. He also wanted to be chief bishop.

And in short tyme this Vitellius
Of thempire took on hym al thestat,
The suerd resseyued of Cesar Iulius,
Vsed a garnement that was purpurat,
Dempte of hymsilff he was most fortunat,
Natwithstonding mor boldli þat tyme atte leste*
Of Aliensois holden was the feeste.

He received the sword of Julius Cæsar, wore purple, and considered himself most fortunate.

941. and] of H.
946. his] is R — whilom bar B, bare sometyme H, bar some tym R 3.
956. in] of B.
958. al] *om.* R.
962. mor boldli þat tyme atte leste] þat tyme mor boldli at the leste B — þat tyme] *om.* H.

The feast of Aliensois was then being held, during which no one was required to do any virtuous labour;

Aliensois was a solempnite
Among[es] Romey*ns* kept be daies olde,
In Frenssh my*n* aucto*u*r recordeth thus, parde,—
And in that tyme of custum no ma*n* sholde,
Nor be statut bou*n*de was nor holde
To do no maner occupaciou*n*
That touched vertu or religiou*n*.

and bound up with it was a custom of granting the requests of all people. So Vitellius asked to be bishop, and no one dared say no.

Dury*n*g this feeste he sholde haue his axy*n*g,
Bi a custum vsid in that cite.
And Vitellius, as empero*u*r & ky*n*g,
Axed that tyme another dignite,
To be cheef bisshop & haue auctorite
Of that estat, with poweer hool & pley*n*;
No ma*n* so hardi to replie ther agey*n*.

He set all wisdom and knowledge at nought and left knighthood and providence, and gave himself up wholly to idleness and gluttony.

From al vertu Vitelli dide varye,
Set at nouht al wisda*m* & science,
Thouhte onto hym was nat necessarye
Ku*n*nyng, knihthod, ma*n*hod nor p*ro*uidence;
Gaf hym onli to slouhthe & necligence,
To glotonye, folwyng his desir[e]s,
Wach al niht with drynk & reresoper[e]s.

As he was a bishop he officiated in the temple, and often he would cast aside the censer and call a kitchen boy to the altar and command him to bring him his dinner.

Beyng a bisshop of ther paynym lawe,
Lik Romey*n* rihtis doyng þ*er* seruise
Tofor the goddes; he wolde hy*m*silf wit*h*drawe
And cast aside censer and sacrefise
And calle a boy in ful vngoodli wise,
A kichen boy, tofor the hih aulteer,
And hym comau*n*did to brynge hy*m* his dyneer!

Always gluttoncus and drunk,

Beyng arrayed in his pontificall,
For the maner void of deuociou*n*,
Lik a ribaude, or lik a wood menstrall
Euer dronclew, & out of al sesou*n*,
Gorge upon gorge, this excessif glotou*n*,
Moste idropik, dra*n*k ofte ageyn[es] lust:
The mor he drank the mor he was a-thrust.

970. vertu or] vnto R, onto J.
978. Vitell J, P.
979. at nouht] anouht R.
994. mynstrall H, R.
996. upon] vp R.

This was a bisshop sacrid for* Sathan,
And an emperour crownid with myschaunce:
Mor lik in poorte a beeste than a man.
Vsed al his poweer in slauhtre & in vengaunce;
To sheede blood was set al his plesaunce,
Takyng non heed nouther of wrong nor riht;
And thus he wex hatful to eueri wiht.

he was a bishop sacred to Satan, more like a beast than a man. As his pleasure lay most in shedding blood without heed to right and wrong, he was hated by all men.

His soudiours forsook hym nih echon, [p. 355]
In al parties bi hym wher thei wer sent;
Thoruh al the contres of Septemptrion
And in al Surrye toward thorient,
Of oon accord & alle of oon assent
Echon forsook hym; with hym bood* nat a man,
And becam seruauntes to Vespasian.

His soldiers deserted him and entered the service of Vespasian.

Vitellius sauh it wolde be non othir,
And he for-feeble [of] dronknesse & outrage, —
And sauh the poweer gan faillen of his brothir,
Whan he had sett* and signed the viage
Ageyn Vespasian to holden his passage:
But al for nouht, bakward wente his partie,
Stood disespeired of euery remedie.

Made weak by drink and excess, and seeing that the expedition he had sent against Vespasian had failed, he despaired,—

Thus Vitellius vnhappi to the werris,
Lik a fordronke vnhappi gret glotoun,*
Whos booste afforn[e] rauht up to the sterris,
Now al his pride in myscheef is come doun,
Fayn for taccorde to this conuencioun:
For litil tresour, which men sholde hym assigne,
To Vespasian thempire to resigne.

a great unhappy drunken glutton, and was glad to resign his imperial dignity for a small compensation.

This was his promys, but he heeld it nouht:
What he saide, his woord was neuer stable;
Certeyn flatereres chaungid hadde his thouht,
And certeyn comouns, that euer be chaungable,
Gaff hym counsail, saide hymsilf was hable
To gouerne thestat imperial,
And non so hable for to reknen al.

But when flatterers told him that he was best able to govern Rome, he broke his promise

999. for] of B.
1011. boode nat with hym H — abood B.
1016. sett] sent B, R, J, R 3, H 5, P. 1019. dispeired R.
1021.] Lik afforn dronke vnhappi stronge glotoun B.
1024. this] his R.
1027. his] my H.
1030. that] þe H.

and began a new war out of presumption, and sent the head of Fabius, Vespasian's brother, who had been killed,

First of Almayne he sent out soudiours,
And of presu*m*pciou*n* a newe werr*e* he ga*n*.
Thouhte that he was amo*n*g othir werreyo*u*rs
Hable to* fihte ageyn Vaspasian.
And of auenture it befill so than,
In thes werris Vespasyanis brothir*
I-slay[e]*n* was; it wolde be non othir.

to Rome. After that he burnt down the Capitol and soon lost the favour of the Romans.

This froward ma*n* callid Vitellius,
Vngracious euere fou*n*de in his entente,
Smet of the hed of seide Fabius,
Brothir of Vespasian, & it to Roome sente,
And aftir that the Capitoile [he] brente.
But suyng on, wit*h*yn*n*e a litil space
Amo*n*g Romey*n*s he loste bothe hap & grace.

Why should I write more of his debauchery? His cook and pastryman did not forsake him; they followed him to the Campania.

Of his riot what sholde I mor entrete? —
For except riot of hy*m* nothy*n*g I reede.
His cook, his pastleer, folk that wer most meete
To serue his lust & appetit*es* to feede,
Forsook hy*m* nat, but went wit*h* hy*m* in deede
Toward Champayne riht as any lyne
Vp to an hill[e] callid Auentyne.

Later on he returned to Rome, hoping to ingratiate himself with Vespasian. Seized at last in his palace, he denied his own name,

Stondyng in hope, but that was but i*n* vey*n*,
Of Vespasian the fauour to recure,
Euene to Roome retournid is agey*n*,
The paleis entrid; & ther hy*m*silff tassure,
Hauy*n*g wit*h* hym non othir creature,
The gatis shet, which was to hy*m* gret shame;
Take at the laste, forsook his owne name.

and was led half naked before the populace, his hands bound behind his back, looking like a madman.

Halff naked he was & haluendel Iclad,
Al allone lik as he was fou*n*de.
So in the cite affor the peeple lad;
Bothe his hondis behy*n*de his bak wer bou*n*de
Wit*h* myhti cheynys & with ropis rou*n*de.
Lik a wood ma*n* of look & of visage,
The peeple to hym hauy*n*g this langage:

1035. he] *om.* H.
1036. werreyo*u*rs] Soudiours H.
1037. to] for to B, R, P, H 5, R 3, H.
1039, 40. *The second halves of these lines are transposed* B.
1043. the said R.
1044. of] vnto R.
1051. lustis H.

"O thou olde lecherous foul glotoun,
A verray coward, to al vertu contrarie,
Cruel, vengable of thi condicioun,
To euery goodman cruel aduersarye,
To all cursid benigne & debonaire,
Roote of al surfetis, hauyng ay delit
To sewe & folwe thi lecherous appetit!"

The people called him a coward, an enemy of every good man, a lecherous foul old glutton,

With such rebukis & castyng of ordure,
With donge & clay was blottid his visage.
In the presence of many a creature,
With cordes drawen he was be gret outrage
Vnto a place callid in ther langage,
Ther most cheeff rakkes or galwes of þe toun,
Wher is of custum doon execucioun.

and threw dung in his face. He was then drawn with cords to the gallows.

Summe remembre he slay[e]n was in haste,
With sharp[e] suerdis dismembred on þe ground,
His careyn aftir into Tibre cast
With a large hook of iren, sharp & round,—
No mor reuerencid than was a stynkyng hound.
Remembryng heer myn auctour seith also
Of this Vitellius, Galba & Ottho,

and despatched with swords. They fastened his carrion to an iron hook and threw it into the Tiber; and no more respect was paid to him than to a stinking hound.

Affermyng thus, as for ther partie, [p. 356]
Thei be namyd among the emperours,
For a tyme thestat did occupie;
And first this Galba, be record of auctours,
Deide at myscheeff, void of al socours,
Eihte monethes regned as lord & sire,
And aftir that cast out of his empire.

Thus, to recapitulate: Galba died in misfortune, cast out of his empire after a reign of eight months;

The thridde moneth, as maad is mencioun,
Ottho deide, proude & ambicious.
And, as I fynde, the domynacioun
Laste eihte monethes of Vitellius.
And for thei wern proud ribaudes* lecherous,
Cruel, vengable, born of cursid lyne,
In wrechchidnesse echon thei dide fyne.

Otho died in the third month of his reign; and Vitellius reigned eight months. As they were all proud dissolute ribalds, they ended in misery.

1074. ay] evir H.
1078. a] *om.* R, H.
1087. a] *om.* H.
1089. Galba] of Galba R.
1101. ribaudes] ribaudi B, P, R, ribaudie J — & lecherous H.

Bochas dampnyth þe Vice of Glotonye.[1]

Bochas, seeing the great iniquity of this froward company, took up his pen to condemn the vice of gluttony.

HEER Iohn Boch*as* sey*ng* the gr*et* offe*n*se
Of this forseid froward co*m*panye,
Took his pen*n*e of enteer dilligence,
And in his studie ga*n* hymsilff applie
To dampne the vice of hatful glotonye,
Fro which[e] syn*n*e, record[e] of Adam,
Al our myscheeuys & sorowis ca*m*.

All our sorrows arose from it, as witness Adam, who in his folly and conceit allowed himself to be governed by a serpent.

Be the outrage of disobeissau*n*ce,
Our said[e] fadir beyng in paradis,
Tween hy*m* and vertu ther roos a gr*et* distau*n*ce,
Cleerli conceyued, he that was so wis,
Aboue creatures be resou*n* bar the pris,
Til [he] of foli wrongli gaff assent
To be gouernid bi a fals serpent.

His innate virtues forsook him and returned to heaven, and for this we have great reason to mourn.

His innat v*er*tues did hy*m* anon forsake
For his assenty*ng*, & did in hast retourne
Ageyn to heuene, wha*n* the infernal snake
In stede of vertu did *with* ma*n* soio*u*rne.
For which we han gr*et* mateer for to mo*u*rne,
Sith that we been difffourmyd in certey*n*,
Be vicious lyuy*ng* of vertu maad barey*n*.

Our vices became dominant, assailing us woeful wretches, when we abandoned the four virtues,

And thus ca*m* in the domynaciou*n*
Of vices alle, & heeld a gret bataille,
The retenv sent fro*m* thynfernal dongou*n*,
Vs woful wrechchis in erthe for tassaille,
Strechchy*ng* ther poweer, & proudli ga*n* p*re*uaille
Thoruh al the world[e] & pocessiou*n* took,
For our demerites wha*n* vertues vs forsook.

Prudence, Temperance, Righteousness, and Fortitude.

Thes said[e] vertues co*m*prised in the nou*m*bre
Of foure reknid: Prudence, Atte*m*perau*n*ce,
Of* vicious lyff tadawed vs fro the slo*m*bre,
Rihtwisnesse taue holde the ballau*n*ce,
And Fortitudo of ther alliau*n*ce;
Wha*n* thei forsake ma*n*ky*n*de to gou*er*ne,
Than of al vertu was clipsed the lant*er*ne.

1114. he that] þat he H. 1115. be resou*n*] *om.* R.
1125. thus] *om.* H.
1134. Of] Fro B, J, H 5, R 3, From R, P.

[1] *The heading is as follows in* MS. J. leaf 146 recto: "Here Bochas ageyne Glotonye compleyneth seieng as it folowith."

Thus thoruh dirknesse vices wer made bold,
The multitude almost innumerable.
Amo*n*ges all reknid of newe or old,
Ther be foure pereilous & reprouvable:
Slouthe, Lecherye, & most abho*min*able,
Fals Auarice bi a gredi desir,
Wit*h* Glotonye, cheef kyndeler of ther fyr.

The four perilous vices are Sloth, Lechery, Avarice, and Gluttony, chief kindler of their fire.

Nature in soth with litil is conte*n*t;
And as my*n* aucto*ur* abidith heer a while,
And to reme*m*bre was su*m*what dilligent
To write, wha*n* Saturn regned in þe ile
Callid Crete, the prophetesse Cibile,
In hir tyme, bi gret auctorite,
The world deuyded prudentli in thre.

Nature is content with little; and my author stops here to write about the Golden World, when Saturn reigned in Crete.

[A Chapitle descryuyng the golden worlde, that is to say whan attemperau*n*ce had hooly the gouernau*n*ce.] [1]

THE olde world, wha*n* Saturn was first ky*n*g,
Regny*n*g in Crete in his roial estat,
Noe, Abraham be vertuous lyuyng
Caused erthli folk to be most fortunat,
The world tho daies callid Aureat;
For sobirnesse and attemperau*n*ce
Hadde in that world hooli the gouernau*n*ce.

Noah and Abraham also lived at that time, and soberness and temperance ruled the world.

Ther was that tyme no wro*n*g nor violence,
Envie exiled from eueri creature,
Dissoluciou*n* & dronken insolence,
Ribaudie & al swich foul* ordure,
Froward surfetis, contrarye to nature,
Ibanshed wern, because attemperau*n*ce
Hadde in that world hooli the gou*er*nau*n*ce.

There was no wrong nor violence, drunken insolence, and froward excesses.

Youthe was bridled vndir disciplyne, [p. 357]
Vertuous studie floured in myddil age,
Dreed heeld the yerde of norture* & doct*r*ine,
Riot restreyned from surquedous out*r*age,
Hatful detracciou*n* repressid his langage,

Youth was bridled under discipline, and virtuous study flowered until middle age; riot was restrained; there was no hateful detraction.

1145. ther] þe H. 1149. ysle R, Isle H.
1163. foul] fals B, H.
1165. wern] was R — Ibanysshid H.
1169. norture] nature B.

[1] MS. J. leaf 146 verso. *There is no initial in* B.

Kouth was charite, because attemperau*n*ce
Hadde in that world hooli the gou*er*nau*n*ce.

Chastity was cherished by knighthood, heretics were punished, and the church held up in spiritual dignity.

Fortitudo stood tho in his myht,
Diffendid widwes & cherisshed chastite,
[Knyhthod in prowesse gaff out so cleer a liht,]
Girt with his suerd of trouthe & equyte,
Heeld up the cherch in spiritual dignite,
Punshed heretikes, because attemperau*n*ce
Had in that world hooli the gouernau*n*ce.

Jurors were honest, promises were kept, forswearing and lying dared enter no town.

Rihtwisnesse chastised al robbo*u*rs
Be egal ballau*n*ce of execusiou*n*,
Fraude, fals meede put bakward fro ioro*u*rs,
Trewe p*ro*mys holde made no dilaciou*n*,
Forsuery*n*g shamyd, durste entre i*n* no tou*n*,
Nor lesyngmongers, because atte*m*perau*n*ce
Hadde in that world hooly the gou*er*nau*n*ce.

The seven deeds of mercy were constantly performed; the rich ready to give alms, and no one was refused a lodging for the night.

That golden world coude loue God & dreede,
Alle the seuene deedis of m*er*cy for to vse;
The riche was redi to do almessedeede:
Who asked herborwe, men dide hy*m* nat refuse.
No man of malis wolde othir tho accuse,
Diffame his neihbour, because atte*m*perau*n*ce
Hadde in that world hooli the gou*er*nau*n*ce.

Merchants and artisans were upright, the plow was held firmly to the furrow, the labourer was never idle.

The trewe marchau*n*t be mesour bouhte & solde,
Deceit was non in the artificeer,
Makyng no balkis, the plouh was treuli holde,
Abak stood idilnesse ferr fro*m** laboreer,
Discreciou*n* marchall at dyneer &* sopeer,
Content with meso*u*r, because attemperau*n*ce
Hadde in that world hooli the gouernau*n*ce.

There was no luxurious excess in clothing (although one could know the lord from his subject); no one boasted or feigned.

Of wast in clothy*n*g was that tyme no*n* excesse,
Men myhte the lord fro*m* his soget knowe,
A differe*n*ce maad tween pouert & richesse,
Tween a p*r*incesse & othir statis lowe,
Of hornyd beestis no boost was tha*n* Iblowe,
Nor cou*n*tirfet feyny*n*g, because attemperau*n*ce
Hadde in that world hooli the gou*er*nau*n*ce.

1176. B *has in place of this line the third of the preceding stanza.* — a] *om.* R.
1179. Punysshed R, H. 1183. bakward] bak H.
1188. That] The H.
1198. fro*m*] fro*m* the B, H. 1199. &] & at B.
1201.] Was set asyde and lost hir gouernau*n*ce R.
1206. was then no boste R.

This goldene world long while did endure,
Was non allay in that metal seene,
Til Saturn cesid, be record of scripture;
Iubiter regned, put out his fadir cleene,
Chau*n*ged Obrison into siluer sheene,
Al up-so-dou*n*, because attemperau*n*ce
Was set aside and lost hir gou*er*nau*n*ce.

This Golden World lasted until Jupiter put his father out of his kingdom, and then temperance was set aside.

Of Martis myneral the metal is so stro*n*g,
Inflexible and nat malliable,
Be sturdynesse to do the peeple wro*n*g
With rigerous suerd, fureous & vengable,
The m*er*ciful gold [of] Phebus nat plicable
To haue co*m*passiou*n*, because atte*m*p[e]rau*n*ce
Was set aside & lost hir gouernau*n*ce.

The metal of Mars is strong and inflexible, and the sword of rigour furious and full of vengeance.

Leed, of philisophres, is callid gold leprous,
Tyn of Iubiter, crasshyng & dul of sou*n*,
Fals and fugitiff is mercurivs, —
The moone is mutable of hir condiciou*n*.
The goldene world is turnid up-so-dou*n*
In ech estat, sith[en] attemperau*n*ce
Was set aside and lost hir gouernau*n*ce.

Lead is called leprous gold, tin is dull of sound, and mercury false and fugitive.

Be Cibilis exposiciou*n*,
Tak of this metal the moralite:
The goldene world was gou*er*ned be resou*n*,
The world of iren was furious cruelte;
The moone is mutable, ful of duplicite,
Lik to this world, because attemp[e]rau*n*ce
Is* set aside and hath no* gou*er*nau*n*ce.

The Golden World was governed by reason, but the world of iron by cruelty; the present world is full of duplicity, like the moon.

Venus, of loueres emperesse & queene,
Of vicious lustis lady and maystresse,
Hir metal coper, that wil ternyssh gr*e*ne,
A chau*n*gable colour, co*n*trarye to sadnesse,
A notabil figur of worldli brotilnesse,
Lik gery Venus, because atte*m*p[e]rau*n*ce
Was set aside & lost hir gou*er*nau*n*ce.

Venus' metal is copper, that tarnishes green, a changeable colour, a figure of worldly mutability.

1222. hir] his H, R 3.
1223. Leed] Bed H.
1224. craisshyng R, J.
1227. The] This R. 1228. sith H, R.
1236. Is] Was B — hath no] lost hir B.
1243. hir] his H.

My author Bochas complained on the cumbrous gluttony of Vitellius and his two fellow emperors, notorious for their debauchery.

My*n* aucto*ur* Bochas ga*n* pitousli co*m*pleyne
On the disordynat comerous glotonye
Of Vitellius & his felawes tweyne,
Alle thre diffoulid *with* horrible lecherye,
Diffamed be sclau*n*dre, noised for ther ribaudie,*
Contrarious enmyes echon tatte*m*perau*n*ce,
Banshed fro ther court[es], myhte haue no gou*er*n-
 au*n*ce.

Gluttony and drunkenness cause fevers, podagra, gout and horrible gangrenous sores.

Of glotonie & riotous excesse, [p. 358]
Wach & reuel & drynkyng al the niht
Kometh vnkouþ feueres & many gr*e*t accesse,
Membres potagre mak[th] men thei go nat riht,
Goutes, mormalles horrible to the siht,
Many infirmytes, because atte*m*perau*n*ce
Was nat of cou*n*sail toward ther gou*er*nau*n*ce.

Prudence was banished from their court; soberness, truth and righteousness stood aside.

Out of ther court ban[y]shed was prudence,
Fortitudo had non interesse
Geyn vicious lyuy*n*g to make resistence,
Cried woluis hed was v*er*tuous sobirnesse;
Trouthe durst nat medle, abak stood rihtwisnesse,
Put out of houshold was attemperau*nce*,
With these thre empero*u*rs koude haue no gou*er*nau*n*ce.

John the Baptist lived in the desert and ate mel sylvester and locusts. His cook was temperance.

¶ Sone of the p*ro*phete callid Zacharie,
The patriark, the holi ma*n* Sey*n*t Iohn,
Victorious cha*m*piou*n* of gredi glotonye,
Lyued in desert, deyntes hadde he non,
Et mel siluestre, lay on the colde ston,
Locustas gadred; his cook was temp[e]rau*n*ce
And of his houshold had al the gou*er*nau*n*ce.

His clothes were woven of camel's hair, and he lived on honeysuckles and drank spring water.

Of kamel heris was wouen his clothy*n*g,
Record the Gospell that ka*n* the trouthe tell,
Honysokeles his moderat feedyng,
Mong wilde beestis whan he dide duell;
To stau*n*che his thrust dra*n*k watir of þe well,
This blissid Baptist, roote of atte*m*prau*n*ce,
Set for cheeff merour of al good gou*er*nau*n*ce.

1245. comberous H.
1248. be] with H—for ther ribaudie] be þ*er* lecherye B—for ther] with H.
1254. podagre R, R 3, P. 1261. Cryed woluyssh was H 5.
1264. Emp*er*our H. 1266. holi] manly H.
1269. Et mel siluestre] Did eat wild honey P.
1270. Locustes P. 1275. Mong] Among H.

Of his diete cato*ur* was scarsete,
His costful foode was vertuous abstine*n*ce,
Rootis of desert his delicat plente,
His riche pymentis, [his] ipocras of dispe*n*se
Heeng nat in costretis nor botelis i*n* þe spence, —
Nat excessiff, because atte*m*perau*n*ce
Hadde of his houshold hooli þe gou*er*nau*n*ce.

Scarcity was his caterer, and his food virtuous abstinence and roots of the desert.

Thus Baptist Iohn bi his moderat foode
The cheef tryu*m*phe of abstyne*n*ce hath begu*n*ne,
This patriark[e] rekned oon the goode,
Content with litil, al suffisau*n*ce hath won*n*e,
As Diogenes in his litil ton*n*e
Heeld hym appaied, because atte*m*perau*n*ce
Hadde of his houshold al the gou*er*nau*n*ce.

He began by moderate diet, the chief triumph of abstinence, and was as content with little as Diogenes in his hogshead,

His ton*n*e to hym was receit & houshold;
And yif I sholde booste of his celeer,
Ther wer no cuppis of siluer nor of gold;
His costful vyntage ca*m* fro the ryueer:
Weel tymed mesour was for his mouth botleer,
And his tastour was attemperau*n*ce,
Which of his houshold had al þe gouernau*n*ce.

who had no cellar or cups of silver and gold. His vintages came from the river, and moderation was his butler.

His conquest was mor soueray*n* of degre
Tha*n* Alisau*n*dris, for al his hih renou*n*;
For he conquered his sensualite,
Made hym soget & seruau*n*t to resou*n*,
Dau*n*ted of prudence ech forey*n* passiou*n*,
His clerk of kechene callid attemprau*n*ce,
Which of his diete had al þe gouernau*n*ce.

His conquest of his senses was greater than the triumphs of Alexander.

Of superfluite, of slouthe & of sleep*e*
This Diogenes stood euer amo*n*g in dreede;
Of worldli fauour he took no man*er* keep*e*;
Strauh was his liteer, a sy*m*ple russet weede:
Turnid his ton*n*e agey*n* the wy*n*d in deede,
Tween hot and cold[e], that attemperau*n*ce
In somer & wyntir had hool the gou*er*nau*n*ce.

His bed was of straw, his garment russet; and he turned his tun according to the wind, and let temperance rule in summer and winter.

1281. his] he H.
1283. nat] *om.* R.
1297. his mouth] þe tyme H.
1313. hool] *om.* R.

¶ Lenvoye.

Noble Princes, The Golden World is turned to lead. Pray God to send down his grace, that temperance may govern your households.

NOBLE Princis, of prudence takith heed
This litil chapitle breefli to comprehende:
The goldene world is turnid into led;
Praieth to God his grace doun to sende
Of his hih mercy, that it may soone amende,
And that this princesse callid attemperaunce
May of your housholdis han the gouernaunce.

Chiefly for love, but also for fear, attend diligently to his precepts; for those who of old ruled by temperance prospered.

Cheefli for loue, parcel eek for dreed,
In your estat whan ye be most shynende,
For your encres & your most gracious speed,
To his preseptis doth dilligentli attende,
Of olde emperour[e]s reedeth the legende:
Whil thei wer reuled be attemperaunce
In long prosperite stood ther gouernaunce.

While temperance and her three sisters held sway, Rome defied its enemies.

Of worldli kyngdames Roome is callid hed,
Whos roial boundis ferthest out extende
In marcial actis, bothe in lengthe & breed,
Rem Publicam bi prowesse to diffende,
No foreyn enmy hardi to offende
Ther hih noblesse, whil attemp[e]raunce
With hir thre sustren hadde* ther gouernaunce.

[How the kynrede of Iacob was destroied / Crist born and deied / Ierusalem destroied, & xj^c M^l slayn bi suerde, hunger, fire & pestilence.] [1]

After the stories of Vitellius, Galba and Otho, a great number of the descendants of Jacob came to Bochas

THE stoori eendid of Vitellyus, [p. 359]
Of his too feeris Galba & Ottho,
How his careyn horrible & hidous,
Drownid in Tibre, was possid to & fro.
Afftir the[r] stori [a]complisshed was & do,
Cam gret noumbre to Bochas, as I reede,
Echon descendid of Iacobis hih kynreede.

like dismayed people, clad in mourning and wet with tears.

In tokne of compleynt & of heuynesse,
Lik folk dismaied, clad in moornyng weede,
For the constreynt of ther wrechidnesse,

1314. goode heede R.
1316. The] This R — into] in R. 1319. thes prynces R.
1323. &] & for H. 1334. hadde] hadden B.
1337. their Careyns H. 1338. was] *om.* H.
1342. tokne] toke H — 2nd of] *om.* H.
1343. dismaied] diffamyd R.

[1] MS. J. leaf 147 verso.

Bespreynt with teres, quakyng in þer dreede,
Cunnyng no recour in so streit a neede,
Resemblyng folk be toknis ful mortall
That wer toward sum* feeste funerall.

Ther ougli cheeris pitous to beholde,
As thei gan aprochen the presence
Of Iohn Bochas to telle ther sorwes olde,
Ther woundis bleedyng, be marcial violence,
Oppressid with hunger, thrust, sodeyn pestilence,
Be foreyn suerd ther lyuys manacyng,
Vpon the deth as beestis abidyng,

Their ugly faces were piteous to look upon, their wounds bleeding; oppressed with hunger, thirst, pestilence and the sword of foreigners,

That wer enclosed narwe in a folde,
Disespeired socour to recure,
To passe ther boundis for dreed thei wer nat bold,
Withynne enfamyne[d], bareyn of al pasture; —
This woful stori remembrid in* scripture,
How that of Iacob the generacioun
Was vengabli brouht to dest[r]uccioun.

they awaited death like sheep in a fold, and lacked all courage to escape.

This patriark callid whilom Israel,
Most rennommed among al naciouns
And most famous, the Bible can weel tell,
Ther lyne out reknid thoruhout al regiouns,
Be goddis beheste took ther pocessiouns,
Maugre Egipciens & Pharaoes pride,
Whan duk Moises be God was maad þer guide.

They were once the most renowned of nations, as the Bible can tell; and in spite of the pride of Pharaoh,

With dreye feet thei passed the Rede Se,
Conueyed be Moises & also be Aaron.
Ther lawe was write, the Bible who list see,
Vpon Syna in tables of hard ston.
And thoruh desert as thei dide gon,
With aungelis mete callid manna, as I reede,
Fourti wyntir ther he did hem feede.

they crossed the Red Sea dry shod, and received the law at Sinai, written on tablets of hard stone.

Afftir Moises, lad be Iosue
Into the lond[e] of promyssioun,
The tuelue lynages of Iacob ther, parde,
He leet make a distribucioun,
And to ech lyne he gaff his porcioun,
Bi promys maad afforn to Habraham,
To Isaak, Iacob, whan thei thidir cam.

They lived for 40 years on angel's food; and after Moses' death Joshua led them into the Promised Land.

1346. Cunnyng] knowyng J, P, H 5.
1348.] Toward that wer sum feeste funerall R — sum] the B.
1360. in] be B.
1367. pocessioun H. 1382. Abraham H, R, J.

Ruled by mighty dukes and judges, they prospered; and at last, when in their pride they wanted a king, Saul was chosen.

Bi patriarkes [&] prophetis that wer sad,
Maugre ther enmyes & ther mortal foon,
Be mihti dukes & iuges thei wer lad,
Gat al the regiou*ns* wher thei dide gon,
Til at the laste, of p*r*ide thei echon
Lik othir naciou*ns* wolden haue a kyng.
Saul was chose; God grau*n*tid þ*er* askyng.

Finally David became king, and of his line Jesus was born.

Thus be patriarkes & be ther allies,
Fro*m* Abraham the gen[e]alogie,
Tolde be p*r*ophetis & be ther p*r*ophesies,
Co*n*ueied to Dauid, which in his regalie
Heeld of Iewes al hool the monarchie,
Of whos kynreede bi processe, thus it stood,
Was Crist I*es*u born of that roial blood.

who became incarnate for our salvation and suffered martyrdom under Herod.

Sent from his fader, as prophetis* det*er*myne,
Took flessh & blood for our sauaciou*n*,
Be the Hooli Goost born of a peur virgyne,
Hadde among Iewes gret tribulaciou*n*,
Vndir Herodes suffrid passiou*n*,
And as the Gospell treuli doth descryue,
The thridde day [he] roos fro deth to lyue.

This blessed Lord was born at the end of December in Bethlehem, and shewn to three kings by a starbeam; and the same Jesus was afterwards condemned by Pilate to die on Calvary.

This blissid Lord, this Lord of most v*er*tu,
Eende of Decembre born [sothly] in Bethlem,
And be the au*n*gel namyd was I*es*u,
Shewed to thre kynges bi a sterre bem, —
This same Ihesus in Iherusalem
Bi conspiraciou*n* of Iewes thoruh envie,
Be Pilat dempt to deie on Caluarie.

Thus the Jews were unkind to him; and for that they were nearly all destroyed.

Thus onto Ihesu Iewes wer vnkynde,
For which thei wern destroied nih echon.
Crist prophecied, the Gospel maketh my*n*de,
How of ther cite ther shold nat leue a ston
Vpon another; for ther mortal foon
Shold hem besege, he told hem so certey*n*,
And make Iherusalem with the soil al pley*n*.

Sin was the cause; for when Jesus came to save them, they did not know him.

With weepyng eyen Crist told he*m* so beforn* [p. 360]
Of ther ruyne and destrucciou*n*;
Syn*n*e was cause sothli that thei wer lorn:
For thei nat* knew, to ther confusiou*n*,

1384. &] *om.* R. 1392. genelogie R, genologie J, Genealogye H.
1398. prophetis] poetis B. 1407. the] *om.* R.
1419. beforn] afforn B. 1420. and] & their H.
1422. nat] ne B.

Tyme of ther notable visitaciou*n*,
Wha*n* Crist ca*m* dou*n*, born heer in erthe lowe
For ther sauaciou*n*, — thei list hym nat to knowe.

Thretti yeer ful cronicleeres write
And su*m*what mor, aftir his passiou*n*,
Amo*n*g the Iewes, pleynli to endite,
Withyn*n*e hem-silff fill a dyuysiou*n*.
Moordrers ros up wit*h*yn*n*e ther owne tou*n*,
So gret a nou*m*bre, wit*h* many an homycide,
That in ther cite no man durst weel abide.

Thirty years after the Passion the Jews became divided among themselves, and there were so many murders that no man dared abide in the city.

Ther presidentis regny*n*g in Iude
Seyng this horrible foul rebelliou*n*
And of moordreris the mortal cruelte
That long endured in that regeou*n*, —
Which for tappese Romey*n*s sente dou*n*
Vespasian wit*h* many a ma*n*li kniht,
Which into Gallile took his weie riht.

The Romans sent down Vespasian to restore order,

And to chastise tho moordreris & robbo*u*rs,
Brente ther contre as he rood up & dou*n*,
So co*n*tynued wit*h* his soudio*u*rs
Til onto tyme the contres envirou*n*
Of Iherusalem entred be the tou*n*
With ther oblaciou*n*s in many sondri wise,
As Pask requered, to do ther sacrefise.

and he laid waste the country at the time the people entered Jerusalem to make their paschal sacrifices.

Tofor tho daies was Iherusalem
Hadde in gret worshep of al naciou*n*s,
Callid p*r*incesse of eueri othir rewm,
Whos fame strechid thoruhout al regiou*n*s,
Ther tresor gret and ther pocessiou*n*s,
Double wallid, of beeldy*n*g most notable,
Dreedy*n*g no*n* enmy, for it was impreuable.

Jerusalem was then called the princess of realms, rich in treasure, double walled, and almost impregnable.

Amo*n*g Romey*n*s was many a ma*n*li ma*n*
Willyng echon of oon affecciou*n*,
Thoruh the knihthod of Vespasian,
Echon to laboure to the destrucciou*n*
Of Iherusalem; for gret dyuysiou*n*
Amo*n*g hem-silf was gun*n*e in the cite
Bi certey*n* capteyns wer i*n* nou*m*bre thre.

The Romans were willing to fight hard to win the city, which was divided against itself.

1425. to] *om.* H.
1426. yeer] yeers R — cronicleeres] cronyclis H, cronycles R 3, cronyculeers R, J. 1430. vp ros R. 1431. an ou*m*bre H.
1432. ther] that R, the J, P — weel] *om.* R.
1439. Gallile] Gaule H. 1451. Ther] The R. 1458. gret] their H.

The tyrants Simon, John and Eleazar were enemies; and there was war both without and within.

Symon, Iohn and Eleazarus,
Horrible tirauntes oppressyng þe poraille,
Of gouernaunce froward and outraious,
Falsli deuided ech othir dide assaille,
Among hem-silf had many gret* bataille:
Werre withoute & werre was withynne;
Thus of vengaunce myscheef dide gynne.

Vespasian tried to make peace among them, but in vain. Returning to Rome as emperor,

Vespasian nat beyng rek[e]les,
For his partie lik a prudent kniht
Be notable menys excited hem to pes;
But al for nouht; blente ther owne siht;
To cheese the beste thei koude nat seen ariht.
And in this while, this noble werreyour
Vespasian was chosen emperour.

he appointed his son Titus to succeed him in Judaea. Jerusalem was besieged and starved.

Bi Alisandre to Roome he went ageyn,*
Resceyued ther thymperial dignite.
His sone Titus he made his cheef capteyn,
His procuratour, to gouerne in Iude,
Besette enviroun Iherusalem the cite,
With men of armys seged it so aboute
That non myhte entre nor non myhte issen oute.

One woman is said to have roasted her child for lack of victuals, which was too horrible a deed!

Stopped ther conduites & ther watris cleer,
Enfamyned hem for lakkyng of vitaille.
A certeyn woman, thus seith the cronicleer,
Rosted hir child whan vitaile did[e] faille, —
She hadde of stoor non othir apparaille, —
Theron be leiseer hirsilf she dide feede,
Which in a woman was to horrible a deede!

The walls were beaten down by engines and two strong towers taken.

Ther myhti wallis with gunnes wer cast doun,
Too stronge tour[e]s take of ther cite,
Resistence gan faillen in the toun,
Thei stood of hunger in swich perplexite.
Titus of knihthod and magnanymyte,
Thoruhout the tour callid Antonyan
Is entrid in lik a knihtli man.

1464. ech] echon H.
1465. gret] strong B.
1469. prudent] manly H.
1472. seen] chese H.
1473. noble] notable H.
1475. went ageyn] was sent B. 1483. lak H.
1485. vitaillis R.

The peeple in streetis lay for hu*n*ger ded,
To beye nor selle no lyfflode in the tou*n*;
Ther was no* soco*ur* nouther of dry*n*k nor bred
In peyne of deth born nouther up nor dou*n*.
Vomyt of oon was the refecciou*n*
Vnto another; ther was such scarsete,
Who redeth Iosephus, the trouthe he* may þ*er* see.

The people lay dead for hunger in the streets: their story can be read in Josephus.

Brent was the te*m*ple maad first be Salamo*n*, [p. 361]
Which had endured, thus writ the cronicleer,
That was so roial bilt of riche ston,
Fulli a thousand & too hundred yeer.
Romey*ns* entred maugre ther porteer
With spere, pollex & suerdis sharp[e] whette,
Lik wode leou*ns* slouh who*m* that thei mette.

The temple, which had stood for 1200 years, was burnt

Ther riche gatis curid wit*h* plate of gold
Wer brente and molte withoute excepciou*n*;
The siluer images that forgid wer of old,
The violent feer made hem ren*n*e dou*n*.
Noble Titus hadde compassiou*n*,
His marcial dukis spared nothy*n*g certey*n*,
List of presu*m*pciou*n* thei wolde* rebelle agey*n*.

together with its rich gates covered with plates of gold, and its silver images.

Eleuene hu*n*drid thousand wer ther slay*n*
Bi suerd, bi hu*n*ger, fyr and pestilence;
Stynk of kareyns that in streetis lay*n*
Caused of deth most sodey*n* violence;
And Titus gaff amo*n*g hem this sentence
— I meene of them that dide alyue duell —
For a peny men sholde thretti sell.

1,100,000 Jews were slain by the sword, starvation, fire, and pestilence; and the stink of corpses caused many more deaths.

So as Iudas sold Crist for thretti pens,
Titus ageyn thouhte of equite,
Of marchau*n*dise to make reco*m*pense,
Thretti Iewes fou*n*de in the cite
For a peny, & for no mor, parde,
Thei to be sold for ther gret out*r*age,
Euer among Sarsyns to lyuen in seruage.

Titus commanded the survivors to be sold to the Saracens at thirty for a penny, as Jesus had once been sold by Judas for thirty pence.

Of the temple a preest that was ful olde,
Too statli lanternis, that wer ful briht & sheene,
Tables, basynes, violes of briht golde
He presented; & thus he dede meene:

An old priest shewed Titus the treasures of the temple in token of its departed glory;

1498. no] non B, R. 1499. nouther] neithir R — nor] ne H.
1502. Iosephus] Ioseph R — he] ye B, R, *om.* J — þ*er*] *om.* J.
1505. riche ston] lyme & stoone H. 1510. Ther] The H.
1516. wolde] list B. 1518. 2nd bi] & H. 1525. of] it H.

That ther tresour sholde weel be seene
Of the temple & shewed to Titus
In tokne it was whilom so glorious.

he shewed also silk and frankincense and the purple vestments and rich pectoral of the high priest.

To shewe eek ther he dede his besi cure,
Silk synamome, franc-ensens withal,
For sacrefise the purpurat vesture,
W*ith* Thymyame, the riche pectoral,
Which ordeyned wern in especial
For the solempne place of placis all,
Sancta sancctor*um*, & so men dide it call.

A prince of the city named John came to Titus, pale with hunger; and Simon was brought to him by duke Terence.

Of the cite a p*r*ince callid Iohn
To Titus cam & shewed his p*re*sence,
Pale for hunger; ther ca*m* also Symon,
Brouht be a duk that namyd was Terence,
Clad in purpil, brouht be violence,
Resceyued of Titus wha*n* this noble tou*n*,
Castellis, tours & wallis wer smet dou*n*.

Eleazar fled; but, trapped in a castle, he incited all who were with him to slay one another.

Into a castell callid Mazadan
Eleazarus hadde take his fliht.
Besegid of Scilla or he the castel wan,
This Eleazar lik a furious kniht
Withyn*ne* the castell the silue same niht
Sterid eueri ma*n*, fadir, child & brothir,
W*ith* sharp[e] suerdis ech ma*n* to slen othir.

Thus Jerusalem, most stately of building, was destroyed.

Thus was this* cite, most statli of beeldy*n*g,
That whilom was of this world cheef tou*n*,
Wher Melchisedek regned, preest & kyng,
Be daies olde, as maad is menciou*n*,
Restorid be Dauyd, bilt newe of Salamou*n*,
P*r*incesse of p*r*ouy*n*ces, was nowher* such anoþ*er*;
Now is it* abiect and refus of al othir.

Jesus gave the Jews thirty years respite before he took vengeance; for the Lord has joy when sinners are contrite and repent:

Vnto the Iewes Crist I*esus* gaf respiht,
Full thretti yeer[e] or he took vengau*n*ce,
In tokne the Lord hath ioie & gret delite,
Wha*n* that syn*n*eres dispose hem to penau*n*ce
Be co*n*triciou*n* and hertli repentau*n*ce.
This blissid Lord, this Lord most m*er*ciable
Lengest abideth or he list be vengable.

1537. so] *om.* R. 1540. the] of H.
1544. R *misplaces here:* "Which ordeyned wer in especiall."
1551. Castell R.
1559. this] the B. 1562, 63 *are transposed in* H.
1564. nowher] neuer B.
1565. is it] it is B — it] *om.* R. 1571. 2nd Lord] kyng R.

He was to them so gracious & benigne,
Bood that thei sholde to hy*m* co*n*uerte soone,
Shewed onto hem many an vnkouth signe:
Dury*ng* tuelue daies eclipsed was the moone;
The peeple astoned, knew nat what was to doone,
But indurat in ther froward entent,
Lik folk abasshed wist nat what it mente.

and although he was gracious to them and shewed them strange signs of what was to come, the people remained obdurate.

Affor the siege, or Titus ga*n* the werre,
Ouer the cite, wherof thei wex afferd,
Ther appeered a comeete & a sterre.
The sterre was shape lich a large suerd;
Touchyng the comeete, ther was neu*er* herd
Of swich another, so fyri, briht and cleer,
Which endured the space of al a yeer.

Before the siege a fiery comet appeared over the city, and a star shaped like a large sword;

Ther festyual day halwid in Aprill, [p. 362]
Ther preestis besi to make oblaciou*n*,
So gret a liht the te*m*ple dide fill,
That al the peeple stondy*ng* envirou*n*
Thouhte it so briht in ther inspecciou*n*,
Passyng the sun*n*e, as it dide seeme;
But what it mente no ma*n* koude deeme.

and on their festival day in April a light shone brighter than the sun in the temple.

As the preestis dide ther besi cure
To offre a calff, ano*n* or thei took heede,
The same calff — a thyng ageyn nature —
Brouht foorth a lamb, the same tyme I reede;
An ougli tokne, which put* hem i*n* gr*e*t dreede,
A contrarie* pronosticaciou*n*,
Shewed onto them of ther subuersiou*n*,

As the priests offered up a calf it brought forth a lamb, which was an evil omen.

With othir toknis froward & co*n*trarye
The* same tyme wer shewed eu*er* amo*n*g;
The brasen dores of the inward sey*n*tuarye,
With iren barres shet, that wer most stro*n*g,
Brood of entaille, rou*n*d and wonder long,
That myht nat meue wit*h* thretti men*n*ys miht,
Opned by hy*m*silff twies on o niht.

There were other froward signs: the heavy brazen doors of the sanctuary opened of themselves thrice on one night.

1585. such H, R, J.
1587. Ther] The H.
1594. the] ther R.
1598. put] took B.
1599. contraire B.
1602. The] Ther B.
1605. rou*n*d] wide H.
1607. thries vpon a H.

Chariots were seen in the air and men-at-arms with gleaming swords and shining armour, who made a feint to assault the city;

Ther wer seyn also charis in the hair,
Men of armes *with* briht suerdes cleere,
Of plate and maile [ther] armure was so fair,
Briht as Phebus wher thei dide appeere.
And as the stori also doth vs lere,
With ther sheltrou*n*s & ther apparaill,
A proffre maad Iherusalem for tassaill.

and one night the priests heard a dreadful sound in the temple, which ended in the awful words, "Let each of us arise and go hence."

To the Iewes it dide signefie
A pronostik of ther destrucciou*n*.
Preestis to the te*m*ple as thei dide he*m* hie
Vpon a niht to doon oblaciou*n*,
Amyd the te*m*ple was herd a dreedful sou*n*;
Of which[e] noise this was the feerful ee*n*de:
"Rys up echon, & let vs hen[ne]s weende."

Four years before the siege one Ananias, the dull son of a peasant, ran through the city in a frenzy, shouting,

And ful foure yeer tofor the siege ga*n*
Oon Ananyas, yong & tendre of age,
Of his berthe sone of a rud[e] man,
Be disposiciou*n* dul of his corage,
Lich as he hadde fallen in a rage
Ran in the cite bamaner frenesie,
Spared nat *with* open mouth to crie.

"A voice out of the east, the south, the north, the west, a voice from the four winds cries out against Jerusalem,

Vnto this noise was maad[e] non obstakle,
But obstynat euere in his entent,
Day of the feeste holde in the Thabernacle,
"A vois," quod he, "out of the orient,
Vois fro the south, fro north & occident,
Vois fro foure wyndis that blowe so brod & wide,
Vois geyn* Iherusalem crieth out o*n* eu*ery* side!

against the temple, against the people, husbands and wives: woe to Jerusalem with a treble woe!"

Vois gey*n** the te*m*ple, agey*n* the peeple also,
Vois ageyn husbondis, vois agey*n* þ*er* wyues:
Wo to Iherusalem with a treble wo
Of hu*n*ger, thrust & leesyng of þ*er* lyues, —
Of suerd & fyr, and many sodey*n* stryues!"
This was the wrecchid lame*n*taciou*n*
Which Anany cried thoruhout the tou*n*.

1608. seyn] slayn R.
1610. ther] *om.* H, R, J, R 3, H 5, P, the Sl.
1614. Iherusalem] ther Cite Ier*usal*em R, J, R 3.
1619. herd] made H. 1620. feerful] dredefull R, J.
1634. fro foure] fro the R — blowe] blew R.
1635. geyn] agey*n* B. 1636. geyn] agey*n* B.
1637. 2nd agey*n*] geyn R. 1638. 1st Wo] Who R.
1642. thoruhout] thoruh H, R, R 3, thurh J, H 5, through P.

Bete he was for his* affray ful ofte,
Whippid, scoorgid eendlong & upriht,
Al-wer-it so he felte [it] ful vnsofte,
Was bi betyng maad feynt & feeble of myht,
He stynte nat to crie so day & niht,
A pronostik shewyng to the cite,
How that riht soone it sholde destroied be.

> Although he was often beaten for his clamour, he did not cease to cry day and night.

Be rehersaile also of Carnotence,
With that cite for syn*n*e it stood so tho,
That yif Romey*n*s be marcial violence
Hadde nat komen & doon hem al this wo,
The erthe sholde han opnid & ondo,
Deuoured the peeple, void of al refuge,
Or drowned the tou*n* be sum sodey*n* deluge.

> And John of Salisbury said that it then stood so with the city for sin, that if the Romans had not come, the earth would have opened and swallowed it.

Breefli to passe, this ve*n*gau*n*ce most t*er*rible
Doon upon Iewes for ther t*r*ansgressiou*n*,
For ther demerites the pu*n*shyng most horrible,
Of Iherusalem fynal subuersiou*n*,
Of the temple, tabernacle & tou*n*,
In Iosephus, who list seen al the deede, —
De bello Iudaico, the surplus he may* reede.

> But you can read all about the end of Jerusalem in Josephus.

¶ Explicit liber Septim*us*.

1643. his] this B, R 3, H 5. 1645. it] *om.* R, J, H 5, P.
1651. for syn*ne*] *om.* R. 1655. peeplis H.
1663. he may the surplus B.

BOOK VIII

¶ Incipit Pro*lo*gus libri octaui.

BOCH*AS* makth heer an exclamaciou*n*: [p. 363]
Ageyn the Iewes gret vnky*n*denesse
Rouht be the Romey*ns*, þ*er* cite & þ*er* tou*n*,
Lich as the stori did heer-toforn expresse, —
Thei disparpiled to lyue in wrechchidnesse,
Bi Goddes hand punshed for ther outrage,
For euere [to] lyue in tribut & seruage.

Bochas exclaims against the great unkindness done to the Jews by the Romans, in punishment by God's hand for their outrages.

Folwyng my*n* aucto*ur*, I caste for to touche
So as I can, rehersyng the maneere
How Iohn Boch*as* liggyng on his couche
Spak to hymsilff & saide as ye shal heere,
"Whi artow now so dul of look & cheere,
Lik a man, thi face berth witnesse,
That hym disposeth to lyue* in idilnesse?"

Afterwards, lying on his bed he spoke to himself, asking, "Why are you so dull and idle?"

"Certis," quod Iohn, "I tak[e] riht good keep,
Of myche trauaile that the out*r*age
Hath be long slombre cast me in a sleep,
My lymys feeble, crokid & feynt for age,
Cast in a dreed, for dulnesse of corage,
For to presume vpon me to take
Of the eihte book an eende for to make."

"Certainly," said John, "it seems to me that the weariness of great labour has overcome me. I am old, and dread to take up the task of finishing the Eighth Book."

"Thow wenist parau*n*tir in thy*n* oppynyou*n*
Bi this labour to gete the a name,
For to reherse the sodey*n* fallyng dou*n*,
And be sum newe processe for to attame,
Of p*r*inces* sittyng hih in the Hous of Fame,
In dyuers bookis, wher thou maist he*m* fy*n*de,
Perpetuelly to putte thi name in my*n*de.

"Perhaps you think you can get yourself a name by this labour, and in some new manner enter the House of Fame.

3. þ*er* (*both*)] þe R. 4. the] their H.
7. to] *om.* R.
12. now] *om.* R, J.
14. lyuen B, R.
17. Hath] hast H.
26. princes] P*r*incessis B, J, P.

"Your remaining days are so few, that you are discouraged. Remember that when men are buried low in the earth there is no reward but of good living.

Thi daies shorte putte the in gret[e] dreed
Of swich a labour to take the passage,
The mor feeble the slowere is thi speed,
Thi* sihte dirkid; & thou art falle in age;
Amo*n*g reme*m*bryng, thy*n*k on this langage:
Wha*n* men be buried lowe in the erthe dou*n*,
Sauf of good lyuy*n*g, farweel al guerdou*n*.

"Worldly goods shall pass, wealth and knowledge shall be forgotten, friendship changes like the moon; but a good name left behind exceeds all riches.

Worldli goodis shal passe, & that riht soone,
Tresour, kun[n]y*n*g and al shal out of my*n*de;
Frenshep chau*n*geth as doth the cloudi moone;
At a streiht neede fewe freendis me*n* do fy*n*de.
But a good name wha*n* it is lefft behy*n*de
Passeth al richesse, yif it be weel diss*er*ued,
And al gold in coffre lokkid & co*n*s*er*uyd.

"Your labour too shall grow dim."
"Sloth spoke to me and bade me cease to labour: 'for your reward shall be small.'"

Of thi labour, the same shal wexe derk;
Bewar Boch*as*, & heerof tak good heed."
"Slouthe spak to me, and bad me leue werk:
For a smal reward thou shalt haue for þi meede,
As be exau*m*ple thou maist othir reede."
This was the langage, I hadde therof routhe,
Atween Iohn Boch*as* and this ladi Slouthe.

Bochas hung his head and was perplexed, knowing

Bochas astoned, ga*n* dou*n* his hed enclyne,
Vpon his pilwe lay hangyng in a trau*n*ce,
Stoode in gret doute, koude nat determyne,
Lik a man hangy*n*g in ballau*n*ce,
To what parti he sholde his pen*n*e auau*n*ce
To proceede as he vndirtook,
Or leue the labour of his eihte book.

not what to do, when Francis Petrarch, the laureate poet, came and sat down at his bedside.

Atwix[e] tweyne abidyng thus a while,
What was to doone in doute he ga*n* fleete,
Halff withyn*n*e & half ouer the stile,
Koude nat discerne to hym what was most meete,
Til Frau*n*ceis Petrak, the laureat poete,
Crownid with laurer, grace was his gide,
Ca*m* and set hym dou*n* bi his beddis side.

32. Thi] The B, R, J, R 3, P.
33. this] thi R.
40. name] Fame H. 49. this] þe H.
50. i*n*clyne R, declyne H. 52. in] in a R.
53. in abalau*n*ce R, in a ballance H 5.
58. What] That R — to fleete R, J.
63. bed side H.

And as Bochas out of his slombre abraide
And gan adawen sumwhat of his cheere,
And sauh Petrak, lowli to hym he saide:
"Wolkome maister, crownid with laureer,
Which han Itaille lik a sunne cleer
With poetrie, pleynli to descryue,
Most souerayn li enlumyned bi your* lyue, —

At this Bochas started up and said, "Welcome, Master, who, like a bright sun, illumined Italy with poetry.

I haue desired, as it is weel kouth,
Of riht hool* herte be humble attendaunce,
To doon you worshep fro* my tendre youth,
And so shal euere, void of al variaunce,
Duryng my lyff; for treuli in substaunce
Ye haue* been lanterne, liht and direccioun
Ay to supporte myn ocupacioun,

"From my tender youth I have done you worship. You have been my guide and example,

As in writyng bookis to compile,
Cheeff exaumplaire to my gret auauntage,
To refourme the rudnesse of my stile
With aureat colours of your fressh langage.
But now fordullid be impotence of age,
Of decrepitus markid with many a signe,
My labour up of writyng I resigne.

reforming the rudeness of my style with your fresh language. "But now I am grown old

I cast[e] me nat ferther* to proceede, [p. 364]
Stonde at abay fordryue with* werynesse."
Quod Franseis Petrak, "leese nat thus thi meede:
Yif men no cause to reporte nor expresse,
In thi laste age thou hast founde a maistresse
Which hath the bridled in sooth (& þat is routhe)
And halt thi rene, and she is callid Slouthe.

and stand at bay, oppressed by weariness." Said Petrarch, "Do not lose your reward thus. Men will say, in your old age you found a mistress, Sloth, who bridled you.

An euident tokne of froward slogardie,
Vpon thi bed thi lymes so to dresse.
Ris up! for shame! for I can weel espie,
Folk that can grone & feele no seeknesse,
Ther chaumbirleyn is callid Idilnesse,
Which leith thi pilwe at euen & at morwe,—
Void hir fro the, and let hir go with sorwe!

"Get up; I know people who groan when they feel no illness. Your handmaiden is idleness,

68. han] shan R. 70. your] hir B.
72. riht hool] rihtful B, R.
73. fro] for B. 76. han B.
85. ferther] foorth B, R, P, forth J.
86. with] for B, R, J.
90. &] *in* R, *om.* H. 92. froward] rowarde H.
97. thi] þe H.

who is most contrary to all virtue and has drawn you away from your library.

To al vertu most froward & contrarye
Is Idilnesse heer in this present lyff,
Which hath the drawe awey fro thi librarie,
Wil the nat suffre to be contemplatiff;
For hir condicioun is to holde striff
With euery vertuous occupacioun,
Which men sholde voide of wisdam & resoun.

"Arouse yourself and open your eyes! "Remember the Book of the Life Solitary, which teaches virtue, and, as I said before, look up and get out of bed. Are you going to stop at the Seventh Book?

In this mateer what sholde I longe tarye? —
Leff thi slombre and up thyn eyen dresse!
The book I-maad of lyff[e] solitarye,
Remembre theron, the which in sekirnesse
Techeth the weie of vertuous besynesse,
Bi and bi, who list reede eueri lyne,
Of contemplacioun moral and dyuyne.

As I seide erst, yit lefft[e] up thi look,
Forsak thi bed, rys up anon, for shame!
Woldestow reste now on thyn seuent book,
And leue the eihte? in sooth thou art to blame!
Proceede forth and gete thi-silf a name.
And with o thyng do thi-silf conforte:
As thou disseruest, men aftir shal reporte.

"Compare light to darkness, cowardice to high renown, virtuous industry to sloth.

Maak a comparisou[n] tween dirknesse & liht,
Tween Idilnesse and Occupacioun,
Tween faire daies and the cloudi niht,
Tween a coward prowesse and hih renoun,
Tween vertuous spech and fals detraccioun;
And to conclude, all vices to represse,
Contrarye to slouthe is vertuous besynesse.

"Industry renews things of old antiquity and causes men to live after they are dead. All were gone had it not been for writers.

Vertuous besynesse, O Bochas, tak good heed,
Renveth alle thynges off old antiquite,
Maketh men to lyuen aftir thei be ded,
Remembreth the noblesse of many gret cite;
And ne wer writers, al wer goon, parde.
Wherfor, Bochas, sith thou art nih the lond,
Suffre nat thi ship to stumble on no sond.

103. to] for to H. 105. voide] use H, R 3. 108. bookis H.
109. sekirnesse] siknesse H.
115. on] at H. 116. eihte] eihte book R.
119. shall afftir H.
125. to] *om.* H. 126. is] & H.
128. Renewith R, J, R 3, H 5.
133. no] the R, J, P.

I meene as thus: the shipp of thi t*ra*uaille,
Which hath passid the se of bookis seuene.
Cast nat anker til thou ha good ryuaille!
Lat no tempest of thundir, rey*n* nor leuene,
Nor no wyndis of the cloudi heuene,
Nor no fals ianglyng of demeres that wil blyue
Depraue thi labour, let thi shipp taryue.

"The ship of your labour has passed the sea of seven books; do not cast anchor until you have come to port.

Haste on thi way, lat Grace crosse þi saille,
Fall on no sond of wilful necligence,
Lat good[e] will be cheef of thi cou*n*saille,
To guye thi* rother set enteer dilligence;
Yif vitaille faille & wyn to thi dispe*n*se,
Yit at the laste, thynk, for thi soco*u*r
Sum roial p*r*ince shal quyte thi labour.

"Hasten on your way, let Grace set your sail and Good-will be chief of your counsel; and at the last, some royal prince will reward your labour.

Thynk, be writy*n*g aucto*u*rs did þ*er* peyne
To yiue p*r*incis ther komendaciou*n*s,
To Remus, Romulus callid fou*n*dours tweyne
Of Rome tou*n*; & of too Scipiou*n*s
Thei wrot the knihthod, prudence of too Catou*n*s,
Of Iulius, Po*m*peye & Hanybal eek also,
Bexau*m*ple of who*m* looke that thou so do.

"Writers have done their pain to commend princes

Of p*ro*phetis thei wrot the p*ro*phecies
And the noblesse of olde Moises,
Of poetis the laureat poesies,
The force of Samson, the strengthe of Hercules;
Of two Grekis, Pirrus and Achilles,
Bi ther writy*n*g — bookis sey the same —
Into this day endureth yit the name.

and to write the prophecies of prophets and the laureate poesy of poets.

And he that can and ceseth for to write
Notable exau*m*ples of our predecesso*u*rs,
Of envie men wil hym atwite,
That he i*n* gardy*n*s leet p*er*she þe holsu*m* flo*u*rs
In sondry caas that myhte do gret soco*u*rs.
Laboure for othir, & spare nat thi t*ra*uaille;
For vertuous labour gey*n* slouthe mai most auaille.

"And he who can and does not write the notable deeds of our predecessors will be censured by men.

135. passid] *om.* H.
144. thi] the B, R, J. 145. expence H. 151. &] *om.* R.
152. the] *om.* R — & prudence H.
153. eek also] too H.
154. whom] them H. 162. and] *om.* R.
166. gret] *om.* H.

"A fair portrait of a prince or person who is dead quickens the heart of his friend;

A thyng remembrid of antiquite, [p. 365]
Is wha*n* ther is set a fair image
Of a p*r*ince of hih or louh degre;
Or of a persone a preent of his visage
Gladeth his freend, quyketh his corage;
And semblabli bexau*m*ple me*n* may fynde
Thynges forgetyn be writyng come to my*n*de.

and in the same manner forgotten merits may be put in mind by writing. The end of our labour is devoted to Christ Jesu."

And for to make our names perdurable,
And our merites to putten in memorie,
Vices teschewe, in vertu to be stable,
That laboure may of slouthe haue the victorie,
To cleyme a see in the heuenli co*n*sistorie —
Despiht of idilnesse & foorthry*n*g of v*er*tu —
Fyn of our labour be youe to Crist I*es*u."

After Petrarch had done speaking, Bochas arose and sharpened his pen. Will had overcome the feebleness of age.

¶ Whan Petrak hadde rehersid this lessou*n*
In rebukyng of vicious idilnesse,
Bochas supprised and meued of resou*n*,
Roos from his couche, ga*n* his pen*n*e dresse.
Will ouercam thympotent feeblesse
Of crokid age, that Boch*as* vndirtook
For tacomplisshe up his eihte book.

And I, John Lydgate, following after, unskilled and more than three score years old, youth and the bright colours of rhetoric faded:—

I folwyng aftir, fordullid with rudnesse,
Mor tha*n* thre score yeeris set my date,
Lust of youthe passid [with] his fresshnesse;
Colours of rethorik to helpe me t*r*anslate
Wer fadid awey: I was born in Lidgate,
Wher Bachus lico*u*r doth ful scarsli fleete,
My drie soule for to dewe & weete.

I was born in Lydgate, where but little of Bacchus' liquor flows. Fordulled by age, I shall proceed in my labour.

Thouh pallid age hath fordullid me,
Tremblyng ioyntes let myn ha*n*d to write,
And fro me take al the subtilite
Of corious makyng in Inglissh to endite, —
Yit in this labour treuli me taquite
I shal proceede, as it is to me dewe,
In thes too bookis Bochas for to sewe.

¶ Explicit prologus libri Octaui.

172. Or] of H — 2nd a] þe H. 174. semblaly R.
175. cometh R. 190. with] for R.
191. yeeris] of yeeres H. 192. with] *om.* R, J, P, H 5.
196. to dewe] ta dew H.

¶ Incipit liber octauus.

[How the proude tiraunt Domytyan Emperour of Rome, and many other Emperours & nobles for ther outrages & wrecchidnesse mischeuesly ended.] [1]

BROTHER to* Titus, sone of Vespasian, [p.367]
Cam next in ordre, as writ myn auctour,
The proude ambicious callid Domycian,
And was in Roome crownid emperour; —
An extorsioneer and a fals pillour,
Proudli comaundid, in his estat up stallid,
Of al the world he sholde a god be callid.

Domitian was an extortioner and pillager, who commanded men to call him god of all the world.

Thoruh hih presumpcioun, of hym it is eek told,
Nouther of tymber koruen nor of ston,
Set up images of siluer and of gold,
In tokne ther was no god but he allon.
Into Pathmos he exiled eek Seynt Ihon,
And ageyn Cristene the seconde next Neroun,
That began first the persecucioun.

He set up silver and golden images of himself and exiled St. John to the Isle of Patmos.

This same tiraunt, regnyng in his estat,
To alle the cite was passyng odious;
Best & most worthi he slouh of the Senat,
And onto all that wer[e] vertuous
Mortal enmy, and most malicious.
And for slauhtre of senatours in the toun
Axed the tryumphe, as maad is mencioun.

He was odious to all Rome, slew senators and was an enemy to virtuous people.

Made among Iewes be ful gret outrage,
Wher-as he hadde grettest suspecioun,
To slen all tho that wer of the lynage
Off Dauid kynreede or kyng Salamoun,
List he wer put out off domynacioun
Among[es] Iewes; this was his meenyng, —
Slouh all tho that wer born to be kyng.

He killed all the Jews of the line of David and Solomon,

204. to] of B — of] to H.
211. is] *om.* H.
221. onto] to H.
225. among] of H.
228. or] or of H, R 3, P, of J.
229. domynacioun] pocessioun H, R 3.

[1] MS. J. leaf 150 verso.

and as God rightly wished to punish him, he was slain one night in his palace. Commodus, who succeeded, was given wholly to his fleshly appetites.

Amyd his* paleis, as God wolde of riht
Punshe a tiraunt & quiten hym his meede,
This Domycian was slayn vpon a niht,
His kareyn aftir vnburied, as I reed.
¶ And Comodus doth aftir hym succeede,
Which was al youe be flesshli appetit
To leue al vertu & folwe his fals delit.

As was then the custom, he habitually went to theatre plays and also slew all the most virtuous senators.

Theatre pleyes of custum he did vse,
As was the custum ther & the vsage;
His liff in vices he falsli did abuse,
In lecherous lustis dispente al his young age,
To the Romeyns did ful gret damage:
For of the Senat that wer most vertuous,
Wer falsli slay[e]n bi this Comodus.

During his time the public library was destroyed by lightning. Finally he was strangled by his concubine.

In his tyme be strook of thundirdent
And firy lihtnyng that cam doun from heuene,
The comoun librarye was of the cite brent,
With roial bookis of al the craftis seuene,
Bookis of poetis mo than I can neuene.
And Comodus, breefli to termyne,
Was slayn and stranglid bi his concubyne.

Helvius Pertinax, who came next on the ring, was old and unwieldy and soon slain.

¶ Helmus Pertynax cam next on the ryng,
Ordeyned aftir emperour of that toun,
Old & vnweeldi, slayn in his gynnyng.
Afftir whom, the book makth menciooun,
Be no title of successioun,
¶ But an intrusour, oon callid Iulian,
Thestat vsurpyng to regne ther began.

Julian, a usurper, followed, and he was killed in battle by Severus, born of the line of Scipio Africanus.

But of the noble lynage Affrican,
Born in Tripolis, a myhti gret cite,
Oon Seuerus, that was a knihtli man,
Gadred of Romeyns a wonder gret meyne.
Bothe maad strong, Iulian mette & he
At Pount Melyn, a cite of Itaille,
And ther was Iulyan slay[e]n in bataille.

Fired by malice, Severus afterwards persecuted the Christians,

¶ Seuerus aftir entrid the empire
And took upon hym the domynacioun,
Vpon Cristene, of malis sette affire,
Began ageyn hem a persecucioun

232. his] the B, R, J. 238. fals] *om.* H. 247. fire R.
253. Helmus] Elius P, Helinus R 3. 259. ther] thei R.
262. knihtli] lykly R.
265. pount Moleyn H, pount meleyn J, poyunt Mellian R, pont Miluian P.

Of tiran*n*ye and fals ambiciou*n*;
¶ But oon of Egipt callid Poscen*n*yus
Agey*n* Seuerus bega*n* to werke thus:

Gadred meyne Seuerus for tassaile,
In purpos fulli, & theron dide his peyne,
First with hym to haue a gret bataille,
Next of thempire the crowne for tatteyne.
But ye shal heere what fill of thes tweyne:
On Poscen*n*yus fill the disconfiture,
And Seuerus thempire doth recure.

and was attacked by Pescennius Niger, whom, however, he defeated.

In his purpos or he myht auaille,
W*ith* oon Albynus, that was a ma*n*li kniht,
He hadde [in] Gaule a ful gret bataille;
Ful gret[e] blood shad in that mortal fiht,
Albynus slay*n* of v*er*ray force & myht.
Seuervs aftir entrid in Breteyne,
Kauht[e] seeknesse & deide of the peyne.

He also fought in Gaul and defeated and slew Albinus. He then went to Britain, where he died of disease.

¶ Aftir Seuerus next ca*m* Antonyne, [p. 368]
Of whom the froward disposiciou*n*,
As alle auctours of hym determyne, —
His besynesse and occupaciou*n*
Set hool in flesshli delectaciou*n*,
So fals a lust his corage did assaille, —
Among[es] Parthois slay[e]n in bataille.

Antoninus next appeared — a wicked man whose whole business and occupation was fleshly delight.

He was slain in battle by the Parthians.

¶ Macrinvs aftir tofor Boch*as* ca*m* dou*n*,
Whilom a prefect in Roome the cite,
Of the Pretoire, and be invaciou*n*
Cam to the imperial famous dignite,
Ocupied a yeer, sat in his roial see,
Til Fortune list hym to disgrade,
Among his knihtis slay*n* at Archelade.

Macrinus, who succeeded Antoninus, reigned one year and was then killed by his soldiers.

¶ Next ca*m* Aurelius surnamyd Antonyne,
A gret ribaud & passyng lecherous,
Yit was he bisshop, as aucto*u*rs determyne,
In the temple of Aliogobolus.
And in his tyme was oon Sabellius,
A fals heretik, of whom* ga*n* the names
Of a sect callid Sebellianes.

The emperor Antoninus Aurelius was a passing lecherous ribald, although a bishop; and in his time the Sabellian sect arose.

272. Pescennius P. 273. to] þe H. 281. his] this H.
286. Briteyn H.
292. hool] holly R. 295. Macrinvs] Marcyus H, R 3.
304. he] the R. 305. Eliagabolus H, R 3, Heliogabalus H 5.
307. whon B.

In his pride he used golden vessels for vulgar purposes, which was contrary to good breeding; and when his knights slew him, his body was thrown into a privy in despite.

This said Aurelius, ageyn[e]s al norture,*
Of fals presu*m*pcioun, in bookis it is told,
Wolde nat pourge his womb bi nature,
But in vessellis that wer maad of gold;
And in despiht[e], wha*n* that he wex old,
Slayn off his knihtis, & nat aftir longe
His carey*n* was throwen in a gonge.

After Antoninus, Marcus Aurelius was elected emperor by the Senate. He defeated Xerxes, king of Persia, and when he sat in judgment,

¶ Aftir this proude forseid Antonyne,
Into thempire be iust eleccioun
Of senatours, as bookis determyne,
Cam Aurelivs, & for his hih renou*n*
Surnamyd Alisau*n*dre, as maad is me*n*ciou*n*.
Fauht with Persiens lik a ma*n*li kniht,
And ther ky*n*g Xerses he put vnto þe fliht.

Ulpian, who made three books of Digests, sat with him.

This Aurelius, this prudent knihtli ma*n*,
Wha*n* he sat iuge in the consistorie,
Ther sat oon with hym callid Vlpian,
A gret cyuylien notable of memorie,
Of whom it is to his encres of glorie
Reported thus, be gret auctorite
He of Digestis made bookis thre.

Marcus Aurelius lost his life by accident in a fight among his soldiers.

Ful pitousli this empero*ur* lost his lyff,
Casueli, as maad is menciou*n*,
Among his kniht*es* bi a sodey*n* stryff,
Wher he was slayn in that discenciou*n*.
Aftir whos eende, for short conclusiou*n*,
Tofor Bochas, the book weel telle can,
Cam Maxymyn*us** & with hym Gordian.

Maximus, who was chosen emperor by his knights, was afterwards a bitter enemy of the Christians,

¶ Maxymynus*, the cronicle doth expresse,
Chose of his knihtis & his soudio*urs*
For his victorious marcial hih prowesse
Doon i*n* Almaigne, & among empero*urs*
Set up in Roome, maugre the senato*urs*.
Afftir strong enmy, as myn aucto*ur* seith,
With al his poweer onto Cristes feith.

309. norture] nature B, R, J.
312. gold] pur*e* golde H.
325. Wlpian R. 329. He of] Off the R.
331. is made H.
336, 37. Maxymynus] Maxynym*us* B, J, Maximymus R, Maxymyns H, R 3.
343. With] Was R.

He was [eek] enmy, his lyff who list to seen,
To cristen clerkis of gret auctorite,
And specialli to olde Origen.
But in his moste furious cruelte,
In Aquileia, a myhti strong contre,
Of a prefect callid Puppien he was slay*n*;
Of whos deth [al] Cristen men wer fay*n*.

and especially of old Origen; and at the height of his cruelty he was slain by a prefect named Puppien.

¶ Next bi the Senat chose was Gordian.
First ageyn Parthois he cast hy*m* to werreie;
Of Ianvs temple wha*n* the werre ga*n*
He made the gatis been opnid with the keye,
Which was a tokne, as olde bookis seye, —
Tho gatis opnyd, to folkis nih & ferr*e*,
That with ther foon the Romey*n*s wolde haue werr*e*.

Gordian made war on the Parthians and opened the gates of the temple of Janus.

With Parthois first this saide Gordian
To holde werr*e* faste he gan hy*m* speede;
And upon hem alwey the feeld he wan.
Afftir he spedde hym into Perse & Meede,
Alwey victorious in bataille, as I reede;
Vpon Eufrates slay[e]n, as I fynde,
Be fals tresou*n*, the cronicle maketh my*n*de.

Always victorious, he was finally slain at the Euphrates by treason.

¶ Next in ordre ca*m* Phelipp be his name,
His sone eek Phelipp ca*m* with hym also,
Myn auct*ou*r Boch*as* reherseth eek the same,
The fadir, the sone baptised bothe too,
Riht sad & wis in what thei hadde to doo,
And wer the firste Cristene of echon
Emper*ou*rs reknid; for ther toforn was no*n*.

Next in order came Philip and his son of the same name. They were the first Christian emperors.

Be Poncivs the martir, as I reede, [p. 369]
In Nicea, a famous gret cite,
Thei wer baptised, and aftir that in deede
Slay*n* in bataille, for thei list nat flee.
Tofor ther deth, both of assent, parde,
Ther treso*ur*s hool, that wer imperiall,
To Cristis cherch, I fynde, thei gaff it all.

Pontius the Martyr baptised them, and both were slain in battle because they would not flee. They gave all their wealth to the church,

344. eek] *om.* R, J.
349. Purpien H. 350. al] *om.* R, J.
357. foon] son*ne* R.
360. the feeld he] he this werr*e* H.
364. tresou*n*] resou*n* R. 369. sad] witty H — what] that J, P — to doo] a doo H.

and Bishop Sixtus assigned St. Laurence to distribute it among the poor. St. Laurence was afterwards martyred by the tyrant Decius, who

The bisshop Sixtus took pocessiou*n*,
Vertuousli assigned it to Laurence
Therof* to make distribuciou*n*
To poore folk in ther indigence;
For which[e] deede be cruel violence
The tirau*n*t Decius ageyn hym* took a striff,
Made hooli Laurence be bren[n]y*n*g lese his lyf.

also caused the two Philips to be slain and by his falsehood and deceit became emperor.

This same Decius, cursid & cruell,
Caused the slauhtre of thes Philippis tweyne;
And for he was sotil, fals & fell,
Be sleihte and falsheed he dide his besi peyne
To thempire be force for to atteyne,
The seuente tirau*n*t be persecuciou*n*
Which ageyn Cristene took first occasiou*n*.

During his time St. Anthony lived on fruit and roots in the desert.

Myn aucto*u*r writ, tyme of this Decivs,
The hooli hermyte, exau*m*ple of parfitnesse,
Be daies olde callid Antonivs,
Lyued in desert ferr out in wildirnesse,
As an hermyte despisyng al richesse, —
Lyued be frut & rootis, as men tell,
And of perfecciou*n* drank watir of þe well.

In punishment of Decius' cursedness God sent a terrible pestilence to Italy.

Vpon Decius for his cursidnesse,
Agey*n* Cristene which gaf so hard sentence,
Thoruh Roome and Itaille, my*n* aucto*u*r berþ witnesse,
In eueri cite was so gret pestilence,
That be the sodeyn dedli violence,
The hertis of me*n*, depe*n*dyng in a trau*n*ce,
To saue ther lyues coude no cheuisau*n*ce.

I will write no more about him. Gallus and Volusian reigned but two years each;

Of this mateer write no mor I can;
To this empero*u*r I nil* resorte agey*n*.
¶ Speke of Gallus and Volusian,
That besi wern, ther labo*u*r was i*n* vey*n*,
Ther tyme but short, as sum*m*e bookis sey*n*;
For Marty*n* writ, an old[e] cronicleer,
In thempire thei regned but too yeer.

381. Therof] Ther for B — a destribuciou*n* H.
384. hym] hem, B, J, R.
385. brennyng] brotling P.
387. thes] þe H.
408. nil] wil B, R, J, H, R 3, H 5, P. 412. cronyculeer R.
413. too] oon R.

Bothe wer slay[e]*n* bi the procuryng
And bi the purchace of oon Emylia*n*,
A Romey*n* kniht, [the] which be slih werky*n*g
To occupie thempire tho began.
Be tiran*n*ye the lordshipe ther he wan,
Whos lordship, for lak of happ & grace,
No lenger laste tha*n* too monethes space.

for both were slain at the instigation of a knight named Æmilian, who himself was emperor only two months.

This litil chapitle, as toforn is seene,
Rehersid hath & toold in woordis pley*n*
Of emperou*r*[e]s almost ful fourteene;
And of alle wer good[e] non but tweyne.
Which to reherse I haue do my peyne,
And to proceede ferther, as I gan,
I mvt now write of oon Valerian.

This little chapter has told of fourteen emperors, of whom but two were good.

HIS sone and he, callid Gallien,
To al Cristene bar gret enmyte,*
Slouh all tho, ther lege*n*de me*n* may seen,
That seruede Crist in trouthe & equite.
Whos persecuciou*n* & hatful cruelte
Abatid was, as I can weel reherse,
Bi oon Sapor that was kyng of Perse.

Valerian and his son Gallien were enemies of the Christians; but Valerian's cruelty was abated by Sapor, king of Persia,

Bi force of armys Sapor, this myhti ky*n*g,
Gan in Asia, & with his host ca*m* dou*n*
Be Tigre, Eufrates, &, knihtli so ridy*n*g
Toward the parties of Septemptriou*n*,
To Kaukasus nat ferr, fro Babilou*n*;
And al Surrye he proudli did assaille,
And Capadoce he wan eek be bataille.

who, riding north from the Tigris and Euphrates, attacked Syria and the Caucasus.

Whom for to meete ca*m* dou*n* Valerian
To Mesopotay*n* with many legiou*n*s.
The werre was strong; but this knihtli ma*n*,
This hardi Sapor, with his cha*m*piou*n*s
The feeld hath won*n*e wit*h* al the regiou*n*s
Affor rehersid; & thoruh Perse he ladde
Valerian bou*n*de with che[y]nys rou*n*d & sadde.

Valerian came down to meet him and was defeated and led to Persia in chains,

He was be Sapor, maugre his visage,
This Valeria*n*, so streihtli brouht to wrak,
Lik a p*r*isoneer bou*n*de to this s*er*uage
Be obeissau*n*ce, that fou*n*de wer no lak,

where he suffered the indignity of having to kneel down and let Sapor step on his back

416. the] *om.* R, J, P, R 3, H 5. 419. happ] helpe H.
420. moneth H. 429. ennyte B. 430. legendis H, R 3.
437. Tigre] Tire H. 439. To] So H. 447. Perse] *om.* R.
451. this] his H, R.

To knele on foure & to profre his bak
Vnto Sapor wha*n* hy*m* list to ride,
Therbi to mou*n*te, for al his gret[e] p*r*ide.

whenever he wanted to mount his horse.

This was thoffise of Valerian, [p. 370]
Be seruytute duryng many [a] yeer;
Wherfor he was callid of many ma*n*
Thassendyng stok into the sadil neer,
Which is in Frensh callid a mou*n*tweer.
This was his offis, to bowe dou*n* his corps
Wha*n* that kyng Sapor sholde worþe upo*n* his hors.

This is Fortune's way with princes and kings; what happens her wheel only knows.

This is the guerdou*n* & fauou*r* of Fortune,
Hir olde maneer to p*r*incis & to ky*n*gis,
Hir double custum vsid in comune
Be sodey*n* chau*n*g[e] of al worldli thy*n*ges.
Aftir tryu*m*phes and ther uprisi*n*ges,
What folwith aftir, hir wheel [weel] telle ca*n*,
I take record of Valeryan:

She shewed herself fickle to Valerian and favourable to Sapor. Yet he was too cruelly vengeable to soil the back of an emperor with his feet!

This ladi Fortune, þe blynde fell goddesse,
To Valerian shewed hirsilf vnstable,
Tauhte hym a lessou*n* of hir doubilnesse;
To kyng Sapor she was fauourable.
But yit he was to cruelli vengable,
With his feet, deuoid of al fauou*r*,
To soille the bak of an emperou*r*.

Princes should remember this and be merciful to their prisoners.

Of olde it hath be songe & cried loude, —
Record on Cirus & many othir mo, —
Kynges of Perse of custum ha[ue] be proude,
Aftir punshid an[d] chastised eek also.
P*r*incis of merci sholde tak heed herto,
Aftir victorie in ther estat notable
To ther p*r*isoneres for to be merciable.

Bochas, who knows how to rebuke tyrants, says to Valerian, "Where are your rubies and sapphires and rich pearls?

My*n* auctou*r* Boch*as* in this mateer weel* ca*n*
Rebuke tirau*n*t*es*, that wer be daies olde;
Turneth his stile, speketh to Valerian:
"Wher be the rubies & saphirs set i*n* golde,
The riche perle & rynges manyfolde

457. a] *om.* R, H, R 3. 458. many a H, J.
460. mounteer H, mountver R 3.
463. fauou*r* & guerdon R.
468. weel] *om.* R — here wele telle I can J.
478. on] of H, R 3. 481. herto] eek hereto R.
484. weel] weel tell B, R, J — *only the* n *in* can *is written* R.
485. wer] *om.* H. 487. the] thy H. 488. The] þi H.

That thou were wont [to] were upon thyn hondis?
Now as a wrech art bounde in foreyn bondis.

Wher thou wer wont of furious cruelte,
Clad in purple withynne Roome toun,
To Crist contrayre in thyn imperial see,
Yaff doom on martirs to suffre passioun,—
Now listow bounde [&] fetrid in prisoun,
To kyng Sapor constreyned to enclyne,
Whan he list ride, bowe nek & chyne.

"You, who were clad in purple and gave judgment on the martyrs in Rome, can now bend your back to King Sapor when he wishes to ride.

Thus artow falle from thyn imperial stage!
Think on Fortune and haue hir in memorie:
She hath the cast in thraldam & seruage
And eclipsed al thyn olde* glorie.
Wher thou sat whilom in the consistorie
As an emperour & a myhti iuge,
List bounde in cheynys and knowest no* refuge.

"Thus you are fallen; think on Fortune, who has cast you into thralldom without remedy.

¶ It is ful ferr fall out of thi mynde
The knihtli deede of worthi Publius,
Of Roome a capteyn, ordeyned, as I fynde,
To fihte ageyn[es] Aristomochus,
Kyng of Asie; of fortune it fill thus:
Whan the Romeyns dide the feeld forsake,
This Publius among his foon was take.

"You have forgotten the example of worthy Publius, who, taken by his enemies in Asia,

This noble prince stondyng in dreedful caas,
His lyf, his worshep dependyng atwen tweyne,
In his hond holdyng a sturdi maas,
Smet out oon of his eyen tweyne
Of hym that ladde hym; the tothir for þe peyne
That he felte and the gret[e] smerte
Took a dagger, rooff Publius to the herte.

and, preferring death to servitude, smote out an eye of the soldier who led him, and he, mad with pain, struck Publius to the heart with a dagger.

Which loued more his worshep than his lyff,
Ches rather deie than lyuen in seruage;
This conceit hadde in his imagynatyff,
And considred, sith he was in age,
To saue his honour it was moor auauntage
So to be slayn, his worshep to conserue,
Than lich a beeste in prisoun for to sterue.

"Publius loved his honour more than his life and did not care to die like an animal in captivity.

489. to] *om.* H, R, R 3, H 5.
494. Yaff] yeve H — martirs] mateers R. 501. olde] eld B.
504. no] *non* B. 508. Aristomachus R, H, Aristonichus P.
515. his] the P.

"As Valerius says, rather than languish in prison a man had better choose to starve to death.

Fortunis chapitle of hy*m* ne* was nat rad;
Of which Valerius maketh mencioun,
Aftir whos co*n*ceit, no ma*n* in vertu sad
Sholde nat longe langwissh in p*r*isou*n*,
But rather cheese, lik his oppynyou*n*,
Of ma*n*li force & knihtli excellence
The deth endure of long abstynence,

as Agrippina did, so that she lay pale and prostrate, in spite of Tiberius, and thus ended.

¶ As whilom dide the p*r*incesse Aggripyne,
Wha*n* she in prisou*n* lay fetrid and Ibou*n*de;
Of hir fre chois she felte so gret pyne
Of hu*n*gir, thrust, in stori it is fou*n*de,
That she lay pale & gruff upon the grou*n*de,
Maugre Tiberye, & leet hir gost so weende
Out of hir bodi; this was hir fatal eende.

"But as for you, Valerian, who with cruel heart made many a Christian die, no such thought ever entered your mind.

Thou stood ferr of of al such fantasie, [p. 371]
I speke to the, o thou Valeryan!
Thi cruel herte of fals malencolie
Made whilom deie many Cristen ma*n*;
And [many] martir, sith Cristis feith bega*n*,
Which for ma*n*kynde starff upon the rood, —
Thei for taquite hy*m* list to sheede her blood.

"You were friendly enough to the Egyptians and their Isis.

Ageyn his lawe thou wer impacient
And importune be persecuciou*n*;
Thou dist fauoure & suffre in thy*n* ente*n*t
That Egipciens dide ther oblaciou*n*,
Ther sacrefises & rihtes up-so-dou*n*
Vnto Isis, of froward wilfulnesse,
That was of Egipt callid cheef goddesse.

and to the Jews and Chaldæans and Cretans; but you killed the Christians and died yourself in prison like a wretch."

Fauourable thou wer in thi desir
To suffre Iewes ther Sabat to obserue,
And Caldeis to worshepe[n] the fyr,
And folk of Crete Saturn for to serue.
And Cristene men thou madist falsli sterue,
Of whos lawe for thou dist nat rechche,
Thou dei[d]est in prisou*n* at myscheef lik* a wrech-
che."

526. ne] it B, R, J, P.
538. gost] breth H. 529. 1st hir] þe H.
542. of] and R, H, R 3, H 5. 546. to] forto R.
547. his] this H — inpacient R. 549. & suffre] suffrid H.
556. to] for to H, R 3.
560. deidest] diest R, deyest H 5, died J, P — lik] as B, R, R 3, H 5.

[How Gallien sone of valerian was slayn] [1]

NEXT in ordr*e* to Boch*as* tho cam dou*n*
Sone of Valerian, oon callid Gallien.
But for the gr*e*te horrible effusiou*n*
Of Cristen blood[e], that me*n* myhte seen
Shadde be Valerian, God wolde it sholde been
Shewed openli to Romey*n*s be vengau*n*ce
Of many a contre sodeyn disobeissau*n*ce.

The reign of Gallienus was disturbed by rebellions, in punishment for the effusion of Christian blood shed by his father Valerian.

Thei of Almeyne the Alpies dide passe
Vnto Rauen*n*e, a cite of Itaille;
Gothis also, proud of cheer & face,
Hadde ageyn Grekis many gret bataille;
And thei of Hungry, armyd in plate & maille,
W*ith* them of Denmark, furious & cruell,
Ageyn Romey*n*s wex of assent rebell.

The Germans came to Ravenna, and the Goths and Danes revolted.

To whos damage in this mene while
Among Romey*n*s it is befalle thus:
Woful werris which called been civile
Gan in the cite, cruel and despitous.
First whan thei mette was slay[e]*n* Gemyvs,
Which first took on hym, in bookis as I reede,
Of hih corage to were purpil weede.

In Rome there were cruel civil wars;

Oon Postumyvs, a myhti stro*n*g Romey*n*,
Kept al Gaule vndir subiecciou*n*;
To ther auail vnwarli aftir slay*n*
Amo*n*g his kniht*es*, for al his hih renou*n*,
Be a sodeyn vnkouth discenciou*n*.
Next Victoryn, hauyng the gou*er*nau*n*ce
Of al Gaule, was aftir slayn i*n* Frau*n*ce.

and Posthumus, who defeated the Franks in Gaul, was slain by his knights. Victorian was slain in France,

But Gallien, of whom I spak toforn,
Sone and heir to Valerian,
His domynaciou*n* off purpos he hath lorn,
In *Republica* [anoon] wha*n* he began,
Lich a contrarious & a froward ma*n*
Wex lecherous and vicious of lyuy*n*g,
At myscheeff slay[e]n; this was his eendy*n*g.

and Gallien, who lost his authority by evil living, died at mischief.

564. myhte] may H.
576. it is befalle] it befill H. 577. The wofull H.
585. hih] gret H, R. 592. anoon] *om.* R, J, H 5.

[1] MS. J. leaf 152 verso.

[How Quyntylyus was moordred by women.] [1]

Quintilius, brother of Claudius, was murdered by women. I do not know why.

¶ Next Gallien ca*m* oon Quyntilius,
A man reme*m*bred of gret attemp[e]rau*n*ce,
Brother of berthe to gret[e] Claudius,
Wis & discreet in all his gouernau*n*ce.
Who may of Fortune eschewe the [sodeyn] chau*n*ce?—
To write his eende shortly in a clause,
Of women moordred; I can*n*at sey*n* the cause.

[Off Aurelian in Denmark born.] [2]

Aurelian, born in Denmark, began a great war against the Goths. His labour was for the profit of Rome.

¶ Of Denmark born next ca*m* Aurelian,
A worthi kniht his enmyes for tassaille.
Agey*n* Gothes a gret werre he began,
Gat victorie in many stro*n*g bataile,
Whos noble co*n*quest gretli did auaille
To comou*n* proffit; for al his werk, parde,
Was to thencres of Roome the cite.

He recovered all the North and asked for the triumph; but one thing, his enmity to Christ, eclipsed his glory.

He recurid al Septemptrion,
And westward had many gret victorie.*
Amo*n*g othir, I fynde [that] he was oon
Axed the tryu*m*phe to be put in memorie.
But ther was o thi*n*g* eclipsed al his glorie,
Which hath the liht of his knihthod wit*h*drawe,
For he was enmy to Crist & to his lawe.

Tacitus and Florianus followed. I can find nothing noteworthy about either of them.

Of whom Boch*as* list no mor now write,
But in his book goth foorth as he bega*n*,
¶ Of oon reme*m*bry*n*g þ*at* callid was Tacite,
Which was success*our* to Aurelyan;
¶ And aftir hym succeded Floryan,
Of which[e] tweyne no reme*m*brau*n*ce I fy*n*de
That is notable to be put in my*n*de.

[How Probus disconfited Romayns and aftir was slayn.] [3]

Probus reigned more than seven years. He defeated Saturninus

Probus aftir regned ful seuene yeer [p. 372]
And foure moneth, which thoruh his hih renou*n*
Gey*n* Saturnynvs, with a [ful] knihtli cheer,

611. victorite B.
612. & among H, And among R 3 — that] *om.* R, J, H 5.
614. o thing] athi*n*g B. 619. was callid H.
626. Saturnynus] Seatour*ns* H, senatours R 3 — ful] *om.* J, P.

[1] MS. J. leaf 152 verso. [2] MS. J. leaf 152 verso.
[3] MS. J. leaf 152 verso.

And brouht hym proudli to subieccio*u*n;
Natwithstondyng that he in Roome tou*n*
Took upon hym of wilful tiran*n*ye
Hooli thempire he for to reule & guie.

and slew Proculus and Bonosus in battle.

Beside the cite callid Agripyne
This seid[e] Probus gey*n* many proud Romey*n*
A bataille hadde, list[e] nat declyne,
Mette Proculus, a myhti stro*n*g captey*n*,
Wit*h* oon Bonosus; & bothe ther wer slayn,
And al ther meyne of verray force & myht
Slay*n* in the feeld; the re*m*nau*n*t put to fliht.

Finally he was himself slain in a tower at Sirmium; let no man trust Fortune.

Aftir this bataille & this disconfiture
Probus was loggid in Smyrme, a gr*e*t cite,
And ther vnwarli of sodeyn auenture
Slay*n* in a to*u*r that callid was Ferre.
But a smal sesou*n* last his prosp*er*ite:
Swich is Fortune; lat no ma*n* in hir truste;
Al wordli thynges she chau*n*geth as she liste!

[How Clarus and his ij. sones were myscheuyd.] [1]

Clarus and his two sons, Numerian and Carinus, next came before Bochas. Born of a noble line in Narbonne, he took Seleucia and Ctesiphon,

¶ Tofor Boch*as* Clarus next ca*m* dou*n*
Wit*h* his too sonys, Numerian & Caryne.
And, as I fynde, he was born in Narbon
And descendid of a noble lyne.
But whan that he most cleerli dide shyne
In his empire, he gat cites tweyne,
Chose & Thelifou*n*t, in Partois wit*h* gret peyne.

but was killed by lightning at the Tigris, and Numerian was blinded.

Beside Tigre, a famous swift ryueer,
He pihte his tentis, & cast hym þ*er* tabide.
A sodeyn lihtny*n*g his face ca*m* so neer,
Smet al to pouder, for al his gret[e] p*r*ide;
And Numerian that stood be his side
Hadde a mark[e] that was sent fro*m* heuene:
Loste bothe his eyen wit*h* the fyry leu[en]e.

639. Smyrne J, Smyryn R 3, Sirmine P — a gr*e*t] þe H.
643. Swich is Fortune] *om.* H — hir] hir curtesye H.
644. as she liste] at hir lust H, as hir list R 3.
645. Carus P. 647. Nabourn*e* H.
651. Choce H — Tholifau*n*t H, Ctesiphon P — Parroys J.
652. Tibre H.
658. wit*h* the] eke wit*h* H, R 3, P — fire R.

[1] MS. J. leaf 152 verso.

Carinus ruled unjustly in Dalmatia and was cast down for his vicious life.

His othir sone Carynus, a good kniht,
In Dalmacia hadde al the gouer*n*au*n*ce;
But* for that he gouerned nat ariht,
He was cast dou*n* & lost al his puissau*n*ce:
Vicious lyff kometh alwey to myschau*n*ce.
Sepcivs chose Dalmacia for to guye,
Amo*n*g his knihtis moordrid of envie.

[How the hardy quene Zenobia fauȝt *with* Aurelian and was take.] [1]

My author now turns to Zenobia; but as Chaucer has already told her story, I will rehearse only its outlines.

MY*N* aucto*u*r heer no lenger list s[o]io*u*rne
Of these empero*u*rs the fallis for to write,
But i*n* al haste he doth his stile to*u*rne
To Zenobia hir stori for to endite.
But for Chauceer dide hym so weel aquite
In his tragedies hir pitous fall tentrete,
I will passe ouer, rehersyng but the grete.

He describes her life in his Book of Canterbury Tales.

In his book of Cau*n*tirbury Talis
This souerey*n* poete of Brutis Albiou*n*,
Thoruh pilgrymys told be hillis & be valis,
Wher of Zenobia is maad me*n*ciou*n*,
Of hir noblesse and of hir hih renou*n*,
In a tragedie co*m*pendiousli told all,
Hir marcial prowesse & hir pitous fall.

She was born of the stock of worthy Ptolemy

Myn aucto*u*r first affermeth how that she
Descendid was, to telle of hir lynage,
Born of the stok of worthi Tholome
Kyng of Egipt, ful notable in that age.
And this Zenobia, expert in al langage,
Wis of cou*n*sail & of gret prouidence,
Passed al othir in fame of elloque*n*ce.

and married Odenathus, King of Palmyra,

Among she was armyd in plate & maille,
Of Palmerencys* weddid to the kyng
Callid Odenatus, prudent in bataille
She was also, be record of writyng,
Hardi, strong, hir lordship defendy*n*g,

661. But] And B, J, P.
667. for] *om.* H. 669. hir] his R, J.
670. so wele did hym quyte H, R 3. 679. p*r*owessis H.
688. Palmerenoys B, Palmerencys J, Palmyrences P, Palmynerois R, H.

MS. J. leaf 153 recto.

Maugre all tho, with hir cheualrie,
Agey*n*[e]s hire that wrongli took partie.

Be Odenatus she hadde sonis tweyne,
Heremanvs callid was the ton,
And Thymolaus, of beute souereyne.
Aftir whos berthe ther fadir ga*n* anon
To occupie the p*ro*uynces euerichon
Of Perse and Mede; bi processe made he*m* fleen,
Of Zenobia, the hardi wise queen.

by whom she had two sons. After they were born their father occupied Persia and Media,

Whil Odenatus wex most glorious
In his conquest thoruhout Perse & Meede,
Slayn he was be oon Meonyus,
Which to the kyng was cosyn, as I reede;
But for because of this horrible deede
And for the moordre of kyng Odenate,
Deide at myscheeff & passed into fate.

and soon afterwards was slain by his cousin Maconius, who was executed for his crime.

Be processe aftir, Zenobia the queen [p. 373]
Took hir too sonis and proudli did he*m* leede
Tofor hir chaar[e], that men myhte he*m* seen,
How thei wer born as p*r*incis to succeede.
Made hem lik kynges be clad in p*ur*pil weede;
Them to diffende this myhti creature,
Hardi as leou*n*, took on hir hir armure.

Zenobia dressed her sons in purple and shewed them to the people as their future princes,

For al hir lordis & knihtis she hath sent,
Maugre the Romeyns proudli ga*n* hir speede,
Al the parties of the orient*
To occupie & hir host to leede.
Of themperour she stood nothi*n*g in dreede,
Callid Aurelian, mette hy*m* in bataille,
With hir meyne hym proudli did assaille.

and in defiance of the Romans continued her husband's conquests in the East,

On outher side that day gret blood was shad;
The strook of Fortune withstant no cr*e*ature:
The queen Zenobia was taken & forth lad;
Fauht first as longe as she myht endure;
With riche stonis frett was hir armvre,
Wi*th* who*m* themperou*r*, so entry*n*g Roome tou*n*,
Of tryu*m*phe requery*n*g the guerdou*n*.

but was defeated in battle and taken prisoner by Aurelian

He dempte it was couenable & sitty*n*g,
This emperou*r*, this proude Aurelian,

695. Herennian P. 696. Timolaus P. 707. &] *om.* H.
709. hir] his R. 715. al] *om.* R. 717. thorient B.

and led in his triumph.

Taxe the tryu*m*phe; it was so gr*e*t a thy*n*g
To take Zenobia [that] such a werr*e* gan
Ageyn* Romey*n*s, this marcial woma*n*.
For I suppose of no woma*n* born
Was neuer queen so hardi sey*n* afforn.

She was brought to Rome in golden fetters, plunged down from her high estate into poverty.

This hardi p*r*incesse, for al hir roialte,*
Whos hih renou*n* thoruh al the world was knowe,
W*ith* stokkis of gold was brouht to the cite,
From hih estat in pouert plongid lowe.
A wynde co*n*trarye of Fortune hath so blowe,
That she, alas, hath pitousli made fall
Hir that in prowesse passed wome*n* all.

Diocletian, who next appeared, was a gardener in his youth.

THE triu*m*phe youe [un]to Aurelian
For þe conquest he hadde upon þis quee*n*
Callid Zenobia, ca*m* Dioclesian,*
Born in Dalmacia, his stori who list seen.
Out of his contre first he dide fleen,
Of garlec lekis, as seith the cronycleer,
Because that he was but a gardener.

Later on he became a soldier and was chosen emperor.

Other menciou*n* is non of his lynage.
Of his berthe forsook the regiou*n*,
Lefft his craff[t] of deluyng and cortilage,
Gaff hym to armys, & be elecciou*n*
Chose to been empero*ur* & regne i*n* Roome tou*n*.
First into Gaule he sente a gret poweer,
And Maxymyan he made ther his vikeer.

He made Maximian his general in Gaul, but the people were rebellious until chastised by Carausius,

His viker ther hadde many gret bataille
Vpo*n* swich peeple that be rebelliou*n*
Gan frowardli co*n*trarye & assaille
Tobeye his lordship withyn*ne* that regiou*n*,
Til Cara*n*synus be co*m*myssiou*n*,
An hardi kniht vndir Maxymyan,
Them to chastise took on hym lik a ma*n*.

who did great damage there to the common weal by robbing the country.

But be processe, the stori doth deuise,
His lordship ther dide gret damage
To comou*n* proffit; for he be couetise

732. that] *om.* R. 733. Ageyn] Geyn B, R, J.
735. beforn R. 736. roialte] cruelte B, J.
739. ploun*g*yng R. 742. that] state R.
745. Deoclesian B. 748. cronyculeer R.
755. into] in H. 760. that] *om.* H, R 3.
761. Carasius P. 766. To] To the R.

The co*n*tre robbed be ful gret outrage,
And to hymsilff he took al the pillage,
And of presu*m*pciou*n* wered the colo*u*r
Of riche purpil lik an empero*u*r.

This Karansynvs of Breteynys tweyne,
Proudli vsurped to be ther gouerno*u*r,
Lik a rebel geyn Roome dide his peyne
And besied hym be marcial labo*u*r,
With many a strau*n*ge forey*n* soudio*u*r;
Hauyng no title nor co*m*myssiou*n*,
Contynued longe in his rebelliou*n*.

He usurped the title of governor and rebelled against Rome,

Wherof astonyd was Dioclesian;
Seyng this myscheef dreedful & pereilous,
Ordeyned in haste that Maxymyan
Was surnamyd & callid Herculius;
Made hym empero*u*r, namyd [hym] Augustus,
Which hadde afforn[e] no mor gou*er*nau*n*ce
But of Gaule, which now is callid F*r*ance.

whereupon Diocletian invested Maximian with the titles Augustus and Herculius and made him co-emperor.

Also mor-ouer this Dioclesian
Made in this while gou*er*no*u*r[e]s tweyne,
Constancius & oon Maxymyan
Surnamyd Galerius. Co*n*sta*n*cius i*n* certeyne,
In this while to wedde dide his peyne
Douhtir of Maxymyan callid Herculius,
Named Theodora, my*n* aucto*u*r writeth thus.

He also appointed Constantius and Galerius governors; and Constantius married Maximian's daughter Theodora,

Be Theodora this Constancius [p. 374]
Hadde sexe childre in trewe mariage,
Brethre to Constanty*n*, the story* tellith þ*us*,
Which aftirward, whan he ca*m* to age,
For his ma*n*hod and marcial corage,
Was chose & maad[e] lord & gouerno*u*r
Of al the world, and crownid empero*u*r.

by whom he had six children, brothers of Constantine, who afterwards became the great emperor.

Caransynvs, which hadde ful seuene yeer,
Lich as I tolde, rebellid in Breteyne
Ageyn the Romey*n*s, a gret extorsioneer, —

768, 69 *are transposed* H. 773. ageyn H.
776. nor] non R.
779] Made in this while gouernours tweyne R.
780] Constancius and oon Maxymyan R.
782. namyd] callid H — hym] *om.* R, J, H 5, P.
784. of] al H. 785. R *omits this stanza.*
794. story] cronicle B, R, J, P — the cronycler seith thus R 3.
799. Carasynus H, R 3, Caramsynus J, Carasius P.

Carausius was murdered by Alectus, who occupied his place three years.

A kniht Alletus that dede at hym disdeyne
Moordrid hym, & aftir ded his peyne
Be force onli and extort tiran*n*ye
Fulli thre yeer his place to occupie.

until slain by Asclepiodatus, who in turn brought all Britain again to subjection.

Til Asclepio was sent fro Roome dou*n*,
Slouh this Alletus, maugre al his myht,
Brouht al Breteyne to subieccciou*n*
Of the Romeyns, lik as it was riht.
And in this while, lik a ma*n*li kniht—
For Italliens ga*n* Romey*n*s disobeye —
Constancius ga*n* proudli hem werreie.

Constantius fought the rebellious Italians and after an early defeat was successful.

He firste with hem had a strong bataille,
His meyne slayn & he put to the fliht.
Trusty*n*g on Fortune, he ga*n* hem eft assaille,
And sexti thousand wer slay[e]n in þ*at* fiht;
The feeld was his thoruh Fortunis myht,
As she that koude dissymule for a while,
And aftirward falsli hy*m* begile.

Diocletian took Alexandria and allowed his soldiers to pillage the city.

I will passe ouer as breeffli as I ca*n*,
Set aside al foreyn incidentis,
Resorte ageyn to Dioclesian,
Which at Alisau*n*dre proudli pihte his te*n*t*es*,
The capteyn slouh, gaff in comau*n*deme*n*t*es*
To his knihtis to do ther auau*n*tage
Wit*h*yn*n*e the cite be robbyng & pillage.

He then began to persecute the Christians in Italy, and was helped by Maximian, by whose sword many a martyr was slain:

Gan agey*n* Cristene gret persecuciou*n*,
Vsed his tiran*n*ye in the orient;*
Bi his biddyng Maxymya*n* ca*m* dou*n*
Toward the parties of the occident.
Bothe these tirau*n*tis wrouhte be assent,
Vndir whos swerd many [a] martire deies,
Slay*n* in Octodoru*n* the legeou*n* of Thebeies.

the Thebæan Legion at Octoduram, St. Alban and Pope Marcellus. Churches were burnt and cities lost their franchises.

At Verolamye, a famous old cite,
Seynt Albon slay*n*; his lege*n*de doth so telle.
And in Roome be furious cruelte
The pope slay*n*, which callid was Marcelle.
Be ther statutis & be ther doomys felle

802. Alectus P. 814. the] *om.* R. 818. As] And R.
823. at] that R. 828. thorient B. 832. a] *om.* B, R, J.
833. in] at H — Octodorn H, R — legeou*n*] region P, Religion R.
835. Albon] abbon R — his] þe H.

Cherchēs wer brent, & tounes* & citees
Loste ther franchise & al ther libertees.

Froward enmy he was to Cristis lawe,
Made many a martir deie for his sake,
Wex feeble & old & gan hym [to] withdrawe
From occupacioun, his reste for to take;
His atturne Maxymyan he doth make.
In his laste age, it is rehersid thus,
Stood in gret dreed[e] of Constancivs,—

When Diocletian grew old and feeble he abdicated in favour of Maximian.

The dreed[e] of hym sat so nih his herte,—
And therupon took swich a fantasie,
Imagynyng he myht[e] nat asterte,
Be fraude of hym but that he sholde deie.
Almost for feer fill in a frenesie,
And of swich dreed, the book makth mencioun,
He slouh hymsilff be drynkyng of poisoun.

During his last days he stood in such dread of Constantius that he fell into a frenzy and slew himself by poison.

¶ As I told erst, in the occident
Maxymyan, callid Herculius,
Regned as emperour; & euere in his entent
To pursue martirs he did ay his labours.
Of whos berthe Bochas fond non auctours;
This to seyne, he coude neuer reede
Wher he was bor[e]n, nor of what kynreede.

Maximian reigned in the west and continued to martyr Christians;

He fynt no mor of this Maxymyan,
Of his uprisyng in especiall,
But that he was bi Dioclesian
Set in dignite callid imperial,
Famous in armys, prudent & marciall,
Daunted all tho that dide ageyn hym stryue,
Slouh Geneyans callid, in noumbre fyue.

and Bochas knows no more about him than that he was a great soldier and that Diocletian made him emperor.

Rood in Affrik lik a conquerour,
Brouht to subieccioun thre sturdi naciouns —
Fortune that tyme did hym such fauour —
Gat Sarmatois with othir regiouns,
Many cites & many riche touns
Bi his conquest of newe that he hath wonne;
Thoruh the world his name shon lik a sunne.

He conquered Africa, Sarmatia, and many other regions, and his name shone throughout the world like a sun.

839. & tounes] in touns B, R, in townes J.
841. he was] *om.* R. 843. to] *om.* R, H 5, P.
851. but] *om.* H. 852. a] *om.* R. 858. labour H.
859. auctour H.
868. Genciauns H, gencians R 3, Genciens H 5, Giauntes P.
872. Sarmacia P. 873. cite H.

Yet Diocletian advised him to resign his dignity,

He was cherisshed in armys fro*m* his youthe, [p. 375]
Dide gret emprises for* Roome the cite;
Yit Dioclesian, as it is weel kouthe,
Cou*n*sailled hym resigne his dignite.
But he was loth to forsake his see,
Sith he was lord & gou*er*ned all,
For to renou*n*ce his stat imperiall.

and finally he did; but afterwards repenting sought to recover his throne.

But be assent of Dioclesian,
As he hymsilff had left al gou*er*nau*n*ce,
So eeuene lik this Maxymyan
Dischargid hymsilf of his roial puissau*n*ce.
But aftirward he fill in repentau*n*ce
And besi was, as dyuers bookis seyn,
Thestat of emperou*r* to recure ageyn,

In this he was opposed by Galerius, for his son Maxentius had already been declared emperor,

Which for to acheue he dede his dilligence.
He was distourbid be Galerius,
For his sone, that callid was Maxence,
Put in pocessiou*n*, my*n* auctou*r* writeth þ*us*;
To which[e] thy*n*g he ga*n* wex envious
And ga*n* ordeyne menys in his thouht
To trouble hym; but it auailled nouht.

and when he found that he could not succeed in his design, and his daughter Fausta had betrayed his intentions, he fled to Gaul and was finally slain by Constantius at Marseilles.

Wha*n* his purpos myhte take no*n* auail
Agey*n* Maxence, as Bochas doth descryue,
His douhtir Fausta, þ*at* knew al his cou*n*sail,
Discurid his purpos; for which he fled[de] blyue
Into Gaule & durste no lenger stryue;
And bi Co[n]stancius in Marcile the cite
Slay*n* sodeynli, lost al his dignite.

[How Galeryus oppressid martirs & cristys feith and mischeuesly ended.] [1]

Next came Galerius, a froward vicious man of evil disposition. We do not know his descent, yet he was set high on the stage of worldly dignity.

NEXT tofor Boch*as* ca*m* Galerivs,
A ma*n* disposid to riot & out*r*age,
Euele entechchid, froward, vicio*us*.
Ther is no stori speketh of his lynage,
Yit was he set ful hih upon the stage
Of worldli dignite, roos up to hih estat;
Yit in his gyn[n]y*n*g he was nat fortunat.

877. for] forn B. 897. his] this R. 898. doth] did R.
899. al] *om.* H. 900. purpos] consail R.
905. disposed R.
906. tecchid J, teched P — froward] frowas R.

[1] MS. J. leaf 154 recto.

He was sent out bi Dioclisian,
And maad emperour bi his auctorite,
Ageyn Narseus, the proude knihtli man,
Regnyng in Perse & lord of that contre,
Which heeld[e] werre with Roome the cite, —
For which Galerius took on hym this emprise,
With mihti hand his pride to chastise.

Diocletian made him emperor and sent him out against Narses, king of Persia.

Galerius entred into Perse-lond;
Kyng Narseus mette hym of auenture;
Hadde a strong bataille, fauht þer hond of* hond;
On Galerius fill the discomfiture,
His fortune suich he myht[e] nat endure.
Clad in purpre, as maad is mencioun,
Of Dioclisian resceyued this guerdoun:

who defeated him.

At ther meetyng, anon or he was war,
Dioclisian made hym for tabide,
To his confusioun, sittyng in his chaar,
To walke on foote be the charis side.
With many rebuk abatid was his pride,
That Galerius for the gret[e] shame
Gan seeke a mene ageyn to gete his name.

When he next met Diocletian Diocletian rebuked him, and sitting in his chariot compelled him to walk on foot alongside, the shame of which impelled

Gan for tassemble his olde soudiours,
Made his ordenaunce be dilligent werking,
Ches out the beste preeuid werreyours;
With a gret host to Perse he cam ridyng
And efft ageyn fauht ther with the kyng,
That the Persiens, maugre al ther myht,
Wer be Galerius that day put to fliht.

him to set out again to Persia to recover his reputation. He fought Narses a second time, and defeating him won great plunder.

The feeld was his, gat ther gret richesse,
Robbed ther tentis, wan ther gret pillage.
In his resort resceyued in sothnesse
With* gret noblesse, because of that viage —
Thus can Fortune chaungen hir visage! —
Of Dioclisian, wher he stood in disdeyn,
With newe triumphe resortid is ageyn.

This cloudi queen stant euer in noun certeyn,
Whos double wheel quauereth euer in doute,
Of whos fauour no man hath be certeyn:

Thus Fortune can change her moods. She stands in uncertainty,

914. &] *om.* R. 920. of] for B, R, J, to P.
923. purpull H. 924. this] his R. 927. chaire H.
935. a gret] agre R — he] *om.* H, R 3.
942. With] In B, R, J, P, H 5. 947. wheel] quele H.

her wheel poised ever ready to turn.

Ther* oon hath grace, anoþ*er* is put oute.
Lat eu*er*yma*n* as it cometh aboute
Take his tourn & neuere i*n* hir assure;
Faillyng in armys is but an auentur*e*!

Afterwards Galerius governed Africa and Italy, but in his old age he persecuted Christ's faith.

Thus Galerius aftir his bataill
On Persiens ga*n* wexen glorious,
Gou*er*nid Affrik & lordshipp of Itaille,
Thoruh al* thorient wex victorious,
Til he for age gan wexen tedious,
His laste daies maligned, as me*n* seith,
Of fals hatreede ageyn[es] Cristis feith.

He set two vicars, Severus and Maxentius, in his empire to help him put down the law of Christ.

And hym to helpen in thes fals mateeris, [p. 376]
It is reme*m*brid to his confusiou*n*,
In his empire he sette too vikeris,
The lawe of Crist toppresse & put dou*n*.*
Gaff hem poweer in eu*er*y regiou*n*
To punshe martirs & putte he*m* to þe deþ;
And in this while ful many on he sleth.

Bi this saide cruel Galerivs,
Which of thempire had al the gou*er*nau*n*ce,
Of cursid herte & corage despitous,
Be his vsurpid imperial puissau*n*ce
Gaf auctorite for to do vengau*n*ce
Vnto tweyne, Seuerus & Maxe*n*ce,
On al Cristen bi mortal violence.

and chose Maxentius emperor, who subsequently quarrelled with Severus. Severus died of the plague at Ravenna.

A certey*n* space, bothe of oon accord,
Thestat of empero*u*r chose was Maxence,
Til Seuerus & he fill at discord.
Ano*n* aftir bi vengable pestilence,
*Withyn*n*e* a cite of notable premyne*n*ce
Callid Rauen*n*e, Seuerus ther was slay*n*,
Of which Galerius, God wot, was nothy*n*g fay*n*.

Galerius next chose Licinius, a Danish knight, to be emperor in opposition to Maxentius,

For which in haste this Galerivs,
Hy*m* to supporte & stonde in his defense,
Ches out of Denmark a kniht Licinius
To been emp*er*o*u*r, thoruh knihtli excellence
For to withstonde & fihte ageyn Maxe*n*ce.

949. Ther] Thei B, Thouh J, though P — is] may be H.
952. an] *om.* R.
956. al] at B.
963, 64 *are transposed in* B, J.
965. punysh H.
979. Rauenna R.

But Maxence, of Romey*n* knihtis all,
Was chose emperou*r* & set up in his stall.

With which eleccio*u*n Galleri*us* wex wood,
Fill in a maner froward frenesie,
His entrailles brent[e], corupt wex his blood,
And of his froward vengable malladie
In euery me*m*bre ga*n* rote & putrefie,
That al the hair aboute hym envirou*n*
To all that felte it was veny*m* & poisou*n*.

but the latter was confirmed in power by his soldiers, whereupon Galerius went mad; his blood became corrupt, his body rotted.

Lik a lazeer, coorbid bak & chyne,
In this while o*n* Cristen most ve*n*gable,
To hym auailed no man*er* medecyne.
But ther was oon in Cristes feith ful stabl*e*
That spak to* hy*m* wit*h* langage ful notabl*e*,
In* woordes fewe co*n*cludyng in s*u*bstau*n*ce,
"The grete Iub[i]ter hath take on the ve*n*gau*n*ce."

He was like a leper, but did not cease his persecutions; and one who was of Christ's faith said to him:

And ouermor, for short co*n*clusiou*n*,
With a bolde spirit to hy*m* began abraide:
"It is nat Iubiter worsheped in this tou*n*,
In the Capitoile set," sothli as he saide, —
"But Iubiter that was born of a maide,
Which wil nat suffre, of that thou dost endure,
That ony medicyne sholde the recure.

"The great Jupiter has taken vengeance on you. Not the Jupiter worshipped in this town and set in the Capitol, but the Jupiter who was born of a maid. He will suffer no medicine to cure you."

Lik a tirau*n*t be ve*n*gau*n*ce furious,
At myscheef deieth, as olde bookis telle,
Perpetueli wit*h* cruel Cerberus
Vpon the wheel of Ixion to duell." —
For his demerites wit*h* Tantalus in hell,
Ther to resceyue his fynal last guerdou*n*
Which coude on martirs haue no co*m*passiou*n*.

It was his ioye for to sheede her blood,
Sent out [his] lettres to dyuers regiou*n*s,
Lik a slih wolff, rauynous & wood,
To slen martirs be dyuers passiou*n*s.
Lik his desert resceyued his guerdou*n*s;
Horrible deth first dide hy*m* he*e*r confou*n*de,
Wit*h* Furies infernal lith now in hell[e] bou*n*de.

It was his joy to slay martyrs, and he received his reward with the Furies in hell.

990. wex] was H, J, P. 999. to] onto B, R, J.
1000. In] In his B, R, J, P, H 5.
1003. to hy*m* began] hy*m* he gan R.
1005. In] mydde H, Myd R 3 — he] I, J, P.
1022. Furies] furious R.

[How maxence the Emperour enmy to cristys feith myscheuesly ended.] [1]

After Galerius, the emperor Maxentius came with a piteous face before Bochas.

AFFTIR Galerius cruel violence
Gey*n* Cristene blood, as Boch*as* heer haþ told,
With pitous cheer themperou*r* Maxe*n*ce
Cam tofor Boch*as*, of age nat ful old,
Famous in armys, sturdi, fressh & bold,
Al-be he entrid nat as enherito*u*r,
Took upon hym to regne as emperour.*

He too was an enemy of Christ's faith; and he was suddenly slain and cast into the Tiber like a rotten dog.

To Cristes feith he was also enmy;
Aftir soone he loste his gou*er*nau*n*ce,
Of infortunye slay[e]*n* sodenly,—
God on tirau*n*t*es* vn-warly takith vengau*n*ce.
Of whos buryyng was maad no*n* ordenaunce,*
For he was nat resceyued of the grou*n*d,
But caste in Tibre lik a roten hou*n*de.

[How Lucynyus enmy to cristes feith was slayn.] [2]

Licinius, the Dane, who became emperor, had an enemy, Maximin, who was slain in Tarsus.

¶ Next tofor Boch*as* cam Lycynyvs,
A kniht of Denmark, born of riht good lyne,
Which had a*n* enmy, the book reherseth þ*us*,
An hardi kniht callyd Maxymyne,
Chose a capteyn *with* themperou*r* Consta*n*tyne;
To Cristes feith he bar gret enmyte,
Slayn ano*n* aftir in Tarce* the cite.

And Licinius persecuted the Christians and suddenly went mad. He allowed no Christian to abide in his house and began a war against Constantine, and, twice defeated,

Of whos deth Lycynyvs was glad, [p. 377]
Gan ageyn Cristene gret persecuciou*n*,
In his proceedyng sodenli wex mad.
Which comau*n*did of fals presu*m*pciou*n*
Wha*n* he bega*n* doon execuciou*n*,
That no Cristene nowher hy*m* beside
Bi no condiciou*n* sholde in his hous abide.

This Licynyvs, which falsli dide erre
Agey*n* our feith Cristen men tassaille,
Gey*n* Co*n*sta*n*tyn of newe he ga*n* a werre;

1029. emperour] gou*er*no*u*r B, J.
1034. ordenaunce] menciou*n* B.
1038. riht good of lyne R.
1043. Tarce] Trace B, J, R 3, R.
1052. Cristen] & Cristen H, R 3. 1053. began H.

[1] MS. J. leaf 154 verso. [2] MS. J. leaf 154 verso.

But of his purpos in sooth he dede faille:
For he was twies discou*n*fited in bataille
Be Consta*n*tyn; onys in Hungrye,
Next in Grece, beside Ebalie.

Thus Constanty*n* thoruh his hih renou*n*
Gat nih al Grece & eueri gret cite,*
Al-be Lycynyvs stood in rebelliou*n*
Geyn Constanty*n*, both on lond & se.
But wha*n* he sauh it wolde non oþ*er* be,
He myht[e] nat escapen in no place,
Put hool hymsilff in Consta*n*tynes g*r*ace.

finally submitted.

But Co*n*stantyn, for his rebelliou*n*,
Gaff iugement in haste that he be ded,
Lest in the cite wer maad dyuisiou*n*
Be Lycinyvs, wherof he stood in dreed.
This same while, as Bochas took [good] heed,
Ther ca*m* toforn hym, w*it*h cheeris ful pitous,
Brethre tweyne, Co*n*sta*n*tyn & Crispus.

But Constantine put him to death to keep the peace.

[Off Constantyne and Crispus & how Dalmacyus was slayn.] [1]

TO Co*n*stanty*n*, of who*m* I spak toforn,
Thei wer sonys, Consta*n*tyn & Crisp*us*.
The same tweyne, of o mooder born,
Cam tofor Boch*as*; his book reherseth thus.
With hem ca*m* eek oon Lycynyvs,
Sone to* Licynyus which in Roome tou*n*
Afforn was slayn for his rebelliou*n*.

Constantine had two sons, Constantine and Crispus,

Constanty*n* his werris to gouerne
Made hem vikeres, the silue same thre.
Echon riht wis, & koude weel discerne
What myhte auaille most to ther cite,
Tencrece the proffit of the comou*n*te.
Ther namys tolde, Constantyn & Crispus,
Tofor reme*m*brid, with hem Licynyvs.

whom, together with a son of Licinius, he made generals.

Whil these thre vikeris vndir the*m*perou*r*
Gouernid Roome, as knihtis riht* famo*us*,
In Alisau*n*dre roos up a gret errou*r*

They governed Rome at the time Arius,

1059. cite] contre B, J. 1069. good] om. R, J, P, H 5.
1077. to] of B. 1087. riht] most B.

[1] MS. J. leaf 155 recto.

a false priest, began his heresy and was excommunicated.

Bi a fals preest Icallid Arryus,
To our beleue a thyng contraryous.
And for he dide ageyn our feith so werche,
Bi a decre he was put out of cherche.

His error was shewn to be damnable by a council of 318 bishops at Nicæa.

Bi a scen at Bithynye ful notable,
In Nicea, a famous gret cite,
This errour was preuid ful dampnable:
Thre hundred* bisshopis wer present ther, parde,
And eihtene, the cronicle who list see.
And alle thes clerkis of o sentence ilik
Preeuyd Arryvs a fals[e] heretik.

During this time Constantine slew his three generals, in favour of his cousin Delmatius,

This same tyme, bookis specefie
How Constantyn of hasti cruelte,
The saide vikeres, nih of his allie,
Feyned a cause to slen hem all[e] thre.
No cause rehersid nor told of equite,
Saf onli this, in which he gan proceede,
To make his cosyn Dalmacivs to succeede.

who was shortly afterwards killed by his own soldiers.

But his fauour was nat fortunat
Toward Dalmacius, nor gracious in sentence,
Among whos knihtes fill a sodeyn debat,
Constantyn ther beyng in presence.
Dalmacius, withoute reuerence,
With sharpe suerdis, to speke in woordes fewe,
Vnto the deth was woundid & Ihewe.

[Off the brethre Constaunce & Constancyus & how Magnencyus & decyus moordred hem self.] [1]

Both Constans and Constantius, young brothers of Constantine, wanted to be emperor, and so they fought one another.

¶ Than cam Constans and Constancius,
Yonge brethre, thus writ myn auctour,
To Constantyn in tyme of Arryvs.
And ech of hem be ful gret labour
Dide his peyne to regne as emperour,
Til at the laste, breefli for to seie,
Euerich of hem gan othir to werreye.

Constans had nine battles with Sapor and finally overcame him.

This saide Constans is entrid Perse-lond;
Nyne tymes he fauht ageyn Sapore,
The same kyng, as ye shal vndirstond,

1092. he] *om.* H. 1093. a scen] a Sene R, a Sceno H, assent J, P, a scene R 3 — at] in H. 1094. Niceyne P.
1096. hundred] C. B. 1102. so nyh R.

[1] MS. J. leaf 155 recto.

That with Romeyns hadde fouht affore.
But fynalli Constans hath hy*m* so bore,
To holde the feelde he myhte nat endure;
For upon hym fill the disconfiture.

His fortune ga*n* to chau*n*gen ano*n* riht, [p. 378]
Wha*n* that he lefte to be vertuous;
He was in Spaigne slay[e]*n* be a kniht,
In Castel Tunge, callid Magnencius.
Than was non lefft but Constancivs;
The Romey*n* kni[h]tis, destitut echon,
Ches hem an empero*ur* callid Vetramon.

But when he ceased to be virtuous, his fortune changed: and he was slain in Spain by Magnentius and succeeded by Vetranio,

¶ This Vetramon was ferr [i]ron*ne* in age,
Barey*n* of witt, koude non lettrure,
Nor in knihthod had no gret corage,
Nor was nat hable to studien in scripture,
Nor lik an empero*ur* no while to endure;
For Consta*n*cius, of who*m* I spak now late,
With this Vetremon cast hy*m* to debate.

who was old and illiterate and no great soldier; and when Constantius made war on him he abdicated.

This Vetremon hath lefft his estat,
List nat werreye agey*n* Consta*n*cius,
Forsook the feeld[e], loued no debat.
But of Spaigne, my*n* aucto*ur* writeth þ*us*,
As I wrot late, how that Magnencius
Geyn Constancivs *with* suerd[e], spere & sheeld
Presumed proudli for to holde a feeld.

Magnentius, however, resisted Constantius, but finally he fled out of cowardice,

To gret damage & hy*n*dry*n*g of the tou*n*,
For many Romeyn thilke day was ded,
Beside a cite which callid was Leou*n*;
Til at the laste, of v*er*ray coward dreed,
Magnencivs, which captey*n* was & hed
Ageyn Consta*n*cius, hath the feeld forsake.
Loo, how Fortune ca*n* hir chau*n*ges make!

Magnencivs for v*er*ray sorwe & shame
Bood no lenger, but gat hy*m* a sharp kniff,
Sool be hymsilff, wher[of] he was to blame,
Roof thoruh his herte & loste [so] his lyff.
His brothir Dencivs, partable of the stryff,

and pierced his heart with a knife. His brother Decius hanged himself.

1131. Castel Tunge] Castiltunge H, Castrell tunge J, Castyl tong P — Mangnencius R, H, Maxencius J, Magvencyus R 3, Magnentius P.
1134. callid] callid hy*m* R, H 5, *om.* P — Vetranion P.
1148. proudli] stoutly H. 1157. gat] gaff R.
1158. wherof] wher R, J. 1160. Demecyus H — the] his H.

Aboute his neeke cast a myhti corde
And heeng hymsilf[e], bookis so recorde.

Constantius made his uncle Gallus governor of France, a false tyrant soon slain and succeeded by Silvanus, who was assassinated.

Constancius ches aftir hy*m* Gallus,
His vncles brothir, to gou*er*ne Frau*n*ce;
Was a fals tirau*nt*, cruel [and] out*r*aious,
Soone aftir slay*n* for his mysgou*er*nau*n*ce.
Another viker for his disobeissau*n*ce,
Callid Siluanvs, be iugeme*n*t was slay*n*;
For which i*n* F*r*ance ful many a ma*n* was fay*n*.

[How Constantyne baptized bi Siluest*er* was cured of his lepre.] [1]

I shall now make a digression to Constantine, because Bochas says little about this notable man.

OFF this mateer sty*n*te I wil awhile
And folwe my*n* owne st*r*ange oppynyou*n*,
Fro Consta*n*ci*us* t*u*rne awey my stile,
To his fadir make a digressiou*n*,
Cause Boch*as* maketh but short me*n*ciou*n*
Of Consta*n*ty*n*, which be record of clerkis,
Was so notable fou*n*de in al his werkis.

Born in Britain, son of St. Helena, and chosen emperor, he was grievously attacked by leprosy

This myhti p*r*ince was born in Breteyne,
So as the Brut pley*n*li doth vs lere;
His hooli moodir callid was Heleyne,
He in his daies most knihtli & enteere.
Of marcial actis he knew al the maneer*e*,
Chosen empero*ur* for his hih noblesse,
Fill to [be] lepre, cronicles expresse.

and advised to bathe in a piscina filled with the innocent blood of children.

His soor so greuous that no medecyne
Mihte auaile his seeknesse to recure;
He [was] cou*n*sailled to make a gret piscyne,
With in*n*ocent blood of childre that wer pure
Make hy*m* cleene of that he did endure.
Thoruh al Itaille childre ano*n* wer souht,
And to his* paleis be ther moodris brouht.

The strange noise and hideous crying of their tender mothers was so dreadful to hear,

It was gret routhe to beholde & see,
Of tendre moodres to heere the sobbyng,
Be furious co*n*streynt of ther aduersite,

1169. a] *om.* H.
1170. I will stynt R, H, R 3, H 5.
1181. he] *om.* R.
1186. piscyne] puyssyne H. 1190. his] ther B, the J.

[1] MS. J. leaf 155 verso.

Hir clothes to-rent, bedewed w*ith* weepy*n*g.
The strau*n*ge noise of ther hidous criyng
Ascendid up, that ther pitous clamour
Kam to the eris of themperou*r*,

Of which[e] noise themperou*r* was agrised.
Wha*n* that he knew grou*n*d & occasiou*n*
Of this mateer, afforn told & deuysed,
This noble p*r*ince gan haue compassiou*n*;
And for to stynte the lamentaciou*n*
Of all the women ther beyng in presence,
Of merciful pite hath chau*n*gid his sentence.

that the emperor was horrified; and climbing high on the stair of mercy he sent them all home unharmed.

This glorious, this gracious emperou*r*
Is clomb of merci so hih vpo*n* the staire,
Spared nouther vitaille* nor his treso*ur*,
Nor his lango*ur* that dide hy*m* so appaire.
W*ith* ful glad cheer[e] maad hem to repaire;
Where thei cam sori to Roome the cite,
Thei hom returned glad to ther contre.

Roial compassiou*n* dide in his herte myne; [p. 379]
Ches to be sik rather than blood to sheede,
His brest enlumyned with* grace which is dyuyne,
Which fro the heuene dide vpon hy*m* spreede.
He wolde nat suffre in*n*ocentis bleede,
Preferryng pite & merci mor tha*n* riht;
He was visitid vpon the next[e] niht.

His heart was penetrated by royal compassion and he chose to be ill rather than shed the blood of innocents.

Petir and Poule to hym dede appere,
Sent fro the Lord as heuenli massagers,
Bad Constanty*n* been of riht good cheere,
"For he that sit aboue the nyne speeris,
The Lord of Lordis, Lord of lengest yeeris,
Wil that thou wete, — haue it weel in my*n*de, —
In mou*n*t Serapti thou shalt thi leche fy*n*de.

The next night Peter and Paul appeared to him and bade him be of good cheer: "You will find your leech on Mt. Serapti.

God of his grace list the to visite,
To sheede blood because that thou dost spare;
He hath vs sent thi labo*ur* for to quyte;
Tidyngis brouht of helthe & thi weelfare
Pope Siluester to the shal declare,

"God has sent us to reward your labour; Pope Sylvester will tell you how you shall be cured."

1195. of] and R, & H, R 3, H 5.
1196. pitous] hidous H.
1203. Of] And H. 1205. 2nd this] & this H.
1207. vitaille] his vitaille B, R, H — his] *om.* H, R 3, P.
1209. hem] home H.
1214. with] bi B, J, P. 1217. m*er*cy and pite R.

As we haue told[e], be riht weel assured,
Of thi seeknesse how thou shalt be recurid,

This Sylvester did, and baptising him, he became well.

To mou*n*t Serapti in al hast that thou seende,
Suffre Siluester come to thi presence."
Souht & fou*n*de, breefli to make an eende,
Resceyued aftir *with* deu reuerence,
Dide his deueer of enteer dilligence,
Lik as the lyff of Siluester hath deuised,
Be grace maad hool, wha*n* he was baptised.

His flesh was suddenly made white by washing in the piscina of holy baptism.

His flessh renewed and sodenly maad* whiht
Be thries wasshyng in the fressh piscyne
Of holi baptem, welle of most deliht,
Wher the Hooli Gost did[e] hym enlumyne.
Enfourmyd aftir be tech*in*g & doctryne
Of Siluester, lik as my*n* auctour seith,
Of alle articles that longe onto our feith.

The font of porphyry was afterwards encircled with a ring of gold, and pearls and fine stones at Constantine's expense.

The font was maad[e] of porfirie stoon,
Which was aftir be cost of Consta*n*ty*n*
With a rou*n*d bie, that dide aboute gon,
Of gold & perle & stonis that wer fy*n*;
Myd of the font, riht up as a ly*n*,
Vpon a piler of gold a lau*m*pe briht,
Ful of fyn bawme, that brente day &* niht.

He also provided of pure gold a pillar, a lamp, a lamb, an image of Our Saviour,

A lamb of gold he did also prouyde,
Set on this font vpon a smal pileer,
Which lik a conduit vpon eueri side
Shad out water as eny cristal cleer,
On whos riht side an ymage most enteer
Was richeli forgid of our Saueo*ur*,
Al of pure gold, that coste gret treso*ur*.

and one of John the Baptist.

And of this lamb vpon the tothir side,
An image set longe to endure
Of Baptist Iohn, with lettres for tabide
Graue coriousli, & this was the scripture:
"Ecce Agnus Dei, that did for man endure,
On goode Friday offrid up his blood,
To saue ma*n*kynde starf upon the rood."

1232. recurid] cured R. 1233. that] *om.* R.
1240] His flessh his senewes maad sodenli whiht B, J; R *and* H 5 *omit* 2nd his.
1241. puyssyne H. 1246. longeth to R.
1253. day &] al the B, J. 1255. this] his R.
1256. conduct R. 1264. was] *om.* R.

He leet also make a gret censeer
Al of gold, fret with perles fyne,
Which be nyhte* as Phebus in his speer
Thoruh al the cherch most fresshli did[e] shyne;
Ther wer fourti stonis iacynctyne.
Appollos temple, my*n* auct*our* writ the same,
Was halwid newe in Seynt Petris name.

Also a great censer of gold and pearls that shone like the sun, and 40 jacinths. He turned the temple of Apollo into St. Peter's

The Romey*n* templis, that wer bilt of old,
He hath fordoon with al ther maumetrie;
Ther false goddis of siluer & of gold
He hath tobroke vpon ech partie.
This goodli p*r*ince, of goostli policie,
Set of newe statutis of gret vertu
To been obseruid in name of Crist I*es*u.

and destroyed the Roman temples and broke the images of the false gods, and enacted new statutes of great virtue.

¶ The firste lawe, as I reherse ca*n*,
In ordre set with ful gret reuerence,
That Crist I*es*u was sothfast god & man,
Lord of Lordis, Lord of most excellence,
"Which hath this day, of his benyuolence,
Cured my lepre, as ye haue herd deuysed,
Be blissid Siluester wha*n* I was baptised.

The first declared that Christ Jesu was truly god and man.

This g*r*acious Lord, my souerey*n* Lord Ihesu,
From hen[ne]s-foorth, for short conclusiou*n*,
I wil that he, as Lord of most vertu,
Of feithful herte & hool affecciou*n*
Be worsheped in euery regiou*n*; —
No ma*n* so hardi my biddeng to disdeyne,
List he incurre of deth the greuous peyne."

"From henceforth I will have him worshipped in every part of my empire upon pain of death."

¶ Folwyng the day callid the secou*n*de, [p. 380]
This Constantyn ordeyned a decre,
That who that euere in [the] tou*n* wer fou*n*de
Or ellis-wher aboute in the contre, —
What-euer he were, of hih or louh degre,
That blasffemed the name of Crist I*es*u,
Be doom sholde haue of deth a pley*n* issu.

The second punished blasphemy of the name of Christ by death.

¶ The thridde day, in euery man*n*ys siht,
Bi a decre confermed & maad strong,
To any Cristene who that dide vnriht

The third provided for the confiscation of one half of the wealth

1269. Al] *om.* H. 1270. nyhte] myhte B.
1272. wer] was R. 1277. Ther] The R.
1281. name] þe name H.
1295. of deth the] the deth off R.

of any man who oppressed or wronged a Christian.

Be oppressiou*n* or [be] collateral wrong,
It should[e] nat be taried ouer long,
Who wer convict or gilti shal nat chese
Be lawe ordeyned halff his good to lese.

The fourth gave to the pope the prerogative of ruling the priests as the king rules his temporal lords.

¶ The fourthe day, amo*n*g[es] Romey*n*s all
This pryuylege pronou*n*cid in the tou*n*,
Youe to the pope sittyng in Petris stall,
As souereyn hed in euery regiou*n*
To haue the reule and iurediccio*un*
Of preestis alle, allone in alle thy*n*g,
Of temporal lordis lich as hath the kyng.

The fifth granted freedom, to the church and the right of asylum to fugitives.

¶ To the cherche he granted gret franchise
The fifte day & special liberte:
Yif a felou*n* in any man*er* wise
To fynde soco*u*r thidir dide flee,
W*it*h*yn*n*e the bou*n*dis fro dau*n*ger to go fre,
To been assurid & haue ther ful refuge
Fro*m* execuciou*n* of any temporal iuge.

The sixth forbade men to build churches without a licence from the bishop.

¶ No ma*n* presume w*it*h*yn*ne no cite, —
The sixte day, he gaff this sentence, —
No ma*n* so hardi, of hih nor louh degre,
To beelde no cherche, but he haue licence,
Of the bisshop beyng in presence;
This to seyne, that he in his estat
Bi the pope afforn be approbat.

The seventh decreed that the tenth part of all the royal possessions should be appropriated annually for building churches.

¶ The seuenthe* day, this lawe he did eek make:
Of all pocessiou*n*s which that be roiall,
The tenthe part [y]eerli shal be take
Be iugis handis, in parti & in all,
Which[e] treso*u*r thei delyuere shall,
As the statut doth pleynli specefie,
Hool & enteer cherchis to edefie.

On the eighth day Constantine took off his royal garments, and kneeling down before St. Peter,

¶ The eihte day meekli he ded hym quite,
With gret reuerence & humble affecciou*n*,
Whan he did of al his clothes white
And cam hymsilf on pilgrymage dou*n*
Tofor Seynt Petir of gret deuociou*n*;
Natwithstondyng his roial excellence,
Made his confessiou*n* in open audience.

1310. fourthe] fourty R.
1315. 2nd alle] on H.
1331. seuenthe] vij te B. 1335. Whiche] wit*h* H.

His crowne take of, knelyng thus he saide
With weepy*n*g eyen & vois most lame*n*table,
And for sobbyng as he myht abraide:
"O blissid I*es*u, o Lord most merciable,
Lat my teres to the be acceptable;
Resseyue my prayer; my request nat refuse,
As man most synful, I may me nat excuse.

removed his crown and confessed, weeping and with a sorrowful voice, that he was a sinful man,

I occupied thestat of the emperou*r*;
Of thi martirs I shadde the hooli blood,
Spared no seyntes in my cruel errou*r*,
The to pursue fell, furious & wood.
Now blissid I*es*u, most gracious & most good,
Peised & considered my*n* importable offense,
I am nat worthi to come in thi presence,

that he had shed the blood of saints and martyrs. "I am not worthy, blessed Jesus, to appear in thy presence;

Nor for to entre into this hooli place,
Vpon this grou*n*d vnhable for to duell,
To opnen my*n* eyen or to left up my face;
But of thi merci so thou me nat repell,
As ma*n* most synful, I come vnto thi well,
Thi welle of grace and merciful pite
For to be wasshe of my*n* iniquite."

but I come to thee to be washed clean of my iniquity."

This exau*m*ple in open he hath shewed,
His staat imperial of meeknesse leid aside,
His purpil garneme*n*t with teres al bedewed;
Suerd nor sceptre nor hors upon to ride
Ther was non seyn, nor baners splaied wide;
Of marcial tryu*m*phes ther was no tokne fou*n*de,
But criyng m*er*ci, themp*er*ou*r* lay plat to grou*n*de.

This example he gave in public, bedewing his garments with tears and laying aside his royal insignia.

The peeplis gladnesse was medlid *with* wepy*n*g,
And ther weepyng was medlid *with* gladnesse,
To seen an emperou*r* and so notable a kyng
Of his free chois shewe so gret meeknesse.
Thus entirmedlid was ioie & heuynesse:
Heuynesse for passid old vengau*n*ce,
With newe reioisshyng of gostli repe*n*tau*n*ce.

The people wept for joy to see so notable an emperor and king shew such meekness.

This ioye was lik a feeste funerall, [p. 381]
In folk of custum that doon ther besi cure
To brynge a corps, which of custum shall

It was like a funeral where the corpse comes to life,

1345. thus nely*n*g R. 1347. as] so as H. 1349. be to þe H.
1352. the] *om.* H, an R. 1354. cruel in myn errour H.
1355. The] Them (*but corrected*) H, Them P — fell] most P.
1369. nor] ne H. 1377. was ioie] wer Ioyes H.

and everybody laughs and weeps at once.

Haue al the rihtis of his sepulture,
And in this tyme, of sodeyn auenture
To lyf ageyn restored be his bonys,
Causyng his freendis to lauhe & weepe attonis.

Thus the people rejoiced and wept by turns to see their emperor asking mercy for his sins.

Semblabli dependyng atween tweyne,
The peeple wepte, & therwith reioisshy*ng*
To seen ther emp*er*o*u*r so pitousli co*m*pleyne,
For his trespacis merci requeryng:
Of ioie and sorwe a gracious medlyng.
That day was sey[e]n gladnesse mey*nt* wit*h* moone,
Wit*h* weepyng lauhtre, & al in o persone.

Afterwards he dug up 12 stones with his own hands and put them into 12 coffins, in memory of the 12 apostles, and built the church of St. Lateran in their name.

Aftir al this he digged up hymselue
Stones twelue, wher he lay knelyng,
[And] putte hem in cofynes tuelue,
On the tuelue postlis deuoutli reme*m*bry*n*g,
Compassed a grou*n*d large for beeldyng,
Beside his paleys caste theron to werche
In Cristes name to sette up ther a cherche.

He also made a law, that if any pauper or cripple became a Christian he should receive a new outfit of garments and 20 shillings.

The place of olde callid Lateranence,
Bilt and edefied in thapostlis name.
Constantynvs bar al the dispense,
Ordeyned a lawe, my*n* aucto*u*r seith the same,
Yif any poore, nakid, halt or lame
Resceyue wolde the feith of Crist I*es*u,
He sholde be statut be take to this issu:

In his promys yif he wer fou*n*de trewe,
That he wer nat be feynyng no faito*u*r,
He sholde first be spoiled & clad newe
Be the costage off the empero*u*r,
Tuenti shillyng resceyue to his soco*u*r,
Of which resseit nothyng was wit*h*drawe,
Be statut kept & holde as for a lawe.

I cannot recount all his noble deeds and victories; but they are all told in the Legend of Sylvester.

It wer to longe to putte [al] in memorie,
His hih prowesse & his notable deedis,
And to reherse[n] euery gret victorie
Which that he hadde with hostis that he ledis;
And to remembre al his gracious speedis,

1394. digged] giggid (*partly erased*) R.
1397. On] Of R.
1398. large for] for large (biggyng) H.
1409. fatour R, H, fantour R 3.
1418. 1st that] *om.* H, R 3 — 2nd that] which H.

The surplusage, who list [to] co*m*prehende,
Lat hym of Siluestre reede the legende.

And among othir, touchy*n*g his visiou*n*,
Which that he hadde, in cronicles men may lere,
Wha*n* that he slepte in his roial dongou*n*,
How Crist to hym did graciousli* appeere,
Shewed hym a cros, & seide as ye shal heere:
"Be nat afferd upon thi foon to falle,
For in this signe thou shalt ouercome he*m* alle."

especially his vision of Christ, who shewed him a cross saying, "By this sign shalt thou conquer,"

Be which auyseou*n* he was maad glad & liht
Thoruh Goddis grace & heuenli influence.
First in his baneer, that shon so cleer & briht,
The cros was bete, cheef tokne of his diffence.
Slouh the tirau*n*t that callid was Maxence,
Aftir whos deth[e], thoruh his hih renou*n*
Of al thempire he took pocessiou*n*.

which so pleased Constantine that he had the cross beaten in his banner, and slaying Maxence, took possession of the whole empire.

In which estat he mey*n*tened trouthe & riht,
Vpon al poore hauyng co*m*passiou*n*,
Duryng his* tyme holde the beste kniht
That owher was in any regiou*n*,
Of Cristes feith thymperial champiou*n*,
Thoruh his noble knihtli magnificence
To alle Cristene protecto*u*r & diffence.

He ruled justly, having compassion on the poor, and was held the best knight of his time.

Aftir his name, which neuer shal appall,
Chau*n*ged in Grece the name of Bizante;
Consta*n*tynople he did it aftir call,
And on a steede of bras, as me*n* may see,
Manacyng of Turkis the contre,
He sit armyd, a gret suerd in his hond
Them to chastise that rebelle in that lond.

He named Byzantium Constantinople; and there he still sits armed on a steed of brass, menacing the country of the Turks.

Reioisshe ye folkis that born been in Breteyne,
Callid othirwise Brutis Albiou*n*,
That hadde a p*r*ince so notabli souereyne
Brouht forth & fostrid in yo*u*r regiou*n*,
That whilom hadde the domynaciou*n*,
As cheef monarche, p*r*ince & president,
Ouer al the world, fro*m* est til occident.

Rejoice, Britons, that your land brought forth such a prince, chief monarch of all the world!

1425. did graciousli] graciousli did B.
1426. ye] *om.* R.
1429. glad] *om.* R.
1432. bete] bor*e* H.
1438. his] this B.
1450. ye] the R. 1455. monarchye H.

When he died the sun was not seen for a month, and there was a great comet in the south that drew towards his palace in Nicomedia.

Tyme of his deth, that moneth of þe yeer
Phebus nat seyn, wit*h*drouh his feruent heete;
And longe afforn[e] large, brod & cleer,
Toward Affrik shewed a gret comete,
Alway encresyng, drouh toward the sete
Of Nichomedie, shon erli & eek late,
Wher in his paleis he passed into fate.

[How Iulian Apostata enmy to cristys bi fals Illusions was chose Emperour and aftir slayn.] [1]

After Constantine came Julian the Apostate, his cousin, a cursed man.

AFFTIR the deth of this marcial ma*n*,— [p.382]
I meene this noble worthi Co*n*sta*n*ty*n*, —
Kometh Thapostata, cursid Iulia*n*,
Which be discent to Constanty*n* was cosyn.
His gynyng cursid, hadde a cursid fyn,
Entred religiou*n*, as bookis specefie,
Vnder a colour of fals ipocrisie.

who entered religion out of hypocrisy, a double iniquity. Fie on such feigned perfection!

It hath be seid[e] of antiquite,
Wher that ther is dissymuled hoolynesse,
It is icallid double iniquite, —
Fih on al suich feyned parfitnesse!
For symulaciou*n* curid wit*h* doubilnesse
And fals[e] semblau*n*t with a sobre face,
Of alle [fals] sect*es* stonde ferthest out of grace.

For a time he devoted himself to religion, and then, wearying of his order, forsook it and gave himself up to necromancy.

A certeyn space, as maad is menciou*n*,
To al perfecciou*n* he did hymsilf applie,
Til he wex weri of his professiou*n*,
Forsook his ordre bi apostacie.
And first he gaff hym to nigroma*n*cye,
Double Apostata, as my*n* aucto*ur* seith,
First to his ordre & aftir to our feith.

Constantius sent this root of hypocrisy to be governor of Gaul, where he conspired to get possession of the whole empire,

Bi ordynau*n*ce of Consta*n*civs,
This said Iulian, roote of ipocresie,
Of gou*er*nau*n*ce froward & vicious,
Was sent to Gaule with gret cheualrie
As viker chose the contre for to guye.

1461. sete] cite R. 1466. the Apostita H.
1468. 1st cursid] *om.* R. 1472. ther] he R.
1473. callid R. 1476. sobre] doubil H, soure J.
1477. fals] *om.* J, P.

[1] MS. J. leaf 157 recto — How] So J.

Gat hym fauour & falsli ga*n* co*n*spire
To haue pocessiou*n* of al the hool empire.

And for he was nat likli to atteyne
To that estat, he did his hert applie
Another mene pley*n*li to ordeyne,
Wikked spiritis to make of his allie,
Beca*m* a prentys to lerne sorcerye,
To haue experience be invocaciou*n*s
To calle spirit*es* wit*h* his coniurisouns.*

and at first not succeeding, allied himself with wicked spirits and became an apprentice to sorcery,

Be fals illusiou*n* in the peeplis sihte,
Of wikked spiritis had so gret fauo*ur*, —
A crowne of laurer upon his hed aliht, —
Made folk to deeme, bi ful fals erro*ur*,
It ca*m* be myracle, to chese hym emp*er*o*ur*.
Which of trouthe as in existence
Was but collusioun* & feyned apparence.

and made the people believe that a crown of laurel alighted on his head by miracle, whereas it was set there by the spirits to whom he sacrificed.

With hem he hadde his co*n*uersaciou*n*,
Spared nat to doon hem sacrefise
Wit*h* cerymonyes & fals oblaciou*n*,
And to thempire he roos up in this wise.
Thestat resceyuyd, first he ga*n* deuyse
Agey*n* Grekis, out of his contre ferre,
To make hy*m* strong with hem to haue a werre.

In this manner he was chosen emperor.

The Feend a while was to hym fauourable,
Gaf hym entre and pocessiou*n*,
And made hym promys for tabide stable
In his lordship and domynaciou*n*,
To haue this world vndir subiecciou*n*;
Of which beheste he stood in pereilous cas,
Folwyng thoppynyou*n* of Pigtagoras.

He made war on Greece; and for a while the devil favoured him.

Following the opinion of Pythagoras,

¶ Pigtagoras hadde this oppinyou*n*:
Wha*n* men deide, anon aftir than
Ther was maad[e] a translaciou*n*
Of his speryt in-tanothir ma*n*,
A maner liknesse; the Bible telle ca*n*,
The double speryt of grace & p*ro*phecie
To Heliseus was g*r*antid be Helye.

who believed in the transmigration of souls,

1491. To haue] off all R — al] *om.* R.
1496. Becam] he becam H, J, R 3.
1498. coniurisouns] coniuraciou*n*s B. 1502. to] *om.* H.
1505. collusioun] intrusiou*n* B, R, J, H 5.
1506. co*n*u*er*saciou*n*s H. 1508. oblacions H.
1511. Agey*n*] geyn H. 1512. haue a] ha H.

he thought that he himself had such a spirit, with all its knowledge and wisdom,

Heeron concludyng, lik his oppynyou*n*,
As Pictagoras affermed in sentence,
He that hadde ful pocessiou*n*
Of suich a speryt, in v*er*ray existence
Sholde haue the same wisdam & science,
The disposiciou*n* aftir hym as blyue,
Which hadde that speryt whil he was heer alyue, —

the spirit of Alexander; and Pluto encouraged him in his belief.

Of gou*er*nau*n*ce and also of nature
Resemblyn hy*m*, of maner*e*s & lyuyng.
And thus be fraude Pluto did his cure
To make Iulian to truste i*n* eueri thyng,
He hadde be berth the sperit of the kyng
Callid Alisau*n*dre, be which he sholde wyn*n*e
This world be conquest, whan-euer hy*m* list begyn*n*e.

So he trusted in Pluto and the infernal gods.

Thus gan he fon*n*e & falle in fantasie
To truste on Pluto & goddis infernal,
Thei sholde enhau*n*ce hym bi his cheualrie
For to posseede and reioysshe al, —
Suerd, sceptre, crowne and staat imperial,
Passe Alisau*n*dre in hono*ur* & in glorie
And hym excelle in tryu*m*phal victorie.

He also trusted Satan, and became a mortal enemy to Christ's law and broke crosses and crucifixes. Jesus he called 'Gallilee' and sometimes 'the Nazarene' in scorn.

He trusted Sathan, be whom he was desceyuid, [p.383]
To Cristes lawe becam mortal enmy;
Wher that euere that he hath parceyued
Cros or crucifix, he brak hem vengabli.
Be fals language he callid traitourly,
Crist I*es*u he callid Gallile,
And of despiht sumtyme Nazare.

He slew many martyrs and was an idolater and renegade.

Ageyn our feith this tirant wex so wood,
[And] ageyn Crist hadde so gret hatreede;
Slouh many martir & falsli shadde hir blood,
An idolatre & renegat in deede.
Heeld mortal werre w*ith* hem of Perse & Meede;
Comyng to Perse, first he ga*n* debate
Geyn Sapor kyng, of who*m* I spak but late.

And he fought many wars

Of Parthois also he entrid thoruh the rewm,
Wher he fond no maneer resistence.
And as he cam forbi Iherusalem,

1528. in] this H. 1529. He that] þ*at* he H.
1543. hym] *om.* H. 1545. Suerd] Off Swerde R.
1550. 1st that] *om.* H. 1552. callith H.
1558. &] an H. 1561. Sapor kyng] kyn Sapor*e* H.

To the Iewes of newe* he gaf licence
To beelde the temple with gret dilligence,
In despiht, of purpos to do shame
To Cristene cherchis, bilt newe in Cristes name.

and let the Jews rebuild their temple, to do shame to Christian churches.

In this while he kauht a gret corage,
In a theatre maad brood in that tou*n*,
Too wilde beestis cruel and sauage
Of seyntis blood to make oblaciou*n*,
Thei to deuoure men of religiou*n*.
And alle Cristene of purpos to destroye,
His lust was set & al his worldly ioie.

In Jerusalem he offered saints to wild beasts and all his joy lay in the destruction of Christians.

Bi an heraud that dide his host co*n*veye,
Of verray purpos to brynge hy*m* in treyne,
Bi strau*n*ge desertis fond out a froward weye.
The heete importable did hym so co*n*streyne,
Brente thoruh the harneys, felte so gr*e*t peyne; —
The drye sondis, the heir infect with heete
Made many a ma*n* ther lyff in hast to lete.

A herald, who guided his army, led him into a desert, where the heat killed many of his men;

This froward tirau*n*t, knowyng no remedie,
Of cursid herte ga*n* Crist I*es*u blasffeme,
And of malicious hatreed & envie,
Wood & furious, as it dide seeme,
Gan curse the Lord, that al this world shal deeme,
Crist I*es*u*s*, which of long pacience
List nat be vengau*n*ce his* malis reco*m*pence.

and this froward tyrant, knowing nothing better, began to curse Christ, of malicious hatred.

A mor cruel was ther neuer non,
Nor mor vengable: nat Cerbervs in hell,
Mortal enmy to goode men euerichon,
Whos blasfemys and rebukis fell,
Be rehersaile yif I sholde hem tell, —
I am afferd the venymous violence
Sholde infecte the heir with pestilence.

A more cruel and revengeful man was never seen, not even Cerberus in hell. His blasphemies would infect the air with pestilence if I were to repeat them.

He cast out dartis mor bittir tha*n* is gall
Of blasfemye & infernal langage;
And in this while amo*n*g his p*r*incis all
A kniht vnknowe, angelik of visage,
Fresshly armyd, to punshen his outrage,

During this while an unknown knight appeared among his princes and thrust a spear into his heart.

1565. or newe] ano*n* B, J, anone P — of newe he gaf] of newe and of R.
1573. to] *om.* H.
1576. heraud] Heronde H, heraude J, herand R, Herauld P.
1579. The] to H — hym] hem H. 1580. the] their H.
1589. his] this B. 1591. nat] *om.* H.

With a sharp spere, thoruh euery synwe & veyne,
Of this tiraunt roof the herte on tweyne.

Some men say this knight was Mercurius.

Bathid in his blood, this tiraunt fill doun lowe,
To God & man froward & odious.
Thouh for that tyme the knibt ne was nat knowe,
Yit summe men seyn it was Mercurivs,
Which bi the praieer of Basilius
This tiraunt slouh, as cronicles don* us lere,
Bi a myracle of Cristes mooder deere.

who, buried before in Cesarea, rose from his grave (a strange thing to see), arrayed himself in his armour, that hung beside his sepulchre, and mounted a horse.

This Mercurius, as bookes determyne,
In Cesaria, a myhti strong cite,
Withynne the contre callid Palestyne,
Buried afforn, roos up at this iourne
Out of his graue, a straunge thyng to see;
An hors brouht to hym, arraied in his armure,
Which heeng toforn beside his sepulture.

The same armour was not seen until the next evening, and Julian was struck down at mid-day.

The same armvre was nat seyn that niht
Nor on the morwe at his graue founde
Til mydday hour, that Phebus shon ful briht,
Whan Mercury* gaf hym his fatal wounde,
His blasfemye for euer* to confounde.
Which thyng accomplisshed, this myracle for to preue,
He and his armure wer ther ageyn at eue.

That was the sudden end of his blasphemy. His last words were, "Thou hast conquered, Gallilee." He cast his blood in the air in despite of Jesus.

Of his blasfemye this was the sodeyn wrak
Which the tiraunt resceyuid for his mede.
The laste woord I fynde that he spak:
"Thou Gallile hast ouercome in deede!"
Took the blood[e] that he did[e] bleede,
This deuelissh man, deying in despeir,
Despiht of Iesu cast up in the heir.

His body was flayed and his skin tanned and nailed to the gate of his palace by the Persian king Sapor.

His bodi flay[e]n & his skyn was take, [p. 384]
Tawed aftir be presept and biddyng
Souple and tendre as thei coude it make, —
Sapor bad so, that was of Perse kyng,
That men myht haue therof knowlechyng
Erli on morwe & at eue late,
He did it naille upon his paleis gate.

1604. his] *om.* R, his oun H. 1605. To God &] To goode a R.
1606. ne] *om.* H. 1607. seyn] seynt R.
1609. don] doth B, J. 1621. Mercurius B, R, J.
1622. euer] euermor B, H, R, P, H 5, R 3.
1630 *is misplaced before* 1628 *in* H, *correction indicated.*
1631. in] in to H.

And to a cite that was callid Kaire,
As cronicles make rehersaille,
This Apostata wolde ofte a-day repaire
To a woman, which hadde in hir entraille
Spiritis closid, to make his dyuynaille.
In whos wombe, bareyn & out of grace,
Of wikkid feendis* was the restyng* place.

During his lifetime this Apostate used to consult a woman in Cairo whose belly was the resting place of evil spirits,

This said[e] woman was a creature,
The which afforn be cursid Iulian,
Be his lyue his purpos to recure,
In sacrifise was offrid to Sathan.
And so as he with cursidnesse began,
Swich was his eende, as all bookis tell,
Whos soule with Pluto is buried deepe in hell.

and whom he afterwards offered up in sacrifice to Satan.

With this tiraunt Bochas gan wex[e] wroth
For his most odious [hatful] fel outrage,
And to reherse in parti he was loth
The blasfemyes of his fell langage;
For nouther furye nor infernal rage
May be comparid, with poisoun fret withynne,
To the fals venym of this horrible synne.

Bochas began to grow angry with this tyrant for his outrages and blasphemies. Neither fury nor infernal rage can be compared to blasphemy.

It is contrarie to alle goode thewes,
And tofor God most abhomynable;
Hatful to alle sauff to cursid shrewes:
For of alle vices verray incomparable,
Most contagious & most detestable,
The mouth infect of suich infernal houndis
Which eueri day sle Crist with newe woundis.

It is contrary to all virtue and abominable to God.

Folk obstynat of purpos for the nonys,
Of disposicioun furious & wood,
Nat afferd to suere [by] Goddis bonys,
With horrible othes of bodi, flessh & blood,
The Lord dismembryng, most gracious, most good,
His feet, his handis, armys, face & hed,
Reende hym of newe, as thei wolde haue hym ded.

Obstinate folk of evil disposition swear horrible oaths by God's bones his body and blood, dismembering him of new, as if they would again have him dead.

The blissid Lord, which is inmortall,
Thouh thei be dedli, thei wolde hym sle ageyn.
Thei be erthli; he is celestiall;

Although they are earthly and he celestial, they have no discretion;

1641. ofte] of R. 1643. his] hir H. 1645. feendis] spiritis B, J, P — restyng] duellyng B. 1648. his] hir H.
1657. furye] *om.* R — nor] nor noon H, R 3, H 5.
1667. Folkis H. 1669. by] *om.* R, J. 1672. armys handis H.

In froward wise thei be ouerseyn;
Discreciou*n* faileth; ther resou*n* is in vey*n*:
Al suich bla[s]ffemye, for short co*n*clusiou*n*,
Proceedith of pride & fals ambiciou*n*.

and it seems to me that they are very ungrateful not to do him reverence, who was nailed on a cross and suffered death for their sake.

It seemeth to me, thei haue foule failed
Of kynd[e]nesse to doon hym reuerence,
Which for ther loue upon a cros was nailed
To paie the* rau*n*sou*n* for ma*n*n*y*s gret offence,
Suffred deth with humble pacience,
Fals rebukyng, spittyng in his visage,
To brynge ma*n*kynde onto his heritage.

It all comes from pride; and Satan is the original cause. Julian was most unfortunate reigning under him.

Fals surquedie that doth the hertis reise
Of suich blasfemo*u*rs, as was this Iulian,
Whos gret empire myht nat cou*n*tirpeise
Ageyn that Lord which is bothe God & ma*n*.
Thorigynal grou*n*d of pride was Satha*n*;
P*r*ince vndir hym most infortunat
Was this Apostata, regnyng in his estat.

What was the end of this cruel felon? He was miraculously pierced to the heart by a heavenly knight.

What was the eende of this tirau*n*t horrible,
This cruel felou*n*, hatful to eueri wiht?
Be sodey*n* myracle to al his host visible,
Ther did appeere a v*er*ray heuenli kniht,
Most fresshli armyd & angelik of siht.
With a sharp spere, sittyng on his steede,
Made the tirau*n*t his herte blood to bleede.

His false gods could not help him nor all his sorcery and invocations.

His false goddis myhte hy*m* nat auaile,
His froward offryng doon to maumetrie,
Nor al his proude imperial apparaille,
His inuocaciou*n*s nor hatful sorcerye:
For this Apostata, that did his feith denye,
Among his knihtis slayn be deth sodeyne;
His soule dampned with Satha*n* depe i*n* peyne.

[How the Emperour Valence / slouh heremytes shad cristen blood destroied chirches & after was brent.] [1]

Bochas next turns to Valens, and first tells us about the perfect holiness

BOCHAS in hast[e] doth his stile dresse
Next to themp*er*o*u*r þ*a*t callid was Valence,
Rehersi*n*g first the parfit hoolynesse

1684. the] ther B, R, J. 1685. þe deth H.
1700. sharp] *om.* H.

[1] MS. J. leaf 158 recto.

Of hermytis, that dide ther dilligence
To lyue in penau*n*ce & in abstynence;
Forsook the world[e], & for Cristes sake
Into desert thei haue the weye take.

of hermits, who forsook this world of variance for Christ's sake,

In this world heer thei list no lenger tarye, [p. 385]
Dyuers & double, of trust nou*n* certeyn;
Ferr in Egipt to lyue solitarye,
Deepe in desertis, of folk nat to be seyn.
The soil was drye; of vitaille ful bareyn;
The frutles treen up sered to the roote:
For Cristes loue thei thouhte that lyff most soote.

and lived far away in the deserts of Egypt, where the soil was dry and there was little food.

This said Valence, of malis frowardli
To thes hermytes, that lyued in gr*e*t penau*n*ce,
Causeles [to hem] was gret enmy,
Troubled hem & did hem gret greuau*n*ce.
Lik a tirau*n*t set al on vengau*n*ce,
Destroied cherchis with peeple that he ladde;
And wher he rood Cristen blood he shadde.

Valens was without cause their enemy. Wherever he rode he destroyed churches and shed Christian blood.

This mene while be robbyng & rauyne
In Mauritayne, which is a gret contre,
Ther was a p*r*ince that callid was Fyryne;
And in Cesarea, a famous gret cite,
For his extorsiou*n* & his cruelte
He took upon hym, proudli ther regnyng,
Maugre [the] Romeyns to be crownid kyng.

In the meanwhile a prince called Firmus took upon himself to reign in Cesarea, in despite of the Romans, so

Theodose the Firste, a ma*n*li ma*n*,
Was sent out his malys to withstonde
Be the biddyng of Valentynyan,
Which that tyme thempire hadde on honde,
Bothe attonys; but ye shal vndirstonde,
Theodose was sent out to assaile
The saide Feryn, and slouh hy*m* in bataille.

Valens sent out Theodosius, co-emperor, against him. Firmus was slain,

Of which Feryn, be ful cruel hate,
In that contre presumptuousli regny*n*g,
Smet of his hed & set [it] on the gate
Of Cesaria; this was his eendyng,
Which be intrusiou*n* afforn was crownid ki*n*g

and his head cut off and set up on the gate of Cesarea.

1716. lenger] lenger no R.
1722. thei] the R — most] so H.
1725. enmy] envye H. 1728. peeplis H.
1734. 1st his *is erased* H — 2nd his] gret H.
1735. ther] the R. 1737. ma*n*] knyht R.
1746. it] *om.* R. 1747] of Cesaria a Cite of gret bildyng H.

In Mauritayne, oppressi*ng* them be dreed,
As ye haue herd, for which he loste his hed.

Returning to Valens, Bochas says, that out of froward cursedness to holy church he slew all the hermits;

In this mateer Boch*as* doth nat soio*u*rne
Be non attendau*n*ce nor no long dillige*n*ce,
But of purpos doth ageyn reto*u*rne
To themperou*r* that callid was Valence,
Which, as I tolde, dide so gret offence
To hooli cherch of froward cursidnesse,
Slouh al hermytes that bood in wildirnesse.

but God would not suffer such a tyrant to live long. The Goths rebelled for the oppression of one of his princes

God wold nat suffre he sholde long endure,
Grau*n*teth no tirau*n*t to haue heer no lo*n*g lyff;
For be sum myscheef or sodey*n* auenture
Thei deien be moordre, *with* dagger, suerd or kniff.
The Gothois whilom agey*n* hym* ga*n* a stryff, —
For his outrage & gret oppressiou*n*
Thei agey*n* Romey*ns* fill in rebelliou*n*.

called Maximus, and became so strong that they defeated Valens himself,

A p*r*ince off his callid Maxymvs
Distressed hem bi so gret tiranye,
Was vpon hem so contrarious,
That thei gadred al ther cheualrie
And wex so strong vpon ther partie,
That bi ther ma*n*hod, it fill of auenture,
Thei on Valence made a disconfiture.

and went on robbing and destroying cities and towns and villages in Thrace. All this while Valens did not cease to persecute the hermits.

Spared nat bi robbyng and pillage,
Slouh & brente many statli place,
Cites, tou*ns* & many smal village,
That wer famous withyn*ne* the lond of Trace.
But al this while Valence ga*n* enchace,
And causeles, of malis voluntarie,
Pursued hermytes that lyued solitarye.

Collecting a new army, he proudly attacked the Goths, who defeated him again. So he fled and hid in a cottage,

And of newe this Valence ga*n* ageyn
Gret multitude of Romey*ns* to purchace,
And with his host[e] proudli be disdey*n*
Agey*n*[es] Gothes ca*m* dou*n* in-to Trace.
But furiousli thei mette hy*m* in the face,
Wher lik a coward he turned his visage,
To saue his lyff lay hid in a cotage.

1759. to haue] *om.* J, P — no] *om.* J, P.
1762. geyn hy*m* whilome H — ageyn hym] *om.* J, P — hym] hem B.
1776. enchace] enhace R.
1779. *This stanza is omitted in* J.

Thus fynalli this emperour Valence,
As ye haue herd, failled of his entent.
The Gothes folwed be cruel violence,
As wilde woluys*, alle of oon assent,
The hous & hym to asshis thei haue brent.
Loo, heer the fyn, ye pryncis taketh heede,
Of tirauntis that* seyntes blood do* sheede!

which the Goths set on fire, and was burnt to ashes. That is the end of tyrants, who shed the blood of saints!

[Off kyng Amarycyus / and how Gracyan and Theodosie destroied temples of fals goddis / & how gracyan was put to flight.] [1]

¶ Aftir Valence, to God contrarious,
In al his werkis most froward of lyuyng,
Tofor Bochas cam Amaricus,
Which of Gothes was whilom lord & kyng,
Of his gret age pitousli pleynyng,
Inflat and bolle, list make no delaies,
Slouh hymsilf to shorte his greuous daies.

After Valens, Hermanric appeared before Bochas; once king of the Goths, he grew old and dropsical and finally slew himself.

¶ Than cam to Bochas* the brother of Valence, [p. 386]
The myhti emperour callid Gracian,
Which hadde afforn[e] had experience
First with his vncle Valentynyan
In thempire, as bookis telle can;
And aftirward Theodosie & he
Hadde gouernaunce of Roome the cite.

Gratian, Valens' brother, and Theodosius ruled Rome.

Theodosie and Gracian of assent
Destroied templis as in that partie
Of false goddis; thei haue also doun rent
The grete idoles & al suich maumetrye,
And ful deuoutli gan chirchis edefye.
And in this while, as Fortune list ordeyne,
On Maxymvs was vikeer in Breteyne.

They destroyed the temples of false gods and pulled down idols and built churches at the time Maximus was governor of Britain.

An hardi kniht, al-be he did[e] varie
From his promys maad be sacrement;
In Breteyne list no lenger tarie,

Maximus was a hardy knight;

1787] In all his werkis most frowarde of entent H.
1789. woluys] beestes B, J, beastes P.
1792. that] the B — do] to B.
1795. Amaricus] Arynacyus H, R 3, Hermenricus P.
1798. bollen H.
1800. to Bochas] doun B — brother] nephew P.
1802, 3 *are transposed* H, R. 1810. mawmentrye H.
1811. deuoute R. 1813. Maxymyan H.

[1] MS. J. leaf 158 verso.

but, breaking his oath, he left Britain and attacked Gratian

But into Gaule of hert & hool entent
Geyn Gracian he sodenli is went.
And as it fill, set be ther bothe auys,
Thei hadde a bataille nat ferr out of Parys.

and put him to flight near Paris, through the bravery of Merobandus, one of his captains.

This Gracian was ther put to fliht
Bi the prowesse of a proud capteyn
Callid Merobandus, was an hardi kniht,
Which with his poweer hath so ouerleyn,
That Gracian was constreyned in certeyn,
Whan his poweer myhte nat availe
Geyn Maxymvs, to fleen out of Itaille.

Maximus was ambitious to be sole ruler of the empire, and Bochas will tell how Fortune threw him down.

¶ This Maxymvs of pride gan desire
In his herte be fals ambicioun
To regne allone, & of the hool empire
In his handis to haue pocessioun.
But in what wise Fortune threw hym doun
With suich othir, that be in nou[m]bre fyue,
In this chapitle Bochas doth descryue.

After Maximus had slain Gratian, Theodosius made war on him

Ageyn this same tiraunt Maxymvs,
Whan that he hadde slay[e]n Gracian,
The noble emperour Theodosius
To venge his deth a werre in hast began,
Because also that Valentynyan
Was wrongli banshed thoruh the cruelte
Of Gracian ful ferr from his contre.

and his general Andragathius who defended the Alps,

With Maxymvs to holde up his partie
Was Andragracian, a ful notable kniht,
Which was maad prince of his cheualrie,
That took upon hym of verray force & myht
To keepe the mounteyns, that no maner wiht
With Theodose, armyd in plate & maile, —
No man sholde ouer the Alpies of Itaile.

and laying siege to Aquileia, took him prisoner and slew him.

Theodose maad a gret arme,
Be grace of God and marcial corage
Leide a seege to Aigle, a gret cite,
And wan the toun, maugre his visage;
Took the tiraunt, and for his gret outrage

1830. the hool empire] al thempire H. 1832. what] that R.
1838. tavenge H — in hast a werre R — gan H.
1841. from] out of H.
1842. Maxymyan H — With] Whiche J.
1843. Andragathius P. 1851. Aquile P — a gret] þe H.

Berafft hym first his roial garneme*nt*
And slouh hym aftir þe rihtful iugeme*nt*.

Whan Andragracian knew that Maxim*us*,
That was his lord, was slay[e]n in swich wise,
Anon for sorwe, the stori tellith thus,
He drowned hymsilf, as Bochas doth deuise.
Thus ca*n* Fortune make folk arise
To thestat of emp*erour*s atteyne,
With vnwar strok yiue hy*m* a fal sodeyne.

Andragathius drowned himself for sorrow.

This Maximvs, of whom I spak tofor,
Tofore his deth[e] made an ordynau*n*ce,
That his sone, which callid was Victor,*
Sholde aftir hy*m* gouerne Gaule & Frau*n*ce,
Whom Arbogastes hadde in gou*er*nau*n*ce —
A gret constable with Valentynyan —
Slouh this Victor* to regne wha*n* he bega*n*.

Before his death Maximus had ordered that his son Victor should govern Gaul, but Victor was slain by Arbogastes, one of Valentinian's generals.

[A good processe how Theodosie wi*th* praiere and smal nou*m*bre gat the victory.] [1]

THA*N* Valentynya*n* wi*th* gr*e*t apparaile
Bi Arbogastes took pocessiou*n*
Of Lumbardie & of al Itaile,
Brouht al that lond to subieccio*u*n.
Tha*n* with his poweer he ca*m* to Gaule dou*n*,
Ther resceyuyd with gret solempnite
At Vyen*n*e, a famous old cite.

Valentinian then took possession of Lombardy and Italy, and entering Gaul was received with great pomp at Vienne.

Arbogastes, of whom I spak now late,
His cheef constable, as ye haue herd deuise,
Of his lord[e] be ful cruel hate
The deth conspired of fals couetise,
Therbi supposyng that he shold arise
Vnto thestat to be chose emper*ou*r,
Whan he wer ded[e], lik a fals tret*ou*r.

Arbogastes, hoping to be made emperor, conspired his death

Vp in a tour he heeng hy*m* trait*ou*rli, [p. 387]
[And] to mor sclau*n*dre & hyndry*n*g of his name,
Reportid outward and seide cursidli,
This Arbogaste, to hide his owne shame, —
His souerey*n* lord to putte in mor diffame, —

and hung him up in a tower, reporting, to hide his guilt, that his lord had hanged himself.

1856. Andragathius P. 1862. hy*m*] hem R.
1865, 69. Vittor B. 1880. of] bi ful H. 1885. And] *om.* R.

[1] MS. J. leaf 159 recto.

Stefli affermed, a thyng that was ful fals,
How he hymsilf[e] heng up bi the hals.

Thus a murderer and traitor, he sought to reign alone with Eugenius, and endeavouring to exclude Theodosius,

Thus lik a moordrer and a fals treto*ur*,
And of condicio*un* hatful and odious,
Laboured sore to be maad empero*ur*,
That he allone with Eugenivs
Mihte exclude Theodosyus,
First to lette hym, he sholde on no partie
Passe thoruh Itaille nor thoruh Lumbardie.

who was in the hills of Lombardy, attacked him there.

Sette espies to brynge hym i*n* a treyne,
Which that tyme, as thei vndirstood,
Lik a iust prynce did his besy peyne,
As he that thouhte nothyng but on good,
In the hilles of Lumbardie abood,
Whom Arbogast, of furious corage,
Cast hym to trouble & stoppen his passage,

Theodosius, scantily provisioned, surrounded by his enemies and deserted by many of his knights, betook himself to prayer.

He and Eugenius beyng of assent
Theodosie mortalli tassaile.
Which whan he knew ther meenyng* fraudule*n*t,
Al-be that he had but scars vitaille,
On eueri cost besette with a bataille,
And of his knihtis forsaken in maneere,
He lefte all thyng & took hym to p*r*aiere.

Falling down on his knee, he said, "O Lord, deliver me out of my distress.

With hym was left[e] but a smal meyne,
Trewe & feithful in ther affecciou*n*.
And first of alle he fill dou*n* on his kne
And to I*esus* ga*n* make his orisou*n*:
"O Lord," quod he, "thyn eres enclyne dou*n*,
And of thi merciful gracious [hih] goodnesse
Delyuere me out of my mortal distresse.

"Consider that although blinded by fleshly lusts I am thy knight.

Considre & see how that I am thi kniht,
Which ofte sithe thoruh my fragilite,
With flesshli lustis bleendid in my siht,
A thousand tymes haue trespasid onto the;
But, gracious I*es*u, of merci & pite
To my requestis benigneli tak heed
Me to socoure in this gret[e] need.

1901. As] And R — on] *om.* H, J, R 3, P.
1903. Whom] Whilome H.
1907. Which] *om.* R — meenyng] mouyng B. R. H 5.
1909. besette] sett H.
1920. ofte] off R. 1925. in] now i*n* H.

My trust is hool, pleynli to co*n*clude,
Thou shalt foorthre & fortune my viage,
W*ith* litil folk ageyn gret multitude
To make me haue gracious passage,
Aftir the prouerbe of newe & old langage,
How that thou maist & kanst thi poweer shewe
Geyn multitude victorie with a fewe.

"My trust is that thou shalt further my enterprise and give victory to few against a multitude.

And as thou sauedest whilom Israel
Gey*n* Phar[a]os myhti strong puissau*n*ce,
And fro the leou*n*s delyueredest Danyel,
And saueddest Susan*n*e in hir mortal gr*e*uau*n*ce,
Saue me this day fro sorwe & myschau*n*ce,
In this myscheef to g*r*ante me this issu,
Tescape fro dau*n*ger be grace of the, I*es*u!

"As thou saved Israel from Pharaoh, and Susannah in her extremity, save me to-day from this peril.

Thi* blissid name be interpretaciou*n*
Is to seyne most myhti Saueo*ur*;
Ther is no dreed nor dubitaciou*n*
That I*esus* is in al worldli labo*ur*
To al that trust hym victorious p*ro*tecto*ur*.
Now, blissid I*es*u, pauys of my diffence,
Make me escape my*n* enmyes violence!

"There is no doubt that thou art the victorious protector of all who trust in thee.

Lat my*n* enmyes, that so gret bost do blowe,
Thouh ther poweer be dreedful & terrible,
That thei may bexperience knowe
Ther is to the nothyng impossible, —
Thou too and thre & oon indiuysible,
Thouh I with me haue but fewe men,
Saue me, I*es*u, this day fro deth; Amen."

"Let my powerful and boastful enemies know by experience that to thee nothing is impossible. Amen."

¶ The day ga*n* cleere, the sun*n*e ga*n* shewe briht,
Wha*n* Theodosie deuoutli lay knelyng,
And be grace adawen gan his siht
Fro cloudi wawes of long pitous weepi*n*g,
His souerey*n* hope set in the heuenli ky*n*g,
I*esus* his capteyn, in whos hooli name
That day escapid fro myscheef & shame.

Dawn found Theodosius still on his knees, almost blinded by weeping, his hope set on Jesus.

The hooli crosse bete in his armure,
Born as cheef standard toforn i*n* his bataile;
God made hy*m* strong[e] in the feeld tendure,

The holy cross was borne as his chief standard, and God gave him victory.

1935. delyuerest R.
1937. &] & all H, R 3.
1940. Thi]This B, R, H 5.
1954. shewe] shyne R, J.

Hardi as leou*n** his enmyes to assaile;
I*esus* his championu*n*, his plate & eek his maile, —
I*esus* allone, set fix in his memorie,
Be whom that day he hadde the* victorie.

One of Arbogast's generals, Arbicio, deserted to the side of Theodosius,

Ther was a kniht, *prince* of the cheualrie [p. 388]
Of Arbogast and [of] Eugenivs,
Which gouerned al hool[i] ther partie,
Arbicio callid, ma*n*li a*n*d vertuous,
Which goodli ca*m* to Theodosius,
Did hym reuere*n*ce, & with riht glad cheer
Saued hym that day fro myscheef & dau*n*geer.

and a miraculous tempest of wind, hail and rain also befell to his advantage.

Whan Theodosie upon his foon ga*n* sette,
Lik a kniht nat turny*n*g his visage,
And bothe batailes togidre wha*n* thei mette,
Of Theodosie texpleite the passage
Fill a myracle to his auau*n*tage:
Be sodeyn tempest of wy*n*dis, hail & rey*n*
Troubled all tho that seeged the mou*n*tey*n*.

Vulcan bent his guns of thunder and lightning, and Æolus awoke the winds in their caverns.

Vlcanvs, which is cheef smyth of heuene,
Gey*n* Arbogastes gan hym reedi make
To beende his gun*n*ys wi*th* thonder & with leuene,
And Eolus his wyndis ga*n* awake
Out of the[r] kauernys, hidous, brou*n* & blake;
Alle of assent be sturdi violence
With Theodosius stooden at diffence

The enemy were scattered, their spears broken, their shields riven asunder. Eugenius was taken captive and beheaded; Arbogastes slew himself.

Agey*n* Eugenivs & Arbogast his brothir,
Ther peeple and thei departed heer & yond*er*
Wi*th* wynd and myst, that non of hem sauh oþ*er*,
Be vnwar vengau*n*ce of tempest & of thu*n*dir,
Ther speres tobrak, ther sheeldes roff assond*er*.
Eugenivs take, aftir lost his hed,
[And] Arbogastes slouh hymsilf for dreed.

1964. leou*n*s B, J.
1965. his] is R.
1967. the] that B.
1968. Ther] Her R — a prince H.
1969. Arbogastes P — 2nd of] *om.* R, J, R 3, H 5, P.
1970. hooli] hool R, J, H 5, whole P.
1977. bothe] *om.* R.
1978. texplete H.
1980. tempestes J, P — haile wynde & reyn H.
1981. seeged] passid H. 1986. ther] the H, J.
1987. Alle] And R.
1990. yond*er*] theer R.
1995. Arbogast P.

Thus can the Lord of his eternal myht
Chastise tirau*n*tis & ther malis represse;
Saued Theodose, his owne chose kniht:
Who trustith hym of parfit stabilnesse,
Goth free fro dau*n*geer, escapeth fro distr*e*sse.
Bookis recorde how Theodosius
Was in his tyme callid Catholicus.

Thus the Lord can chastise tyrants and save those who trust in him.

This myracle God list for hy*m* werche,
Made hym victor for his gret meeknesse.
[Afforn and] afftir fou*n*de onto the cherche
As Cristis kniht; I take onto witnesse
His submyssiou*n* & his deuout hu*m*blesse;
Of hastynesse wha*n* he was vengable,
He to the cherch[e] yald hymsilf coupable.

God worked this miracle and made Theodosius victorious for his great meekness; and once when he was revengeful he afterwards devoutly submitted himself to the church.

The caas was this, as I reherse can:
In Thesalonica, a famous old cite,
Beyng bisshop Seynt Ambrose in Mela*n*,
Certeyn iuges* for to doon equite
And sitte in doom hauyng auctorite,
Natwithstondyng ther com*m*yssiou*n*
Wer slayn be comou*n*s entryng in the* tou*n*.

Certain judges in Thessalonica were slain by the commons; and the emperor in his anger

Wherof* themp*er*ou*r* was nothyng* glad nor fay*n*,
But comau*n*ded of hasti wilfulnesse,
Wha*n* he knew his iuges wer so slay*n*,
That his knihtis sholde hem thidir dresse,
Entre* the cite be cruel sturdynesse,
Wi*th* suerd & pollex & daggeres sharp*e* whette,
Indifferentli slen al tho þ*at* thei mette.

ordered his knights to enter the city and massacre the people.

Bi whos biddyng the cite to encou*m*bre,
That day was slayn many an in*n*ocent:
Fyue thousand ded reme*m*brid in that nou*m*bre,
Moordrid in hast withoute iugeme*n*t
Bi them that wern vnto* the cite sent.
But whan Ambrose herde of this cruel deede,
Lik a iust prelat thus he gan proceede:

Five thousand were murdered, including many innocent.

St. Ambrose heard of this cruel deed,

As ye haue herd[e] how this vengau*n*ce ga*n*,
Be Theodosie to chastise the cite,
The same emp*er*ou*r* cam aftir to Melan,

and afterwards when he met Theodosius on the porch of

2001. recordeth R. 2012. Milayn H. 2013. iuges] Iewes B.
2016. in the] into B, R, in to the J. 2017. Wherof] Therof B, J — nothyng] nouther B, H, nothir R 3, nouthyr H 5.
2021. Entre] Entred B, R, J. 2028. vnto] into B.

the cathedral church at Milan, he forbade him to enter.

Wolde haue entrid at a solempnite
The cathedral cherch in his most rialte;
Bisshop Ambrose at the porche hy*m* mette,
And of purpos manli hym withsette.

saying, "I advise you to go away; you are a cruel homicide and shall not enter this church in spite of your power. You can remain outside for a while.

Quod the bisshop, "I cou*n*seil the withdrawe,
Into this cherch thou shalt haue no*n* entre.
Thou hast offendid God and eek his lawe.
Be nat so hardi nor bold, I charge the,
To sette thi foot nor entre in no degre;
Because thou art a cruel homycide,
Maugre thi myht thou shalt a while abide.

"Go home to your palace and don't let yourself be seen for eight months. God has disdain for all such murderers.

Vnto thi paleis hom ageyn retourne,
This eihte monethes looke thou be nat sey*n*;
Passe nat thi bou*n*dis, doo meekli ther soio*u*rne:
For, trust me weel and be riht weel c*er*teyne,
Al suich moordrers God hath he*m* in disdeyne.
Blood falsli shad, haue this in reme*m*b*r*ance,
Callith day and niht to hym to do ve*n*gau*n*ce.

"During these eight months do not presume to enter the church,

Ageyn[e]s the, for this gret offence [p. 389]
Of in*n*ocent blood shad ageyn[e]s riht,
Be iust auctorite I yiue this sentence:
This eihte monethes acou*n*tid day & niht
To entre the cherch thou shalt nat come i*n* siht,
Resou*n* shal holde so iustli the ballau*n*ce
Til thou haue fulli acomplisshid thi penau*n*ce.

and take good heed of what I have said; for you'll get no more of me this time, and don't kill any more innocent people."

What I haue seid[e] tak [t]heerof good heede,
For this tyme thou gest no mor of me.
Withdrawe thy*n* hand in*n*ocent blood to sheede
For any rancour or hasti cruelte."
That to behold the gret humylite
Of themperou*r*, considred eueridee1,
It wolde haue perced an herte maad of steel.

It would have pierced a heart of steel to see the emperor's humility; for bursting into tears and sobs he went home to his penance

With hed enclyned he spak no woord* ageyn,
Brast on weepyng with sobbyng v*n*stau*n*chabl*e*,
His purpil weede bedewed as with rey*n*,
Returnyng hom with cheer most lame*n*tabl*e*,
So contynued in his purpos stable,
Wit*h* al the toknys of feithful repentau*n*ce
In lowli wise acomplisshed his penau*n*ce.

2039. shal H.
2059. I haue] have I R. 2066. no woord he spak B.
2068. as] all R. 2071. the toknys] *om.* H.

Gaf exau*m*ple to p*r*incis euerichon
In caas semblable, that werke of wilfulnesse
To execucion*n* for to proceede anon,
Meynteene ther erro*u*r & froward cursidnesse,
Diffende ther trespas, mey*n*teene ther woodnesse,
Ferr out of ioynt, yif it shal be declarid,
To Theodosie for to be comparid.

with a most lamentable face. An example to princes, who out of perverse cursedness defend their trespasses.

To the cherche he meekli did obeye,
[Lik] Goddis kniht did lowli his penau*n*ce,
Wher ther be sum*m*e that wrongli it werreye,
Holde therageyn*n* be froward mey*n*tenau*n*ce.
Touchyng this mateer set heer i*n* r*e*me*m*b*r*ance,
As men disserue, — lat eu*er*y wiht tak heede —
He that seeth al quiteth he*m* ther meede.

He obeyed the church and meekly did his penance, in contrast to those who wrongly resist,

Theodosivs list nothyng abregge
To shorte the yerde of his correcciou*n*;
Forsook the platte, of rigo*u*r took the egge,
Meekli to suffre his castigaciou*n*;
To bowe his chyne was no rebelliou*n*,
Bi meek confessiou*n* knowy*n*g his trespace,
Be Seynt Ambrose restored ageyn to g*r*ace.

and, accepting his punishment to the full, was finally restored to grace.

Vertuous p*r*incis may exau*m*ple take
Of Theodose, how thei the Lord shal queeme,
He nat froward amendis for to make,
His sceptr*e*, his suerd, his purpre, his diadeeme
Soget to Ambrose, what hym list to deeme,
Obeied al thyng; & for his gret offence
To hooli cherch to make recompence.

Virtuous princes may take example of Theodosius, how they shall conciliate the Lord. He subjected himself to Ambrose

He knew[e] that God was his sou*er*eyn Lord,
To hooli cherch how gretli he was bou*n*de,
Gruchched neuer in thouht, will nor woord,
Hooli on Crist his empire for to fou*n*de.
Wher vertu regneth, vertu wil ay rebou*n*de;
And for this p*r*ince obeied tal vertu,
Hath now his guerdou*n* aboue wit*h* Crist I*es*u.

and holy church without complaint, and now has his reward with Christ above.

2078. Ferr] for*e* H, For R 3 — it] all H.
2081. Lik] *om.* R, J.
2082. it] *om.* H.
2087. nothyng] no while H.
2093. Be] *om.* H — restored] restorde hy*m* H.
2099. his] this H.
2105. ay wil R.
2106. tal] to al H, callid R.
2107. his] *om.* H.

[How knightys and gentylmen chese Aleryk kyng / and comou*n*s chese Radagasus whiche ended in myschef.] [1]

All peoples are descended from Noah and his three sons, as the Bible says. From Japhet came seven nations:

IT is remembrid of antiquite,
In the Bible, aftir Noes flood,
How bi dissent[e] of his sonis thre,
Of ther lynage pleynli and ther blood
Al kynreedis dilatid been abrod;
And [in] my*n* aucto*u*r, as it is maad[e] mynde,
Of Iaphet ca*m* seuene naciou*n*s, as I fy*n*de.

Gaul, Galatia, the Goths, Italians, Tyre, Scythia and Thrace.

The peeple first of Gaule & Galathe,
Of Magoth Gothes & folkis of Itaile,
Tire, Sithia, with many gret contre
Stondy*n*g in Asia, as be rehersaile;
But in Europe sta*n*t Trace, it is no faile.
Gothes, Sithiens of purpos did ordeyne
Among hemsilff[e] gou*er*nou*r*[e]s tweyne:

In Thrace the Goths and Scythians had two governors, Alaric, chosen by the gentry, and Radagaisus, chosen by the commons.

Knihtis, gentilmen chose* Alericus
To be ther p*r*ince and haue the souereyn*n*te,
Wher the comou*n*s chose Radagasus.
The Gothes first, for grettest surete,
With kyng Alerik been entred þe cite,
Into Roome to fynde ther soco*u*r,
That tyme Honorius beyng emp*er*o*u*r.

The emperor Honorius granted Alaric Gaul, Spain and France, but Stilicho was sent down against him afterwards,

Be grau*n*t of whom, al the hool contre
Youe to Alerik, of Gaule, Spaigne & F*r*ance,
Ther for tabide & holde ther his see,
Gothes, Spay[g]nolffs vndir his obeissau*n*ce,
Takyng on hym al the gou*er*nau*n*ce,
Til Stillicon out of the occident
To meete with them was dou*n* fro Roome sent,

and Alaric put him to flight.

That tyme Honorie beyng emper*ou*r. [p. 390]
Stillicon ga*n* Allerik enchace
Wit*h* many a proud[e] sturdi soudeo*u*r,
For to fihte thei chose haue ther place;

2122. chosen B — Alaricus R, P, R 3, Alaricas H.
2124. Radagusus H. 2127. ther] their H.
2130. Spayn Gaule & Frau*n*ce H.
2135. them] hym R.
2139. place] space R.

[1] MS. J. leaf 160 recto.

But Allerik stood so in the grace
Of Fortune, that be verray myht
Stillicon he putte vnto the fliht.

Radagasus and Alerik of assent
Haue concludid and ful accordid be
Thoruh Itaille for to make her went
Toward Roome, and entre that cite,
Maugre Romeyns to haue the souereynte.
Tofor ther entring gan the toun manace,
The name of Rome to chaungen & diffface.

Radagaisus and Alaric then decided to conquer Rome, and threatened to change its name, to the disgrace of the Romans.

For euermor the toun to doon a shame
Ther purpos was, as ye haue herd deuise;
First of alle to chaungen the touns name,
Dempt themsilff hable to that emprise.
But Fortune thouhte al othirwise,
Lik hir maneeres to do most damage,
Whan she to men sheweth fresshest hir visage.

They thought themselves able to do this; but Fortune thought otherwise.

Hir condiciouns be nat alwey oon;
Stoundemeel of custum she can varie;
For she was first froward to Stillicon,
And to Radagasus eft ageyn contrarie:
In o poynt, she list[e] neuer tarie,
To Radagasus hir fauour did faille,
Be Stillicon he venquisshid in bataille.

Although she had been froward to Stilicho, she now, favoured him. Radagaisus was defeated,

Al his pride myht nat make hym speede;
Fortune list[e] so for hym ordeyne,
That he was fayn, at so streiht a neede,
To flee for socour to an hih mounteyne,
Of al vitaille nakid & bareyne,
Wher for hunger he felte so gret greef,
Nih al his peeple deide at* myscheeff.

and fled to a mountain, where his soldiers died of hunger;

Of al socour destitut and bareyn,
Sauh no remedie, took hym to þe fliht;
Be the Romeyns he was so ouerleyn,
Take at myscheef, & maugre al his myht
In cheynis bounde & dampned anon riht
For to be ded; his peeple, as it is told,
Many on slayn, summe take & summe wer sold.

and finally he was captured and sentenced to death.

2146. that] þe H.
2149. chaungen] daunger R.
2161–63 *are transposed in* H, *but correction indicated.*
2170. at] for B.

No one was more proud than king Radagaisus. His power did not last long.

Ther was no[n] proudere nor mor surquedous
In thilke dayes, pleynli to descryue,
Than was this said[e] ky*ng* Radagasus,
Which took on hym with Romey*ns* for to stryue.
His poweer short, was ouertourned blyue;
For Fortune of malys hadde a lust
To slen this tirau*n*t with hu*n*ger & with thrust.

He was vainglorious because people called him king of the Goths. His memory was soon forgotten.

Among[es] othir proud[e] p*r*incis alle
Reioysshed hy*m*silf bamaner [of] veyn*g*lorie,
Because that men in contres ded hy*m* calle
Kyng of Gothes; short is the memorie
Of hy*m* rehersid or writyn in historie, —
To yiue exau*m*ple, in deede me*n* may fynde
The name of tirau*n*t*es* is soone put out of my*n*de.

[How Ruffyne chamberleyn *with* Theodosie vsurped to be Emperou*r* and therfor*e* by honoryus dampned & his heed smet of.] [1]

High climbing up by usurpation to imperial estate has often a sudden fall.

HIH clymby*ng* vp haþ ofte a*n* vnwar fall
And specialli wha*n* it is sodeyne,
Fro lowh degre testat imp*er*iall,
Wha*n* fals ambiciou*n* the ladder doth ordeyne,
Be vsurpaciou*n* presumptuousli tatteyne
Aboue the skies with his hed to perse;
Fro whens he ca*m* wer shame to reherse.

And this is especially true of those men whose beginnings are often a shame to rehearse—men who do not wish to know themselves, like Rufinus,

I meene as thus; al suich hasti cly*m*byng
Of them that list nat he*m*silf for to knowe
And haue forgete the grou*n*d of þ*er* gyn*n*yng,
Be froward fame with worldli wyndis blowe,
To reise ther name* boue Sagittaries bowe, —
Record on Ruffyn*, which proudli gan desire
Be fals intrusiou*n* to occupie thempire.

once an officer of Theodosius, who tried to become emperor by intrusion.

The which Ruffyn was whilom chau*m*birley*n*
With Theodosie, and holde a ma*n*li kniht;
Yit in o thyng he was foul ouersey*n*,

2180. ky*ng*] *om.* R. 2181. took] *om.* R — on] vpon H.
2189. historie] memorye H. 2194. testat] to thestate H.
2197. skies] sterris R — with his hed] his hede with H, R 3.
2199. as] *om.* H. 2202. worldli] clowdy H.
2203. names B, J — aboue H.
2204. Ruffyn] Ruffia B, R, J — on] off R.
2206. whilome was H. 2207. and] was R.

[1] MS. J. leaf 160 verso.

Be couetise bleendid in his siht
To spende his labour, & hadde no ground of riht.
Be themperour Honorius he was sent
For to gouerne al the orient.

Bi processe Ruffyn was maad vikeer,
Callid aftir vikeer Imperial,
Took upon hym hooli and enteer
Be auctorite, [as] cheef and princepal,
Hymsilf allone to gouernen al,
As most hable; thus he dede deeme,
Beforn all othir to were a diadeeme;

He was sent by Honorius to the East and called Vicar Imperial. Afterwards he seized the whole empire

Of hymsilff so moche he ded[e] make, [p. 391]
In port and cheere [the] most ambicious.
At Constantynople vnwarli he was take,
First bounde in cheynys and aftir seruid thus:
Be trewe iugement of Honorivs,
His hed smet of and his* riht hand in deede;
This was his eende; of hym no mor I reede.

and made much of himself; but he was taken in Constantinople and bound in chains, and his head and right hand were cut off.

[How Stillicon and othir of lik condicion ended in myscheff.][1]

AFFTIR whos deth to Bochas ther cam oon,
Swich another lik of condicioun,
Afforn remembrid, callid Stellicon,
Whos sone Euterius, as maad is mencioun,
Purposed hym to haue pocessioun
Of thempire hool; pleynli thus he thouhte,
And bi what mene the weie his fadir souhte.

Stilicho next appeared to Bochas. His son Eucherius proposed that they should take possession of the Empire;

Compendiousli to tellyn of thes tueyne,
Fro dyuers contres toward Septemptrioun
To gadre peeple, thei dide her besi peyne,
Of many dyuers straunge nacioun.
Ageyn Honorivs thei cam togidre doun,
[And] as thei mette, Fortune made hem faille,
Bothe attonys slay[e]n in bataille.

so they collected an army of various peoples and were defeated and slain by Honorius.

2209. Be] to H.
2223. aftir] aftirward R.
2225. hed] he R — his] in his B.
2230. Eucherius P.
2239. And as] All R, and H, R 3 — made] dyd R.

[1] MS. J. leaf 160 verso.

Their evil beginning had an evil end. Constans and his father Constantine also took upon themselves to usurp power in the Empire.

Ther gynnyng cursid hadde a wengable fyn;
Aftir whos deth I reede of othir tweyne:
¶ Of oon Constans, his fadir Co*n*stanty*n*,
Which Constanty*n* took on hym in certeyne
To regne in Gaule, and aftir that ordeyne,
In that contre to be gouerno*u*r,
Ther to co*n*tynve as lord and empero*u*r.

Constans turned monk, but his father had him taken out and made a knight.

His sone Constans kaute a deuocio*u*n
Of conscience, and forthwith ano*n* riht
Was shaue a monk, & made his professio*u*n.
His fadir aftir of verray force & myht
Leet take hy*m* out, gaf hym the ordre of kniht;
Both of assent gan make hemsilue*n* strong
Toppresse the contre & do the peeple wrong.

Both of them then oppressed the people, and, joining together with one Gerontius,

This said[e] Constans, as my*n* aucto*u*r seith,
Was confederat, of hatful cruelte,
With oon Herencivs, assurau*n*ce maad & feith,
As brethre suorn for mor auctorite.
And for to make the nou*m*bre up of thre,
Constantyn was sworrn with hem also
To been al oon in what thei hadde ado.

conquered many cities in Spain. Gerontius traitorously slew Constans,

Thes said[e] thre sworn and Iioyned thus,
Conquered in Spaigne many gret cite;
But in this while this seid Herencivs,
Traito*u*r and fals, ful of duplicite,
His fellawe slouh agey*n* his oth, parde.
Thus was Constans thoruh fals collusiou*n*
Of Herencivs moordred be tresou*n*.

and shortly afterwards he himself was killed by his own soldiers. As a rule men receive their just reward.

Herencivs aftir lyued but a while;
Be his owne knihtis he slay[e]n was also.
Fraude for fraude; deceit is quit *with* gile;
It folweth euer & gladli cometh therto:
Men resceyue ther guerdou*n*s as thei doo.
Lat men alwey haue this in reme*m*brau*n*ce,
Moordre of custum wil eende with myschau*n*ce.

Among others who ended in mischief were Attalus and Heraclian,

¶ Amo*n*g suich othir, thus eendi*n*g i*n* myscheef,
Cam Attalus and oon Eraclyan;
For no prowesse, but to ther gret repreeff

2241. Ther] The R. 2250. &] *om.* H, R 3.
2257. Herencius] Heroncyus H, R 3, henricius J, Gerontius P.
2261. ado] to do R. 2262. Ioyned R, H. 2264, 68. Gerontius P.
2275. wil eende] eendith H. 2277. and] an R.

Reme*m*brid heer; ther stori telle ca*n*,
Ageyn Romey*n*s whan thei rebell[e] gan,
Be Honorivs afforn maad officeeres
And of thempire callid cheef vikeres.

who rebelled against Honorius.

First Attalus for his tiran*n*ye,
Whan he in Gaule was maad [a] gou*er*nou*r*,
Went into Spaigne with a gret co*m*panye,
Did his peyne and fraudulent labo*u*r
Be fals sleihte to be maad empero*u*r.
Take and bou*n*de, exilid for falsnesse,
His hand smet of, eendid in wrechidnesse.

Attalus tried to be made emperor in Spain and was exiled and his hand cut off.

OFF Eraclyan the ende was almost lik,
Yit was he promoot to gret prosp*er*ite,
Maad gouerno*u*r & lord of [al] Affrik,
Of consuleer roos to the dignite,
Rood thoruh Libie and many gr*e*t contre,
With thre thousand shippes ga*n* to saille
And with seuene hundrid taryue [vp] i*n* Itaille.

Heraclian, governor of Africa, became a consul and attempted to invade Italy with 3700 ships.

Swich nou*m*bre of shippis neu*er* afforn was* sey*n*,
Lik as it is acou*n*tid be writyng;
His naue passed the naue in certeyne
Of myhti Xerses, that was of Perse ky*n*g,
Or Alisau*n*dre; but yit in his comyng,
Toward Itaille whan he sholde aryve,
The se and Fortune ga*n* agey*n* hym stryve.

His navy was larger than that of mighty Xerxes or Alexander.

At his arryuaile he hadde a sodey*n* dreed, [p. 392]
Cause Honorius had sent dou*n* a capteyn*n*,
Constancivs callid, gou*er*nou*r* and hed
Of al the Romey*n*s, to meete hym o*n* the pley*n*;
For which Eraclya*n* tournid is agey*n*,
As I fynde, ga*n* take his passage
Toward the cite that callid is Cartage.

When he arrived, he lost courage because Honorius had sent down Constantius to give him battle, and sailed for Carthage,

Thus Fortune list hir poweer shewe:
Or he ca*m* fulli to that noble tou*n*,
With sharp[e] suerdis he was al to-hewe
Among his knihtis thoruh fals occasioun*
As thei fill at a discenciou*n*.

where he was cut to pieces by his knights.

2292. al] *om.* R.
2297. was] wer B, were J.
2312. noble] *om.* R. 2314. occasioun] collusiou*n* B
2315. at] as R — a] *om.* H.

Of intrusioun began first this quarell,
Ageyn Romeyns whan that he gan rebell.

¶ Bochas rehersith here be vhom Rome cam to nou3te.[1]

Almost every prince whose story Bochas told in his Eighth Book ended in wretchedness,

OFF many myscheuys heer afforn rehersid,
Summe drawe along & summe shortli told,
And hou Fortune hath hir wheel reuersid,
Be tragedies remembrid manyfold
Toforn be Bochas, of princis yong & old,
In the eihte* book rehersid the processe,
Echon almost eendid in wrechidnesse.

especially those who tried to become emperor without just title. Yet the estate of emperor has gone to ruin,

Namli all tho that dide most desire
Be wrong title themsilff to magnefie,
To haue lordshipe & gouerne the empire,
Thestat imperial proudli to occupie.
Which estat, pleynli to specefie,
As ferr as Pheebus doth in his speere shyne
Among al lordshipe is drawe onto ruyne.

and Rome came to nought, as John Bochas rehearses.

Fro myn auctour me list[e] nat discorde
To telle the ground whi Roome is com* to nouht;
Be an exaumple I cast me to recorde
What was cheef cause, yiff it be weel souht,*
Be a stori that cam onto the thouht
Of Iohn Bochas, which, as ye shal lere,
Ful notabli is rehersed heer.

It happened in the time of Odoacer, a king and a great governor, yet a ravenous robber,

Which exaumple and stori rehersyng,
Ceriously folwyng myn auctour,
Odoacer, whilom a famous kyng,—
A kyng be name & a gret gouernour,
But of his lyuyng a rauynous robbour,
Out of whos court wer merci & pite
Banshed for euere with trouthe & equite.

2316. this] the R.
2319. along] long R.
2323. eihte] seuent R, vij^te H 5, viij^te B.
2331. lordshippis R. 2333. is com] cam B, J.
2335. out souht B, J. 2336. the] his H.
2337. Of] bi H. 2339. and] in H.
2340. folwen H.

[1] *The following chapter-heading is in* MS. J. leaf 161 recto: "A good processe why Rome was destroied / and for the same or like cause many other Rewmes."

In that regiou*n* wher m*er*ci is nat vsid,
And trouthe oppressid is with tiran*n*ye,
And rihtwisnesse be poweer is refusid,
Fals extorsiou*n* supporteth robberie,
And sensualite ca*n* haue the maistrie
Aboff resou*n*, be toknes at a preeff,
Which many a lond haue brouht o*n*to myscheeff.

without mercy or pity. Many a land has been brought to ruin when sensuality has the mastery of reason.

Ther is no rewm may stond in surete,
Ferme nor stable in verray existence,
Nor contune in long prosp*er*ite,
But yif the throne of ky*n*gli excellence
Be supportid with iustise and clemence
In hym that shal as egal iuge stonde
Tween riche & poore, with sceptr*e* & suerd* i*n* honde.

No realm can stand secure unless the throne is supported by clemency and justice.

A cleer exau*m*ple, this mateer for to grou*n*de, —
So as a fadir that is naturall,
Or lik a moodir which kynd[e]li is bou*n*de
To fostre ther childr*e* in epsecial,
Riht so a kyng in his estat roiall
Sholde of his offis dilligentli entende
His trewe leeges to cherisshe [hem] & diffende.

Just as fathers and mothers are bound to foster their children, so should kings cherish and defend their subjects,

Be good exau*m*ple his sogettis tenlumyne;
For temp*or*al rewmys sholde, as in figure,
Resemble the kyngdam which [that] is dyuyne,
Be lawe of God & lawe eek of nature,
That *res publica* long tyme may endure,
Void of discord and fals duplicite,
As* o bodi in long prosp*er*ite.

giving them a good example; and temporal kingdoms ought to resemble the kingdom that is divine.

Nouther ther regne nor domynaciou*n*
Haue of themsilff non other assurau*n*ce;
Thestat of kynges ga*n* be permyssiou*n*
Of Goddis grace & of his purueyau*n*ce,
Be vertuous lyff and moral gou*er*nau*n*ce,
Long to contune bothe in pes and werre
Lik her desertis, & pu*n*she hem wha*n* thei erre.

There is no other assurance for them; inasmuch as the estate of kings began by the permission of God; and God will treat them as they deserve.

Thei sholde be the merou*r* and the liht, [p. 393]
Transcende al othir be vertuous excellence,
As exau*m*plaires of equite and riht,

Kings should excel all other men in virtue and discretion;

2346. nat] na H. 2348. be] wit*h* H.
2359. suerd & sceptr*e* B, J. 2363. special H.
2366. hem] *om.* J, P, H 5. 2369. that] *om.* R.
2373. As] Of B, J. 2374. nor] no H.

So be discrecioun of natural prouidence
To tempre ther rigour with merci & clemence;
What shal falle afforn[e] caste al thynges,
As apparteneth to princis & to kynges.

they must remember the past and prepare for things to come and resist vices.

Thynges passed to haue in remembrance,
Conserue wisli thynges in presence,
For thynges to come afforn mak ordenaunce,
Folwe the tracis of vertuous contynence,
Ageyn all vices to make resistence
Be the vertu of magnanymyte,
Which is approprid to imperial mageste,

They should be stable in joy and adversity,

Brothir to force, auctours seyn echon,
Which conserueth the roial dignite
In suich a mene stable as eny ston, —
Nat ouer glad for no prosperite,
Nor ouer sad for non aduersite;
For lyff nor deth his* corage nat* remewe
To God and man to yeld hem that is dewe.

arm themselves against fleshly lusts and exclude all slanderous people, flatterers and ribalds from their palaces.

Geyn flesshli lustis arme hym in sobirnesse,
Voide al surfetis of froward glotonye,
Gredi appetites be mesure to represse,
Out of his hous auoide al ribaudie,
Rowners, flaterers and such folk as kan lie,
War in his doomys he be nat parciall,
To poore doon almesse, to vertuous liberall.

In their dress they should shew themselves kings; but virtuous living deserves more praise than clothing.

In his array shewe hym lik a kyng
From other princis bamaner difference,*
So that men preise his vertuous lyuyng
Mor than his clothing, ferr from his presence;
And let hym thynken in his aduertence,
Truste theron, verraily certeyn,
As he governeth men wil reporte & seyn.

For companions let them have notable, experienced princes, who know the difference between good and evil;

Lat hym also for his gret avail
Haue such aboute hym to be in presence,
Notable princis to be of counsail,
Swich as toforn haue had experience
Tueen good and euel to knowe the difference.

2385. with merci] *om.* H. 2392. to] an H, *om.* R 3.
2394. to] to þe H. 2400. his] my B — nat] to B.
2403. of] and R. 2405. hous] thouht H, R 3.
2410. difference] apparence B, J. 2411. that] *om.* R.
2414. verraily] verrey H.

And sixe thynges, hatful of newe & old,
To banshe hem out in hast fro*m* his houshold.

¶ First them that loue to lyue i*n* idilnesse,
As such as nouther loue God nor dreede,
Coueitous peeple that poore folk oppresse,
And them also that doon al thyng for meede,
And symulaciou*n*, clad in a double weede,
And suich as ca*n* for ther auau*n*tages
Out of oon hood[e] shewe too visages.

and they must not be idle, covetous, deceitful, or

Lat hym also uoid out at his gate
Riotous peeple that loue to wachche al niht,
And them also that vse to drynke late,
Ly longe abedde til ther dyner be diht,
And such as list nat of God to haue a siht,
And rekles folk that list nat heere masse,
Tauoide his court, & let hem lihtli passe.

riotous, with late drinking and lying long abed, or have about them reckless people who do not go to mass.

For suich defautis, rehersed heer toforn,
Nat onli Roome, but many gret contre
Hath be destroied & many ky*n*dam lorn,
In olde cronicles as ye may reed & see.
Fals ambiciou*n*, froward duplicite
Hath many a rewm & many a lond encloied,
And been in cause whi thei haue be destroied.

Not only Rome but many another kingdom has been destroyed for such faults:

Iherusalem was whilom t*r*ansmygrat,
Ther trewe p*ro*phetis for thei hadde i*n* despiht;
And Baltazar was eek infortunat,
For he in Babilou*n* folwed al his deliht.
Darye in Perse had but smal respiht,
Sodenly slay*n* and moordred be tresou*n*,
The same of Alisau*n*dre wha*n* he* dra*n*k poisou*n*.

Jerusalem because the Jews scorned their true prophets; Belshazzar for his luxury in Babylon; Darius was suddenly slain, and Alexander poisoned.

Discord in Troye grou*n*did on couetise,
Wha*n* be fals tresou*n* sold was Palladiou*n*;
Roome and Cartage in the same wise
Destroied wern, for short conclusiou*n*,
Amo*n*g hemsilff for ther dyuisiou*n*.
Rekne othir rewmys that been of latter date,
As of dyuisiou*n*s in F*r*ance that fill but late.

Troy was lost by covetousness; Rome and Carthage were destroyed by civil strife, such as fell but late in France.

2424. nouther] nouthis R. 2427. a] *om.* R.
2428, 29. avau*n*tage, visage H. 2430. uoid] avoide H.
2439. many a H. 2442. *both* a's *om.* H, 2nd a *om.* R.
2443. been in cause] be the cause R.
2450. he] that he B, H, R. 2452. sold] slayn H.
2457. of] in H — in] of H.

The chief fault has been in the ruling princes; and I shall tell as an example the story of Odoacer.

Al thes defautis rehersid heer breefli,
Outsouht the roote & weied in balau*n*ce,
Cheeff occasiou*n*, to telle bi and bi,
Hath been in p*r*incis that haue had gou*er*nau*n*ce.
And specialli to putte in reme*m*brau*n*ce,
For an exau*m*ple telle as kometh to my*n*de
Of Odoacer the stori, as I fynde.

He was born in Pannonia, and as he had no ancestry he began a conquest of theft and robbery.

Born in Prevs and hardi of corage, [p. 394]
At his begyny*n*g hymsilf to magnefie,
Thouh no menciou*n* be maad of [his] lynage,
Hauyng no title of blood nor au*n*cetrie,*
His co*n*quest gan of theffte and robberye,*
Gadred peeple of sondri regiou*n*s,
Entred Itaille with many naciou*n*s.

He invaded Hungary and defeated Orestes, who fled to Pavia

With his soudio*u*rs first he gan assaille,
With multitude entry*n*g ano*n* riht,
Kyndames of Hungry & contres of Itaille;
Mette in his passage with a Romey*n* kniht
Callid Horestes, in steel armyd briht:
The feeld wás take and put in iupartie;
Horestes fledde for soco*u*r to Pauye.

and was there taken prisoner and afterwards slain.

Streihtli beseged and the tou*n* Iwon*n*e,
Fond for the tyme non othir cheuisau*n*ce,
The nexte morwe at risyng of the sun*n*e,
Bou*n*de in cheynis tencres of his greuau*n*ce,
Sent to a cite that callid was Plesau*n*ce,
Ageyn[e]s whom Odoacer was so fell,
Leet hym be slayn be iugement ful cruel.

Odoacer then marched on Rome and was crowned king of Italy.

Aftir whos deth, be sodey*n* violence
Odoacer is passid thoruh Itaille,
Entred Roome, fond no resistence;
For ther was non to yiue hy*m* bataille.
Zeno themp*er*o*u*r durste hy*m* nat assaille,
So that be force and rauynous werky*n*g
Of al Itaille he was crownid kyng.

2461. Hath] Have H.
2467. his] *om.* R.
2468. of blood nor au*n*cetrie] but theffte and robberye B, J.
2469. gan of theffte and robberye] gan*n*at of blood nor au*n*cetrie B, gan nought of blood and au*n*cetrie J.
2474. Kyngdam H, R 3, Kyngdom P. 2478. to] i*n* to H.
2482. in] wit*h* H.
2490. durste] did H.
2491. rauynour R.

Hadde al Roome vndir subiecciou*n*,
Fortune a while list [hym] nat [to] faille,
Zeno therof hadde indignaciou*n*,
Gan werke ageyn hym, in hope it sholde [a]uaile.
And therupon the lordship of Itaille
He gaf of purpos, his poweer com*m*itty*n*g,
To Theodorik, that was of Gothes kyng.

The Emperor Zeno resigned his power to Theodoric the Goth,

So that Theodorik in hope to haue victorie,
Ageyn Odoacer ga*n* make resistence;
And his name to putte[n] in memorie,
Took vpon hy*m* be knihtli excellence
For the Romeyns to stonde[n] in diffence.
Mette hy*m* proudli with his cheualrie
Beside a ryueer that callid was Sowcye.

who attacked Odoacer on the Sontius

With ther batailles togidre wha*n* thei mette,
Beside Leglere that stant in Lumbardie,
With rou*n*d[e] speres & sharp swerdis* whette,
Odoacer, for al his tiran*n*ye,
Was put to fliht, discou*n*fited his partie.
And Fortune than, [which] ca*n* best chau*n*ge & varie,
At vnset hour was to hym contrarie.

in Lombardy and defeated him.

Hym & his poweer the Romey*n*s haue defied;
He brente her vynes and to*u*r[e]s envirou*n*,
Because the entre was to hy*m* denyed,
And to Rauen*ne* he is descendid dou*n*.
But maugre hym he was take i*n* that* tou*n*
Be Theodorik; lat ech tirau*n*t tak heed,
Odoacer comau*n*did to be ded.

Retreating through Italy, Odoacer laid waste the land, but was finally captured in Ravenna and (let every tyrant take heed) beheaded.

¶ Myn aucto*u*r Bochas of entenciou*n*,
For the tyme, as kam to reme*m*braun*c*e,
Toward Romey*n*s maketh a digressiou*n*,
To them recordyng the gret[e] variau*n*ce,
The vnwar chau*n*ges, the gery contenau*n*ce
Of Fortunis fals t*r*ansmutaciou*n*,
Thes same woordis rehersyng to the tou*n*.

My author now makes a digression, recording the many vicissitudes of Rome.

2494. hym] *om.* J — list hym nat to faille] was to hy*m* favourable H, R 3 — to] *om.* R, J.
2497. the] ther R. 2501. Ageyn] Geyn R.
2504. in] at H. 2508. legle H.
2509. swerdis] speres B. 2512. which] *om.* R.
2515. to*u*res] tou*n*s R.
2518. that] the B, J.
2519. tirau*n*t] man H.
2525. guery R, H.

¶ The wordes* of Bochas a-geyne Rome.[1]

Rome, remember the days of your greatness. You once shone like a sun through the world; now all is turned to ruin.

REMEMBRE o Roome & calle ageyn to myn*d*e
The daies passid of thi felicite,
Þi* marcial co*n*quest, þi tri*um*phes left behyn*d*e,
Thi grete victories most of auctorite,
Thi famous laudes songe in ech contre,
Which like a sonne* thoruh al þe world did shyne,
Now al attonis is turnid to ruyne!

Your lordship extended from east to west; but the golden letters of your name are now darkened and defaced.

From est to west thi lordship did atteyne,
Aboue al poweers most excellent & roiall;
But now fro Roome dou*n* into Almayne
Thestat t*r*anslatid which is imperial;
Name of thi senato*ur*s, name i*n* especial,
The golden lettres dirkid & diffacid,
And from reme*m*b*r*ance almost out araced.

City of cities, to which the Alps and all the mountains of Lombardy were once subject

Cite of cites, whilom most glorious, [p. 395]
And most fresshli flour*yng* in cheualrie,
To which the Alpies & mou*n*teyns most famo*us*
Wer lowli soget of al Lumbardie,
Til that discord, dyuisiou*n* and envie
Amo*ng* yoursilf hath clipsed the brihtnesse,
Bi a fals serpent brouht in bi doubilnesse.

and kings and princes tributary, you were brought to nought when divided against yourself.

Kynges, p*r*incis wer to the tributarye,
Of al prosp*er*ite so fulsum was the flood,
Among yo*ur*silf til ye bega*n* to varie,
The world[e] thoruhout soget to you stood,
Til ye ga*n* shewe too facis in o hood:
What folwed aftir, Fortune hath so prouided,
Ye cam to nouht wha*n* ye ga*n* be deuyded.

Lacking in prudent senators, in knighthood and soldiers, the community stood desolate;

Vnpurueied of prudent senato*ur*s,
Thi marchau*n*dise turnid to pouerte,
Of knihthod barey*n*, nakid of soudio*ur*s,
Disconsolat stant al thi comou*n*te,
To*ur*[e]s, wallis broke of thi cite,

2530. Þi] Þ*at* B, þe H.
2533. a sonne] be report B, R, H 5 (whiche thurgh all the world by report did shyne J).
2537. into] in R. 2541. out racid R.
2542. most whilom R.
2549. to] *om.* R. 2553. o] oon H.

[1] wordes] workis B.

That whilom wer a paradis of deliht, —
Now al the world hath the but i*n* despiht.

and now all the world has you in contempt.

Cause, to conclude, of al thi wrechidnesse,—
Fals ambiciou*n*, pride and lecherie,
Dyuysiou*n*, malicious doubilnesse,
Ranco*ur*, hatreed, couetise [&] envie,*
Which set aside al good[e] policie;
In breef rehersed, for short co*n*clusiou*n*,
Haue be cheeff grou*n*d of thi destrucciou*n*.

Your wretchedness arose from false ambition, pride, lechery, division, deceit, anger, hatred, covetousness and envy.

[How the kynges Trabstila and Busarus were brouht to subiecciou*n* and made tributaryes to Theoderyk.] [1]

AFFTIR thes myscheuys told of Rome tou*n*,
Ca*m* Trabstila kyng of Gepidois
Wit*h* other tweyne, as maad is me*n*ciou*n*:
Busar that was kyng of Bulgarois,
Wit*h* Pheletevs, regny*n*g in Ragois.
Alle thes thre, breeffli for to seyne,*
Cam attonys to Bochas to co*m*pleyne,

Ther rewmys stondyng toward Septe*m*triou*n*.
And to reme*m*bre of the firste tweyne,
Wer brouht attonis to subiecciou*n*
Bi Theodorik, that did his besi peyne
Them to conquere, & proudli did ordeyne
That thei wer neuer hardi to rebell
Ageyn* Romey*n*s nor take no quarell.

After these calamities told of Rome, Trasilla, king of the Gepidae, Busar, king of the Bulgars, and Philete, king of the Rugii, all of whom reigned in the north, came complaining to Bochas.

The first two were conquered by Theodoric

To Theodorik thei wer maad tributarye,
Most wrechchidli bou*n*de[n] in seruage,
Neuer so hardi aftir for to varie
In peyne of deth duryng al ther age.
Of seruitute, loo, heer the surplusage,—
Of all wrechchis most wrechchid thei be fou*n*de,
Thei that to thraldam co*n*streyned bee*n* & bou*n*de.

and bound wretchedly in servage.

2566. *is transposed after* 2568 *in* B, *but correction indicated.*
2569. be] the R. 2571. Trasilla P.
2573. Busa P, Busarus J.
2574. Pheteus H, Philitheus P, J — Rugiois P.
2575. seyne] feyne B.
2583. Ageyns B.
2590. Thei that] That thei R — that] to þ*at* H.

[1] MS. J. leaf 162 verso.

Virtuous freedom is the greatest of treasures, transcending all riches found in earth.

Tresour of treso*urs*, yif it be weel souht,
Is vertuous fredam with large liberte;
Wit*h* worldli goodis it may nat be bouht,
With roial rubies, gold, stonis nor perre;
For it t*r*anscendith and hath the souereyn*n*te
Aboue al richessis that been in erthe fou*n*de,
A ma*n* at large freeli to stonde vnbou*n*de.

[How Philitee lost his kyngdom.] [1]

The third king, Philete, lost his kingdom and his life when attacked by Odoacer.

¶ Next thes too kynges, i*n* ordre as ye may see,
To Iohn Bochas ga*n* shewe his presence
The thridde kyng, callid Phelete,
Which bi Fortunys sodeyn violence
Loste his kyngdam, and be cruel sente*n*ce
Of Odoacer, the tirau*n*t merciles,
Loste his liff and ca*m* no mor in pres.

The Emperor Marcian was murdered by his soldiers;

Thes sodeyn chau*n*ges to reede wha*n* I ga*n*,
Sauh so ofte the wheel turne up & dou*n*
¶ Of Fortune; ther ca*m* oon Marcian,
Of whom is maad no*n* othir me*n*ciou*n*,
Sauff be a sodey*n* coniuraceou*n*
He moordred was, [he] beyng in*n*ocent,
Amo*n*g his knihtis, which slouh hy*m* of assent.

and young Leo, who justly succeeded his father of the same name,

¶ Than tofor Bochas to shewe[n] his p*re*sence
Ther ca*m* oon that callid was Leou*n*,
Which kauht a title be no violence,
But made his cley*m* be iust successiou*n*
Afftir his fadir, and took pocessiou*n*,
Which of a Leou*n*, my*n* aucto*u*r seith the same,
Beyng emp*er*o*ur*, bar the same name.

was tyrannously put out of his realm by Zeno and forced to become a monk.

This yonger Leou*n*, agey*n* al trouthe & riht,
Be tiran*n*ye, as maad is me*n*ciou*n*,
Thoruh cruel Zeno, that was an hardi kniht,
Was put out of his pocessiou*n*,
Constreyned to lyue in religiou*n*;
But to what ordre that he did[e] weende,
I fynde nat; but ther he made a*n* eende.

2591. of] o H.
2600. Philite P. 2604. and] *om.* H.
2605. begane H. 2606. offten H — vp so dou*n* H, J.
2609. a] *om.* R.

[1] MS. J. leaf 162 verso.

[How Symak and Boys his son in lawe were banys-shed and aftir Iuged to die.] [1]

AFFTIR thes myscheuys Symak gan [p. 396] hym drawe
Toward Bochas with a ful pitous face;
Bois cam with hym, that was his sone in lawe,
Which among Romeyns gretli stood in grace.
But in this mateer breefli for[th] to pace,
The said[e] Bois, only for his trouthe
Exilid was; alas, it was gret routhe!

Symmachus and his son-in-law Boetius were great favourites in Rome; and Boetius was exiled for his uprightness.

For comoun proffit he was onto the toun
In mateeres that groundid wer on riht
Verray protectour and stedfast championn
Ageyn too tirauntis, which of force & myht
Hadde in the poraille oppressid many a wiht
Be exacciouns and pillages gunne of newe
Vpon the comouns, ful fals & riht vntrewe.

He was protector and champion of the city against two tyrants,

Whan* Theodorik, of Gothes lord & kyng,
Took upon hym be fals intrusioun
To regne in Roome, the peeple oppressyng
Bi his too prouostis, as maad is mencioun, —
Did in the cite gret oppressioun,
Confederat as brothir onto brothir:
Coniugast, and Trigwill was the tothir.

Conigastus and Trigguilla, provosts of Theodoric;

Compendiousli this mateer to declare,
To saue the comoun Bois stood in diffence;
For lyff nor deth he list nat for to spare
To withstonde of tirauntes the sentence.
Kyng Theodorik of cruel violence
Banshed hym bi hatful tirannye,
He and his fadir tabide in Pauye.

but his struggle against them brought him into disfavour with Theodoric, who banished him and his father to Pavia.

Aftirward Theodorik of hatreede,
Lik a fals tiraunt, of malis & envie
Yaf iugement that bothe too wer dede.
Bot touchyng Boys, as bookis specefie,
Wrot dyuers bookis of philosophie,
Of the Trynite mateeres þat wer dyuyne,
Martird for Crist & callid Seueryne.

Afterwards they were both condemned to death.

2626. Simachus P. 2628. Boetius P.
2639. riht] eke R. 2640. Whan] Than B.

[1] MS. J. leaf 162 verso.

[Off kyng Arthur*e* and his co*n*quest*es* / of the co*m*moditees of Englond / and he was destroied by his Cosyn Mordrede.] [1]

Was there ever a prince who could make himself secure in Fortune's grace?

WAS eu*er* p*r*ince [that] mihte hy*m*silf assure
Of Fortune the fauo*ur* to restreyne?—
Lik his desir hir g*r*ace to recure
Tabide stable & stonde[n] at certeyne?
Amo*n*g alle rekne Artho*ur* of Breteyne,
Which in his tyme was holde of eu*er*y wiht
The wisest p*r*ince and the beste kniht.

Arthur of Britain was in his time held to be the wisest prince and best knight; and Bochas tells his story in this chapter.

To whom Bochas gan his stile dresse,
In this chapitle to reme*m*bre blyue
His grete conquest & his hih noblesse,
W*ith* synguler deedis that he wrouhte his lyue.
And first he gyn*n*eth breefli to descryue
The siht of Breteyne & of that contre,
Which is enclosed w*ith* a large se,

Britain is surrounded by a large sea and lies far to the west, north of Spain and near France. It has many rivers, hot baths and divers minerals,

Set ferr westward, as ye shal vndirstond,
Hauy*n*g Spaigne* set in the opposit,
Of a smal angle callid Ing[e]lond,
Frau*n*ce aboute hym, descryuy*n*g thus his siht,—
With many a ryueer plesau*n*t of deliht,
Hote bathes [&] wellis ther be fou*n*de,
Dyuers myneres, of metallis ful habou*n*de.

and is abundant in food. London has ships, Winchester wine, Worcester fruits, Hertford cattle, and the Cotswolds wool.

Aboute which ren*n*eth the occian,
Riht plenteuous of al man*er* vitaille,
The name of which at Brutis first bega*n*.
Londene hath shippis be the se to saille,
Bachus at Wynchestre gretli doth auaille,
Worcetre w*ith* frutis habou*n*deth at the fulle,
Herford w*ith* beestis, Cotiswold with wolle,

There are hot baths in Bath, York has timber, Cornwall mines,

Bathe hote bathes, holsum for medecyne,
York mihti tymber for gret auau*n*tage,
Cornewaile myneres in to myne,

2671. deedis] *om.* H.
2475. westward] west H.
2676. Spaigne] in Spaigne B. S.
2680. &] *om.* H, R 3.   2684. at] & H.
2686. Wynchestre] Westmynstre H, Westmenstre R 3.
2691. Cornewale H.

[1] MS. J. leaf 163 recto.

Salisburie beestis ful sauage,
Whete, melk & honi, plente for eueri age,
Kent and Cau*n*tirburi hath gret com*m*odite
Of sondri fishes ther taken in the se.

Salisbury wild cattle, Kent and Canterbury have plenty of fish.

Bochas reherseth, ther is eek in Breteyne
Fou*n*d of geet a ful precious stoon,
Blak of colour & vertuous i*n* certeyne
For siknessis many mo than oon,
Poudir of which wil discure anon,
Yif it be dronke (thouh it be secre),
Of maydenhod the broke chastite.

As Bochas says, jet is found in Britain, and its powder when drunk will quickly discover broken chastity.

Ther been eke* perlis fou*n*de in muskel shell*es*;
And thei [be] beste that haue most whitnesse.
And, as the book of Brutus also tell*es*,
How kyng Artho*u*r, to speke of worthynesse,
Passed al kynges in marcial prowesse;
Touchyng his lyne & his roial kynreede,
Who that list see, in Brutus he may reede.

There are also pearls, and the whitest are the best. King Arthur surpassed all kings in martial prowess, and his line is described in the Brut.

His fadir callid Vter Pendragou*n*, [p. 397]
A manli kniht and famous of corage,
Of fals envie moordrid be poisou*n*;
His sone Artho*u*r, but yong & tendre of age,
Be ful assent of al his baronage
Be successiou*n* crownid anon riht,
Callid of Europe the moste famous kniht.

His father was Uther Pendragon, and after he had been murdered by poison, Arthur was crowned king.

Curteis, large and manly of dispence,
Merour callid off liberalite,
Hardi, strong and of gret prouidence.
And of his knihtli magnanymyte
He droof Saxones* out of his contre,
Conquered bi prowesse of his myhti hond
Orcadois, Denmark and Houlond,

Arthur was courteous and a mirror of liberality, hardy and of great foresight. He drove out the Saxons and conquered the Orkneys, Denmark and Holland, Ireland, Norway, Gaul, Scotland and France, by the counsel of prudent Merlin. He founded the order of the Round Table,

Hirelond, Norway, Gaule, Scotlond & F*r*ance.
As Martis sone to the werris meete,
Wrouht bi cou*n*sail, and bi the ordynau*n*ce
Of prudent Merlyn, callid his p*ro*phete.
And, as I fynde, he leet make a seete,

2693. whete melk] whetmele H.
2697. geet] gret R.
2703. eke] of B, R, J.
2717. dispence] expense R. 2721. Saxones] Saxoyns B.
2723. holonde H, Holande R 3. 2727. Merlyn] Marly H.

Amon[g] his Bretou*n*s most famous & notable,
Thoruh al the world callid the Rou*n*d[e] Table.

and chose out the most famous knights and bound them by statute

Most worthi knihtis, preeued of ther hond,
Chose out be Arthou*r* this ordre haue begun*ne*;
Ther famous noblesse thoruh eu*er*y Cristen lond
Shon be report as doth the mydday son*ne*;
To Famys paleis the renou*n* is vp ron*ne*,
Statutis set be vertuous ordenau*n*ce,
Vndir p*ro*ffessiou*n* of marcial gou*er*nau*n*ce.

to be always armed, except when they slept, and to sustain rightful quarrels

The firste statut in the[r] registre fou*n*de,
Fro which thei sholde nat declyne of riht,
Be ful assurau*n*ce of oth and custu*m* bou*n*de,
Ay to be armyd in platis forgid briht,
Except a space to reste* hem o*n* the niht,
Seeke auentures, & ther tyme spende
Rihtful quarellis to susteene & diffende.

and help the weaker party if justice were on his side.

The feebler parti, yif he hadde riht,
To ther poweer manli to supporte,
Yif that thei wern requered of any wiht
Folk disconsolat to bern vp & conforte,
At alle tymes me*n* may of hem* reporte,
No man*er* wise thei do no violence
And agey*n* tirau*n*t*es* make knihtli resistence,

They were bound to comfort the disconsolate and to resist tyrants, so that widows and maidens were protected and children restored to their inheritance, and always ready to make themselves strong in the defence of holy church and their country.

That widwes, maidnes suffre no damage
Be fals oppressiou*n* of hatful cruelte,
Restoren childre to ther trewe heritage,
Wrongli exiled folk to ther contre,
And for hooli chirchis liberte
Reedi euere to make hemsilue strong,
Rather to deie tha*n* suffre hem [to] haue wro*n*g.

For comou*n* proffit, as chose champiou*n*s,
Pro republica defendyng ther contre,
Shewe ay themsilff[e] hardi as leou*n*s,
Honoure tencrece, chastise dishoneste,
Releue al them that suffre aduersite,
Religious folk, haue hem i*n* reuerence,
Pilgrymes resceyue that faille of þ*er* dispence.

They performed the seven deeds of mercy in arms

Callid in armys seuene deedis of m*er*cy,
Burie* soudiou*r*s that faile* sepulture,

2742. reste] resten B. 2744. quarell R.
2749. At alle tymes] þ*at* al tyme H. 2755. to] for R.
2767. Burie] Buried B, J — faile] failed B, J.

Folk in p*r*isou*n* delyuere hem graciousli,
Swich as be poore, ther rau*n*sou*n* to recure.
Wou*n*did peeple that languisshe & endure,
Which *pro republica* ma*n*li spent her blood, —
The statut bond to do suich folkis good.

To putte hemsilff neuer in auenture
But for mateeres that wer iust & trewe,
Afforn prouided that thei stood[e] sure,
The grou*n*d weel knowe, wer it of old or newe.
And aftir that the mateer wha*n* thei knewe,
To proceede knihtli & nat feyne,
As riht requereth*, ther quarelis to darreyne.

and never put themselves in adventure except for just causes.

A clerk ther was to cronicle al ther deedis,
Bi pursyuau*n*tis maad to hym report
Of ther expleit and ther goode speedis,
Rad & songe, to folk gaff gret confort.
Thes famous knihtis maky*n*g ther resort
At hih[e] feestis, euerich took his seete
Lik ther estat, as was to them meete.

There was a clerk, who recorded their deeds; and at high feasts each took his seat according to his rank.

Oon was voide* callid the se pereilous,
As Sang Real doth pley*n*li determyne,
Noon to entre but the most vertuous,
Of God prouided to been a pure virgyne,
Born bi* discent taco*m*plisshe & to fyne,
He allone, as cheeff and souereyne,
Al auentures of Walis & Breteyne.

One seat was empty, called the See Perilous, and only the most virtuous could place himself there.

Among al kynges renom*m*ed & famous, [p. 398]
As a briht son*n*e set amyd the sterris,
So stood Artho*u*r notable & glorious,
Lik fresh[e] Phebus casty*n*g his liht aferris.
In pes lik Argus; most marcial i*n* þe werris;
As Ector hardi, lik Vlixes tretable,
Callid among Cristene, ky*n*g most hono*u*rable.

Arthur was to other kings as a bright sun set amidst the stars; he was Argus, Hector, Ulysses in one.

His roial court he did[e] so ordeyne,
Thoruh ech contre so ferr sprad out þe liht,
Who that euer thidir ca*m* to pleyne,

The light of his royal court spread abroad through other realms, and

2779. requered B, J — ther] þe H — quarell R.
2781. pusyuau*n*tis R, pusivau*n*tis H, purcevauntys J.
2784. Thes] þe H.
2786. estat] staat R.
2787. voide] wide B, wilde J.
2788. seyn Greall H, seyn Geral R 3, Seyn Greal P, Sank Riall J.
2791. bi] of B, J.

there was always a knight ready at hand to defend the oppressed.

Be wrong oppressid*, & requered of riht,
In his diffence he sholde fynde a kniht
To hym assigned, fynalli tatende
Be marcial doom his quarel to diffende.

The challenges of strange knights were also accepted,

Yif it fill soo that any straunge kniht
Souht auentures, and thidir cam fro ferre
To doon armys, his request maad of riht,
His chalenge seyn, wer it of pes or werre,
Was accepted, to the court cam nerre,
Lik as he cam with many or allone,
Thei wer delyuered; forsake was neuer one.

and there was a school of martial doctrine for the young,

Ther was the scoole of marcial doctrine
For yonge knihtes to lernen al the guise,
In tendre age to haue* ful disciplyne
On hors or foote be notable excersise;
Thyng take in youthe doth help in many wise,
And Idilnesse in greene yeeris gonne
Of al vertu clipseth the sheene* sonne.

and all wronged people, widows and maidens of any nation, were received, and a knight assigned to their defence.

Widwes, maidnes, oppressid folk also,
Of extort wronges wrouht be tirannye,
In that court, what nacioun cam therto,
Resceyuid wer; ther list no man denie.
Of ther compleyntis fond reedy remedie,
Maad no delay, but foorth anon[e] riht
Them to diffende asigned was a kniht.

The knights were also bound to tell truthfully to the registrar all that befell during their adventures;

Eek bi ther ordre thei bounde wer of trouthe,
Be assuraunce & be oth Isworn,
In ther emprises, and lette for no slouthe,
Pleynli to telle how thei haue hem born,
Ther auentures of thynges do beforn,
Riht as it fill, spare in no maneere
To telle ech thyng onto ther registreer.

and their statements were sworn.

Thyng openli doon or thyng that was secre,
Of auentures as betwixe tweyne,
Or any quarel take of volunte
Treuly reporte, and platli nat to feyne,
Them to be sworn, the statut did ordeyne,
No[uh]t conselid of worshep nor of shame,
To be registred reporte the silue same.

2804. oppressid] repressid B. 2809. aventure H.
2817. haue] lerne B. 2821. sheene] cleer B, clere J, cleare P.
2825. wer ther] ther thei H. 2841. conselid] cownsailid H.

And to conclude, the statutis han vs lered,
Eueri quarel grou*n*did on honeste,
In that court what kniht was requerid,
In the diffence of trouthe and equite,
Falshod excludid and duplicite,
Shal ay be reedi to susteene that partie,
His lyff, his bodi to putte in iupartie.

Every honest quarrel was defended to the death.

Thus in Breteyne shon the cleer[e] liht
Of cheualrye and of hih prowesse,
Which thoruh the world[e] shadde his bemys
  briht,
Welle of worshep, co*n*duit of al noblesse,
Imperial court al wrongis to redresse,*
Hedspry*n*g of hono*u*r, of largesse cheef cisterne,
Mero*u*r of ma*n*hod, of noblesse the lanterne.

Thus the clear light of chivalry shone in Britain;

Yit was ther neuer sey*n* so briht a son*n*e,
The someres day in the mydday speere
So fress[h]li shyne, but sum skies don*n*e
Mihte percas courtyne his bemys cleere;
Oft it fallith, wha*n* Fortune makth best cheere
And falsli smylith in hir double weede,
Folk sey*n* expert, than is she most to dreede.

but the sun is never so bright but that sometimes a passing cloud throws it into the shadow; and Fortune often smiles most kindly when she is most to dread.

Thus wha*n* the name of this worthi kyng
Was ferthest sprad be report & memorye,
In eueri rewm his noblesse most shyny*n*g,
Al his emprises co*n*cludyng wit*h* victorie,
This double goddesse envied at his glorie
And caste menys be sum maner treyne
To clipse the liht of knihthod i*n* Br*e*teyne.

Thus, while Arthur was flowering in his strength,

Thus whil Artho*u*r stood most honourable
In his estat, flouryng in lusti age,
Among his knihtis of the rou*n*d[e] table,
Hiest of p*r*incis on Fortunis stage,
The Romey*n*s sente to hym for truage,
Gan make a cleym froward & outraious,
Takyng ther title of Cesar Iulivs.

the Romans sent to him for tribute, outrageously claiming a title from Julius Cæsar.

The same tyme, this myhti kyng Artho*u*r [p. 399]
Conquered hadde Gaule & also F*r*au*n*ce,

2852. the] al þe H — his beemys shad so briht H, R 3.
2854. redresse] represse B, J. 2858. 2nd the] *om.* R.
2861. best] *om.* R. 2863. she] *om.* H — to] *om.* H.
2864. this] þ*at* H. 2870. Eclipse H.
2876. Gan] Gayn R. 2877. ther] þe H.

This happened at a time after Arthur had been victorious in France.

Outraied Frolle, and lik a conquero*ur*
Brouhte Parys vndir obeissau*n*ce,
Took hem to grace, & with his ordenau*n*ce
Gat al Au*n*goie, Au*n*gerys* & Gascoyne,
Peitow, Nauerne, Berry & Burgoyne.

He conquered Paris, Gascony, the country of Poitiers and Touraine, and kept possession for nine years.

Cessed nat, but ded his besi peyne,
Most lik a kniht heeld forth his passage,
Gat al the lond of Peiteres & Towreyne,
Ther cites yolde, to hym thei did homage;
To be rebell thei fond no*n* auau*n*tage,
Soio*ur*ned in F*r*ance, as seith the cronicleer,
Heeld pocessiou*n* the space of nyne yeer.

He held a feast in Paris, and divided the lands of France among his princes and barons.

Heeld a feeste ful solempne at Parys, —
Al the contres which he gat in F*r*au*n*ce,
Lik a p*r*ince ful prouident & wis,
Which hadde of fredam most* roial suffisau*n*ce,
Of al his conquest the contres in substau*n*ce,
For his p*r*incis and barou*n*s so prouided,
Lik ther desertis he hath hem deuided.

To Kay he gave Anjou and Maine, to Bedevere Normandy, to Berel the Duchy of Burgundy.

To his senescall that was callid Kay
Au*n*goye* & Meyn he gaff al that partie;
To his botleer, was maad[e] no delay,
Callid Bedewar, he gaf Norma*n*die;
To a barou*n*, nih cosyn of allie,
A ma*n*li kniht which namyd was Berell,
Gaff the duchie of Burgoyne eu*er*ydeell.

and reserving other lordships for himself, returned to Britain and convened a great parliament in Cærleon.

Thus he departid lordships of that lond,
Wher he thouhte was most expedient;
Sum*m*e he reserued in his owne hond,
Ageyn to Breteyne reto*ur*nid of entent,
Sent out writtes, heeld a gret parleme*n*t,
Afftir which he made a feeste anon
In the contre Icallid Gloumorgon,

Ten kings were there ready to obey Arthur, thirteen earls, many barons,

At a gret cite namyd Carliou*n*,
As [it] is reme*m*brid be writyngis,
Cam many p*r*ince and many fressh barou*n*,
In nou*m*bre, I fynde, that ther wer te*n* ky*n*ges,
Reedi tobeie Artho*ur* in alle thynges;

2883. Au*n*gerys] Au*n*gorys B. 2885. nat] *om.* R.
2894. prouident] prudently H. 2895. most] ful B, J.
2900. Au*n*goyne B, P.
2902. Bedwar R, Bedwer*e* H.

Present also, as it was weel seene,
Ther wer of erlis reknid ful thretteene.

Al the knihtes of the rounde table,
Feste of Pentecost, a feeste princepal,
Many estatis famous & honourable
Of princis, barouns born of the blood roial
Wer ther present*, and in especial
Al tho that wern be oth & promys bounde
To brothirhede* of the table rounde.

and all the knights of the Round Table.

And it fill so, whil that kyng Arthour
As appartened sat in his estat,
Ther cam tuelue sent doun be gret labour
Of olde mene chose [out] of the Senat,
Sad of ther port, demvre & temporat,
Richeli clad, of look and off visage,
Greihored [echon], sempte of riht gret age.

Then came twelve richly clad old Romans chosen by the Senate to present the claims of Rome.

First cunnyngli, as thei thouht it due,
Cause of ther comyng & pleynli what thei mente, —
First of assent the kyng thei gan salue,
Next aftir that thei tolde who them sente,
And ther lettres meekli thei presente,
Concludyng thus, to speke in breef langage,
How the Romeyns axe of hym truage.

They saluted the king and meekly presented their credentials, demanding immediate payment of the tribute,

Custumyd of old sith go many [a] day,
Whan that Cesar conquered first Breteyne,
The kyng requeryng to make hem no delay.
Arthour abood, list nothyng to seyne;
But al the court gan at hem disdeyne;
The proude Bretouns of cruel hasti blood
Wolde hem haue slay[e]n euene ther thei stood.

which they said dated back to the time of Cæsar's conquest. Arthur was silent, but his court would have slain the Roman envoys.

"Nay," quod Arthour to al his officeeres,
"Withynne our court thei shal haue no damage;
Thei entred been and kome as massageris,
And men also gretli falle in age.
Let make hem cheer[e] with a glad visage."
Took his counsail of suich as wer most wise,
With this ansuere seid in curteis wise:

"Nay," said Arthur, "they shall have no damage in our court."

2924. ther present] present ther B.
2926. brothirhede] brothreed B. 2927. whil that] þat while H.
2930. of] *om.* R. 2931. temperate H.
2933. echon] *om.* J — gret] *om.* R.
2935. what] þat H. 2946. hasty cruel H.
2948. his] these R. 2954. this] his R.

His answer was, "You threaten me with war,

"Yo*ur* lettres rad and pleynli vndirstonde,
The teneur hool rehersid in this place,
Touchi*n*g the charge which ye haue tak o*n* honde,
To yiue ansuere rehersid in short space,
Be woord & writyng ye gretli me manace,
How ye purpose with many strong bataille
Passe the mou*n*teyns me felli for tassaille.

but you need not trouble to come the entire way; I will shorten your journey, with God's grace."

It nedeth nat suich conquest to a-legge [p. 400]
Ageyn[es] Bretou*n*s of non old truage,
Of comyng dou*n* yo*ur* weie I shal abregge,
With Goddis grace shorte yo*ur* passage.
Mak no delay, but with my barou*n*age
Passe the se withoute long tarieng
To meete Romeyns at ther dou*n* komy*n*g."

At their departure they were given rich gifts, and, returning to Rome, reported Arthur's bounteous liberality.

This was the ansuere youe to the massagers.
At ther departy[n]g bar with he*m* gret richesse,
The kyng bad so vnto his officeeres.
Ageyn to Roome in haste thei ga*n* he*m* dresse,
Pleynli reportyng the bounteuous* largesse
Of worthi Artho*u*r, considred all[e] thynges,
Of Cristendom he passed all othir ky*n*ges.

They told Lucius that he excelled all others in chivalry, and that his knights were the best in Europe;

Arthuris court was the so*u*rs and well
Of marcial power*, to Lucyvs thei tolde,
And how that he all othir did excell
In chuialrie, with who*m* ther wer withholde
The chose knihtis, bothe yong & olde,
In al Europe, who ca*n* considre ariht,
Of al noblesse the torchis be ther liht.

they said further, that he would pay no tribute, for he held no land of the Romans.

He cast hym nat to paien no truage,
Seide of the Romey*n*s [how] he heeld no lond,
Which to* diffende he wil make his passage,
"Of yo*ur* cleymys to breke atoo the bond;"
And knihtli preeue [it] with his [owne] hond,
"Ye haue no title, ye nor yo*ur* cite,
Agey*n* the Bretou*n*s, which euer haue sto*n*de free."

2956. tenour R, H.
2972. thai gan i*n* hast H.
2973. the] *om.* H — bounteuous] plenteuous B, J.
2975. othir] *om.* H.
2977. power] prowesse B, J, P.
2984. how] *om.* R. 2985. to] for to B, R, J.
2987. it *and* owne *are supplied from* MS. Harley 1766, *om.* in B, R, J, P, H 5, H, R 3.
2989. haue] hath R.

With al the kyngdames soget to Rome tou*n*,
Kynges, p*r*incis aboff the hih mou*n*tey*n*s,
With Lucyus thei be descendid dou*n*
To meete Bretou*n*s upon the large pley*n*s.
Arthour[i]s comy*n*g gretli he disdeyns,
Because he hadde, pleynli to descryue,
In multitude of peeple swich[e] fyue.

The Romans came down with Lucius to meet the Britons on the plains; and Lucius, who had five times the number of Arthur's men, was contemptuous.

At Southhamptou*n* Arthou*r* took the se
With al his knihtis of the Rou*n*de Table,
Behynde he leffte to gouerne the contre
His cosyn Modred, vntrusti & vnstable,
And, at a preef, fals & deceyuable,
To whom Arthou*r* of trust took al the lond,
The crowne except, which he kept i*n* his hond.

Arthur took ship at Southampton, and left his traitorous cousin Mordred as regent.

Fro Southhamptou*n* Arthou*r* ga*n* to saile
With al the worthi lordis of Breteyne,
At Barbeflu fond good arryuaile;
He and his p*r*incis ther passage did ordeyne
Thoruh Normandie, F*r*ance & eek Burgeyne
Vp to a cite callid Augustence,
Wher he first fond of Lucyus the p*re*sence.

He landed at Harfleur and marched to meet Lucius and found him at Augusta.

So large a feeld nor suich a multitude
Of men of armys assemblid o*n* a pley*n*
Vpon a day, shortli to conclude,
Togidre assemblid afforn wer* neu*er* sey*n*.
Lucivs hadde on his partie certey*n*
Estward the world[e] al the cheualrie
Brouht be the mou*n*teyns dou*n* toward Germanye.

Never before was such a large army seen as that of the Romans.

Ther wardis sett, in ech a gret bataile,
With ther captey*n*s to gouerne hem & guye,
Arture with Bretou*n*s the Romei*n*s gan* assaile,
Fond many Sarsyns vpon that partie.
The Bretou*n* Gaufride doth pley*n*li specefie,
As he of Arthure þe prowesse doth descryue,
He slouh that day of Sarsyns ky*n*ges fyue.

There were many Saracens with the Romans, and Geoffrey says that Arthur slew five of their kings;

3000. Modred] moordred R.
3003. kept] toke H.
3005. worthi lordis of] lordis of worthi H.
3006. Barbeflu] Barflue J, Harflue P.
3011. suich] so gret R. 3013. day] playn H.
3014. wer] was B, J. 3017. the] *om.* R.
3019. hem] *om.* H.
3020. gan] did B, J.

and the slaughter was so great that it were tedious to describe it.

The grete slauhtre, theffusiou*n* of blood
That was that day vpon outher side,
Ech ageyn othir so furious was & wood,
Lik for the feeld as Fortune list prouide,
That yiff I sholde theron longe abide
To write the deth, the slauhtre & the maneere,
Touchyng the feeld wer tedious for to heere.

To conclude, Lucius was slain and the proud Romans were put to flight;

To conclude & leue the surplusage,
In that bataile ded was many a kniht,
The consul Lucyus slay[e]n in that rage,
The proude Romey*n*s be force put to fliht.
Of gentilesse Arthou*r* ano*n* riht
Leet the bodi of Lucyus be caried
Ageyn to Roome; it was no lenger taried.

and, like a king, Arthur saw that his dead princes and lords and knights were buried.

The worthi p*r*incis and lordes that wer dede,
And ma*n*li knihtis abidyng with Arthou*r*,
Lik a kyng solempneli took heed
That thei wer buried be dilligent labou*r*.
And in this while, lik a fals tretou*r*,
His cosyn Modred did his besi peyne
To take fro hym the kyngdam of Breteyne.

In the meanwhile Mordred wanted to be king in Britain,

and persuaded the people to rebel against Arthur,

So as the stori pley*n*li maketh my*n*de, [p. 401]
Modred falsli, to his auau*n*tage,
Entreted hem that wer lefft behy*n*de,
Vnder colou*r* of fraudulent langage,
Gaff hem* gret fredam; & þei did hym homage,
That be his fals[e] co*n*spiraciou*n*
Brouht al Breteyne into rebelliou*n*.

making fair promises and granting great freedoms.

Be faire behestis & many freendli signe
Drouh the peeple to hym in sondri wise,
Shewed hym outward goodli & benigne,
Gaf libertes & grau*n*ted gret frau*n*chise
To make Bretou*n*s ther souerey*n* lord despise.
And purueyau*n*ce he ga*n* ordeyne* blyue
To keepe the portes, he shold[e] nat aryue.

But when Arthur heard of this false treason he

Whan kyng Arthour hadde knoulechi*n*g
Of this fals tresou*n* and al the purueiau*n*ce
That Modred made, he, lik a ma*n*li kyng,

3026. That] ther H. 3034. rage] orage (*perhaps; the* o *is mutilated and may stand for another incomplete letter*) H.
3040. And] a H — knyht H.
3050. hem] hym B. 3055. hym] *om.* R.
3058. ordeyne] make B, J. 3061. this] his R.

Lefte Burgoyne & al the lond of F*r*ance,
Cast on Modred for to do vengau*n*ce;
Took the se, [&] with gret apparaile
Cast at Sandwich to make his arrivaile.

sailed home and landed at Sandwich,

Modred was reedi w*ith* knihtis a gr*e*t nou*m*br*e*,
Made a strong feeld to meete hy*m* on the pley*n*,
In purpos fulli Artho*ur* to encou*m*bre,
At which aryuaile slay[e]n was Gaway*n*,
Cosyn to Artho*ur*, a noble kniht certay*n*;
Eek Au*n*guisel was slay[e]*n* on the stronde,
Kyng of Scottes, or he myhte* londe.

where he met Mordred. There Gawaln and Anguisel, king of the Scots, were slain.

Maugre Modred Artho*ur* did aryue,
The grou*n*d recurid lik a ma*n*li kniht
(For feer of whom, ano*n* aftir blyue
The seid[e] Modred took hym to the fliht),
Toward Londene took his weie riht,
The gatis shet, & kept was the cite
Agey*n* Modred; he myhte haue no*n* entre.

Arthur landed in spite of Mordred, and after defeating him went to London and shut the gates.

In al haste to Cornewaile he fledde,
The suerd of Arthure he durste nat abide,
List he shold[e] leyn his lyff to wedde;
Yit for hymsilff[e] thus he ga*n* prouide,
With multitude gadrid on his side
Put lyf and deth that day in auenture,
That day to deie or the feeld recure.

Mordred fled to Cornwall and collecting a fresh army fought Arthur once more.

In Fortune ther may be no certay*n*,
Vpon whos wheel al brotilnesse is fou*n*did:
Moodred that day in the feeld was slay*n*
And noble Arthour to the deth was wou*n*did.
Be which the feeld of Bretou*n*s was co*n*fou*n*did,
Of so gret slauhtre & goode knihtis lorn
Vpon oo* day, men haue nat herde* toforn.

In this fight Mordred was slain and Arthur mortally wounded.

Afftir the bataile Artho*ur* for a while
To stau*n*che his wou*n*dis & hurtis to recure,
Bor[n] in a liteer ca*m* into an Ile
Callid Aualou*n*; and ther of aue*n*ture,
As seid Gaufrid recordeth be scripture,
How kyng Artho*ur*, flour of cheualrie,
Rit with his knihtis & lyueth in Fairye.

After the battle Arthur was borne to an isle called Avalon, where, as Geoffrey records, he still rides out with his knights and lives in Fairy-land.

3067. a] & R. 3070. rivaile H. 3073. myhte] ca*m* to B.
3081. Cornwall H. 3087. feeld] feel R.
3094. oo] a B — herde] seyn B, seen J. 3098. Aualon P.

Thus the sun of Britain was translated to the sky, where he sits crowned in the heavenly mansion, the first of the nine worthies.

Thus of Breteyne translatid was þe sun*n*e
Vp to the riche sterri briht dongou*n*, —
Astronomeeres weel r*e*herse kun*n*e, —
Callid Arthuris constellaciou*n*,
Wher he sit crownid in the heue*n*l[y] ma*n*siou*n*
Amyd the paleis of stonis cristallyne,
Told among Cristen first of þe worthi nyne.

Britons still believe old Merlin's prophecy that Arthur shall come again some day to reign in England.

This erro*u*r yit abit amo*n*g Bretouns,*
Which fou*n*did is vpo*n* the p*ro*phecie
Of olde Merly*n*, lik ther oppynyou*n*s:
He as a kyng is crownid in Fairie,
With sceptre and suerd, & w*ith* his regalie
Shal resorte as lord and souereyne
Out of Fairye & regne in Breteyne,

At any rate his epitaph says, "Here lies King Arthur, who shall reign again."

And repaire ageyn the Rou*n*de Table;
Be p*ro*phecie Merlyn set the date,
Amo*n*g[es] p*r*incis kyng inco*m*parable,
His seete ageyn to Carliou*n* t*r*anslate.*
The Parchas sustren spon*n*e so his fate;
His epitaphie recordeth so certeyn:
Heer lith ky*n*g Artho*u*r, which shal regne agey*n*.

Now I will return to Bochas, but first I'll write a lenvoy on Mordred's treason.

Vnto Boch*as* I wil agey*n* reto*u*rne,
Afforn r*e*hersid parcel of his prowesse,
Theron tabide me list no mor soio*u*rne,
But to reme*m*bre the gret v*n*kynd[e]nesse,
The co*n*spiraciou*n*, þe tresou*n*, the falsnesse
Doon to kyng Artho*u*r be his cosy*n* Modrede,
Make a Lenvoye, that al men may it reede.

[Lenvoy.]

This tragedy of Arthur bids princes to beware of treason. Nothing is more perilous.

THIS tragedie of Artho*u*r heer folwy*n*g [p.402]
Bit p*r*incis all bewar of fals tresou*n*;
For in al erthe is no*n* mor p*er*eilous thi*n*g
Than trust of feith, wher is decepciou*n*
Hid vndir courtyn of fals collusiou*n*.
For which men sholde — I holde þe cou*n*sail good —
Bewar afforn euere of vnkynde blood.

3103. briht] *om.* H. 3107. the] that R.
3109. Bretouns] Breteyns B.
3118. princis kyng] kyngis p*r*ince H, R 3.
3119. translate] to translate B, J. 3120. sponne] span H.
3127. 3rd the] & H, R 3. 3129. it] *om.* R.
3133. Than] That H — of] on H. 3135. men] none R.

The world [is] dyuers, Fortune ay chaungyng,
In euery contre & eueri regioun;
At a streiht neede fewe freendis abidyng;
Long abscence causeth deuisioun:*
And yif princis be fals ambicioun,*
Nih of allie, shewe too facis in oon hood,
Lat men bewar euere of vnkynde blood.

The world is always changing. At a need we have few steadfast friends. Men must always beware of unkind relations.

Who was mor hardi of princis heer regnyng
Or mor famous of marcial renoun
Than whilom was, his enmyes outraieng,
Arthur, cheef sonne of Brutis Albioun?
But, for al that, the disposicioun
Of Fate and Fortune, most furious & wood,
Caused his destruccioun be vnkynde blood.

Who was more hardy and famous than Arthur? Yet he was destroyed by unkind blood!

What mor contrarious to nature in shewing
Than fair pretence, double of entencioun,
Gret alliaunces frowardli werkyng?
Hid vndir flours, a serpent cast poisoun,
Briht siluir scaled, damageth the dragoun;
Ech werm sum parti tarageth of his brood.
And what mor pereilous than vnkynde blood?

What is more evil than fair pretense, like a silver-scaled serpent hidden under flowers? What more perilous than unkind blood?

Noble Princis, on Arthour remembryng,
Deemeth the day of Phebus goyng doun:
Al is nat gold that is cleer shynyng,
Afforn prouided in your inward resoun,
Fals vndirmynyng & supplantacioun,
Remembryng ay with Arthour how it stood,
Be conspiracioun of vnkynde blood.

Noble Princes, remember the story of Arthur, and do not deem the day fair until the sun has set.

¶ An exclamacion a-geyn men þat been vnkynde to þeir kynrede.[1]

AGEYN* kynreedis & vnkynde alliaunces,
Bochas makth heer an exclamacioun
Vpon Modred, which with his ordenaunces
Caused of Arthour fynal destruccioun,
The sunne eclipsyng of Brutis* Albioun,

Bochas here exclaims upon Mordred, who caused the destruction of Arthur, notwithstanding that he trusted him above all men.

3137. The] This R. 3138. contre] court R.
3139. abidyng] fyndyng H. 3140. deuisioun] discencioun B, R, J.
3141. ambicioun] deuisioun R, B, J, derision R 3.
3146. Than þat H. 3156. brood] bloode H, R 3.
3165. Ageyn] Yeyn B. 3169. Brutis] Brutus B, J, P.

[1] *The following heading is in* MS. J. leaf 165 verso: "An exclamacioun of Bochas ageyn kynredys vnkynde."

Natwithstondyng, pleynli to descryue,
He trusted hym abof al men on lyue.

It is strange and hateful to God for any man to be unkind to his kindred.

It is a merueile & vnkouth to deuise,
Be what occasiou*n* or be what corage,
That a ma*n* sholde in any man*er* wise
Be fou*n*de vnkynde vnto his lynage.
Hatful to God, that in any age
Blood ageyn blood born of o kynreede
Conspire sholde of malis or hatreede.

It were vain to tarry on this matter. The story of Arthur and Mordred is well known.

In this mateer it wer but vey*n* to tarie,
The stori knowe of Artho*u*r & Modrede,
Be blood allied, in werkyng most co*n*trarie,
Which made many Bretou*n* kniht to bleede;
For be vsurpi*n*g, conspiry*n*g and falsheede
Of seide Modred, most infortunat,
Caused al Breteyne to stond[e] desolat.

All Britain stood desolate without her king; and the light of the Round Table was darkened and eclipsed by Mordred, the forsworn knight.

First desolat be absence of ther kyng,
Callid in his tyme of kynges most notable,
The desolaciou*n* of knihtis abidyng,
Whilom in Breteyne famous & honourable,
Brethre echon of the Rou*n*de Table,
The which be Moodred, the false forswor kniht,
Stod longe eclipsed & dirked of his lyht.

The monarchy was divided, that once stood whole, and all concluded in duplicity.

The liht of noblesse þ*at* shon thoruh al Breteyne
Be fals Modred was dirkid off his bemys;
The monarchie departid was o*n* tweyne,
That stood first oon wit*h* his marcial stremys.
But aftirward the brihtnesse of his lemys
Drouh to declyn be fals deuisiou*n*,
Which hath destroied ful many a regiou*n*.

Adieu welfare and prosperity where there is no concord. Trees cannot thrive when separated from their bark.

Al this processe vpon* duplicite
Pley*n*li co*n*cludeth, & blood that is* vnky*n*de.
A-dieu weelfare and al prosp*er*ite,
Wher* pes & concord been Ilefft behy*n*de:
Trees may nat thryue departid fro þe ry*n*de, —

3171. on] of R — on lyue] alive H. 3172. a] *om.* R.
3173. occasiou*n*] comp*ar*isou*n* H. 3175. vnto] to R.
3185. to] *om.* H. 3187. his] this R. 3190. Brethren R.
3191. 1st The] *om.* H, R 3 — forsworn R, J.
3198. declyn] dirknesse R. 3200. vpon] vpon a B, R, J, H 5.
3201. blood that is] that is blood B, J, H 5, that is blode is R, on bloode þat is H.
3203. Wher] Ther B, J.

A pley*n* exau*m*ple in Arthure & Modrede,
Who ca*n* co*n*ceyue, & list ther stori reede.

[Off Gesevye kyng of venandre and of iij. othre kynges / and how they were destroyed.] [1]

AFFTIR al these v*n*kouth strau*n*ge* thi*n*gis, [p. 403]
Tofor Iohn Boch*as*, as made is me*n*ciou*n*,
Ther ca*m* toforn hym fyue myhti ki*n*ges
For to co*m*pleyne ther desolaciou*n*.
First Giseli[n]e, kyng off the regiou*n*
Callid Venandre, in werris ful co*n*traire
Vnto a p*r*ince callid Balisaire.

Among five mighty kings, Gelimer, king of the Vandals, came first to complain his desolation.

And to this saide noble Balisaire,
Ful ren*n*omed that tyme in cheualrie,
The kyng of Gothes was also aduersaire;
And bothe attonis of hatrede & envie
Assentid fulli to hoolde chau*m*partie
Geyn Balisair, which thoruh his hih renou*n*
Took hem bothe and cast hem in p*r*isou*n*.

Together with the king of the Goths he was an enemy of Belisarius, who took them both captive and put them in prison.

Ther is no mor of the*m* in Boch*as* fou*n*de.
But aftir them, in ordre be writy*n*g,
¶ Ca*m* Amarales, with many bloodi wou*n*de,
Which in his tyme was of Maures kyng.
Withoute cause or title of any thyng
Vpon Ian Sangwyn ga*n* werreye agey*n* riht,
Which thoruh al Affrik was oon the best[e] kniht.

Then came Amarales, king of the Moors, who fought John the Sanguinary without cause

The saide Ian, armyd in plate and maile,
Mette Amarales in Affrik on a sond,
And heeld with hym a myhti stro*n*g bataile,
And lik a kniht slouh hym with his hond,
Droof al his peeple proudli fro þ*at* lond.
And in my book ther is no*n* othir my*n*de
To be reme*m*brid of hym that I ca*n* fynde.

and was slain; and that is all I can find remembered about him.

¶ Than Syndual, of Brentois lord & ky*n*g,
Tofor Bochas put hymsilf in pres,
Ga*n* shewe his myscheef, pitousli pleyny*n*g,

Then Sindbal the Herulian began to describe his misfortune,

3207. strau*n*ge v*n*kouth B. 3211. Gelymer P. 3212. Vandalia P. 3214. And to this saide noble] Vn to this noble saide H. 3219. Geyn] gey H. 3223. Amarales] Attila P. 3226. Ian] Iohn H, P. 3228. The] This H. 3229. Amarales] Attila P. 3232. his] that R. — þat] þe H. 3235. Brentois] Bretonys R, Breto*un* J, Briteyns H, Brentoys R 3, Brentois P.

[1] MS. J. leaf 165 verso.

for he made war on Narses, a Roman knight.

Wha*n* he heeld werre, wilful & rek[e]les,
Ageyn a *pr*ince callid Narsates,
A Romey*n* kniht, fers, hardi & riht strong
In his diffence wha*n* men wold doo*n* hy*m* wro*n*g.

who was an eunuch, and captured Sindbal and hanged him.

This Narsates, of cas or auenture,
Thouh he in deede was a ma*n*li kniht,
He failled me*m*bres in soth of engendrure.
His aduersaires he put echon to fliht,
Took ther kyng, & foortwith ano*n* riht,
As the cronicle pley*n*li doth recorde,
On hih[e] galwes he heng hy*m* with a corde.

Soon afterward king Totila the Ostrogoth met Narses with a great army, and he too was defeated and slain.

Of Narsetis aftir this victorie,
¶ Kyng Totila hadde ful gret disdeyn;
With a gret host, most pompous in his glorie,
Kam upon hym & mette hym on a pley*n*.
With multitude thow he wer ouerleyn,
Kyng Totila, which many ma*n* beheeld,
Of Narsates was slay[e]n in the feeld.

[Trusimond kyng of Gepedois.] [1]

Turisund, king of the Gepidæ, requested Bochas to write his adversity and the unhappy fate of his daughter Rosamond, to whom Fortune was contrary all her life.

IN ordre nexte Boch*as* doth [so] write,
Of Gepidois how ki*n*g Trusimou*n*de
Requered hym that he wolde endite
The grete aduersites in which he did habou*n*de,
And of his douhtir callid Rosymou*n*de
The vnhappi chau*n*ce to marken & descryue,
To who*m* Fortune was co*n*trarye al hir lyue.

Alboin, king of Lombardy, slew Turisund in battle and afterwards married Rosamond.

Alboinvs kyng of Lumbardie,
Which many lond heeld i*n* subiecciou*n*,
Conquered Beeme, Pragve & Hu*n*grie,
The lond of Gepidois, with many regiou*n*,
Fauht with ther kyng, as maad is me*n*ciou*n*,
Slouh in bataille the said[e] Trusimou*n*de,
Weddid aftir his douhtir Rosamou*n*de.

3238. reklesses R.
3239. ycalled Narses P — Narsates] Narsarses H.
3242. Narses P, Narsates H.
3249. Narsates H, R, J, Narsetes R 3, Narses P.
3252. on] in H, R. 3256. so] *om.* R, J, H 5.
3257. Trusimou*n*de] Eurismou*n*de H, Ewrysmonde R 3, Trusmonde J, Turisounde P.
3263. Albonius *or* Alboinus B. 3266. regiou*n*] dongou*n* H.
3268. Eurismou*n*de H, R 3, Trusmond J, Turisounde P.

[1] MS. J. leaf 165 verso, in margin.

Myn auctour gretli comendeth hir beute
And writ also she was but yong of age,
Whos stori first, whan I dide see
How vngracious was also hir mariage,
I gan wexe pale in my visage,
Gretli astoned, confus of verray shame
To write this stori in hyndryng of hir name.

(And when I first read her story and knew how ungracious her marriage was, I grew pale and confused at the thought of writing in detraction of her name.

I wil forbern and breefli passen heere,
The surplusage lihtli ouerpasse;
For bi and bi to telle al the maneere
Of fellonies that did hir herte enbrace,
It sholde blotte this book & eek difface.
For which I caste treuli & nat faille
Touching hir stori to make rehersaille.

So I will forbear and pass over the rest lightly; for it would blot this book to tell the manner of all her sins.)

[How Albonyus was moordred by his wif / and how she aftir most vicious was moordred also.] [1]

KYNG Alboinus, as ye shal vndirstonde,
Afftir many conquest & victorie,
Which he hadde [had] both on se & londe,
To putte his name* & triumphes in memorie,
Leet crie a feeste to his encres of glorie;
At which[e] feeste, solempne & princepall,
So as he sat in his estat roiall,

After his victories King Alboin let cry a feast to put his triumph in memory,

and as he sat in his royal estate

Parcel for pride, parcel for gladnesse, [p. 404]
The queen present, the said[e] Rosamounde,
Take and supprised he was with dronk[e]nesse,
Of myhti wynes which þat day did habounde,
Sent a goblet of gold, as it is founde,
Vnto the queen, with licour ful plesaunt,
Bad to hir fadir [she] sholde drynke a taunt.

he became drunk, and bade Queen Rosamond drink a taunt to her father.

She dempte it was a maner moquerie,
First hir name and worshep to confounde,
To bidde hir drynke a taunt for hir partie
To hir fadir, the said[e] Trusymounde,
Slay[e]n afforn with many bloodi wounde

She looked upon it as an insult to drink to her father, whom Alboin had slain, and determined to be revenged.

3276. this] his R — hir] his H.
3284. Albynus H, R 3, Albonyus R, Albonius *or* Alboinus B.
3287. names B. 3288. of] and R.
3294. which þat day] þat day which H, R 3.
3301. Eurismounde H, Ewrismounde R 3, Trusmond J, Turisounde P. 3302. bloodi] mortall H.

[1] MS. J. leaf 166 recto.

Be Albonius, thoruh his vnhappi chau*n*ce, —
Of which rebuk she cast to do vengau*n*ce.

She waited a long time, and at last persuaded a squire named Peredeo to murder her lord,

She bar the rancou*r* ful long in hir ente*n*t,
Which day be day gan renewe & encrece.
A certey*n* squiecr she made of hir assent,
Which taco*m*plisshe she wolde neu*er* cese.
A*n*d on another squiecr she ga*n* prese,
Callid Peredeus, accorded al in oon,
This false moordre texecute anon.

which he did, although Alboin defended himself to the last with a broken spear.

The day was set; whil he lay & sleep*e*
Fill upon hym *with* sharp suerdis grou*n*de:
Hir lord was slayn, alas, he took no* keep*e*!
Or he deide of Fortune he hath fou*n*de
A speris hed[e] to a tronchou*n* bou*n*de,
Hymsilf defendyng in that mortal striff;
But slayn he was be tresou*n* of his wiff.

After the murder Rosamond took all Alboin's treasure and fled with Hilmichis, her squire, to Ravenna.

¶ Aftir this moordre tescape fro dau*n*geer,
This Rosamou*n*de fledde awei be niht.
With hir went[e] Melchis hir squieer;
Took a ship, sailed be sterre-liht,
To Rauen*n*e thei took the weie riht,
Lad with hem for refut & socou*r*
Of kyng Alboyne al the hool treso*u*r.

She then married Hilmichis, but growing tired of him, — for her affections were promiscuous, —

Aftir she was [I]weddid to Melchis,
Ma*n* of this world[e] stood most in hir grace.
Hir loue appallid, set of him no pris;
For she nat koude be content in o place.
Hir ioie was euere newe thing to p*ur*chace,
Tassaie manye, plesid neu*er* *with* oon,
Til bexperience she preuid hadde echon.

had an affair with the Provost of Ravenna. Hilmichis she sought to murder.

Prouost of Rauen*n*e & cheef gou*er*no*u*r,
For thexcellence of hir gret beute
Aboue al women loued hir paramo*u*r,
Whan she entred first in that cite.
And thoruh hir fraude and duplicite

3303. Albonoys R.
3304. to] *om.* H.
3312. whil] whan H.
3314. he] or he H — no] *om.* H, no*n* B, R.
3321. Melchis] Helmiges P — hir] his H.
3325. kyng Alboyne] Albonyus J, Alboinus P.
3326. wedded to Helmiges P. 3329. o] no H.
3331. manye] *om.* H — neu*er* *with*] *with* nevir H.

She caste moordre in hir froward auys
Hir newe husbonde that callid was Melchis.

One hot day when he was thirsty after bathing, she gave him a goblet of poisoned wine.

The hote somer in lusti fressh[e] May,
The same Melchis for heete & weerynesse
Hymsilff to bathe wente a certey*n* day,
Kauht a gret thrust of* feyntise in sothnesse.
And Rosamou*n*de, of infernal falsnesse,
Took a goblet, *with* lic*our* gret foisou*n*,
Gaf hym drynke wyn medlid with poisou*n*.

After he had drunk up half, his body began to swell and he grew deadly pale, and, suspecting treason, compelled her to drink the rest. They both died.

He drank up half, & therwithal he ga*n*
Brest and beli to suelle & arise,
Intoxicat, wex dedli pale & wan;
And wha*n* he dide hir tresou*n* aduertise,
He made hir drynke in the same wise,
Maugre hir wil, she myht it nat r*e*streyne, —
Guerdou*n* for moordre, — thei deide bothe tweyne.

I find little profit in this chapter, except that it reminds us that murder always cries vengeance before God.

In this chapitle but litil frut I fynde,
Sauf onli this, to putte in reme*m*brau*n*ce,
That men sholde calle agey*n* to my*n*de,
Moordr*e* affor God requereth ay vengau*n*ce.
This funeral stori weied in ballau*n*ce,
Wrouht be Melchis, co*m*passid first & fou*n*de
Be fals tresou*n* of cursid Rosamou*n*de.

Rosamond slew Alboin, and afterwards she and Hilmichis killed one another.

Slouh first hir lord Albonivs, as I seide,
Tueyne of hir squieres did execusiou*n*,
Out of his slep*e* whan he did abraide.
Lat cou*n*tirpeise what was ther guerdou*n*:
Ech moordrid othir be drynkyng of poisou*n*;
Melchis drank first, & next drank Rosamou*n*de;
At them it ga*n*; to them it did rebou*n*de.

Both lost their lives; treason punished by treason; murder for murder.

Cou*n*tirpeised o moordre for another:
Albonivs slay*n* be Rosamou*n*de his wiff
Bassent of Melchis, & aftir ech to other
The poisou*n* partid; ther ga*n* a fatal striff.
Moordre quit for moordre, thei bothe lost her lyff.
Who vseth falsnesse, ful weel afferme I dar,
Shal with falsnesse be quit or he be war.

3339. newe *is repeated in* H. 3341. Helmiges P
3343. of] on B.
3352. it] hir R. 3359. Helmiges P.
3361, 69. Alboinus P. 3364. ther] hir H.
3366. 2nd drank] *om.* H.

As men give, so shall they receive; and as they deserve, such shall be their reward.

As thei departed, suich part ageyn þei took; [p. 405]
As men disserue, suich shal be ther meede.
This froward story, eende of the Eihte Book,
Of Rosamounde & Melchis wrought in deede,
For short conclusioun biddith men take heede,
Thei shal resceyue ageynward * suich mesour
As thei mesure vnto ther neih[e]bour.

3378. Helmiges P.
3380. resceyue ageynward] ageynward resceyue B, P.

¶ Finis libri octaui.

¶ Incipit IX*us* liber Bochasii.

BOOK IX.

[How the Emperour*e* Maurycyus his wif and his childre wer slayne atte Calcedonye.][1]

TO F*r*anceis Petrak as Boch*as* vn*der*took,[p.407]
In eschewi*n*g of slouthe & idilnesse,
As he bega*n* taccomplissh* up his book,
Assurau*n*ce maad to doon his besynesse;
Which thi*n*g reme*m*brid ga*n* his pen*n*e dresse,*
The Nyhnte Book, so God wold send hy*m* grace,
It to parfo*u*rme yif he had lyff & space.

As Bochas had promised Francis Petrarch to do his best, he now made ready his pen to finish his Ninth Book.

At the gyn*n*yng sothli of his labour,
In his studie to hym ther did appeere
Mauricivs, the mihti empero*u*r,
Which ga*n* co*m*pleyne, rehersi*n*g the maneere
How he bi Phocas, cruel of look & cheere,
Destroied was — wiff, childre & kynreede —
The slauhtre kouth, who list ther stori reede.

And as he began, the mighty Emperor Maurice came, complaining how he and his family had been murdered by Phocas

The said[e] Maurice, as writ Bochas Iohn,
Was be Phocas brouht to destrucciou*n*,
His wiff, his childre slay[e]*n* euerichon
At Calcedoyne, as maad is me*n*ciou*n*,
Aftir whos deth he took pocessiou*n*.
The said[e] Phocas, as put is in memorie, —
Gaf Panteou*n* onto Seynt Gregorie,

in Chalcedon.

The same Phocas gave Saint Gregory the Pantheon,

Which was a temple of old fundaciou*n*,
Ful of idoles upset on hih[e] stages.
Ther thoruh the world of eueri naciou*n*
Wer of ther goddis set up gret images,
To eueri kyngda*m* direct wer ther visages,
As poetis & Fulgence be his lyue
In bookis olde pleynli doth descryue.

an old temple full of the idols of all nations.

Eueri image hadde in his hand a belle,
As appartened to euery naciou*n*,
Which be crafft sum tokne sholde telle

Each image had a bell in its hand, that rang when the

3. taccomplissh] acco*m*plisshed B, R.
5. *is misplaced at end of stanza* B.
18. Calcedoyne] Macedoyn H, R 3. 21. Pantheon P.
29. his] *om.* H. 30. appartened] app*er*tenyth H, p*er*teyneth J, P — naciou*n*] Regiou*n* H.

[1] MS. J. leaf 166 verso.

kingdom to which it beloneed fell in revolt against Rome.

Whan any kyngdam fill in rebellioun
Or gan maligne ageyn[es] Roome toun;
Swich to redresse with strong & mihti hond
Sent a prince to chastise al that lond.

The said temple was turned into a Christian church by Pope Boniface.

The saide temple bilt of lym & ston,
Pope Boniface*, bookis specefie,
Wher it was first callid Pantheon,
Set up crossis upon ech partie,
Halwid it to martirs & Marie, —
Yeer be yeer[e] gynnyng off Nouembre
The feeste holde, the martiloge doth remembre.

The Emperor Maurice was slain in Asia in the city of Chalcedon; and 24 years afterwards Phocas was put to death by Heraclius.

In Asie this emperour Maurice was slayn,
In the cite that callid is Calcidonye,*
Al his houshold and many good Romayn
Bi Phocas and Perciens, as had is in memorie.
And Phocas afftir, for al his veynglorie,
Slayn be Eraclivs, thouh he* was emperour
Foure and twenti* wyntir and cheef gouernour.

[Off Machomet the fals prophete and how he beyng dronke was deuoured among swyn.] [1]

After the death of Phocas, Muhammad appeared. He was a false prophet and a magician, born of low kindred in Arabia, and an idolater all his life.

AFFTIR the deth of Phocas, as I tolde,
That Eraclius to regne first began,
Cam Machomeet, in his tyme Iholde
A fals prophete and a magicien,
As bookis olde weel reherse can.
Born in Arabia but of low kynreede,
Al his lyue an idolastre in deede.

When he grew older he was the first to use camels for carriage, and journeyed to Egypt and studied the Bible.

And whan that he greuh to gretter age,
Deceyuable in many sondri wises,
With chamelis vsid first cariage:
Wente to Egipt [to] fette marchaundises,*
Fals and double, sotil in his deuises;
To Iewes & Cristene sondry tymes sent,
Lerned the Olde a[nd] Newe Testament.

37. Pope] *blotted and erased* B, J — Bonifas B — bookis] as bookis J, as bokes P.
44. callid is] is callid H — Calcidonye] Calcidoine B.
48. he] who P — thouh he] he than B. 49. xxiiijti B.
56. ydolatre R, H, R 3.
57. that] *om.* H — gretter] gret H. 59. camelis R, H, R 3.
60. to] *om.* H, R 3, P, H 5. 60 *and* 61 *are transposed in* B.

[1] MS. J. leaf 167 recto.

As bookis olde recorde* in that partie,
This Machomeet, this cursid fals[e] ma*n*,
Out of Egipt faste ga*n* hy*m* hie
Toward a contre callid Corozan,
Wi*th* a ladi that hihte Cardigan, —
Thoruh his sotil fals[e] daliau*n*ce
Be crafft he fill into hir aqueyntau*n*ce.

This cursed man then went to Khorasan with a lady named Khadija, who was attracted by his false subtle talk

He wrouhte [so] be his enchau*n*teme*n*tis
And be fals menis off nigromau*n*cie,
Hir enclynyng toward his ententis;
For bothe he koude riht weel flatre* & lie.
Saide openli that he was Messie,
Iewes abidyng vpon his comyng,
As grettest p*ro*phete and ther souerey*n* ky*n*g.

and fooled by his necromancy; for he was an accomplished flatterer and liar.

Thus the peeple he brouht in gret erro*u*r
Bi his techi*n*g & his fals doctryne;
He wex among hem a gret gou*er*no*u*r.
The saide ladi he dede also enclyne,
As to a p*ro*phete which that was deuyne
Sent from aboue, as she did vndirstonde;
For which she took hy*m* vnto hir husbonde.

He openly said he was Messiah, and became a great prophet among the people; and for that reason the lady married him.

His lynage [be]gan at Hismael; [p. 408]
Hadde a siknesse, fil* ofte sithes dou*n*,
In his excus[e] seide that Gabriel
Was sent to hym fro*m* the heuenli ma*n*siou*n*
Be the Hooli Goost to his instrucciou*n*:
For the au*n*gel shewed hym* so sheene,
To stonde upriht he myhte nat susteene.

He was an Ishmaelite and an epileptic, and excused his fits by saying, "I must always fall down when the Angel Gabriel comes to instruct me."

On his shuldre[s] wer ofte tymes sey*n*,
Wha*n* he to folk[is] shewed his presence,
Milk whit dowes, which that piked grey*n*
Out of his eris; affermy*n*g in sentence
Thei ca*m* be grace of goostli influence
Hym to visite, to shewe & specefie
He was the p*ro*phete that callid was Messie.

Milk-white doves sat on his shoulders, by spiritual influence, he claimed; but it was only to pick grain he had put in his ears.

Newe lawes he did also ordeyne,
Shewed signes be fals apparence;
Lik Moises, hymsilf he did[e] feyne

He made new laws and feigned to be a prophet like Moses; and as

64. recorden B. 67. Coriozan P. 68. Cardican P.
74. riht weel flatre] flatre weel B, J. 79. &] and bi R.
82. a] *om.* H. 86. fil] ful B. 90. hym] hymsilf B.
92. shuldris R, R 3, H 5, shuldirs H, shuldre J, P.
93. folkis] folk R, H 5, folke P. 101. feyne] fyne H.

an evidence of his powers he hung pots of milk and honey on the horns of a great bull.

A *pro*phete of most excellence.
And therupon to shewe an euidence,
Smale pottis wit*h* milk & hony born,
Of a gret bole wer hangid o*n* ech horn.

symbolizing the plenty which was to come from his spiritual working.

Made the peeple yiue credulite
To his doctryne and [his] froward techi*n*g:
Be mylk & hony figurid was plente,
Be the merit* of his gostli werki*n*g.
And thus he was at his begyn*n*yng
Take of Sarsyns, as thei ga*n* to [hym] drawe,
Which bi fals erro*u*r bond he*m* to his lawe.

He soon converted the Saracens, and his clerk Sergius wrote down his laws and miracles.

A clerk of his, callid Sergius,
Wrot his lawes & thes myracles thre:
First of the dowes, how thei ca*m* to hy*m* thus,
As heer-toforn rehersid was by me,
How milk & hony wer tokne[s] of gr*e*t plente,
And of the bole, afforn be crafft maad tame,
Bi fals deceitis to getyn hy*m* a name.

He was made a prince of the Arabs and Turks, and collecting an army, made war on Heraclius and captured Alexandria.

Of Arabiens & Sarsyns, as I reede,
And of Turkis maad p*r*ince & gou*er*no*u*r,
Wit*h* Hismaelites & folk of Perse & Mede
He gadred peeple, ga*n* wexe a werreio*u*r,
Ageyn Heraclius, the mihti empero*u*r,
And vsurped to ride in tho cuntres,
Gat Alisau*n*dre wit*h* many mo cites.

Failing to become king, he said that he was sent to provide prophets to guide the people; and, as he was lecherous of heart, he set up an image of Venus.

Of tho parties desirous to be kyng,
Of that purpos wha*n* he was set aside,
To the peeple falsli dissymulyng,
Told he was sent p*ro*phetis to prouide
For tho contrees, for to been ther guide.
And for he was lecherous of corage,
He made of Venvs sette up an image.

He made the Saracens worship on Friday, just as the Jews do on Saturday, and told the people to drink water, although he got drunk himself on good wine.

Made Sarsyns to worshep the Friday,
Semblabli his stori doth expresse,
So as Iewes halwe the Satirday, —
Al his werkis concludy*n*g on falsnesse.
Wha*n* he drank wyn [he] fill in dronk[e]nesse;
Bad the peple, lik a fals propheete,
Drynk[e] watir, & good wyn to lete.

109. merit] meriht B.
111. hym] *om.* R, H 5 — Sarazyns J.
114. thes] his H. 129. dissymulyng] dissemblyng R.

As I seide, the heretik Sergivs,
Wit*h* hym of cou*n*sail froward & contrar*ie*,
Foon to our feith, he and Nostorivs,
From hooli chirch[e] gretli thei gan varie.
On whos errou*r*s Bochas list nat tarie
Mor to write[n] of this Machomeete,
A nigroma*n*cien & a fals prophete.

Bochas did not care to dwell on his errors or on those of the Nestorians; but all his false laws are to be seen in the Koran.

Who list to seen his lawes euerichon
Youe to Sarsyns, his book ca*n* ber witnesse,
As thei be set in his Alkerou*n*,
Echon in ordre grou*n*did on falsnesse.
Lik a glotou*n* deied in dronk[e]nesse,
Bi excesse of mykil dry*n*kyng wyn,
Fill in a podel, deuoured amo*n*g swyn.

Finally, when drunk, he fell in a puddle and was devoured by hogs.

This was the eende of fals[e] Machomeete,
For al his crafftis of nigromancie,
The funeral fyn of this seudo p*ro*phete,
Dronklew of kynde, callid hymsilf Messie,
Whom Sarsyns so gretli magnefie.
Iohn Boch*as* let be for a queen of Frau*n*ce,
Mor of his errou*r*s to putte i*n* reme*m*brau*n*ce.

That was his end, for all his magic. John Bochas then turned to Brunhilde, a queen of France,

[How Brounchild / queene of Fraunce slouh hir kyn / brought the londe in diuisiou*n*, and aftir was honged / and hewen in pecys smale.] [1]

SHE ca*m* arraied nothi*n*g lik a queen,
Hir her v*n*tressid; Bochas took good heed,
In al his book he had afforn nat seen
A mor woful creature in deede.
Wit*h* weepi*n*g eyen, totorn[e] was hir weede,
Rebuki*n*g Bochas, he had lefft behy*n*de
Hir wrechidnesse for to putte i*n* my*n*de.

who came to him with dishevelled hair and torn garments and weeping eyes.

Vnto my*n* aucto*u*r she sodenli abraide, [p. 409]
Lik a woma*n* that wer with wo chekmaat.
First of alle thus to hym she saide:
"Sumtyme I was a queen of gret estat
Crownid in Frau*n*ce; but now al desolat

She said: "Once I was a great queen; but now I am desolate and almost ashamed to tell my woe.

144. thei] *om.* H. 157. pseudo H.
160. a queen of Frau*n*ce] it did hym grevau*n*ce H.
162–532 *are omitted in* H.

[1] MS. J. leaf 167 verso.

I stonde in soth. Bru*n*nechild[e] was my name,
Which to reherse I haue a man*er* shame.

"You wrote all about Arsinoe and Cleopatra and Rosamond, and it seems you have forgotten me.

Thou wer besi to write the woful caas
Withy*n*ne thi book off Arsynoe,
Dist seruise to queen Cleopatras,
Of Rosymou*n*de thou writ also parde;
And among alle thou hast forgete me,
Wherbi it seemeth thou dost at me disdeyne, —
List no parcel to writen of my peyne."

When Bochas heard this he was embarrassed, for he knew nothing about her. "No," he replied, "I never read your story." "I'll tell it to you then."

Whan Bochas herd, of cheer he wex riht sad,
Knowyng nothi*n*g of that she ded endure.
"I-wis," quod he, "afforn I haue nat rad
In no cronicle nor in no scripture
Of yo*u*r woful froward auenture."
¶ "No?" quod she, "I pray you tak good heede,
So as thei fille I wil reherse in deede."

"You women," said Bochas, "never tell anything to your own discredit.

Bochas with Bru*n*nechilde ga*n* debate ano*n*:
"Sothli," quod he, "this the condiciou*n*
Of you wom*m*en almost euerichon;
Ye haue this maner, withoute excepciou*n*,
Of your natural inclynaciou*n*,
Of your declaryng this obseruau*n*ce to keepe:
Nothyng to seyn contrarye to yo*u*r worshepe.

"Nature teaches you to hide all your faults and to look most innocent when you have been most wicked.

Nature hath tauht you al that is wro*n*g texcuse,
Vndir a courtyn al thyng for to hide;
With litil grey*n* yo*u*r chaff ye ca*n* abuse;
On yo*u*r diffautis ye list nat for to bide:
The galle touchid, al that ye set aside;
Shewe rosis fresshe; weedis ye leet passe,
And fairest cheer[e] wher ye most trespace.

"And if you now tell me your story, you will shew very little of your vices, and only a fool would believe you."

And yiff ye shal telle yo*u*r owne tale,
How ye be fall[e] fro Fortunis wheel,
Ye will vnclose but a litil male,
Shewe of yo*u*r vices but a smal parcel:
Brotil glas sheweth brihter tha*n* doth steel;
And thouh of vertu ye shewe a fair pretence,
He is a fool that yiueth to you credence."

174. Bru*n*childis R, Brounchilde J, Bru*n*kildys R 3, Brunchildys H 5, Brunichilde P.
180. forgotyn R, forgoten J. 188. you] the R.
200. On] Onto R — fortabide R.
203. fairest] faireth R.

¶ Quo[d] Brunnechild, "I do riht weel espie
Thou hast of wommen a fals oppynyoun,
How that thei can flatre weel & lie
And been dyuers of disposicioun; —
Thou myhtest haue maad an excepcioun
Of hih estatis & them that gentil been,
Namli of me, that was so gret a queen."

Said Brunhilde, "I see you have a false opinion of women; but you might have made an exception of me. I was a great queen."

¶ "Your hih estat boff Kynde hath no poweer
To chaunge in nature nouther cold nor heete:
But let vs passe and leue this mateer,
Theron tabide or any mor to plete;
Of your compleynt seith to me the grete.
Be weie of seruise to you I shal me quite,
As ye declare take my penne & write."

"Your high estate cannot alter your nature," answered Bochas; "but I'll not argue. Tell me your complaint and I will write it down."

¶ "Tak heed," quod she, "& with riht good auis
Fro the trouthe bewar that thou nat varie!
Whilom in France regnid kyng Clowis,
Hadde a sone that namyd was Clotarye,
Clothair an heir which callid was Lotarie;
And this Lotarie, namyd the secounde,
Hadde sonis foure, in stori it is founde.

"Be sure you write the truth," said she. "Once there was a king in France named Clovis,

To the cronicle who can taken heed,
As it is Iput in remembraunce,
Whan ther fadir, the myhti kyng, was ded,
Atween thes foure partid was al France,
Ech be hymsilff[e] to haue gouernaunce,
Be oon assent, as brothir onto brothir,
Weryng her crownis, ech quit hem onto othir.

and the kingdom was divided amongst his four great-grandchildren.

The same tyme, I, callid Brunnechild, —
Me list nat varie fro the old writyng, —
Hadde a fadir namyd Leuychild,
Of al Spayne souereyn lord and kyng.
My saide fathir, to ful gret hyndryng
Of bothe rewmys (the fame ronne ful* ferre),
Tween Spaigne & Fraunce gan a mortal werre.

"I was the daughter of Athanagild, king of Spain, who unfortunately began a war on France.

The brethre foure, in Fraunce crownid kynges,
Ageyn my fadir made strong diffence,
Of marcial pride & fortunat chaungyngis,

"The four brothers made a strong defence,

227. Clowis] Cloduice P.
229. an] had an R, R 3.
241. leuygilde R.
244. full] so B, J, P.

Whan thei mette be mortal violence,
Of sodeyn slauhtre fill suich pestilence
On outher parti, the feeld lik a gret flood
With the terrible effusioun of blood.

and finally to have peace I was given in marriage to Sigebert, then reigning in France."

To bothe reumys the werris wer importable, [p. 410]
Causid of deth[e] passyng gret damage;
Souhte menys, wex be assent tretable,
Of blood sheedyng tappese the woful rage.
Bi oon accord I was youe in mariage
To Sigibert, regnyng tho in Fraunce,
Tueen bothe rewmys to maken alliaunce."

"No, no," said Bochas, "that isn't so; we are not going to agree. You were first the wife of Chilperic. The chronicles say so."

¶ "Nay, nay," quod Bochas, "I deeme it is nat so;
Tween you & me ther mut begynne a striff.
Beth auised; taketh good heed herto:
The first assuraunce of mariage in your lyff,
Of Chilperik ye wer the weddid wiff,
Cronicles seyn, what-euer ye expresse,
In this mateer wil bere with me witnesse."

"Although some books have it as you mention, at any rate I was given when very young to Sigebert.

¶ "Thouh summe bookis reherse so & seyn,
Lik as ye haue maad heer mencioun,
Ther rehersaile stant in noun certeyn;
For be thassent of outher regioun,
Spayne and Fraunce in ther conuencioun
Ordeyned so in my tendre age,
To Sigibert I was youe in mariage.

"It was an unhappy marriage: Hymenæus was not there, and Tisiphone and her sisters bore the torches;

Ymenivs was nat ther present,
Whan we took our chaumbre toward niht;
For Thesiphone, hir sustren of assent,
Infernal goddessis bar the torchis liht.
And as the torchis shewid dirk or briht,
Therbi the peeple present, oon & alle,
Dempte of the mariage what sholde befalle.

and of old times, according as the torches burnt dark or bright, the marriage was deemed fortunate or otherwise.

This custum vsid of antiquite:
Fro ther templis of goddis & goddessis,
At mariages of folk of hih degre
Torchis wer born, of whom men took witnessis,
As thei wer dirk or shewed ther brihtnessis,
The difference seyn in ech estat,
Yif it wer toward or infortunat.

264. Chilperis R. 274. Himeneus P.

Of this mariage short processe for to make,
The torchis brente, & yit thei wer nat briht, —
Shewed out komerous smokes blake;
Of consolaciou*n* lost was al the liht.
Thus in dirknesse wastid the firste niht:
Ther vers, ther songis of goddis & goddessis
Wer al togidre of sorwe and heuynessis.

"At my marriage the torches gave out heavy black smoke and turned the light to darkness.

Thes wer the toknis the niht of mariage,
Pronostiques of gret aduersite;
Yit of nature I hadde this auau*n*tage
Of woma*n*heed and excellent beute;
And lik a queen in stonis & perre
I was arraied, clad in purpil red,
Wit*h* a crowne of gold upo*n* myn hed.

"Such were the prognostics, although I was very beautiful and arrayed like a queen.

Solempneli crownid queen of Frau*n*ce,
Which for to seen folk faste ga*n* repaire.
Of al weelfare I hadde suffisau*n*ce,
Clomb of Fortune ful hih vpon the staire.
A sone I hadde, which callid was Clotaire,
Be Sigibert, be record of writyng,
Thridde of þ*a*t name in Frau*n*ce crownid ky*n*g.

"I had a son named Clotaire by Sigebert, the third of the name crowned in France;

So wolde God the* day wha*n* he was born
He hadde be put in his sepulture,
In sauaciou*n* of blood shad heer-toforn:
Caused the deth of many creature,
As dyuers bookis recorden in scripture,
Grou*n*d and gyn*n*yng, as maad is me*n*ciou*n*,
Withyn*n*e this lond of gret deuysiou*n*.

but would to God he had been put in his sepulchre the day he was born, for he was the cause that many a man died."

He with his brethre, of who*m* I tolde late,
At hym begon*n*e the first occasiou*n*" —
¶ "Nat so," quod Boch*as*, "ye faillen of yo*u*r date.
Who was cheef cause of [this] discenciou*n*?"
[¶] "Sothli," quod she, "to myn oppynyou*n*,
Amon[g] hem-silff, I dar weel specefie,
The cheef gyn*n*yng was fraternal envie."

"Not so," said Bochas, "who was chief cause of this dissension?" "Really," she replied, "I think it was fraternal jealousy."

¶ "Keep you mor cloos; in this mateer ye faille.
Folwyng the tracis of your condiciou*n*,
Ye halte foule in yo*u*r rehersaille:
For of your owne imagynaciou*n*
Ye sewe the seed of this discenciou*n*

"Be careful, you are not telling the truth. You yourself were chief cause."

298. womanhode R. 309. the] that B — wha*n*] that J, *om.* P.
311. here beforn R.

Among thes kynges, yif ye taken heed,
Bi which in *France* many ma*n* was ded."

At this Brunhilde changed her expression and grimly said to Bochas, "A few moments ago you knew very little about my life; now you sit over me as a judge.

¶ Tha*n* Brun*n*echild[e] ga*n* to chau*n*ge cheere;
To Bochas seide with face ful cruel,
"Nat longe agon thou knew nat the maneer
Of my lyuyng but a smal parcel;
Me seemeth now thou knowest euerideel,
So that ye may withoute lenger striff
Sitte as a iuge, that knowe so weel my lyff.

"When these brothers were at discord, Chilperic, brother of King Sigebert, was slain,

Whan thes brethre stoden at discord, [p. 411]
Ech ageyn other bi mortal violence,
Vndir colo*ur* to tretyn of accord
With a maner feyned dilligence,
Chilperik ther beyng in presence,
Whilom brothir to Sigibert the kyng,
Was slayn among hem be fals conspiryng.

and also Sigebert, who sought to avenge his death."

"No," said Bochas, "he was murdered because of your deceit and evil life.

On whos deth auengid for to be,
As Sigibert did[e] hymsilff auau*n*ce,
Among the pres he slay[e]n was parde . . ."
[¶] "Nat so," quod Bochas, "but of fals gou*er*nau*n*ce,
Of yo*ur* mysleuyng fill this vnhappi chau*n*ce,
That Sigibert was moordred in sothnesse
Oonli be occasiou*n* of your doubilnesse.

"You loved another, and through your outrage and folly the king was slain while hunting in the Forest of Compiègne."

Folwyng the traces* of newefangilnesse,
Geyn Sigibert ye wrouht[e] ful falsli,
Wha*n* ye loued* of froward doubilnesse
Landrik the erl of Chau*m*payne & of Bry;
For bi your outrage & your gret foly
The kyng was slay[e]n, and ye did assente,
In a forest on huntyng whan he wente,

"Alas," she exclaimed, "Bochas, Bochas, you know too much; but how do you know about the slaughter of Sigebert, done by my assent, if you were not there?"

Which callid was the forest of Compyne."
¶ "Alas!" quod she, brak out in co*m*pleyny*n*g,
"Bochas, Boch*as*, thou dost sore vndermyne
Alle the surfetis doon in my lyuyng!
Thou knowest the slauhtre of Sigibert the ki*n*g,
Which that was wrouht, alas, be myn assent, —
How knowist thou it, that wer nat ther present?

329. many a R.
334. eueri] eueril R.
346. the pres] thres R.
351. traces] tras B, trace R, traces J, P.
353. loued] loueden B R.

Of thes debatis and of al this werre,
With rebukis rehersed heer in veyn,
In rehersaille gretli thou dost erre;
For which I caste — be riht weel certey*n* —
In my diffence to replie agey*n*.
It was nat I; for she that thou dost meene
Was Fredegu*n*dus, the lusti yonge queene.

"You are wholly wrong. It was not I, but the lusty young Queen Fredegond whom you mean.

This Fredegunde, thou shalt [weel] v*n*dirstonde,
Riht womanli and fair of hir visage, —
Chilperik was whilom hir husbonde;
For hir beute took hir in mariage.
Bi hir treynys & hir gret outrage
He was aftir, the stori who list reede,
At myscheef slayn; thou shalt so fy*n*de in deede."

"Chilperic was once her husband, and it was through her wiles and outrages that he was afterwards slain."

[¶] "Thouh ye be langage make strong diffence
In thes mateeres, which cause me to muse,
I haue agey*n* you lost my pacience,
That so sotilli wolde yo*u*rsilf excuse.
Contrariousli yo*u*r termys ye abuse;
For Clotaire*, I haue so rad, parde,
Was nat engendred of Sigibert nor of the.

"Although you defend yourself well, I've lost patience with you for your subtile excuses.

I reme*m*bre ful weel that I haue rad
That Childepert*, thouh ye therat disdeyne, —
Record of aucto*u*rs that prudent been & sad, —
How he in trouthe was gendrid of you tweyne,
Which in his deyng (me list nat for to feyne*)
Lefft sonis two, the story ye may* reede, —
Theobart & Thederik to succeede."

"Clotaire was not your own son nor Sigebert's, but Childebert was; and he left two sons, Theudebert and Theuderich."

¶ "Boch*as*," quod she, "thouh thou turne vp-so-dou*n*
Thes said[e] stories, rehersid heer in deede,
Folwy*n*g of malis thyn own* oppynyou*n*,
Maugre thi wil[le], foorth I wil proceede
As I bega*n*; tak therto good heede:
First Theodorik, thou shalt vndirstonde,
Cosyn germyn was to myn husbonde,

"Bochas, although you turn these stories upside down out of malice, I will go on as I began, in spite of you.

365. al] *om.* R.
371. Fredegundis R, R 3, Fredegundys J, H 5 — Was] It was J, P.
372. weel] *om.* J.
384. Clotaire] Colataire B, Colotaire J, Colatayre H 5.
387. Childepert] Chilperik B, Chilperike P.
390. feyne] seyne B. 391. may] do B.
395. of malis thyn own] the malis of thyn B.
397. therto] heer to R, herto H 5.

"Theuderich was cousin german to my husband, and he slew his brother Theudebert and all his family. Whatever you say, this is the truth."

Kyng of Burgoyne that tyme, and non other.
He of hatreede and indignacioun
Slouh Theobart, which that was his brother,
His wiff, his childre, for short conclusioun,
Which in the myhti famous regioun
Of Autrasie regnid as lord & kyng.
What-euer thou seist, this soth & no lesyng."

"No," said Bochas, "it was quite otherwise. I cannot let you go on in this way. Whether you like it or not, you caused Theudebert's death.

¶ "Nay," quod Bochas, "it was al otherwise;
I may nat suffre how ye go ther among.
Al this langage of newe that ye deuise,
Brouht to a preef, concludeth vpon wrong.
What sholde we lenger this mateer drawe along?
Yoursilf wer cause, wher ye be lothe* or fayn,
Be Theodorik that Theobart was slayn.

"And it was all because of your burning covetousness to rule the country yourself."

The ground heerof gan parcel of envie,
Bi your froward brennyng couetise,
Which that ye hadde onli to occupie,
To reule the lond aftir your owne guise.
And yif I shal pleynli heer deuise
Of thes myscheeuys rehersed, God do boote,
Ye wer your-silff[e] ground, cheef cropp & roote."

Said Brunhilde, "I see you have lost all your reverence for me and only want to shew your cruelty.

¶ Quod Brunnechild, "I conceyue wel & se, [p. 412]
Ye for your part haue lost al reuerence,
Your-silf enarmed to shewe your cruelte
Ageyn[e]s me, touchyng the violence
Of too slauhtris rehersed in sentence:
First how Theodorik his brothir slouh in deede,
Callid Theobart, a pitous thyng to reede;

"Afterwards Theuderich was himself poisoned and his wife and children slaughtered."

Hymsilff[e] aftir stranglid with poisoun,
His wiff, his childre hewe on pecis smale . . ."
¶ "As ye," quod Bochas, "mak heer mencioun,
Sum part is trewe, but nat al your tale;

"Some of this is true, but not all. You had better

For I suppose ye sholde wexe pale
For shame of thyng which ye canat excuse,
Whan Theodorik begynneth you taccuse.

grow pale for shame; you slew them yourself."

He put on you the crym of fals tresoun;
Ye slouh his wiff and his childryn also;
Hymsilf also ye moordred with poisoun:

405. Autrasie] Austriche P. 410. concludyng R.
412. lothe] leef B, wroth R, R 3, H 5.
419. do] to R, be H 5. 427. Theobart] Theodobert R, H 5, Theodobart R 3, Theobert P. 435. on] vpon R.

I wolde wete what ye ca*n* seyn herto?"
¶ "Alas," quod she, "alas, what shal I do!
Was neuer woma*n*, in hih nor louh estat,
Al thyng considred, mor infortunat!

"Alas," said she, "what shall I do! Was there ever a more unfortunate woman!

Fortune of me set now but litil prys,
Bi hir froward furious violence
Turny*ng* hir wheel & visage of malys,
Causeth to me that no ma*n* yeueth credence,
Had in despiht, void of al reuerence,
And thoruh Fortunys mutabilite
Sool [and] abiect and falle in pouerte.

"Fortune cares little for me now; she allows no man to believe what I say, or to hold me in respect, — abject and alone and fallen in poverty!

¶ O Boch*as* Iohn, for short conclusiou*n*,
Thou must ageyns me þi stile now auau*n*ce.
I haue disserued to haue puniciou*n*,
And alle the p*r*incis & barou*n*s now i*n* F*r*ance
Crie out on me & axe on me vengau*n*ce;
Refuge is non nor recure i*n* this thi*n*g,
Thouh that Clotaire my sone* be crownid ky*n*g.

"O Bochas John, I have deserved punishment and there is no refuge for me, though my son be crowned king.

For my defautis foul & abhomynable,
Tofor the iuges of al the parleme*n*t
I was foriugid & fou*n*de also coupable,
Of euery crym co*n*vict be iugeme*n*t,
Myn accusours ther beyng present,
Of oon & othir stondyng a gret route,
Markid with fyngris of folk þ*a*t stood aboute.

"I was found guilty by the judges of all the parliament; and people pointed me out with their fingers, so that I shut my eyes for very shame.

For verray shame I did my*n* eyen close,
For them that gaured & cast on me þ*er* siht;
But as folk may be toknys weel suppose,
Myn eris wer nat stoppid half ariht.
Taken be force & lad forth with myht,
Be the hangma*n* drawe ouer hill & vale,
Disme*m*brid aftir & hewe on pecis smale.

"Taken out by force, I was drawn by the hangman and cut up into small pieces.

With my blood the pament al bespreynt,
Thanked be Fortune, such* was my*n* auenture,
The soule partid, my bodi was so feynt.
Who radde euer of any creature
That mor wo or torment did endure!" —

"Who ever read of a woman who endured more torment than I."

438. herto] therto R. 448. and] *om.* J.
453. 2nd on] of R.
455. Clotaire my sone] wit*h* Clotaire my soule B, R, J.
461. a] ther a R.
470. pament] paume*n*t R, pavment R 3, payvment H 5.
471. such] which B, J, P.

Praied Bochas to haue al thyng in mynde,
Write hir lyff & leue nothyng behynde.

Lenvoye.

The tragedy of Brunhilde is froward and grievous to read. She was deceitful and an instigator of treason.

THIS tragedie of Brunnechild the queen,
To hir stori who list yiue attendaunce,
Froward to reede, contagious to seen,
And contrarie to al good gouernaunce,
Born in Spayne, crownid queen of Fraunce,
Double of hir tunge, vpfyndere of tresoun,
Caused al that lond stonde at dyuisioun.

No man could escape her wiles; mistress of murder and dissension.

From hir treynys ther koude no man fleene,
Sours & hedspryng of sorwe & myschaunce;
Shad hony first, stang aftir as doon beene,
Hir myrre medlid with sugrid fals plesaunce.
What she saide includid variaunce,
Maistresse of moordre & of discencioun,
Caused al that lond stonde at dyuysioun.

The princes of Gaul could not stand her outrages and excesses, which almost brought their country to ruin.

Princis of Gaule myhte nat susteene
Gret outrages nor the gret gouernaunce
Nor the surfetis doon in hir yeeris greene,
Brouht that kyngdam almost to vttraunce;
Alle of assent cried on hir vengaunce.
The fame aroos, how al that regioun
Bi hir falsnesse stood at dyuisioun.

The knife of murder was ground keen by her malice; she spared neither her kin nor her friends.

The knyff of moordre grounde was so keene
Bi hir malys of long contynuaunce,
Hir corage fret with infernal teene,
Spared nouther kyn nor alliaunce.
Peised hir surfetis & weied in ballaunce,
As Bochas writ, she was thoccasioun
Which made al Fraunce stonde at dyuisioun.

¶ Here Bochas in maner excusith the vorrching of Brunnechild.[1] [p. 413]

BOCHAS astonid, gan inwardli meruaile,
Fill in a maner of ambiguite
Of Brunnechildis merueilous rehersaile, —

486. doon] *om.* R. 492. outrages] greuaunces R.

[1] *The following heading is in* MS. J. leaf 169 recto: "Bochas mervelyng of the malice and cruelte of Bronnchild/writeth thus."

How any woma*n* of resou*n* sholde be
So ful of malis & froward* cruelte,
To slen hir kyn & setten at distau*n*ce
Be dyuysiou*n* al the rewm of F*r*ance.

Bochas marvelled how any woman could be so full of malice and perverse cruelty.

Bochas dempte it was nat credible
That a woma*n* sholde be so vengable,
In hir malis so venymous or terrible
Of slauhtre or moordre [for] to be coupable.
The stori suspect, heeld it but a fable,
Onli except that she did hym excite
Wi*th* gret instau*n*ce hir story for to write.

He thought it incredible that a woman should be so terrible in her rage as to be guilty of murder.

Hir cry on Boch*as* was verray importune,
To sette in ordre hir felicites
With hir vnhappi chau*n*ges of fortune,
Hir disclau*n*dres and gret aduersites,
With hir diffame reportid in* contres;
No verray grou*n*de fou*n*de in bookes olde,
But of confessiou*n* that she hirsiluen tolde,

He held her story but a fable, except for her insistence; and it came not from old books but was her own confession.

That myn aucto*ur* with* sole*m*pne stile
Reherse sholde hir deedis disclau*n*drous,
Hir flouryng yeeris also to co*m*pile,
Medlid with hir daies that wer contrarious,
Hir fatal eende froward & furious, —
Wherof encou*m*bred of verray weerynesse,
Toward Eraclyus he gan his pen*n*e dresse.

And finally, overcome by very weariness, he turned his pen to the Emperor Heraclius.

[How Eraclyus the Empero*ur* sustened heresye fill in to dropesy and sikenesse incurabl and so died.] [1]

AFFTIR Phocas, with gr*e*t hono*u*r & glorie
Crownid emp*er*o*u*r of Roome þe cite,
In whos tyme, lik as seith þe storie,
The Romey*n*s stood in gret perplexite
Bi them of Perse that roos with Cosdroe,
Which took upon hy*m* to be lord and sire,
As a tirau*n*t to trouble the empire.

After Phocas became emperor the Romans were greatly embarrassed by the Persians under Chosroes,

509. froward] of B. 515. or] and J — for] *om* R.
523. in] be B, by J. 525. confessions R.
526. with] rehersed with B, J. 533. H *begins again.*

[1] MS. J. leaf 169 verso.

who conquered many provinces in Asia, and, froward to Christ, besieged Jerusalem, until Heraclius smote off his head.

Gat many prouynce & many famo*us* rewm
Thoruh al Asie, as the cronicle seith,
Gan approche toward Iherusalem;
Afforn the tou*n* proudli a siege he leith,
As a tirau*nt* froward to Cristes feyth.
But Eraclius, maugre al his miht,
Smet of his hed & slouh hym lik a knyht.

In his youth Heraclius slew many Saracens, and was a famous knight and a seeker after relics.

And bi grace, which that is dyuyne,
This famous p*r*ince, this Eraclius
In his begy*n*ni*ng* slouh many proud Sarsey*n*,
Holde in tho daies notable & glorious,
And in his conquest passyng[ly] famous.
Dyuers reliques & the cros he souhte,
And fro tho cuntres many of he*m* he brouht.

No man was more fitted to rule the empire; but he became a heretic

Was non so famous holde in his daies
As Eraclius thempire for to guye,
Nor mor manli fou*n*de at al assaies
Of hih prowesse nor in cheualrye.
But wha*n* he ga*n* susteene heresie,
God took from hym, wit*h*yn*ne* a litil space,
His hap, his weelfare, his fortune & his g*r*ace.

and upheld the doctrines of the Monarchianites. After that he was never fortunate.

He ga*n* susteene & folwe certey*n* rihtis,
Of wilfulnesse and froward fantasie,
Of a sect callid Monachelites,
Which is a sect of froward heresie;
And sith that he drouh to that partie,
The stori tellith, for al his hih estat,
This Eraclius was neuere fortunat.

Once dreaded on land and sea, Grace and Fortune left him, and he suffered with such a dropsy that his thirst could never be quenched.

Wher he was first drad on se & lond,
Na*m*li off Sarsyns, for his* cheualrie,
Grace & Fortune fro*m* hy*m* wit*h*drouh ther hond;
For whan that he fill into heresie,
He was trauailed with suich a dropesie,
And therwithal he hadde a froward lust
Euere to drynk, & euere he was a-thrust.

In tho daies fou*n*de was no leche,
Al-be that thei wer souht o*n* ech partie,
The saide p*r*ince that koude wissh or teche,

549. begyning] gy*n*nyng H. 551. passyngly] passyng J, R, H 5, P. 553. tho] þe H.
558. to susteen H, to sustene R 3.
568. first drad] drad first H, R 3. 569. for] for al B, J.
576. that] though H — o*n*] in R, R 3.

Hym to releue of his idropesie,
Maad feynt & feeble *with* a gret palisie:
Thus in siknesse he hath his daies spent,
Be vengau*n*ce slay*n* *with* infernal torme*n*t.

No physician was able to relieve him, and he finally died in torment.

Of Heraclius this was the woful eende, [p. 414]
As is rehersed, slay[e]n with seeknesse,
Out of this world[e] wha*n* he sholde weende,
Al hool thempire stood in gret distresse,
Force of Sarsyns dide hem so oppresse;
And day be day drouh [vn]to declyn
Be his successour callid Constanty*n*,

That was his sad end; and all the empire stood in distress because of the Saracens.

[How Constantyne the sone of Eraclyus supportyng errour and heresye was moordred in a stewe.] [1]

Which was his sone, as maad is me*n*ciou*n*.
In whos tyme thoruh his gret folie
Sarsyns dide gret oppressiou*n*,
Spoillyng the contres of al Lumbardie.
And Consta*n*ty*n*, of wilful slogardie,
Wasted his daies til that he hath brouht
Al thempire almost onto nouht.

His son Constantine succeeded; and during his reign the Saracens did as they would,

Geyn Cristes feith in especial
He ga*n* of malys his wittis to applie,
And was therto enmy ful mortal,
As* cheeff supporto*u*r of fals heresie.
And toward Roome faste he gan hy*m* hie,
Spoilled templis of many riche image,
And be water took aftir his passage.

while he wasted his days, an enemy to Christ's faith, until the empire was almost brought to nought.

To Constantynople he hasted hy*m* ful blyue,
Be Cecile the weie was most* meete;
At Siracuse I fynde he did aryue,
And for the sesou*n* was excessiff of heete,
Which in his labo*u*r made hym for to sueete,
And secreli he ga*n* hymsilf remewe
To be bathed in a preue stewe.

He hastened from Rome to Constantinople, and stopping over at Syracuse, where it was very hot, secretly went to a brothel for a bath;

578. dropesie R, J. 581. torme*n*t] Iugement H.
583. is] *om.* R. 595 *is misplaced at foot of column* R.
596. Geyn] All R. 599. As] And B, J — fals] all H.
603. To] *om.* H, R 3 — ful] *om.* H, H 5.
604. Be] To — most] almost B, R, J, H 5.
607. hym] his H. 608. remewe] renewe H.

[1] MS. J. leaf 169 verso.

and there his own knights fell upon him and slew him.

Of enmyte ther he was espied;
His owne knihte*s*, lik as it is fou*n*de,
Be co*n*spiracio*un*, certeyn of them allied,
Fill upon hy*m* with sha[r]p*e* swerdis* grou*n*de.
And merciles, with many mortal wou*n*de,
Thei slouh hy*m* ther, on hy*m* thei wer so wood,
Amyd the stewe, nakid as he stood.

They chose their own emperor; but Constantine, the next heir,

Aftir whos deth thei did hemsilf auau*n*ce
To chese a kniht bor[e]n in Armenye,
Of thempire to take* the gou*er*nau*n*ce
And to supporte falsli ther partie.
¶ But Consta*n*tyn, succeedyng of allie,
Beyng next heir, the trouthe for to sue,
To hym that was moordred in the stue,

a notable man, who was wiser than his father, slew all the conspirators.

Callid Consta*n*tyn, as his fadir was,
Riht notable in actis marciall,
Mor wisli gouerned, stood in othir caas:
Lik a p*r*ince, be iugeme*n*t roial,
Of ma*n*li herte and corage natural
The conspiratou*r*s first of alle he sleth,
That wer assentid to his fadris deth.

To his great renown he caused 289 bishops to assemble for the defence of Christ's faith against old heresies.

To gret encres of his famo*us* renou*n*,
Grace of God dide hym enlumyne,
Consta*n*tynople, in that roial tou*n*
Olde heresie[s] to cessen and to fyne.
Too hundrid bisshoppis [eihty] & eek nyne
He made assemble, thoruh ma*n*li prouidence,*
Of Cristes feith to stonde at diffence.*

He also restored churches and justly punished all heretics, without respect of person or favour.

He was eek besi cherchis to restore,
Al heretikes ma*n*li to withstonde,
Ther oppynyou*n*s examyned weel before,
And wha*n* the trouthe was weel v*n*dirsto*n*de,
Lik Cristis kniht list for no ma*n* wonde
To pun[ys]shen hem ius[t]li be rigo*u*r,
Withoute excepciou*n* of persone or fauo*u*r.

I read little more about him in Bochas

Of hy*m* in Boch*as* litil mor I reede,
Nor of his empire I fy*n*de no*n* oþ*er* date, —
Spared no*n* heretik, nouther for gold nor meede,

613. swerdis] speris B, sperys J. 619. to take] took B, J, toke P. 623. was moordred] moordrid was H. 631. famo*us*] fadris R. 635. eihty] *om.* J — eek] eke also J. *The second halves of lines* 636, 37 *are transposed* B, J, P. 647. nor] no H.

Consta*n*tynople he passid into fate;
Wha*n* Bulgarience ga*n* with hy*m* debate,
A froward peeple, wilful & rekles,
Gaff hem a tribut, he for to lyue i*n* pes.

except that he paid tribute to the Bulgars for the sake of peace and died in Constantinople.

[How Gisulphus was slayn, and his wif ended mischeuesly in lecherye.] [1]

NEXT ca*m* Gisulph*us* to Boch*as* o*n* þe ryng,
A famous duk & notable i*n* his lyff,
W*ith* weepi*n*g eyen pitousli pleyny*n*g,
W*ith* whom also ca*m* Rymulde his wiff,
Which þ*at* lyueden euere in sorwe & striff.
Yit was she bothe of berthe & of lynage
Riht excellent, & fair of hir visage.

Gisulf and his wife Romilda lived always in sorrow and strife, although she was of an excellent family and very beautiful.

Sixe childre hadde this famous queen
Bi Gisulphus begety*n* in mariage,
Wonder semli and goodli on to seen,
And fortunat be processe of ther age,
Al-be ther fadir felte gret damage
Be the werris he hadde in his lyuy*n*g
W*ith* Cathanus that was of Narroys kyng.

They had six children, who were at first happy in spite of their father's wars with Cacanus, King of the Avars,

This Cathanvs w*ith* many strong bataille [p. 415]
Is descendid, and took the weie riht
Of duk Gisulphus the londis to assaile;
Togidre mette in steel armyd briht;
Gisulphe slay*n*; his peeple put to fliht.
And Cathanus with strong & myhti hond
Took pocessiou*n*, co*n*quered al his lond.

who slew Gisulf and conquered all his land.

Aftir whos deth Romulde the duchesse,
Gretli astoned, pale of hir visage,
To the castel off Forgoil gan hir dresse
With hir knihtis of strong & fel corage.
Cathanus made aftir his* passage,
Leide a siege, caste hym to iuparte
His lyff, his bodi rather tha*n* departe.

Romilda retired with her knights to the castle of Foroiulanum;

649. Bulgariens R, H, R 3. 655. Romilda P.
663. felte] fell in R. 664. the] ther R.
665. Cathanus] Cathamus J, Cathenoys H, Cacanus P — Narroys] Bauars P.
673. Rymulde H, J, Romilde P.
676. hir] his R. 677. his] hir B.

[1] MS. J. leaf 170a.

and as she stood on the wall and saw Cacanus riding about in armour

Aboute the castel armyd as he rood,
Lik a p*r*ince sat knihtli on his steede,
Vpon the wallis as Romuldus stood,
Fresshli beseyn[e] in hir purpil weede,
And of the seege gan to taken heede,
Hir look, vnwarli, as she cast a-side,
And sauh the kyng tofor the castel ride,

and looking like a prince and manly knight, she fell in love with him,

So lik a p*r*ince and a ma*n*li kniht;
She gan on hym looke wondir narwe:
The god of loue persed thoruh hir siht,
Vnto hir herte markid hir with his arwe;
The firy ty*n*dis of his bren*n*yng harwe
Made the soil so pliau*n*t of hir thouht,
That of hir castel she set almost riht nouht.

and, agreeing to yield the castle, presented herself to him in his tent.

And for taco*m*plisshe the hool entenciou*n*
Of hir fals lust in al man*er* thy*n*g,
She is agreed be co*m*posiciou*n*
To yeeld the castel in haste onto the ky*n*g,
She for to come withoute mor tarieng,
Lik a duchesse hirsiluen to presente,
Wher-as the kyng sat armyd in his tente.

Her people were taken prisoner, her four sons fled. Cacanus lay with her one night and then despised her.

The peeple withyn*n*e p*r*isoneeres take,
Hir foure sonis took hem to the fliht;
Loue caused that she hath forsake
Hir blood, hir kyn, wher it wer wro*n*g or riht.
And Romulde the space but of* a niht
With Cathanus hadde al hir deliht,
And euere aftir he hadde hir in despiht.

Repulsed by the king, she cohabited with twelve men of his household and afterwards sank so low as to be acquainted with the grooms of the stable

And bi the kyng whan she was refusid,
Tuelue in nou*m*bre that duelled i*n* his hous
Most frowardli hir beute haue abusid,
Of hir nature she was so lecherous.
Al to reherse it is contagious,
How she wex afftir so abhomynable
To been aqueynted with gromys of þe stable.

It wer but veyn to tarie on this mateere
Or any long processe for to make,
Hir stori is co*n*tagious [for] to heere.

682. Rymuldis H — Romuldus stood] Rymuldus abood J, Romilde abode P.
691. firy ty*n*dis] fire teyndis R. 693. nouht] *om.* R.
698. withoute] with R. 705. but of] of al B, J.
715. on] in R, H, R 3, H 5.

But fynalli at myscheef she was take,
For a spectacle fichched on a stake,
Set up alofte, myn auctour tellith so,
Deide in distresse for constreynt of hir wo.

It is a foul story; and finally she was impaled on a stake and died.

[Off Iustynyan the fals extorcioner exiled by Patrycyan/after bothe nose & eien kut from his hede.] [1]

BY exaumple, so as fressh armure
Thoruh long[e] resting leseth his brihtnesse,
Fret with old rust, gadreth gret ordure,
Is diffacid of his fressh cleernesse,
Semblabli the Romeyns hih prowesse
Gan for tappalle, alas, & that was routhe! —
Whan thei hem gaff to necligence & slouthe.

Just as new armour if unused becomes tarnished, so the Romans lost their prowess when they grew slothful.

Who in knihthod list haue experience
Must eschewe riotous idilnesse,
Be prouident with enteer dilligence,
Large with discrecioun, manli with gentilesse,
To hih emprises his corage dresse,
And be weel war, upon ech partie,
Hym to preserue fro rust of slogardie.

Knights must avoid riotous idleness and keep themselves from the rust of indolence.

The which[e] vice gretli hath appeired,
As is remembrid of old antiquite,
Caused ofte Romeyns be dispeired,
Be froward lustis hyndred ther cite
And appallid ther old prosperite;
For which defautis cam to pleyne blyue
To Iohn Bochas emperour[e]s fyue.

It was this vice that hurt the prosperity of Rome; and five emperors and five kings came to Bochas to complain their sloth.

As many kynges of the same noumbre,
Which be slouthe wern afforn oppressid,
Whom that slouthe whilom did encoumbre,
Ther names heer bi and bi expressid,
To myn auctour thei han her cours Idressid
Lik ther degrees to speke in wordes fewe:
¶ Iustynyan first did* his face shewe,

Justinian Temerarius,

Nat Iustynyan whilom so vertuous, [p. 416]
And of prudent gouernaunce so notable,
But Iustynyan Temerarivs,

723. resting] rustyng H. 738. disespeyred H.
744. slouthe] slouhe R. 749. did] gan B, J, P.
751] And so notable off prudent gouernaunce R, R 3, H 5, & so noble of prudent governaunce H.

[1] MS. J. leaf 170c.

an irresponsible man of bad character, was exiled by Patrician for extortion,

Double of his deedis, fals & deceyuable,
Of his promys dyuers & vnstable,
Whilom exilid be Patrician
For extorsiou*n*s that he in Roome ga*n*.

and his eyes and nose cut off. Leontius was put down by Tiberius,

His nase, his eyen Patrician gaf i*n* charge
To be kut of, be furious cruelte.
And of thempire þ*at* was so wide & large,
¶ Leoncius next gou*er*nid the cite;
And thoruh Fortunis mutabilite
The same Leonce be Tiberie was cast dou*n*,
His eien put out, deied afftir i*n* prisou*n*.

and Tiberius was served in the same fashion and imprisoned for a thief.

¶ Tiberius afftir seruid on the same,
His nose kut of, from his see put dou*n*;
For a rebuk and a perpetuel shame,
To a cite that callid was Cersou*n*,
W*ith*oute merci, fauour or rau*n*sou*n*
Exilid he was, prisowned as a theeff,
Bi long[e] turment deide at myscheef.

[How Philip the Emperour died at myschef.] [1]

Philippicus was an odious heretic and iconoclast, who knocked down the images of the holy saints,

¶ Next to Boch*as* ca*m* Phelipp on the ri*n*g,
Whos empire no while did endure.
Lik an heretik cursid of lyuyng
And odious to eueri creature,
Beet dou*n* images & many fressh picture
Of hooli seynt*es*, which in ther templis stood,
Wherbi Romey*n*s dempte that he was wood.

for which the Romans thought he was mad, and Anastasius put him out of the empire and blinded him.

Pursuid he was bi a manli kniht
Callid Anastaise, and put out of his place;
And in Cicile, of verray force & myht
He did his eyen out of his hed arace,
Be iugement his visage to difface,
Semblabli as he be gret outrages
Of Cristes cherch diffaced the images;

Anastasius then took possession, and the empire was divided.

Deide at myscheeff dirkid with blyndnesse.
¶ Than Anastaise took posessiou*n*,
In whos tyme, bookis ber witnesse

755. Patrician] Leoncian P. 764. Tibery H — on] of J, P.
769. he was] was he R.
778. manli] myhty H. 779. Anastasius P, anastasie R.
780. in] *om.* R. 784. cherch] Chirchis R.

[1] MS. J. leaf 170d.

And cronicles make me*n*ciou*n*,
Of thempire was maad dyuisiou*n*:
That first was oon, partid [was] on tueyne
Wherof my*n* auct*our* in maner doth co*m*pleyne.

¶ Bochas in maner compleynyth of þingis deuidid in too.[1]

AS he reherseth in his oppynyou*n*
And therupon doth a grou*n*d deuise,
Cause & rote of ther deuisiou*n*
Took origynal of fals couetise;
And ceriousli he tellith heer the guise,
Into the cherch whan richesse brouht i*n* p*r*ide,
Al perfecciou*n* anon was set aside.

As Bochas says, the cause of this division was covetousness; and when wealth brought pride into the church, all perfection was abandoned.

The poore staf and potent of doctryne,
Whan it wer chau*n*gid & list nat for tabide
In wilful pouert, but gan anon declyne,
On statli palfreyis & hih hors to ride,
Sharp heires wer[e]n also leid aside,
Tournid to copis of purpil & sangwy*n*,
Gownis of scarlet furrid w*ith* hermyn.

When the monks rode on stately palfreys and high horses, and laid aside their haircloth for scarlet gowns trimmed with ermine,

Slendre fare of wyn & water cleer,
W*ith* abstinence of bred maad of whete
Chau*n*gid tho daies to many fat dyneer,
W*ith* confect drynk of ipocratis* sueete;
And sobirnesse dide his bou*n*dis lete,
Scarsnesse of foode lefte his olde estat,
With newe excesse gan wexe delicat.

and exchanged their simple fare for rich feasting, and no longer kept sober,

Gostly lyuyng in the cherche appallid,
Caused Greekis withdrawe hem i*n* sente*n*ce
From the pope, in Petris place stallid,
And list to hym do non obedience.
Fals auarice caused this offence,
That the Grekis dide hemsilf deuide
Fro the Romeyns for ther gret[e] p*r*ide.

the spiritual life of the church grew faint, and the Greeks withdrew themselves from the Romans.

790. 2nd was] *om.* R.
791. myn auct*our* in maner] in maneer my*n* Auctour H.
796. the] his R. 809. confect] comforte H. confort R 3 — of ipocratis] & ipocras B, J, of ypocras R.

[1] *The following heading is in* MS. J. leaf 170d: "How Anastace was co*m*pellid to leve the Empire to be a preste and lyve in pouerte."

Thus covetousness and evil ambition brought in division. Take record of Anastasius, who was put out of the empire by Theodosius,

Thus coueitise and [fals] ambicioun
Did first gret harm among* the spir*it*ual,
Brouht in discord and dyuysioun
Among princis in ther estat royal.
Who clymbeth hiest, most pereilous is his fall,
Record I take of forseid Anastase,
Be Theodosie put out of his place.

and finally took orders and died in poverty.

This Theodosie dide his besi peyne [p. 417]
On Anastace suich werre for to make,
That maugre hym he did hym so constreyne,
That he was fayn thempire to forsake.
For feer and dreed he did upon hy*m* take
The oordre of preest from the imperial see,
Content with litil, lyued in pouertee.

[How the hede of Lupus kyng of Lumbardie was smet of by Grymaldus.] [1]

Four mighty kings of Lombardy appeared to Bochas, with hair grown long and beards reaching to the navel.

AFFTIR thes chau*n*ges r*e*me*m*brid be wr*i*ti*n*gis,
Lik as I haue told heer i*n* partie,
Ca*m* to Boch*as* foure myhti ki*n*gis
Regnyng echon of old in Lu*m*bardie.
Afftir the maner and guise of barbarie
Thei wern arraied, & in ther passage
Wi*th* her forgrowen bodi and visage.

They wore many-coloured garments, broad baldrics, large golden buckles and pendants, breeches embroidered with pearls,

Ther berdis rauhte ouer ther nouele dou*n*;
Ther garneme*ntes* of colo*urs* manyfold,
Wi*th* brode baudrikis enbracid environ*n*,
Large bokelis & pendau*n*tis of fy*n* gold.
Ther brech enbrowdid aftir the guise of old,
Fret with perle, leg stukkid to the kne,
Pleynyng to Bochas of ther adu*er*site.

and shoes laced with gold wire and set with strange stones.

Ther shon wer racid fresshli to the ton,
Richeli transuersed with gold weer,
And theron sette many a strau*n*ge ston,
Gey*n* Phebus liht that shon ful briht & cleer.
Thes Lombard kynges gan tapproche neer,

820. fals] *om.* J, R 3, H 5. 821. among] in B, J, R.
825. of] on H. 835. partie] Iup*ar*tye H.
841. rauhte] rauh H — 2nd ther] þe H, the R 3, J.
846. stukkid] stokkid H. 848. to] vnto R.
850. strau*n*ge] riche H.

[1] MS. J. leaf 171a.

And first of alle the proude kyng Lupus
Vnto Bochas ga*n* his co*m*pley*n*t[e] thus:

¶ "Bochas," quod he, "as for my partie,
For to reherse be short conclusiou*n*,
On Grymaldus, a p*r*ince of Lumbardie,
Hath me enchacid out of my regiou*n*
And cruelli me cheynid in p*r*isou*n*.
And aftir that he did a sergau*n*t sende,
Smet of myn hed, and ther I maad a*n* eende."

Lupus complained that Grimoaldus first chased him from his kingdom and then sent a sergeant to smite off his head.

[How the hede of Alexyus was smet of by Co*m*pertou*n*.] [1]

Aftir this eende rehersed of Lupus,
For to declare his mortal heuynesse,
¶ Next in ordre ther ca*m* Alexius,
A Lombard ky*n*g famous of richesse,
Which took on hym of surquedous prowesse
For to compasse the destrucciou*n*
Of a p*r*ince Icallid Co*m*pertou*n*,

Which wered also a crowne in Lumbardie.
Atwixe bothe was werre & gret distau*n*ce,
But al the peeple and lordis of Pauye
W*ith* myhti hond and marcial gou*er*nau*n*ce
The saide Alex brouhte to myschau*n*ce;
And Compertou*n*, escapid from al dreed,
Of mortal vengau*n*ce leet smyte*n* of his hed.

Alahis took upon himself of pride to destroy another Lombard prince called Gunibert;

but the people of Pavia defeated him, and he too lost his head.

[How Arypertou*n* was drowned with his rychesse.] [2]

Aftir whos deth pitousli pleyny*n*g,
¶ Tofor Iohn Boch*as* cam Aripertou*n*,
Of Lumbardie whilom lord & kyng,
Which, lik a fool, of hih presu*m*pciou*n*
Al causeles took occasiou*n*
Of volu*n*te, ther is no mor to seye,
Ageyn the duk off Bagorois to werreye.

Aribertus, like a fool, made war on the duke of Bavaria,

864. Alexius] Alahus P. 868. Co*m*pertou*n*] Guniberte P.
873. Alex] Alexius R, Alahis P. 877. Arithberto*n* P.
879. Which] & H — hih] his R.
882. Bagorois] Baier*n*oys H, R 3, Bauaroies P.

[1] MS. J. leaf 171b. [2] MS. J. leaf 171b.

and losing, fled to Pavia with his treasure,

Thes princis tweyne taken haue the feeld,
Of* Ariperton the parti gan appeire;*
His aduersaire anon as he beheeld,
His coward herte ga*n* to disespeire.
Into Pauye for feer he ga*n* repeire,
Took his tresour in purpos ano*n* riht,
For verray dreed to take hy*m* to the fliht.

and then took ship and was drowned in a tempest. Such is the fate of those who begin predatory wars against their neighbours.

Took a vessel and entrid is the se,
With sodeyn tempest assailed & dirknesse,
His barge pershid bi gret aduersite
And he was drownid with al his gret richesse.
Loo, heer the fyn of worldli wrechidnesse,
Namli of them, to gete gret treso*u*rs
That gyne werre agey*n* ther neih[e]bo*u*rs.

[How Dediere by pope Adryan and Charles of Fraunce was put to flight & died at mischef.] [1]

Next, Desiderius, king of Lombardy, appeared. Whereas his father Agilulf had offended the pope,

NEXT to Bochas, *with* heuy look & cheere,
Kyng of Lu*m*bars shewed his p*re*sence,
Callid in his tyme noble Dedieer,
Notable in armys & of gret excellence.
And wher his faddir hadde don offence
To the pope and ful gret duresse,
This kyng caste the damages to redresse.

Desidirius sought to make amends by presenting the Holy See with the city of Faenza,

Agistulphe was his fadris name,
Which to the pope did gret aduersite;
For which his sone to encrece his fame,
Of roial fredam and magnanymyte
And off benigne liberalite,
Gaff to the pope *with* hu*m*ble reuerence
A statli cite that callid is Fayence.

together with great treasure and a mighty castle in Ferrara.

Therwith he gaff gret treso*u*r & gret good, [p. 418]
As he that list of freeda*m* nat to spare,
A mihti castel which on Tibre stood
Withyn*n*e the bou*n*dis & lordship of Ferare,
Which is a cite, pleynli to declare,

884. Of] And B, And of J, P — appeire] to appeire B, to peyre R, H 5. 885. aduersaries H.
892. His barge] And he was H. 893. And] for H.
899. Dedieer] Desidere P. 904. Agistulphe] Agilulphe P.
910. is] was H — Fayence] Fauence P. 913. castel] Cite H.

[1] MS. J. leaf 171 verso.

Of antiquite, my*n* aucto*ur* tellith so,
And stant upon the ryuer of the Po.

This Dedieer regnyng in Lu*m*bardie
Gan wexe famous at his [be]gyn*n*yng,
Hadde gret name vpon ech partie;
But in this eerthe is nothi*n*g abidy*n*g:
Al stant on chau*n*g; & Fortune in werky*n*g
Is fou*n*de vnstable & double of hir visage,
Which of this ky*n*g chau*n*ged the corage.

He grew famous and prospered; but nothing abides here on earth; Fortune is unstable,

Ther he was first large on eueri side,
Liberal fou*n*de in many dyuers wise,
His goodliheed was chau*n*gid onto p*r*ide
And his largesse onto couetise.
Of doublenesse he ga*n* ano*n* deuise
To cleyme ageyn, as ye shal vndirsto*n*de,
His seide giftis out of the popis ho*n*de.

and the king became proud and covetous and decided to take his gifts back again.

Which Dedieer hadde made alliau*n*ce,
As the cronicle maketh menciou*n*,
With kyng Pepy*n* regnyng tho in F*r*ance.
Afftir whos deth, to haue pocessiou*n*
And ful lordship of al that regiou*n*,
He gan of newe fallyn at distau*n*ce
Bothe with the pope & with the ki*n*g of France.

He had also allied himself with Pepin of France, so as to get possession of his kingdom after his death,

Of presumpciou*n* thes werris he bega*n*
Ageyn his promys, of double variau*n*ce;
Pope in tho daies was hooli Adria*n*,
Which to stynte this* trouble & gr*e*t myschau*n*ce,
Requered helpe of the ki*n*g of Frau*n*ce.
And grete Charlis, in Bochas as I reede,
Ca*m* to the pope to helpyn in this neede.

and now he fell out with both Charlemagne, who succeeded Pepin, and Pope Adrian.

Charlis that tyme was trewe* protecto*ur*
To hooli cherche, ther pauys and diffence;
Which of hool herte and dilligent labo*ur*
With Dedieer be ma*n*li violence
He mette in Tuscan, of kingli* excellence;
Hadde a bataile to preeve ther bothe myht:
Charlis victor; Dedier put to fliht.

Charlemagne was a true protector of the church, and, meeting Desiderius in Tuscany, put him to flight

925. Ther he] The R. 929. anon he gan R.
938. 2nd with] *om.* H, R, R 3. 939. thes] the R.
942. this] the B, J, P. 945. this] his R.
946. trewe] cheef B, chief J, P.
950. knigli] knihtli B, J — of] & H. 951. bothe] bothis R.

and laid siege to Pavia, where he took refuge. Starvation forced him to surrender,

As I fynde, he fledde into Pavie;
Worthi Charlis leide his* siege afforn,
Constreyned hem upon ech partye,
For lak of vitaile thei wer almost lorn;
Thei wanted[e] licour, greyn and corn.
Be sodeyn constreynt & gret aduersite
To kyng Charlis thei yald up the cite.

and he was sent to prison in France, where he died at mischief. He was the last king of the Lombards.

Kyng Dedieer was sent into Fraunce,
With myhti cheynis fetrid in prisoun;
Lik a wrech, in sorwe & in* penaunce,
Deide at myscheef; ther geyned no raunsoun,
Which hadde afforn so gret pocessioun.
Aftir whos day, as be old writyng,
Among Lumbardis was neuer crownid kyng.

[Off pope Iohn a woman with child and put doun.] [1]

Rounded and shorn like a bishop and wearing the broad tonsure and vestments of a priest, Pope John, a

AFFTIR thes princis rehersed heer-toforn,
Drownid in teres cam a creature,
Lik a bisshop roundid* & Ishorn;
And as a prest she had a brod tonsure,
Hir apparaille outward & vesture,
Beyng a woman, wherof Bochas took heed,
Lik a prelat shapyn was hir weede.

woman, a beardless prelate, who unworthily sat in the chair of St. Peter, appeared drowned in tears before Bochas.

She was the same that of yore agon
Vnworthily sat in Petris place;
Was afftirward callid Pope Iohn,
A berdles prelat, non her seyn on hir face.
Of hir berthe namyd was the place,
Mayence, a cite stondyng in Itaille,
Vpon the Reen, ful famous of vitaille.

In her youth she devoted herself to the liberal sciences

In hir youthe and in hir tendre age
Forsook hir kyn, and in especiall
Caste she wolde for hir auauntage

954. his] a B, J, P. 959. thei] *om.* R, H, R 3, H 5.
961. myhti] *om.* R. 962. 2nd in] gret B, J, H 5.
969. roundid] Iroundid B, I rounded J.
972. wherof] theroff R. 973. hir] his R.
975. Vnworthily] vnworthly R.
979. Mayence] Magonice P — stondyng] not standing P.
980. of vitaille] it is no faile H.

[1] MS. J. leaf 171 verso.

Yiue hir to konyng, bodi, herte & all.
And [in] the science[s] callid liberall,
In alle seuene, bi famous excellence,
Bi gret studie she hadde experience,

and became famous for her learning.

Hir name kouth in many dyuers lond.
To shewe hir cunnyng first whan she began,
Serchyng prouynces cam to Ing[e]lond,
No wiht supposyng but that she was a man;
Cam to Roome, hir stori telle can,
Tauhte gramer, sophistre [and] logik,
Redde in scoolis openli rethorik.

She went to England, where all people thought she was a man, and taught grammar, logic and rhetoric in Rome.

In the tyme of emperour Lotarie, [p. 419]
Afftir the deth, as maad is mencioun, —
Fro myn auctour yif I shal nat varie, —
That the pope which callid was Leoun,
The saide woman be eleccioun
Istallid was, supposyng no wiht than
Be no tokne but that she was a man.

In the time of the emperor Lothair, after the death of Pope Leon, she was herself made pope by election and

The book of sortis aftir that anon,
Of auenture tournid up-so-doun;
She was callid & namyd Pope Iohn,
Of whos natural disposicioun
Fill bi processe into temptacioun:
Quik with childe, the hour cam on hir than;
Was delyuered at Seynt Ihon Lateran.

called Pope John. Falling into temptation, she was gotten with child, delivered at St. Lateran

Afftir put doun for hir gret outrage,
I wil on hire spende no more labour,
But passe ouer al the surplusage
Of hir lyuyng and of hir gret errour;
Tourne my stile to themperour
Callid Arnold, & write his pitous chaunce,
Sone to Charlis, the grete kyng of Fraunce.

and afterwards put down for her great outrage.

[How arnold son to Charles of Fraunce was eten with lys and so died.] [1]

To this Charlis, as bookis determyne,
He was sone nat born in mariage,
But begetyn of a concubyne;

Arnulph, a natural son of Carloman, king of France,

991. No wiht] Nouht R, nouht H. 993. and] *om.* R.
1015. Charlis the grete] Charlemaine P.

[1] MS. J. leaf 172 recto.

undertook to reign without title as emperor of the Romans.

Took upon hym of surquedous outrage,
W*ith*oute title of berthe or lynage,
To succeede be fraude and fals labour
Among Romeyns to regne as empero*ur*.

But he spent all his days in mischief and died eaten up by lice and worms.

He was vngracious sitty*ng* i*n* that estat,
In myscheeff spente his daies euerichon,
W*ith* lees and wermys maad infortunat,
Thoruh skyn and flessh fret onto þe bon.
Crafft of medecyne nor soco*ur* was ther non,
So deepe [he] was fret in his entraille;
Deide in distresse; no leche myhte auaille.

¶ Thauctour geyn the pride of Princis.[1]

Bochas pauses for a while to write angrily of the sins of tyrants, counselling them to remember this proud Arnulph,

MYN auctour Boch*as* stynt heer for a while,
Sharped his pen*ne* of ente*n*ciou*n*,
Gan of angre to t*r*ansport his stile
To write off tirau*n*tis for ther* transgressiou*n*,
Moor wood & fell tha*n* any scorpiou*n*,
Them cou*n*seillyng, wha*n* thei be most bold,
For to reme*m*bre on this proude Arnold.

who was not attacked by wolves or lions or ravenous bears or wild boars or mighty champions, but murdered by worms.

He ne was nat in his pride assailed,
Nat with wolues, tigres nor leou*n*s,
With rauynous beres nor wilde boor* t*r*auailed,
Nowthir with othir myhti champiou*n*s,
Which haue conquered many regiou*n*s;
But with wermys engendrid of his ky*n*de
The saide Arnold was moordrid, as I fy*n*de.

Although of the blood of Charlemagne, he was so tormented by lice and worms that he could not endure the pain.

In suich disioynt the sayd[e] Arnold stood,
With lees and wermys fret agey*n* nature,
That was so nih[e] born of Charlis blood,
Impotent the peyne to endure.
Which was in sooth an vnkouth auenture,
That a p*r*ince myht nat be socourid
Of smale wermys for to be deuourid.

A good example for princes to consider how

A gret exau*m*ple, who list considre & see,
To p*r*incis alle for tabate ther pride.
Lat hem considre ther fragilite,

1023. that] his H — estat] state R. 1031. of] for H. 1033. for ther] the B, J. 1035. counseillyng] cou*n*sailid H. 1036. on] vpon H. 1039. nor] *with* H — boor] wolues B, bores J, P. 1044. Arnolphe R. 1046. nihe] myhty R.

[1] *The following heading is in* MS. J. leaf 172 recto: "Bochas counceyleth p*r*incys to remembre on Arnold."

To seen an emperour [for] to abide*
Thassaut of wermys — & ley ther bost aside,
In this Arnold wisli aduertise
How God hath poweer ther pompe to chastise.

God has power to chastise their pomp.

Deth of Arnold dide my penne encoumbre
For the gret abhomynacioun.
¶ Than onto Bochas cam the tuelue in noumbre,
Callid Pope Iohn, as maad is mencioun,
Entryng be fraude and fals eleccioun,
To Goddis lawe froward & contrarie,
Nat lik a pastor but a mercenarie.

The death of Arnulph disgusted me. Then came Pope John, called the Twelfth,

[Howe pope Iohn the xij^{the} for lechery & vicious lif was put doun.] [1]

Callid afforn he was Octauyan,
Nothing resemblyng Petris gouernaunce.
Fro the tyme in Roome that he began
To sitte as pope, he gaf his attendaunce
To folwe his lust & his flesshli plesaunce, —
In haukyng, huntyng stood his felicite,
And among women conuersaunt to bee.

who entered by fraud and spent his time in hawking, hunting and in intercourse with women,

Vnto surfet, riot, glotonye [p. 420]
He gaff hym hooli; took of God non heede;*
Gretli disclaundrid he was of lecherie;
Kepte in his court, withoute shame or dreed,
A noumbre of wommen, in cronicle as I reed.
Too cardinales of purpos did entende
His vicious lyff to correcte & amende.

and gave himself wholly to riot, gluttony and excess. He took no heed of God; and when two cardinals tried to correct him

And of entent thes cardynalis too
The cherch esclaundrid cast hem to redresse;
Made lettres, sent hem to Otto,
Duk of Saxonye*, that he sholde him* dresse
Toward Roome, and of [his] hih noblesse

and sent letters to Otto, Duke of Saxony, requesting him to reform the mischief,

1054. to abide] tabide B — for] *om.* H, R, J, R 3, H 5.
1060. the] ther H, R 3. 1062. Entryng] Entrid R.
1064. but] lik H.
1073. non] no R — heede] keepe B, kepe J, P.
1080. esclaundrid] disclaundrid H, ensklandrid H 5.
1082. Saxonye] Saxoyne B, Saxone R — him] hem B.
1083. hih] *om.* R, J.

[1] MS J. leaf 172 recto.

On hooli cherche to haue compassiou*n*,
Make of this myscheef iust reformaciou*n*.

John cut off the nose of the one and the hand of the other.

This Pope Iohn, whan he hath parceyued
Of his* cardynales the maner of writy*ng*,
And how the duk the lettres hath* resceyued,
He to do vengau*n*ce made no tarieng;
Bood no lenger, this iugement yiuyng:
Kitt of the nose felli of the ton,
Hond of the tothir; and ech was callid Iohn.

The Emperor wrote to him, but without avail; and finally he was deposed by cardinals. I don't want to write any more about him.

The emperou*r* did[e] his lettres sende
To this pope of hool affecciou*n*,
Of his defautis he sholde hy*m* amende.
But ther was fou[n]de no correcciou*n*;
For which he was deposid & put dou*n*
Bi cardynalis for his cursidnesse;
Me list no mor write of his wrechidnesse.

Seeing all this mischief, my author prepared openly to describe the faults of prelates,

¶ For his defautis & his gret out*r*age
This Iohn put dou*n*, as ye haue herd deuise,
Myn auctour aftir kauht a gret corage,
Seyng this myscheef in many sondri wise,
In hooli cherch[e] which that did arise
Among prelatis, cast hymseluen blyue
Ther diffautis openli descryue,

their pride and their presumption; but remembering a verse in the Psalter, "Do not touch my prophets nor malign against them,"

Of ther pride and ther presu*m*pciou*n*.
And whil he gan studie in this mateer,
He ga*n* remembre anon in his resou*n*
Vpon a vers write[n] in the Sauteer:
"Touche nat my p*ro*phetis, ne neih hem nat to ner,
Nor ageyn hem, be[th] war in deed & thouht,
In no wise that ye maligne nouht."

he withdrew his hand and turned to Duke Charles of Lorraine.

For this cause, as ye shal vndirstonde,
Touchyng this mateer, pleyn*l*i as I reede,
Myn aucto*u*r [Bochas] gan withdrawe his honde,
Lefft his purpos, and foorth he ga*n* proceede, —
To whos presence, or that he took heede,
Cam a p*r*ince, Duk Charlis of Loreyne;
Hym besouhte to write his greuous peyne.

1085. reformaciou*n*] informacion R.
1087. his] thes B, thise J, these P. 1088. hath] haue B.
1096. was] *om.* R. 1101. Iohn] Pope R.
1105. cast] cauht H. 1110. writen] *om.* R.
1111. my] *om.* R. 1112. beth war] bewar B, J.
1117. ga*n*] can R.

[Off Charles of Loreyn confounded with hunger.] [1]

¶ This duk of Loreyne, as ye shal conceyue,
Hadde werre with the kyng of Fraunce
Callid Hewe Capet; and, as I apparceyue,
An archebishop, the kyng to do plesaunce,
Of hatreede made his ordenaunce
[A]geyn this duk, await upon hym kepte,
That he hym took abedde whil* he slepte.

This duke was at war with Hugh Capet and was taken in bed by an archbishop,

The said bisshop gan falsli vndermyne
This worthi duk, bi ful fals tresoun,
Which, as I fynde, was callid Ancelyne;
And he was bisshop that tyme of Leoun.
Which be fraude & fals collusioun
Took this prince that was duk of Loreyne,
And to the kyng he brouht hym bi a treyne.

Ascelin of Laon,

who delivered him to the king, who in

Bi whom he was delyuered to prisoun,
To Orlyanes, and with cheynis bounde.
What was his eende is maad no mencioun;
But in a pet horrible & profounde,
Mischeeff with hunger did hym so confounde,
That, I suppose, this duk of Loreyne
Consumyd was for constreynt of his peyne.

turn sent him to prison in Orleans, where he was confined in a horrible deep pit and probably died of hunger.

[How kyng Salamon whilom kynge of Hungery was put to flight.] [2]

AFFTIR to Bochas in noumbre þer cam doun
Princis foure; and ech for his partie
Ther greuys tolde; and first king Salamon,
Which that whilom regned in Hungrie,
Bothe fool & coward, bookis specefie,
Void of resoun, noised of ignoraunce,
And, at a poynt, koude no purueiaunce.

Four princes then appeared to Bochas. The first, King Salomon of Hungary, a fool and a coward,

Fortune also did at hym disdeyne;
For he was nouther manli nor coraious.
Ageyn[es] whom wer worthi princis tweyne;

1123. Hewe] huhe R, heugh H, hugh J, R 3 — apparceyue] parceyue R. 1127. whil] whan B.
1128. The] This R, H. 1130. Which] & H — was] he was H.
1135. delyuered] committid H. 1144. Ther] That R.

[1] MS. J. leaf 127c. [2] MS. J. leaf 127d.

was chased out of his region by two notable and virtuous princes, Ladislaus and Geysa,

Zerta was oon, with Laudisalus,
Famous in armys, notable and vertuous; —
Bothe attonis geyn Salamon cam doun
And made hym fleen out of his regioun.

and Bochas wrote no more about him.

Thoruh his vnhappi froward cowardise, [p. 421]
Ther was in hym founde no diffence;
Fliht was his sheelde, list nat in no wise
Geyn his enmyes make resistence;
Failled herte to come to presence
To saue his lond, he dradde hymselue so sore,
Of whom Bochas writ in his book no more.

[How Petro kyng of Hungery was slayn.] [1]

King Pietro of Hungary was malicious and foolish enough to offend Charles of France, who put out his eyes and slew him.

¶ Anothir kyng heer put in remembrance
Callid Petro, regnyng in Hungrye,
For his defautis ageyn the kyng of France
Icallid Charlis, of malis & folie,
Be indignacioun, this* was his tormentrie:
His eyen put out, — ther was no bet socour —
And aftir slayn be doom of themperour.

[How Diogenes the emperour was take and eiene put out.] [2]

Ernest, Duke of Swabia, who opposed the Emperor Henry, was banished to dwell with savage beasts in a forest, where he was slain.

¶ Afftir to Bochas ther cam tweyne on þe ryng,
Duk of Sweue, Hermest, as I reede,
Geyn* themperour first maliciousli werki[n]g,
Herry themperour regnyng tho in deede.
But for his malis, this was his fatal meede:
Banshed to duelle among beestis most sauage,
Slayn in a forest for his gret outrage.

After Constantine of Greece died, Diogenes, a knight, succeeded him in Constantinople,

¶ Whan Constantyn departed from this lyff,
Which of al Grece was lord and gouernour,
Be mariage of hire that was his wiff,
A kniht Diogenes was maad emperour;
Fortune to hym dide so gret fauour,

1152. Zerta] Herta J, Geysa P. 1159. make] made H.
1164. Petre H. 1167. this] that B, J.
1171. Sueuie P — earnest P.
1172. Geyn] Ageyn B, J, R 3, P. 1173. Henry P.
1175. among] mong R 3 — most] *om.* J, P.

[1] MS. J. leaf 172 verso. [2] MS. J. leaf 172 verso.

Constantynople holdyng in his hond,
As souereyn prince of al Grekis lond.

Yet ther wer* summe that gruchched þerageyn 1184
And hadde of hym gret indignacioun.
The kyng of Perse, Belset Tarquemayn,
From hym be force took many a regioun;
Mesopotanye to his pocessioun 1188
Took be strong hand, thoruh his cheualrie,
Maugre Diogenes, & al-most al Surrie.

although some men grumbled, among them Belsech Turcoman, who took Mesopotamia and nearly all Syria away from him.

Belset Tarquemayn made hymself so strong,
Bi manli force Diogenes tassaile; 1192
And for Diogenes thouhte he did hym wrong,
He gan ordeyne gret stuff & apparaile;
A day assigned, thei mette in bataile,—
Diogenes of froward auenture 1196
He and his knihtis brouht to disconfiture.

Diogenes considered himself wronged and met Belsech in battle, but was defeated

Take he was and brouht be gret disdeyn,
In whom as tho ther was no resistence,
To kyng Belset callid Tarquemayn. 1200
And whan he cam onto his presence,
Ageyn[e]s hym was youe this sentence:
To lyn doun plat, and the kyng Belsette
Sholde take his foot and on his throte it sette. 1204

and brought before his conqueror, who after compelling him to lie down on the ground, set his foot on his throat in despite.

This was doon for an hih[e] despiht,
Diogenes brouht foorth on a cheyne,
Withoute reuerence, fauour or respiht,
At gret[e] feestis assigned was his peyne; 1208
And aldirlast put out his eye[n] tweyne.
The wheel of Fortune tourneth as a ball;
Sodeyn clymbyng axeth a sodeyn fall.

Diogenes was afterwards exhibited at festivals and finally his eyes were put out.

[How Robert duk of Normandie fauht with turkes was named to the crowne of Ierusalem & died at mischef.] [1]

A WORTHI prince spoke of in many rewm, 1212
Noble Robert, duk of Normandie,
Chose to the crowne of Iherusalem;

Duke Robert of Normandy was a worthy prince.

1184. wer] was B, H 5, P. 1186. Belset] belsate H, Belsech P—Tarquemayn] Tarquenyayne J, Tarquynyan H, Turcomane P. 1191. Tarquynyan H, Tarquenyan J.
1200. Belsech Tarcomene P — Tarquynyayn H.
1204. throte] bak H, bake R 3.

[1] MS. J. leaf 173 recto.

He refused the crown of Jerusalem, which lost him Fortune's favour.

But for cause he dide it denye,
Fortune ay hadde onto hy*m* enuye.
The same Robert next in order was
That ca*m* to pleyne his fall onto Bochas.

Together with Godfrey de Bouillon he fought the Turks and Saracens,

For Cristis feith this myhti champiou*n*,
This Duk Robert, armyd in plate & maile,
W*ith* ma*n*li Godfrey, Godfrey Bolliou*n*,
Agey*n*[es] Turkis fauht a gret bataille,
For Cristes feith that it sholde auaille
To susteene his lawe in ther entent
To alle the kyngis of the occident.

who sought to destroy Christ's faith, and with the aid of the kings of England, Normandy and France defeated them.

Of Turkis, Sarsyns was so gret a nou*m*bre,
Geyn Cristis lawe gadred a puissau*n*ce,
The feith of Crist falsli to encou*m*bre:
But ther wer maad[e] hasti ordenau*n*ce
Be kynges of Inglond, Norma*n*die & Frau*n*ce;
First to socoure did his besi peyne
Godfrey Bolliou*n*, that was duk of Loreyne,

Robert was chosen king of Jerusalem;

Which on Sarsyns made a disconfiture,
Maugre Turkis, for al ther cruel myht.
In which bataille Crist made hym to recure
The feeld that day for to supporte his riht,
Wher said Robert was fou*n*de so good a kniht,
That for his noblesse, be report of writy*n*g,
Of Iherusalem was namyd to be kyng.

but he would not accept, because his older brother William had died in England and he was the next heir.

Assentid nat onto the eleccíou*n*, [p. 422]
Because of newe that he did vndirstonde
His elder brothir, for short co*n*clusiou*n*,
Icallid William was ded in Inglond;
Knowyng hymsilf[e] next heir to that lond,
Forsook Iherusalem, and lik a ma*n*li kniht
Cam to Inglond for to cleyme his riht.

He went to England and found his younger brother Henry crowned king, who said he was rightful heir, Robert being king of Jerusalem.

And yit or he cam he hadde knoulechi*n*g,
His yonger brothir, [that] callid [was] Herry,
Had take upon hym to be crownid ky*n*g;
Told his lordis and p*r*incis fynalli
He was next heir; entrid rihtfulli
As enherito*u*r to succeede in that rewm,
His brother beyng kyng of Iherusalem.

1229. ordenau*n*ce] purveiaunce H. 1238. of] and R.
1240. onto] to R. 1247. And] *om.* H, R 3.
1248. yonger] yong R. 1249. upon] on H. 1252. As] an R

God wot the cas* stood al in oþ*er* wise:
The said[e] Duk Robert of Norma*n*die
Purposed hym be marcial emprise
Fro*m* his brother to take the regalie.
Took his p*r*incis and his cheualrie;
Thouhte he wolde, lik a ma*n*li kniht,
Arryue in Inglond and reioysshe his riht.

So Robert proposed to take the kingdom by force,

Bothe in o feeld assemblid on o day,
The brethre tweyne, ech with stro*n*g partie
To darreyne, and make no delay,
Euerich with othir to holde chau*m*partie.
But whan the lordes this mischeef did espie,
Thei besied hem and wer nat rek[e]les
Atween the brethre to refourme pes.

and both sides met on the field of battle; but before the fight began, the lords intervened, and the brothers

The said[e] brethre wer fulli co*n*descen*d*did
Vpon this poynt, for short co*n*clusiou*n*,
As in thaccord was iustli co*m*prehendid:
Herry to holde and haue pocessiou*n*
Duryng his lyff of al this regiou*n*,
And Robert sholde haue for his partie
A sum*me* of gold with al Norma*n*die.

agreed to let Henry keep his crown in England, Robert to have Normandy and £3000 a year.

Thre thousand pou*n*d, put in reme*m*b*r*ance,
Ech yeer to Robert sent fro this regiou*n*,
Of which[e] pay to make ful assurau*n*ce
Was leid hostages, as maad is me*n*ciou*n*.
But yit of newe fill a discenciou*n*
Atwixe the brethre, of hatreede & envie,
For certey*n* castellis that stood in Norma*n*die,

But a new quarrel broke out about certain Norman castles,

Which castel[lis] longed of heritage
Vnto the kyngis iuredicciou*n*,
Of which the duk took his auau*n*tage,
Maugre the kyng, & heeld pocessiou*n* —
Torned aftir to his confusiou*n*.
And wha*n* the ky*n*g did this thing* espie,
With strong[e] hond ca*m* into Norma*n*die,

which belonged by inheritance to the king, and of which Robert took possession.

Wher the duk was leid a siege aboute.
Made ordenau*n*ce to recure his riht;
Gat the castel; took his brother oute;

Henry came to Normandy with a strong force, took his brother Robert

1254. cas] cause B, J, H 5. 1259. Thouhte] thouh H.
1261. 1st o] the H, a R, R 3, H 5 — 2nd o] a R, J, R 3, P.
1282. castell R.
1287. did this thing] this thi*n*g did B, J, P.

and put him in prison, where he remained 14 years until he died.

Emprisowned hy*m* of verray force & myht;
Lefft hym allone out of men*n*ys siht
Fourteene yeer, the cronicle writ so;
Ther he deide in myscheeff and in wo.

While Bochas was busy with his book, the Emperor Henry IV. came to him to complain of his son's great unkindness;

¶ Whil Bochas was besi in his labo*ur*
His book taco*m*plissh with gret dilligence,
To hym appeered the grete empero*ur*
Callid Herry, shewyng his presence;
Gan co*m*pleyne of the grete offence
Doon to hym, the myscheeff and distresse,
Bi his sonys gret vnkyndenesse.

for he bound his father in chains and let him die in prison.

The which[e] sone was callid eck Herry,
Gretli accusid of ingratitude,
Cause he wrouhte so disnaturalli:
Took his fadir with force & multitude,
Bou*n*de and cheynid, shortli to co*n*clude;
And aftirward, ther geyned no rau*n*sou*n*,
At gret myscheef deied in prisou*n*.

[How Iocelyne prince of Rage for pride slouthe & lecherie died in pouert.] [1]

Next in order came Josselyn, with sad and dead visage. He was prince of Rages, a famous city, but gave himself to lechery and

NEXT in ordre, with trist & ded visage,
Vnto Boch*as* to shewe his heuynesse
Ca*m* Iocelyn, lord & p*r*ince of Rage,
Which is a cite famous of richesse.
And this prince, myn aucto*ur* berth witnesse,
Was gretly youe to slouthe & slogardie,
And al his lust he sette in lecherie.

idleness and neglected his realm and lost his reputation to such a degree

Lefft his lordship out of gou*er*nau*n*ce,
For lak of wisdam & discreciou*n*;
In flesshli lust[es] set al his plesau*n*ce;
And to the contres aboute hy*m* envirou*n*
He was nat had in reputaciou*n*:
Certey*n* princis, my*n* aucto*ur* doth descryue,
Of his lordship cast hy*m* to depryve.

that several kings laid siege to his city and,

Amongis which the p*r*ince of Alapie, [p. 423]
Callid Sangwyn, the stori who list see,
To Iosalyn hauyng gret envie,

1292. Enprisowned R. 1293. of] of his R.
1299. shewyng] shewid H. 1309. At] A R.
1319. lustes] lust J, P. 1325. Sagnine P.

[1] MS. J. leaf 173 verso.

Leide a siege to Rages his* cite,
He beyng absent ferr fro that contre.
And thus for slouthe & wilful necligence,
Rages was take be myhti violence.

And Iosalyn comau*n*did to p*r*isou*n*;
To hym Fortune was so contrarious:
Lost his lordship and domynaciou*n*.
Loo, heer the fyn of folkis vicious;
Slouh, delicat, proud and lecherous,
Deide in pouert, in myscheef & in neede;
Of vicious p*r*incis, loo, heer the fynal meede!

capturing him, put him in prison, where he died. Such is the final reward of proud and vicious princes.

[How the Emperou*r* Andronycus slouh all that wer*e* of the blood Roial cherysshed vicious peple and aftir was honget.] [1]

AS verray heir and trewe successou*r*
Bi elecciou*n* and also bi lynage,
Ca*m* Andronic*us*, as lord & emperou*r*,
Consta*n*tynople, crownid yong of age,
Next to Bochas, w*ith* trist & pale visage,
Besechyng hym to doon his besi cure
To reme*m*bre his woful auenture.

Andronicus I., who was the rightful emperor in Constantinople, came to Bochas and besought him to remember his story.

Among Grekis, be stori and scripture,
This Andronicus gouernid nat ariht;
Ageyn[es] lawe & eek ageyn nature,
Fou*n*de with his sustir flesshli on a niht;
Bothe of assent[e] took hem to the fliht,
Ageyn[es] hym his cosyn was so fell,
Lord of that contre callid Emanvell.

He did not rule justly and, discovered one night with his sister, fled for fear of his cousin Manuel.

For a tyme stood as a ma*n* exilid
For his discenciou*n*s and many v*n*kouth stryff;
Bi his p*r*incis afftir reconciled,
Stondyng in hope he sholde amende his lyff.
But in the tyme that he was fugitiff,
He was maad lord, & stood so for a while
Regnyng in Pontus, of Asie a gret ile.

For a time he was an exile, but afterwards his princes, hoping he would amend his life, became reconciled to him, and he reigned in Pontus.

In this while Emanuel was ded,
Fall in gret age, the stori tellith thus,

1327. his] the B, J. 1331. to] vnto R.
1341. crownid] crowny*n*g R. 1347. eek] *om.* H.
1349. took] to R. 1352. 2nd a] *om.* R. 1355. his] *om.* H.

[1] MS. J. leaf 173d.

Manuel died and left a son called Alexius, who had a tutor of the same name.

Hauyng a child, & he, who list take heed,
Whil he duelled in his fadris hous
Among Grekis callid Alexivs;
And the tuto*ur* he was assigned too
Icallid was Alexivs also.

This tutor took all the power in Constantinople to himself;

The same that was assigned his tuto*ur*,
Took upo*n* hym al the gouernau*n*ce
And ful poweer as lord & emperou*r*,
Hadde al thempire vndir his obeissau*n*ce;
P*r*incis, lordis gaff to hym attendau*n*ce;
Wher that he was present or absent,
Ech thyng was doon at his comau*n*deme*n*t.

but he was a tyrant, and his subjects decided to call Andronicus back to the imperial throne.

I meene as thus: he had al in his hond
Co*n*sta*n*tynople, cite of gret substau*n*ce;
But for extorsiou*n*s which he did in the lond
On his sogettis, and for mysgou*er*nau*n*ce,
Amo*n*g the lordis it fill in reme*m*brau*n*ce,
Alle of assent in hert[e] gan desire
Calle Andronicus ageyn to his empire.

No sooner was Andronicus in Constantinople than he slew all the royal blood except a prince called Isaac.

Bassent restorid and crownid emperou*r*,
Consta*n*tynople entry*n*g the cite,
Besied hym be fraudulent labou*r*
Al the blood born of the imperial see
For to be slayn, of vengable cruelte,
Be iugement of this Andronicus,
Except a p*r*ince callid Isacivs.

He was as evil and revengeful in old age as in his youth, and

Thus in effect the trouthe was weel seene,
He was vengable last in his old age,
Riht as he was in his yeeris greene,
Felli gouerned, ful off fals outrage,
Last of alle, malicious of corage.
Took to cou*n*sail, in Grece he was thus namyd,
Al suich as wern disclau*n*drid or diffamyd.

associated with defamed men, homicides and ribalds, sparing no woman

Homycides he hadde in his housholde,
Tirau*n*tis that wrouhte ageyn[es] rihtwisnesse;
Cherisshed all that hardi wern and bolde
Widwes, wyues & maidenes to oppresse;*
Ribaudie was callid gentilesse;
Spared nouther, he was so lecherous,
Women sworn chast nor folk religious.

1393. or] & H. 1397. toppresse B.

Hadde also no maner co*n*science
To pile his sogettis falsli be rauyne;
Took what hym list be iniust violence;
To alle vices his youthe he did enclyne.
And alle that wer[e]n of the roial lyne
Wer slayn echon, except Isacivs,
As I told erst[e], bi Andronicvs.

and pillaging his subjects by unjust violence.

As I fynde, for hym in haste he sente, [p. 424]
For this purpos to come to his presence,
To moord[e]ren hym, this was his entente;
Be dyuers toknes and many euidence,
And fully knew the fyn of his sentence,
He lik a p*r*ince list [to] come no neer;
Smet of the hed[e] of the massageer.

He sent for Isaac with the intention of murdering him; but Isaac smote off the head of the messenger

And afftir that, of ma*n*li prouidence,
Mid the cite shewed hy*m* lik a kniht;
Praied lordis to yiue hym audience,
P*r*incis, iuges for to doon hy*m* riht,
That he myht declaren in ther siht
Gret iniuries, damages outragious
Wrouht bi themperour callid Andronicus.

and prayed the lords and princes of the city to do him justice, saying,

"O citeseyns, that knowen al the guise
Of yo*u*r emperour callid Andronicus;
Nat empero*u*r, so ye list aduertise,
But a tirau*n*t cruel & furious,
A fals moordrer, vengable, despitous,
Hath of newe, of* frowar[d] fals corage
Slayn of thempire hooli the lynage.

"O citizens, you know that the cruel tyrant Andronicus has slain all the royal blood

Ther is alyue left non of the blood
Sauf I allone of the roial lyne;
For Andronicus lik a tirau*n*t wood
Hath slay[e]n echon, breeffli to termyne;
His suerd of vengau*n*ce thei myhte nat declyne.
Now purposeth of mortal tiran*n*ye,
Slen me also that am of ther allie.

except me alone, whom he now purposes to destroy.

Requeryng you in this consistorie,
O citeseyn[e]s that heer present bee,
To remembre and calle to memorie
How this famous imperial cite
Hath ay be redi to doon equite,

"I beg you to remember that this city has always been ready to do justice and

1405. And] To R. 1413. to] *om.* R — neer] were R.
1427. of] and B, R, P, & H 5. 1435. ther] þis H.

repress the wrong of tyrants.

Besi also of ther hih noblesse
Wrong of tirau*ntes* manli to represse.

"Philosophers and poets say that the blood of tyrants is a noble sacrifice, and, since you are just, weigh this matter in balance."

Philisophres and poetis eek deuise,
In ther sawes prudent and notable,
Blood of tirau*n*tis is noble sacrefise
To God aboue*, whan thei be vengable.
And sith ye bee rihtful, iust & stable,
In yo*u*r werkis void of variau*n*ce,
Weieth this mateer iustli in ballau*n*ce."

The people agreed to put down Andronicus and set up Isaac. The tyrant betook himself to a fortress,

The peeple echon, alle of oon assent,
For outrages of this Andronicus
Put hym dou*n* be rihtful iugement,
In whos place set up Isacius.
The said tirau*n*t, froward & furious,
Gan maligne and hy*m*siluen dresse
In his diffence to take a forteresse.

but was captured, stripped of his garments, one of his eyes rent out, and

It halpe hym nat to make resistence,
So as he stood[e] void of al fauo*u*r;
Segid he was, and be violence,*
Maugre his myht[e], rent out of that to*u*r;
Spoilled cruelli; fond no bet soco*u*r,
Stood al nakid, quakyng i*n* his peyne;
And first rent out oon of his eien tweyne.

compelled to ride backwards on an ass, holding fast to his tail, to the delight of all the people.

And ouermor he hadde this reward,
Withoutyn help[e], soco*u*r or respiht,
Rood on an asse, his face set bakward,
The assis tail holdyng for despiht.
Whom to beholde the peeple hath deliht;
To poore and riche thoruhout the cite
Hym to rebuke was g*r*antid liberte.

After that, he was taken out of the city in a cart and hanged amidst a terrible clamour until he died.

Afftir al this, in a carte sette
And vengabli lad out off the tou*n*,
Be doom Ihangid on an hih gibet.
The peeple on hym, to his confusiou*n*,
Made [a] clamo*u*r and terrible sou*n*,
Wolde neuer fro the galwes weende
Til in myscheeff bi deth he made an eende.

1445. noble] notable H, R 3. 1446. aboff B.
1459. violence] benivolence B.
1467. for] so of H.
1472. vengabli] vengable R.
1475. a] *om.* R, J, H 5 — and] and a H, R 3, P.

Lenvoye.

IN this tragedie, ageyn Androni*cus*
 Bochas maketh an exclamaciou*n*,
And ageyn alle p*r*incis vicious,
Whil thei haue poweer and domynaciou*n*
Be tiran*n*ye vse extorsiou*n*,
Concludyng thus:* that ther fals lyuy*n*g
Of riht requereth to haue an euel eendy*n*g.

Bochas exclaims against all tyrannous, vicious princes, and says that justice requires them to have an evil end.

Indifferentli this tirau*n*t lecherous
Of wyues, maidenes maad no*n* excepciou*n*,
Folwyng his lust, froward & disclau*n*derous,
Spared no wom*m*an of religiou*n*.
Made widwes breke ther professiou*n*
Be violence; peise weel al this thyng,
Of riht requereth to haue an euel eendi*n*g.

This lecherous tyrant made no exception of wives and maidens, and even oppressed widows and nuns.

Most in [m]ordre he was contagious, [p. 425]
Of in*n*ocent blood to make effusiou*n*;
Vengable also ageyn al vertuous;
Ageyn his kynreede souhte occasiou*n*
To slen the lyne fro which that he ca*m* dou*n*.
Which considered, al suich fals werkyng
Of riht requereth to haue an euel eendi*n*g.

He shed innocent blood and hated all virtuous men.

Bochas manaceth p*r*incis out*r*aious,
Which be ther proud hatful ambiciou*n*,
To God & man of wil contrarious,
Hauyng in herte a fals oppynyou*n*,
Al tho that been in ther subiecciou*n*
Thei may deuoure, ther poweer so strechchi*n*g,
Which shal nat faille to haue a*n* euel endy*n*g.

Bochas threatens such outrageous princes, proud and contrary to God, who think they can devour all men who are subject to them.

Noble princis, ye that be desirous
To perseuere in yo*u*r domynaciou*n*,
And in al vertu to been victorious,
Cherissheth trouthe, put falsnesse dou*n*,
Beth merciable, mesurid be resou*n*,
Of Andronicus the surfet*es* eschewyng,*
That ye bi grace may haue a good eendi*n*g.

Noble Princes, if you wish to keep your crowns, cherish truth, put down falseness and be merciful.

1480. And] *om.* R. 1483. thus] this B.
1489. widwes] widwes maidenys H, wyfes J.
1492. contagious] contrarious H, R 3. 1496. that] *om.* H.
1509. falsnesse] falshede J, P.
1511. eschewyng] shewyng B, R, H 5.

[Off Isacyus made blynde & taken at mischeff.][1]

Isaac then became emperor, but a brother of Andronicus clapped a red-hot basin to his face and blinded him.

AS is rehersed, wha*n* Isacivs
Had al thempire in pocessiou*n*,
Tauenge the deth[e] of Andronic*us*,
Constantynople, in that roial tou*n*,
A brother of his be force ther ca*m* dou*n*
With a bacyn, bren*n*yng briht as gleede,
Made hym blynde; of hym no mor I reede, —

He lay await for Isaac like a thief and, seizing him, put him in prison.

Except Isacivs was taken at myscheeff
Of hym that wrouhte to his destrucciou*n*;
Liggyng await as doth a preue theeff,
Took themperou*r*, put hym in p*r*isou*n*,
Vengabli dide execusiou*n*,
As is reme*m*brid, with a bacyn briht,
Bren*n*yng red hot; and so he loste his siht.

Isaac's son Alexius expected to succeed, but he was murdered by his tutor.

A sone he hadde callid Alexivs,
Tendre of age, cast hym to succeede.
Bi his tuto*u*r, fals and contrarious,
Moordred he was at myscheef, as I reede;
The same tuto*u*r purposyng in deede
Of thempire, be fals collusiou*n*,
Be fraude & meede to haue pocessiou*n*.

Savagetus, sultan of Egypt, then came in haste together with two mighty sultans of Damascus, piteously weeping.

In this chapitle of hy*m* no mor I fynde
Rehersed heer in ordre be writyng;
But to myn auctour, þe p*ro*cesse maketh mynde,
[¶] Ther ca*m* in hast Sangot of Egipt kyng,
And with hym cam pitousli weepyng
Mihti p*r*incis, soudanys [bothe] tweyne,
Regnyng in Damas, ther fallis to co*m*pleyne.

The one was Salethus and the other Cathebadinus.

Of Allapie Salech was the ton,
Regnyng in Damas of his deu[e] riht;
Cathabadyn ther beyng eek soudon,
Which in tho daies was holde a ma*n*li kniht
And riht notable in eueri man*n*ys siht.
And for the soudon of Babilon a-ferre
Callid Saladyn oppressid was with werr*e*,

1513. wha*n*] than H. 1530. at myscheff he was H.
1537. of Egipt Sangot i*n* hast H — Sangor R, Sauagetus P (*om.* in hast). 1540. Damas] Sirie P.
1541. Of] Of al H, R — Alopie J, Alopye P.
1543. Cathebaden P — ther] the R. 1546. a-ferre] of ferr R.

[1] MS. J. leaf 174 verso.

For soco*u*r sente to thes p*r*incis tweyne,
To come in haste with al ther cheualrie
Hym to supporte, and doon ther besi peyne
Enforce ther miht to susteene his partie.
Whos request thei list nat [to] denye;
Abood no lenger, but made hemsiluen stro*n*g
To stonde with hym, wher it wer riht or wro*n*g.

Saladin, sultan of Babylon, sent to them for aid in his wars,

Of this mateer the substau*n*ce to co*n*clude,
Thes p*r*incis ca*m*, Salech & Cadabadyn;
For ther gverdou*n* thei fond ingratitude
In this forseid soudon Saladyn;
Fou*n*de hym vnkynde; pleynli this þe fyn,
From ther estat, as it was aftir knowe,
Disgraded hem, brouht hem dou*n* ful lowe.

but rewarded them with ingratitude and put them from their estate,

Of hym in soth thei hadde non oþ*er* meede
For ther labo*u*r nor for ther kyndenesse.
What fill aftir, in Bochas I nat reede;
For he foorþwith leueth this processe,
[¶] And vnto Robert doth his stile dresse,
Callid Ferenty*n* regny*n*g in Tarence,
Loste his lordshep be sodeyn violence:

and that is all Bochas says about them. Robert Surrentine, who reigned in Tarentum, lost his kingdom by violence;

This to seyne, he regned but a while;
This saide Robert loste his gou*er*nau*n*ce.
¶ Next to Boch*as* cam Guillia*m* of Cicile,
Kyng of that contre, a lord of gret puissau*n*ce;
Loste his kyngda*m* thoruh Fortunis variau*n*ce,
His eyen tweyne rent out of his hed;
Afftir deide in myscheef & in dreed.

and William of Sicily, who next appeared to Bochas, died in mischief and dread after his eyes had been put out.

Which Guylliam regnyng in Cecile [p. 426]
Was be discent[e] born nih of allie
To Robert Guiscart, as bookis do co*m*pile,
That whilom was duk of Norma*n*die,
Which of his manhoode & gret policye,*
With his brothir, ful notable of renou*n*,
Brouhte al Naples to ther subiecciou*n*.

He was a near relative of Robert Guiscard, once Duke of Normandy, who, together with his brother Roger, conquered Naples.

His brother name callid was Roggeer,
Which hadde a sone to been enherito*u*r,
Callid Tancret, as seith the cronicleer;

1552. to] *om.* J, P, R 3. 1556. Cathebadyn P. 1561. Disgratid R. 1567. Forentyne R, Forentyn H, R 3, H 5, Surrentine P. 1580] Gretli delityng in cheualrie B, R, J, H 5. *Supplied from* H, *which agrees with* R 3.

Roger had a son called Tancred, who reigned in Sicily.

Which took on hym to regne as successour.
Thus in Cecile Tancret was gouernour,
Ageyn[e]s whom, be title souht a-ferre
Of alliance began a mortal werre

against whom a war was begun for the sake of Constance, Roger's daughter, who wanted to become a nun.

For a maide that callid was Constaunce,
That douhtir was to this duk* Rogeer,
Which was set of spiritual plesaunce
To be religious, of hool hert & enteer.
And be record off the cronicleer,
This Constaunce hath the world forsake
And to religioun hath hir bodi take.

It had been foretold that her marriage would cause the desolation of the kingdom.

Of this Constaunce, the silue same yeer
That she was born, as maad is mencioun,
Ther was a clerk, a gret astronomeer,
Tolde of hir birthe be calculacioun,
She sholde cause the desolacioun
Of that kyngdam bi processe of hir age,
Bi the occasioun oonli of mariage.

Enemies of Tancred moved Emperor Henry to take Constance out of her convent; and with the dispensation of the pope she was married, and Tancred put from his right.

Summe that wern to Tancret gret enmy,
Be ther vngoodli excitacioun
Meued themperour that callid was Herry
To take Constaunce from hir religioun.
And bi the popis dispensacioun
She weddid was; themperour bi his myht
Bi title of hire put Tancret from his riht.

For a long time however he withstood the emperor, but finally died of the pest,

With a gret noumbre of Italiens
Themperour entrid into that regioun;
But be fauour off Siciliens,
Tancret long tyme stood in pocessioun:
But thoruh Fortunys transmutacioun,
The same tyme, to conclude in sentence,
The saide Tancret deide of pestilence.

and his young son William then resolved to defend the country.

His sone Guilliam, that was but yong in deede,
With Siciliens cast hym nat to faille
To keepe his lond and his riht posseede;
Meete themperour with statli apparaille,
Made hym reedi with hym to haue bataile.
But themperour to gretter auauntage
Caste otherwise of fraude in his corage.

1588. whom] hom R. 1591. this duk] the kyng B, J, P. 1593. &] *om.* R. 1594. cronyculer R. 1602. hir] his R, H. 1603. the] of H. 1604. that] tyme R. 1612. into] in R. 1617. pestilence] sentence R. 1622. haue] *om.* H.

Feynyngli duryng this discord,
Themperour caste another wile,
Bi a fals colour to fallen at accord,
And yonge Guilliam vngoodly to beguyle;
Vnder trete taken in Cecile,
Falsli depryued off his regio*u*n,
Sent to Itaille and throwe in p*r*isou*n*,

But the emperor, under colour of a treaty, deprived him of his kingdom and threw him into prison,

Be weie of trete, the stori who list see;
Al concluded vndir fals tresou*n*.
With Guillia*m* take wer his sustres thre,
He perpetueli dampned to p*r*isou*n*,*
His eien put out for mor co*n*fusiou*n*,
Deied in pouert, lost his enheritau*n*ce:
Loo, heer the fyn of worldly varyau*n*ce!

where his eyes were put out and he died.

Ferther to write as Ihon Boch*as* bega*n*,
Aftir that Guilliam was put fro*m* his rewm,
¶ To hy*m* appeered Guyot Lycynyan,
Chose afforn kyng of Iherusalem ,—
Whos knihtli fame shon like the son*n*e-bem, —
Which bi his noblesse he whilom did atteyne,
Godfrey present, that was duk of Loreyne.

After William, Guy de Lusignan, king of Jerusalem, appeared, a knightly man,

But bi the soudon namyd Saladyn
He was enchacid out of that dignite —
Al worldli pompe draweth to declyn! —
So for the constrey*n*t of his aduersite,
The yeeris passid of his prosp*er*ite,
Wente into Cipre as a fugityff;
What fill afftir, I reede nat i*n* his lyff.

whom Saladin chased out of his realm; and he became a fugitive in Cyprus. I do not know what happened afterwards.

¶ To make his co*m*pleynt afftir hy*m* ca*m* oon
Which hadde stonde in gret perplexite,
Erl of Bryen*n*e, & was callid Ihon,
Which aftirward was kyng of the cite
Callid Iherusalem, and [had] also parde
A fair[e] douhtir, yong & tendre of age,
Ioyned aftir to Frederik in mariage.

John, Earl of Brienne and king of Jerusalem, had a fair daughter who married Emperor Frederick II.,

Beyng that tyme lord and emper*our*, [p. 427]
Was desirous aboff al othir thyng
Of Iherusalem to be gouerno*ur*

but John, instead of keeping his kingdom of Jerusalem

1626. caste] cast all H, R 3, P.
1634. sustren R. 1635, 36 *are transposed in* B, R, J, H 5, P.
1641. Guido Lusignan P.
1651, 52 *are transposed in* H, *but correction indicated.*

and becoming king of Sicily, as he desired, was made a captain of mercenaries in Lombardy.

And of Cecile to be crownid kyng;
Which aldirlast, for his sotil werky*ng*
Constreyned was, dou*n* fro that partie,
To be a capteyn for soud in Lumbardie.

[Off Herry the eldest sone of Frederyk the secounde myscheued by his Fadir.] [1]

Henry, eldest son of the Emperor Frederick II., lame and ill, thin and pale from imprisonment, came complaining to Bochas.

NEXT to Boch*as*, crokid, halt & sik,
Oon callid Herry ca*m* for to co*m*pleyne,
The eldest sone onto Frederik,
Which bi seeknesse hadde felt gret peyne,
Megre and pale, contract in eueri veyne,
Of whos lang*ou*r the cheef occasiou*n*
Was that he lay so long tyme in *pr*isou*n*.

His adversity was caused by his father's perverse cruelty.

Al his disese and gret aduersite
Icausid was, for short co*n*clusiou*n*,
Bi his fadris froward cruelte,
As Bochas aftir maketh menciou*n*.
And this Herry bi generaciou*n*
Sone to Frederik, lik as it is fou*n*de, —
I meene Frederik callid the secou*n*de.

First king of Sicily and of Jerusalem, his renown shone.

This saide Herry be discent of lyne
Of Cicile first was crownid kyng,
And of Iherusalem, whos renou*n* dide shyne
Thoruh many a lond[e] at his begyn*n*yng;
And Fortune also in hir werkyng
Was to this Herry, passyngli notable
In al his werkis, inly fauourable.

He was affable and constant and popular among the people; but

Off his persone had this auau*n*tage:
To al the peeple he was riht acceptable,
Weel comendid in his flouryng age,
Of cheer and face and look riht amiable,
And of his port verray demuer & stable,
Callid in his gyn*n*y*n*g, such fauo*u*r he hath won*n*e,
Of *pr*incis alle verray liht & son*n*e.

it often happens that a cloudy day follows a bright morning,

But ofte it fallith, that a glad morweny*n*g,
Wha*n* Phebus sheweth his bemys cleer & briht,
The day su*m*tyme, therupon folwyng,

1666. To be] been H. 1681. This] The H.
1687. inly] & inly H, R. 1690. his] this R.
1695. morny*n*g H, J, morning P.

[1] MS. J. leaf 175 b.

With sum dirk skie is clipsid of his liht;
And semblabli, thoruh Fortunys myht
This saide prince, bi hir fals variaunce
Fond in hir wheel ful noious fell greuaunce.

Who may the furies of Fortune appese,
Hir troubli wawes to make hem calm & pleyn;
Wher men most truste thei fynde most disese,
Wher double corages stonde in noun certeyn.
A shynyng day is ofte meynt with reyn:
Thus of Frederik the grete vnstabilnesse
Hath brouht his sone in myscheef & distresse.

and no one can allay the troubled waves of Fortune. The great inconstancy of Frederick brought him to distress.

This Frederik set up in gret fauour
Be the popis dilligent bisynesse,
Vnto thestat lefft up of emperour;
But thoruh his hatful froward vnkyndenesse,
Of couetise fill into suich* excesse,
Took upon hym patrymonye to guie,
Of Cristes cherch that part to occupie.

Frederick, made emperor by the pope, became so covetous that he took upon himself the management of the church's patrimony, and

Fill in the popis indignacioun,
Counsail nor trete myhte not* auaile,
But of malis and [fals] presumpcioun
Caste with the pope to haue a gret bataile.
The saide Herry his fadir gan counsaille,
Ageyn the cherch to do no violence
But hym submytte with humble obedience.

thereby incurring the pope's enmity, determined to make war on him. Herry advised his father to do no violence to the church,

This striff enduryng atween thes gret estatis,
Frederik made his sone be accusid
To hym of crym, *Illese Magestatis*,
Wolde nat suffre he sholde been excusid;
But lik a man maliciousli refusid,
Be his fadris cursid fals tresoun
He was comaundid to deien in prisoun.

and for this advice Frederick accused him of *lèse majesté* and threw him into prison.

Summe bookis sey[e]n he was take & brouht
To his fadir of doom to ha[ue] sentence,
But lik a man passid sorwe & thouht,
Which to his lyff hadde non aduertence,
Furiousli and with gret violence,

Some books say that when he was brought in sorrow to his father for judgment, his horse fell down and he broke his neck.

1700. prince] princesse H.
1704. most truste] trust most R.
1713. into suich] in suich in B. 1715. part to] party forto R.
1717. not] non B, noon J, R 3, none P.
1720. The] And the R. 1725. Lesæ Maiestatis P.

As he was lad, alas, on hors[e]bak,
His hors fill dou*n* & so his nekke he brak.

Other books rehearse that he died in prison after long confinement, and that he tumbled off a bridge and was drowned.

Sum*me* bookis reherse of hym & seyn,
His fadir took geyn hym occasiou*n*;
And wha*n* he hadde longe in cheynis leyn,
At gret myscheeff he deied in prisou*n*.
And sum*me* sey[e]*n* [how] that he fill dou*n*
Of a bregge, Bochas reherseth heer,
And drownid was in a deep ryueer.

¶ Bochas makith a comendacion of trewe love a-tween kynrede.[1]

[p. 428]

Bochas commends all such as are naturally disposed to be upright to their kindred.

NEXT in ordre my*n* aucto*u*r did his cure
To make a special come*n*dacio[u]n
Of swich as been disposid be nature
An[d] bi ther kyndli inclynaciou*n*,
As blood requereth and generaciou*n*,
Taquite hymsilff in thouht, in will, in deede,
W*it*h*o*ute feynyng onto ther kynreede.

Especially when no unkindness is found in them, in spite of adversity, and when they are merciful and sincere.

Specialli that non vnkynd[e]nesse
Be fou*n*de in them for non aduersite;
To considre, of naturel gentilesse
To them approprid is merci & pite;
And tauoide the fals duplicite
That was in Frederik, which so v*n*kynd[e]li
Leet slen his sone that callid was Herry.

Pity is a natural trait, and parents are bound by law, nature and reason to foster their children and

Pite is approprid to kynreede,
Fader and mooder be disposiciou*n*
To cherisshe ther childre & [eke] feede
Til seuene yeer passe, lawe maketh me*n*ciou*n*,
As thei are bou*n*de of nature and* resou*n*.
That tyme passid, ther tendirnesse tenclyne
Vnto fourtene* to* vertuous disciplyne.

1736. he] *om.* R. 1741. how] *om.* J — that] þe H.
1749. in thouht in will] in will i*n* thouht H, in wil thouht R 3 — 2nd *and* 3rd in] *om.* J — 3rd in] & R 3 — in thought, wil, & dede P.
1760. eke] *om.* H, R, R 3.
1762. As] And as J, P — nature and] naturel B, natural J.
1764. fourtene] Fortune B, J — to] be B, bi R, R 3, J, by P.

[1] *The following heading is in* MS. J. leaf 175 verso: "A commendacion of Bochas of suche as be kynde to theire kynrede."

Than afftirward in ther adolescence,
Vertuousli to teche hem & chastise,
Norissh hem in doctryne & science,
Fostre in vertu vices to despise,
To be curteis, sad, prudent & wise;
For whan thei gynne with vertu in that age,
Gladli aftir, thei do non outrage.

to teach them virtue during their adolescence.

As it longeth to euery gentil lyne,
And blood roial, be kyndli influence,
To fader, mooder shewe hymsilf benigne,
Of humble herte don hem reuerence,
Ay to remembre in ther aduertence
On sexe princis wrouhte the contrarie,
For which Fortune was ther aduersarie.

Every gentle line and all royal blood should shew filial reverence; but there were six princes who wrought the contrary.

Euerich to other founde was vnkynde;
In cursid blood may be no kyndenesse;
Of oon tarage sauoureth tre & rynde,
The frut also bert[h] of the tre witnesse;
And semblabli the fadris cursidnesse,
With mortal suerd, in nature repreuable,
Ageyn the child is ofte seyn vengable.

Each was cruel to his children. There may be no kindness in cursed blood.

¶ Among[es] which Brutus is reknid oon,
Next in ordre folweth Manlius,
Slouh ther childre be record euerichon;
Phelipp Manlius & also Cassius,
And cruel Heroude, fell and malicious;
Frederik also most vengabli
Slouh his sone that callid was Herry.

These princes were Brutus, Manlius, Philip Manlius, Cassius, Herod and Frederick; and

This Frederik beyng ay contrarye
Toward his sone, nat gracious nor benigne,
From hooli cherche vngoodli he gan varie
And therageyn[es] frowardli maligne;
And lik a man obstynat & vndigne
Deied a-cursid thoruh mysgouernaunce,
Withoute confessioun outher repentaunce.

this Frederick, who was neither gracious nor benign to his son, and who maligned against holy church, died accursed, without confession or repentance.

1768. Fostre] fostre hem H.
1772. H *writes* 1723 *at beginning of this stanza but indicates correction with* "vacat."
1779. was founde R. 1790. Herodes P.

[How Manfroy kyng of Poyle was slayn.] [1]

Manfred, king of Naples, was put down and slain for his tyranny: what avails sceptre or sovranty to a tyrant?

¶ Nexte to Bochas of Poille cam þe kyng,
Began his fall and compleynt specefie,
Callid Manfroy; and for his fals werking
Put doun & slayn, cause of his tirannye.
Loo, what auailleth sceptre or regalie
To a tiraunt, which of violence
List to Godward haue non aduertence!

[How Encys kyng of Sardany died in prisoun.] [2]

Enzio, king of Sardinia, was conquered by the people of Bologna and died in prison.

¶ With look[e] doun-cast, dedli pale of cheere,
Of Sardania Encis next cam doun;
Kyng of that lond, to telle the maneere
How he werreied ageyn the mihti toun
Callid Bononia, to his confusioun;
Be them venquisshed, & with cheynys rounde,
Deied in prisoun, so long he lay ther bounde.

[a water makith theves blynde & trewe men to see.] [3]

John Bochas says that in Sardinia there are no serpents and wolves, but that there is a well whose water makes thieves blind, and is a medicine to honest folk.

¶ Folwyng myn auctour callid Bochas Iohn,
In Sardynia, as he maketh mynde,
Serpent nor wolff in al that lond is* non,
Hauyng a welle, which of veray kynde
Theuys eyen the watir maketh blynde;
To trewe folk, as he doth diffyne,
Water therof is helthe and medecyne.

[An erbe who tastith it shal die lauhyng.] [4]

There is also an herb that makes people laugh themselves to death if they taste of it; even to touch it is dangerous.

Ther groweth also an herbe, as bookis seie, [p. 429]
Which that is so dyuers of nature,
Who tasteth therof lauhhyng he shal deie,
No medecyne may helpe hym* nor recure;
The touch therof stant eek in auenture, —

1800. Poille] Naples P.
1802. Maufron H, Manfrede P.
1808. Encius P. 1816. is] was B, H.
1819. folk] farlk R — diffyne] dyuyne J, devyne R 3, diuine P.
1824. hym] hem B.

[1] MS. J. leaf 176 recto.
[2] MS. J. leaf 176 recto.
[3] MS. J. leaf 176 recto.
[4] MS. J. leaf 176 recto.

Yiff it entre his mouth in any side,
He shal alyue for lauhtre nat abide.

[Another Frederyk was slayn bi Iugement of his brothir.] [1]

¶ Ther was anothir froward Frederik,
Sone to Alfonce, that was kyng of Castile,
Of corage wood and [also] fren[e]tik;
His owne brothir falsli to begile,
Began a werre lastyng but a while,
Whos purpos was his brother to deceyue
And the crowne of Castile to resceyue.

Another froward Frederick, son of Alphonse of Castile, made war on his brother for the sake of the crown;

This Frederik cam with a gret bataile
Ageyn his brother for the same entent;
Off his purpos yit he dide faille:
God nor Fortune wer nat of assent.
Take in the feeld[e] and be iugement
Of his brothir, for his gret trespace
Slay[e]n openli; gat no bettir grace.

but neither God nor Fortune were with him. He was captured and slain.

[How Manymettus and Argones died at mischef.] [2]

[¶] Manymettus, of Perce lord and kyng,
Cam next in pres, distressid with gret peyne,
Vpon Fortune pitousli pleynyng,
His aduersite did hym so constreyne;
For ther was oon which did at hym disdeyne
Callid Argoones, void of title or lyne,
Geyn Manymet[tus] proudli gan maligne.

Maumetus, king of Persia, came in great distress, complaining on Fortune; for Argones was hostile to him without cause.

Which Argones for his presumpcioun
Take at mischeef be sodeyn violence,
His doom was youe to deien in prisoun,
Of noun poweer to make resistence;
But Fortune, that can no difference
In hir* chaunges atwixen freend & foo,
Caused hem to deie at myscheef bothe two.

However, for his presumption Argones was captured and sent to prison to die there, and Maumetus also died at mischief.

1830. also] *om.* R.
1842. Maumetus P. 1848. Maumetus P.
1853. difference] diffence R. 1854. hir] his B, H.

[1] MS. J. leaf 176 recto.
[2] MS. J. leaf 176 recto.

[How Charles kyng of Jer*usa*lem and of Cecile for Auaryce and avoutrie died at mischef.] [1]

Noble Charles, king of Jerusalem and Sicily, came with such good cheer and knightly manner to Bochas,

AFFTIR thes forseid, rehersed i*n* se*n*tence,
As Boch*as* procedeth* in his stile,
Kam noble Charlis u*n*to his p*re*sence,
Kyng of Iherusalem and also of Cicile;
Of whos comyng my*n* aucto*ur* a gret while
Astonid was, to seen his knihtli face
With so good cheere com into the* place.

that it seemed as if he stood high on Fortune's wheel, defying her power.

For bi his port, who that beheeld hy*m* weel,
Considred first his look & his visage,
It sempte he trad upon Fortunys wheel,
And of his noble marcial corage
Hadde of hir poweer getyn auau*n*tage,
Shewyng hym-silf so fressh on ech partie,
Hir and hir myht did vttirly diffye.

Of royal lineage and famous alliance, he was brother of St. Louis;

First to come*n*de his roial hih lynage,
And of his vertuous famous allyau*n*ce,
As be writyng and preisyng with langage
The name of hym specialli tauau*n*ce,
Seith he was bor[e]n of the blood of Frau*n*ce;
And to encrece mor souerey*n*li his prys,
Writ he was brother onto Seynt Lowis.

and I also read that, as Phœbus outshines all the other spheres, so does France surpass all other lands both in peace and war.

Gaff to F*r*ance this comendaciou*n*:
So as Phebus passeth ech othir sterre,
Riht so that kyngdam in comparisou*n*
Passeth eueri lond, bothe nih & ferre,
In policie, be it of pes or werre;
For it transcendith, in pes be prouidence,
And in werre be knihtli excellence.

These words were not written by Bochas, but by one Laurence, the translator of this book, to commend France.

Thes woordis be nat take out of my*n* aucto*ur*,—
Entitled heer for a reme*m*brau*n*ce
Bi oon Laurence, which was a translato*ur*
Of this processe, to come*n*de Frau*n*ce;
To preise that lond set al his plesau*n*ce,

1856. Afftir] Whan H, R 3 — i*n*] was in H, R 3.
1857. procedeth] reherseth B.
1862. com into the] komen into B, R. 1864. &] *om.* H.
1867. hir] his H. 1872. with] bi H, of J, P.
1877. this] his R. 1882. in pes be] bi pes of H.
1886. a] *om.* H. 1887. this] his R.

[1] MS. J. leaf 176 recto.

Seith influence of that roial lond
Made Charlis so worthi of his hond.

Of whos noblesse Pope Vrban hadde ioie,
Hym to encrece for vertuous lyuyng,
Which that tyme was duk of Aungoie,
Aftir chose of Cicile to be kyng.
Of Pope Vrban requered be writyng,
Toward Rome that he shold hym dresse
Of kyng Manfroy the tirannye toppresse.

Pope Urban also had joy in Charles, and while he was Duke of Anjou asked him to come to Rome

Ageyn the pope and hooli cherchis riht
This same Manfroy dide gret extorsioun.
Noble Charlis, as Goddis owne kniht,
Cam with strong hond up to Roome toun;
Which in his komyng gaf pocessioun
To Guyot Maunfort for to haue the garde
In his passage and gouerne the vaunwarde.

and defend the church against King Manfred. Charles came with Guy de Montfort,

Toward Roome with gret ordenaunce [p. 430]
Thei passed ouer the boundis of Itaille;
This manly kniht, this Charlis born in France,
Ladde with hym many strong bataille
The popis enmy manli for tassaille.
But al this while, to stonden at diffence
The said[e] Charlis fond no resistence.

leading many a strong company, and found small resistance.

Entryng Roome to be ther protectour,
Ful weel resceyuyd at his first entryng,
Chose and preferrid for cheef senatour
Bi the pope, most glad of his komyng;
Of Cicile was aftir crownid kyng,
And of Iherusalem, as maad is mencio[u]n,
Graunted to hym fulli pocessioun.

Entering Rome he was chosen chief senator by the pope, and afterwards crowned king of Sicily and Jerusalem.

Which in his gynnyng bar hym tho so weel,
Entryng that lond with knihtly apparaille,
Of Cassyne gat first the strong castel,
At Bonnevente hadde a gret bataille
With kyng Manfroy, whos parti did[e] faille.
To reherse shortli his auenture,
Charlis on hym made a disconfiture.

After taking Monte Cassino, he fought a great battle at Benevento,

1899. same] saide H.
1903. Monforth R, Maufroit H, Manfort J (Guido of Mountfort P).
1904. vawarde H, vawward P.
1906. ouer] wer H, R 3. 1910. stonden] stoden H.
1921. Cassile R. 1922. Beneuent P. 1925. made] had H.

where Manfred was slain. He then put down a rebellion in Sicily and

In which[e] bataile kyng Manfroy was slay*n*;
And noble Charlis took pocessiou*n*,
Wherof Romey*ns* wer ful glad & fayn.
Yit in Cicile ther was rebelliou*n*,
But thei wer brouht onto subieccioun.
Than* Coradyn, record of old writing,
Sone of Conrade cleymed to be kyng.

at Talliazzo defeated and slew Conradin, son of Conrad IV., who claimed the throne.

Gan make hym strong, proudli took his place
At Aligate, a famous old cite.
Noble Charlis *with* knihtli cheer & face
Fill upon hy*m*, made hym for to flee.
And to sette reste in the contre,
Tauoide trouble & make al thi*n*g certay*n*,
Gaff iugement Coradyn to be slay*n*.

Charles then had entire possession of Sicily, and

Among kinges notable and glorious,
Charlis was put, as maad is menciou*n*,
Lik a p*r*ince strong and victorious
In ful pesible and hool pocessiou*n*
Of Cicile and al that regiou*n*,
Ageyn[e]s whom was non dissobeissau*n*ce,
Yolde of hool herte to his gouernau*n*ce.

Fortune favoured him. His son married Mary, daughter of Stephen of Hungary;

Be title also off his alliau*n*ce,
Fortune gretli did hy*m* magnefie;
For as it is Iput in reme*m*brau*n*ce,
The noble p*r*incesse that callid was Marye,
Douhtir to Steuene regnyng in Hu*n*grye,
Iioyned was and knet in mariage
To Charlis sone, tencres of his lynage.

and by the authority of the pope Charles was made king of Jerusalem.

The same Charlis be auctorite
Of the pope, so as hy*m* list ordeyne,
Was eek maad kyng of the gret cite
Callid Iherusalem, of tou*n*s most souereyne;
Be which[e] title he bar crownis tweyne.

His brother Louis

His brothir Lowis, olde bookis seye,
The same tyme in Egipt ga*n* werreye.
Gat al the contrees abouten enviro*un*,
Which that Sarsyns did falsli occupie;

1930. onto] to R.
1931. Than] Yit B, R, J, P, H 5 — Corandyne J, Conradine P.
1934. Agliate H, Talliatozzo P — an olde famous R, H, R 3, H 5.
1942, 43 *are transposed in* H, *but correction indicated.*
1945. no disbeissau*n*ce R. 1950. p*r*incesse] processe R.
1951. Stephene P. 1952. knet] knet was R.

Brouht hem ageyn[e] to subiecciou*n*
Of Iherusalem, that lond to magnefie:
Cartage in Affrik, with al ther regalie,
And alle the contrees beyng afforn co*n*trarye,
To kyng Charlis becam tributarye.

conquered the Saracen countries about Egypt, and all became tributary to Charles.

Thus* while he sat hiest in his glorie,
Lik Phebus shyny*n*g in his mydday speere,
With many conquest and many gret victorie,
Whan his noblesse shon most briht & cleere,
The same tyme, with a frowny*n*g cheere,
Fortune ga*n* fro*m* Charlis turne hir face
And hym berafte his fauo*u*r and his grace.

But when he sat highest in his glory, Fortune turned her face away from him.

This lady Fortune doth* seelde in oon co*n*tune,
She is so gerissh of condiciou*n*,
A sorceresse, a traitour i*n* comune,
Caste a fals mene to his destrucciou*n*,
Oon of his sonys slay[e]n with poisou*n*,
Which did eclipse, my*n* aucto*u*r doth expresse,
A ful gret part of [al] his old gladnesse.

She is a sorceress, a traitress to men, and seldom continues in one. A son of Charles was poisoned, and

He was disclau*n*drid of the grete* vice
Which apparteneth onto tiran*n*ye,
I meene the vice of froward auarice,
Which is cont*r*arie gretli to cheualrie;
Diffamed also of fals auoutrie,
Which was susteened thoruh his mey*n*tenau*n*ce
Wit*h*yn*n*e that lond[e] be a kniht of Frau*n*ce.

he himself accused of avarice and defamed of adultery committed at his court by a French knight

The same kniht abidyng in his hous, [p. 431]
Al Cicile troublid with that deede:
The grete offence was so disclau*n*drous,
Thoruh al the regiou*n* that it bega*n* to spreede;
For thilke woma*n*, pley*n*li as I reede,
Was wyff to oon which suffred this offence
And to be vengid dide his dilligence.

with the wife of John of Procida, who determined to be revenged,

Iohn Prosithe pleynli was his name,
Which cast hym fulli auengid for to be,
That kyng Charlis sholde ber the blame,
Sleñ al Frensh-men that bood in that contre,
Withoute grace, merci or pite.

and that King Charles might bear the blame, instigated a massacre of all the Frenchmen in the country.

1965. ther] þe H. 1968. Thus] This B, J.
1975. doth] did B. 1979. his] *om.* R. 1981. al] *om.* R.
1982. the grete] al the B, R, J, H 5. 1988. that] þe H.
1993. thilke] thirk R — I] *om.* R. 1995. dide his] he did R.
1996. Procida P.

The king of Aragon was called in, and

And for to doon ful execuciou*n*
Requered was the kyng of Arragou*n*.

Charles lost Sicily and Jerusalem, and became so poor that he prayed for death.

Loste of Cicile al hool the regiou*n*
With the obeissau*n*ce of many gret cite,*
And of Iherusalem the pocessiou*n*;
Fill be processe in gret aduersite,
And last, constreyned with gr*e*uous pouerte,
To God most meekli, with ful heuy cheere,
Soone to be ded[e]; this was his praieere.

He grew sick and languished until he fell into age and finally died. There is no more about him.

Supprised he was with sorwe in his corage;
Loste his force; fill into malladie;
Languisshed foorth til he gan falle i*n* age,
Agey*n* Fortune fond no remedie.
And be thoccasiou*n* of fals auoutrie
Fill to myscheeff; and for sorwe & dreed
This Charlis deide; no mor of hy*m* I reede.

¶ Lenvoye.

Just as Phœbus is often darkened after a bright morning, so it was with Charles. Men do not praise the fair day until eve.

LYK as Phebus in su*m* fressh morweny*ng*
Aftir Aurora þe day doth clarefie,
Fallith ofte that his briht shyny*ng*
Idirkid is with su*m* cloudi skie:
A liknesse shewed in this t*r*agedie,
Expert in Charlis, the stori doth weel preeue,
Youthe & age reknid ech partie,
The faire day men do preise at eue.

He was nearly related to St. Louis, wise, manly, virtuous and a flower of chivalry, until adultery came into his court.

The noble fame of his fressh gyn*n*yng, —
To Seyn[t] Lowis he was nih of allie, —
Riht wis, riht manli, riht vertuous of lyuy*n*g,
Callid of knihthod flour of cheualrie,
Til mey*n*tenau*n*ce of auout[e]rie
Cam into his court to hurte his name & gr*e*ue,
His lyff, his deth[e] put in iupartie:
The faire day men do preise at eue.

Lik desertis men haue ther guerdonyng:
Vertuous lyff doth p*r*incis magnefie;
The contrarie to them is gret hyndryng, —

2003. the] that R. 2004. cite] contre B.
2017. mornyng H, J, H 5, morning P.
2023. ech] his R — partie] trulyJ.
2024. day] lady R — do] doto R. 2026. Seynt] *om*. H.
2028. 1st of] for H.

Folk expert the trouthe may nat denye.
Cerche out the reward of cursid lecherye:
Where it is vsed, the houshold may nat preue;
In this mateer to Charlis hath an iye,
The faire day to preise toward eue.

Men are rewarded according to their deserts; and what is the reward of lechery?

Noble Princis, all vices eschewyng,
Your hih corages lat resoun modefie;
Withdrawe your hand fro riotous wachching;
Fleeth flesshli lustis and vicious companye;
Oppressith no man; doth no tirannye;
Socoure the needi; poore folk doth releeue;
Lat men reporte the prudent policie
Of your last age whan it draweth to eue.

Noble Princess, withdraw yourselves from riot, fleshly lusts and vicious company, oppress no man and assist the poor. Let men report your prudent policy when your age draws to eve.

[Off Hugolyne erle of Pyse slayn in prisoun.] [1]

OFF Charlis story rad þe woful fyn,
As ye haue herd þe maner & the guise,
To Ihon Bochas appeered Hugolyn,
Callid whilom the noble Erl of Pise,
Til the Pisanys gan ageyn hym rise;*
Most vengably, cruel & vnkynde,
Slouh hym in prisoun; no mor of hym I fynde, —

Ugolino, earl of Pisa, was slain in prison by his subjects, who arose against him

[Athon kyng of Ar[me]nye / put from his ri[ght] by his brothire.] [2]

Sauff his childre, of hatreede and envie,
Wer moord[e]rid eek in a deep prisoun.
¶ Next with his compleynt the kyng of Armenye
Cam tofor Bochas, that callid was Achoun,
A Cristene prince ful famous of renoun;
For our feith, from which he list nat erre,
Geyn Tartarynes long tyme he heeld gret werre.

and slew his children also. Aiton, king of Armenia, a famous Christian prince who fought the Tatars, was

2045. doth] do H.
2050. As] as her H. 2053. rise] hem arise B.
2055. mor of hym I ne fynde H.
2056. hatreede] malis H, malice R 3.
2057. *is misplaced at end of stanza* H — eek] also R.
2058. *The paragraph mark is misplaced at the beginning of the next line in* B — Armonye R.
2059. Aiton P.
2062. Tantarynes H, Tartarians P, Tartaryens H 5.

[1] MS. J. leaf 177 recto.
[2] MS. J. leaf 177 recto, *margin pared by binder*.

treasonably robbed of the throne by his brother Sabath, who cast him in prison and blinded him.

This manli kyng, in knihthod ful famo*us*, [p. 432]
It was shewed, his stori who list reede,
Hadde a brother fell and despitous
Callid Sabath, desirous to succeede,
Stede of his brother the ky*n*gdam to posseede;
Be fals[e] tresou*n* reued hy*m* of his riht,
Kept hym in hold[e] and put out his siht.

But another brother chased Sabath from the country and, capturing him, cast him in prison, where he died. Lo, how the Lord can reward treason and murder!

This Sabath loste bothe happ & grace,
His other brother, as maad is me*n*ciou*n*,
Be strong hond[e] put hy*m* fro*m* his place,
Chacid hym out of that regiou*n*.
Take be force and fetrid in prisou*n*,
Deide ther; no ma*n* list hym visite:
Loo, hōw God ca*n* tresou*n* and moordre quite!

[How pope Boneface the viij[the] was take by the Lynage de Colu*m*pnys / ete his hondes & died in prisou*n*.] [1]

About the year 1300, Pope Boniface the Eighth

AMO*N*G thes woful froward p*r*incis thre
Which shewed hem so ougli of þ*er* cher*e*,
Pope Boneface be gr*e*t adu*er*site,
Eihte of that name, gan taproche neer.
A thousand thre hundred acou*n*tid was þe yeer
Fro Cristes berthe be co*m*putaciou*n*,
Whan that he made his lamentaciou*n*.

laid an interdict on all France;

This same pope kauhte occasiou*n*,
Which vndir Petir kepte gou*er*nau*n*ce,
To interdicte* al the regiou*n*,
Tyme of kyng Phelipp regny*n*g þ*er* in F*r*ance;
Directe bollis dou*n* into Constau*n*ce
To Nicholas, maad[e] be Boneface,
Archidekne of the same place.

but the prelates and bishops of France proved that he injured the church, and

Off hooli cherche the prelatis nih echon,
Bisshoppis of Frau*n*ce felli haue declarid,
Preuyng be poyntis many mo tha*n* oon
In a gret seen[e] pleynli & nat spared,

2063. ful] most H. 2076. moordre & tresou*n* H — tresou*n*] reson R.
2077. thre] iij B. 2080. taproche] approche R.
2081. hundred] C B — was] *om.* R.
2086. interdicte] Interducte B, Entirdite H.
2088. into] vn to H. 2091. nih] nyth R.
2094. seene] sene R, H, H 5, R 3, synne J, Scene P.

[1] MS. J. leaf 177 verso.

Be hym the cherche was hurt & nat reparid;
Put on hym crymes of gret misgou*er*nau*n*ce,
Denou*n*cid* hym enmy to al the lond of F*r*ance.

denounced him as an enemy of the country.

Put [up]on hym many gret outrage,
Wro*n*gli how he hadde doon offence
To a cardynal born of the lynage
De Colu*m*pnis, a kynreede of reuerence;
For which[e] cause he kept hy*m* i*n* absence
Out of the court, drouh wher he was born;
Be which occasiou*n* the pope his lif hath lorn.

They accused him of many outrages, especially of wronging a cardinal of the house of Colonna,

De Columpnis the lynage hath so wrouht:
Took Boniface for his old cruelte;
Wi*th* gret poweer & force thei haue hy*m* brouht
Into a castel which stood in the cite,
Callid Sancti Angeli; gaf auctorite
To a cardynal, & be com*m*yssiou*n*
Poweer to doon ful execusiou*n*.

whose family took Boniface and imprisoned him in the fortress of St. Angelo,

Of thes mateeris hangyng in ballau*n*ce
Atween parties, wer it riht or wrong,
Bothe of Romeyns, prelatis eek of F*r*ance,
The pope ay kept withyn*n*e the castel stro*n*g,
Of auenture, nat bidyng ther riht long,
Fill in a flux, and aftirward for neede,
For hunger eet his hondis, as I reede.

where he fell in a flux and afterwards ate his hands for hunger.

Hour of his deyng, it is maad menciou*n*,
Aboute the castel was merueillous lihtny*n*g,
Wher the pope lay fetrid in prisou*n*, —
Non such afforn was seyn in ther lyuy*n*g.
And whil Boch*as* was besi in writyng,
To write the fall[e] of this Boniface,
The Ordre of Templeris ca*m* toforn his face.

It is said that marvellous lightning played about the castle when he died.

[How the ordre of Templers was founded and [Iaques] wi*th* other of the ordre brent.] [1]

¶ Croniclers the trouthe ca*n* recorde,
Callyng to my*n*de the first fundaciou*n*,
And olde aucto*u*rs therwithal accorde,

2097. Denou*n*cid] Denou*n*cyng B, R, H 5, J.
2108. the] their H. 2113. it] it be H, R 3.
2121. the] this H, R 3. 2125. afforn R.

[1] MS. J. leaf 177 verso. Iaques *is supplied from* P.

The Order of Templars was founded at the time when Godfrey de Bouillon won Jerusalem, by

Of thes Templeeris how the religiou*n*
Gan thilke tyme wha*n* Godfrey Bolliou*n*
Hadde won*ne*, that noble knihtli man,
Iherusalem, that ordre first began.

certain knights who fought there.

Bi certeyn knihtis which did her besi peyne,
Whan the said[e] cite was first won*ne*
Be noble Godfrey, duk whilo*m* of Loreyne,
Ther crownid kyng, this ordre thei begon*ne*, —
Olde bookis weel reherse kon*ne*, —
Takyng a grou*n*d of pouert & meeknesse,
To fou*n*de this ordre did her besynesse.

Their guiding principles were poverty, humility and chastity, and they lived in the temple not far from the city.

Ther begyn*n*yng ca*m* of deuociou*n*,
The grou*n*d Itake of wilful pouerte;
And made first ther habitaciou*n*
Be the temple, nat ferr fro the cite,
In tokne of clen*n*esse sworn to chastite,
Of the temple lik to ther desirs
Took that name & callid wer Te*m*pleeris.

Pope Honorius gave them license to wear a white habit, to which Eugenius added a red cross.

Pope Honorie gaff hem* auctorite, [p. 433]
Of hooli cherche beyng that tyme hed;
A whiht habit thei bar for chastite;
Eugenivs afftir gaf hem a cros of red.
And to diffende pilgrymes, out of dreed,
Geyn Saresyn[e]s thoruh ther hih renou*n*,
This was cheef poynt of ther professiou*n*.

So long as they lived in perfection their fame spread;

Whil thei lyuede in wilful pouerte,
Thes crossid knihtis in mantlis clad of whiht,
Ther name spradde in many ferr contre;
For in perfecciou*n* was set al ther deliht.
Folk of deuociou*n* kauht an appetiht
Them for tencrece, gaf hem gret almesse,
Bi which thei gan encrece in gret richesse.

but as they increased in numbers and wealth they lost their virtue and gave themselves up to luxury and vice.

Bi processe withyn*ne* a fewe yeeris,
The nou*m*bre gret of ther religiou*n*;
And the fame of thes seid Templeeris
Gan spreede wide in many regiou*n*.
Ther sodeyn risyng, of ther pocessiou*n*,
With tou*n*s, castellis, thei gaf hem to delices,
Appalled in vertu, which brouht in many vices.

2136. thei] first H. 2147. hem] hy*m* B.
2156. name] names H. 2160. encrece] wexe H 5.
2162. ther] that R. 2165. Ther] þe H.

It wer to longe for to rekne hem alle;
But among other I fynde ther was oon,
A ma*n*li kniht, folk* Iaques did hy*m* calle,
Gret of auctorite among hem euerichon,
As cronicles reme*m*bre of yore agon.
The which[e] Iaques in the rewm of F*r*ance
Was born of blood to gret enheritau*n*ce.

A knight named Jacques de Molay, a Frenchman born to rich inheritance, was of great authority among them,

The same Iaques, holde a manli kniht
In his gyn*n*yng, fressh, lusti of corage,
Hadde a brother, be elder title of riht
Occupied al hool the heritage,
Because Iaques yonger was of age,
Which myht[e] nat be no condiciou*n*
Nothyng cleyme of that pocessiou*n*.

and as his older brother kept possession of the heritage,

His elder brother occupied al,
Whil this Iaques was but of low degree,
Wonder desirous with hy*m* to been* egal,
Alway put bak be froward pouerte.
And to surmou*n*te, yif it wolde bee,
Fond out a mene lik to his desirs,
Was chose maister of thes Templeeris.

and Jacques had always been held back by poverty, he finally got himself appointed grand master,

Was promootid be free eleccìou*n*
Bi them that sholde chesyn hy*m* of riht;
Wherbi he hadde gret domynaciou*n*,
Richesse, treso*ur*, gret poweer & myht.
Of his persone was eek a ma*n*li kniht, —
The same tyme, put in reme*m*brau*n*ce,
Phelipp Labele crownid kyng in F*r*ance.

wherethrough he obtained great power and wealth.

Which hadde of Iaques gret indignaciou*n*,
To alle the Templeris and al ther cheualrie,
Caste weies to ther destrucciou*n*,
Gaf auctorite his lust to fortefie,
Dou*n* fro the pope, bookis specefie,
Clement the Sexte, concludyng yif he may,
Alle the Templeeris destroie hem on a day.

Philip IV. of France, who hated the Templars, determined to destroy them.

2169. fynde] rekne H.
2170. folk] Folkis B.
2184. with hy*m* to been] to been (be) with hym B, J, P, H 5.
2186. bee] ha be H, R 3, have be R, H 5.
2187. to] *om.* H.
2195. Labele] la bele R, J, R 3, label H 5, Le Bele H, la Bele P.
2199. to] forto R.
2202. a] oo H.

He had them suddenly imprisoned for certain horrible crimes; and their friends advised them to plead guilty and beg for mercy.

For certeyn crymes horrible to heere,
Alle attonis wer set in prisou*n*,
Bi ther freendis touchi*ng* this mateer*e*
Cou*n*seilled to axe merci & pardou*n*,
That thei sholde be pleyn confessiou*n*
Requere m*er*cy, knelyng on a rowe,
And as it was ther trespas been aknowe.

Jacques and three others were detained, while the rest, tied to stakes ready for burning, were led to believe that the king would pardon them if they confessed.

Iaques was take, and with hym othir thre,
Kept in holde and [in]to prisou*n* sent.
And the remnau*n*t for ther iniquite
Ordeyned wern be open iugement
To myhti stakes to be teied and brent.
The kyng in maner lik to doon he*m* grace,
So thei wolde confesse ther trespace.

They would not confess, but cried piteously that they were innocent until they died.

But al for nouht; thei wer so indurat,
Alle of accord[e] and of o corage
To axe mercy verray obstynat.
The fire reedi, al with o langage,
Whan the flawme approched ther visage,
Ful pleynli spak [&] cried pitousli,
Of ther accus how thei wer nat gilti.

Fro ther purpos list nat to declyne;
But with o vois echon[e] an[d] o sown
Fulli affermed til thei did[e] fyne,
How ther ordre and ther religiou*n*
Igrou*n*did was upon perfecciou*n*,
And how ther deth, verraili in deede,
Compassid was of malis & hatreede.

Jacques was taken to Lyons and there publicly confessed and was burnt to ashes.

The saide Iaques, of whom I spak toforn, [p. 434]
Brouht to a place which callid was Leou*n*,
Tofor too legatis, or that his lyff was lorn,
Al openli made his confessiou*n*:
He was worthi, for short conclusiou*n*,
For to be ded be rihtful iugeme*n*t.
This was his eende; to asshes he was brent.

2207. That thei] Thei that R.
2208. rowe] trowe R.
2222. &] *om.* H, R, J, R 3, H 5, P — pitousli] spitously R.
2224. to] *om.* R.
2235. He] And R.

¶ Here Bochas makith a comendacion of thre Philisophris for their pacience.[1]

YIUYNG a pris to philisophres thre,
Boch*as* comendith w*ith* gret dilligence
How ech of hem was in his contre
Souereynli be vertuous excellence
Off old come*n*did for ther pacience,
Which may be set and crownid in his stall
As emperesse among vertues all.

Bochas now commends three philosophers who were of old time praised for their fortitude and patience.

Mong Siciliens first Theodorus,
For pacience hadde in gret reuerence;
Among Grekis, the stori tellith vs,
Anaxerses for his magnificence,
Bi force of vertu grou*n*did o*n* pacience,
Because he was [both] vertuous & wis,
For suffrau*n*ce gat hym a souerey*n* pris.

Theodorus of Sicily, Anaxarchus of Greece and

Among[es] Romey[n]s put in reme*m*br*a*nce,
S[c]euola, bothe philisophre & kniht,
For his marcial hardi strong constau*n*ce,
Wha*n* that he heeld amyd the flawmys liht*
Hand and fyngres aboue the coles briht,
Til the ioyntes, fallyng heer & yonder,
From the wirste departid wer assonder.

Scævola of Rome, who allowed his hand to be consumed by fire.

¶ First Theodorus, born in the famo*us* ile,
Be pacience gret peynes enduryng,
Cheeff philisophre callid of Cicile,
W*ith* cheynys bou*n*de upon the grou*n*d liggy*n*g,
On his bodi leid gaddis red bren*n*yng,
Suffryng this peyne, list it nat refuse,
Bi kyng Iherom, the tirau*n*t Siracuse.

Theodorus was bound in chains and burning gads were laid on his body, and

For comou*n* proffit suffrid al [t]his peyne,
Long tyme afforn[e] liggyng in prisou*n*;
Which bassent of mo than on or tueyne

he suffered all for the sake of the common weal; for he

2238. pris] laude H. 2254. For] bi H.
2255. liht] briht B, H, R, J — flawmys] flame P.
2256. aboue] among P.
2258. wirste] wrest R, J, P, wrost R 3, wristis H 5.
2264. this] his R, H, J.
2265. Siracuse] of Siracuse H, R 3, P. 2266. this] his J.

[1] *The following heading is in* MS. J. leaf 178 b: "Bochas here co*m*mendith Theodorus with othir ij philosophres for their*e* pacience notably."

was one of the conspirators who slew the tyrant Hiero

Was the most cheef be conspiraciou*n*
To brynge the tirau*n*t to his destrucciou*n*;
For no peyne that he myhte endure,
The co*n*iuraciou*n* he wold nat discure.

and chose rather to die in mischief than discover the names of his fellows. He believed that no man should spare to slay a tyrant, and bore his torture in patience until he died.

Rather he ches in myscheeff for to deie,
Than the* name openli declare
Of hy*m* that slouh the tirau*n*t, soth to seie.
Thouhte of riht no man sholde spare,
For comou*n* proffit, helthe and weelfare
To slen a tirau*n*t, deemyng for the beste,
Alle a regiou*n* for to sette at reste.

For which[e] title, he list to suffre deth,
Al [t]his torment took most pacientli
Theodorus, til he yald up the breth,
Gruchched nat with noise nor loude cry;
Amyd whos herte rootid [so] feithfulli
Was comou*n* proffit, Boch*as* writ the same,
Among Siciliens to getyn hy*m* a name.

Anaxarchus, to prevent mortal wars, rebuked the tyrant Nicocreon of Cyprus, who

¶ Grekis also comende aboff the sterris
Anaxerses and gretli magnefie,
Cause that he to stynte mortal werris
List nat spare taquiten his partie
In rebukyng ma*n*li the tiran*n*ye
Of Nicocreou*n*, tirau*n*t ful mortall,
Regnyng in Cipre in his estat roiall.

in a rage bade men cut out his tongue. But Anaxarchus said he should have no advantage of it,

Spared nat nouther for deth nor dreed
Hym to rebuke bi vertuous langage.
The tirau*n*t badde kutte [out] of his hed
His tu*n*ge in haste; but he with stro*n*g corage
Saide he sholde haue non auau*n*tage
Of that me*m*bre, which, maugre al his miht,
Hadde tolde hym trouthe in [the] peeplis siht.

and biting off his tongue chewed it in small pieces which he spat in the tyrant's face.

Off his manace sette litil tale,
Boot of his tunge, of hardi strong corage,
Chewed it al on pecis smale;
Of manli herte thouhte it no damage;
Spit it out into the visage

2274. the] be B, bi J.
2277. þe welfare H, R 3. 2279. at] a R.
2281. this] his R, H.
2296. out] *om.* R, J, P, H 5.
2302. hardi] harde H. 2305. Spet R.

Of the tirau*n*t; gat so the victorie,
To putte his name euermor i*n* memorie.

¶ And S[c]euola, egal to thes tweyne, [p. 435]
For comou*n* proffit, be iust co*m*parisou*n*,
Put hym in pres[e]; did his besi peyne
To slen Porsen*n*a, enmy to Roome tou*n*.
For tacomplisshe his entenciou*n*
Took a strong dart, riht passyngli trenchau*n*t,
With al his myht[e] cast at the tirau*n*t.

Scævola, who missed the tyrant Porsenna with his dart,

Of his marke cause he dide faille
To slen his enmy aftir his entente,
Which in Tuscan with many strong bataille
[A]geyn[es] Romey*n*s with his knihtis wente,
This S[c]euola his owne hande brente,
Cause that he failled of his art,
To slen Porsen*n*a be casti*n*g of his dart.

burnt off his hand in bright red coals for love of his city,

To declare the force of his ma*n*heede
Vpon hymsilff auengid for to bee,
As I haue told, in briht[e] coles rede
His hand he brente for loue of his cite,
Onli taquite his magnanymyte,
Of feruent loue his cite for tauaille,
To slen the tirau*n*t cause he did[e] faille.

deeming that he deserved such punishment.

Thus for to putte the marcial suff*r*ance
Of thes notable philisophres thre
In perpetuel mynde and reme*m*brau*n*ce,
How thei hem quite ech lik his degre
For ther purparti vnto the comou*n*te,
Cause al ther ioie and ther inward deliht
Was for avail of the comou*n* proffit.

All the joy of these noble philosophers lay in their being of avail to the common weal.

First Theodorus put hy*m*silf in pres
For Ciciliens to deien in prisou*n*;
And for Grekis noble Anexerses,
His tunge torn, felt gret[e] passiou*n*;
And S[c]euola for Romeyns & ther tou*n*
Suffred his hand, be short auiseme*n*t,
Tokne of trouthe, in colis to be brent.

Theodorus, who died in prison for the Sicilians, Anaxarchus, who tore his tongue, and Scævola, who burnt off his hand, were

A martirdam it was, in ther maneer
Of ther corage to haue so gret co*n*stau*n*ce;

2313. strechau*n*te H. 2315. his] this R.
2318. Ageynes] Geyn R, J, P, H 5.
2319. he brente H, R 3, P. 2343. ther] *om.* R.

constant until death, and are now crowned with laurel for their patience.

Wer so stable of bodi, hert and cheer,
For comou*n* proffit, of face & contenau*n*ce,
Vnto the deth withoute variau*n*ce;
Gat the tryu*m*phe be souereyn excellence,
With laureer crownid for ther pacience.

As Phœbus surpasses a little star, so does patience shew its bright beams above all other virtues.

Lik as Phebus passeth a litil sterre,
Hiest vpreised in his mydday speere,
So this vertu, in trouble, pes & werre,
Cald pacience most fresshli doth appeere
Among vertues to shewe his bemys cleere;
For pacience knet with humylite,
Wher thei abide ther may no*n* erou*r* bee.

It appeases the hearts of tyrants and

Tirau*n*tis hertis this vertu doth appese,
Modefieth ther cruel fell woodnesse.
Rage of leou*n*s, who list lyue in ese,
Of folk prostrat his malis doth represse.
Al ou*r* ioie bega*n* first with meeknesse;
For of Iuda the hardi strong leou*n*
A maidnes meeknesse fro*m* heuene brouht dou*n*.

vanquishes champions. It was the meekness of a maid that wrought our redemption.

In bataille & myhti stro*n*g sheltrou*n*s,
Avys with suffrau*n*ce wyn*n*eth the victorie;
Pacience venquissheth champiou*n*s;
Lownesse in vertu be many old historie,
And meeknesse, perpetuel of memorie, —
Al to conclude, grou*n*did on resou*n*, —
A maidnes meeknesse wrouhte ou*r* rede*m*pciou*n*.

A Comendacion of pacience in stede of a Lenvoy.[1]

Virtue of virtues, O noble Patience, laud, honour and reverence be given to thee,

VERTU of vertues, o noble Pacience,
Wit*h* laureer crownid for v*er*tuo*us* co*n*stau*n*ce,
Laude, hono*u*r, prys and reu*er*ence
Be youe to the, pryncesse of most plesau*n*ce,
Most ren*n*om*m*ed be anxien reme*m*brau*n*ce;
Of who*m* the myhti marcial armure
Geyn al vices lengest may endure.

Grou*n*d and gyn*n*yng to stonden at diffence
Ageyn Sathanis infernal puissau*n*ce;

2361. with] at H, R, R3. 2364. Batailles H.
2367. be] wit*h* H — old] obstynat R 3.
2368. of] in R. 2369. grou*n*de H.

[1] *The following heading is in* MS. J. leaf 179 recto: "Bochas here co*m*mendith humylyte."

Laureat queen, wher thou art in presence,
Forey*n* outrages haue no gouernau*n*ce;
Conduit, hedspri*n*g of plentevous habu*n*dau*n*ce,
Cristal welle, celestial of figure,
Geyn alle vices whiche lengest may endure.

the ground upon which we may stand against Satan, which may longest endure against all vices.

Cheef fou*n*deresse be souerey*n* excellence [p. 436]
Of goostli beeldyng and spiritual substau*n*ce,
Emperesse of most magnificence,
With heuenli spiritis next of alliau*n*ce,
Wi*th* lyff euerlastyng thi tryu*m*phes to auau*n*ce,
And ioie eternal thi noblesse to assure*
In the aureat Throne perpetueli tendure,

Foundress of spiritual up-building, empress of most magnificence

Thre iherarchies ther beyng in presence,
Wi*th* whom humylite hath souerey*n* aquey*n*tau*n*ce,
Wher osan*n*a with deuout dilligence
Is sung of au*n*gelis be long co*n*tynuau*n*ce,
Tofor the Throne keepy*n*g ther obs*er*uau*n*ce
Syng Sanct*us* Sanct*us*, record of scripture,
Wi*th* vois memorial perpetueli tendure,

in the heavenly throne where hosannah is sung by angels,

The bren*n*yng loue of Cherubyn be ferue*n*ce,
Parfit in charite, dilligent obeissau*n*ce;
And Seraphyn with humble obedience,
And Ordres Nyne be heuenli concordau*n*ce,
Domynaciones with vertuous attendau*n*ce,
Affor the Trynyte syng fresshli be mesure,
With vois memorial perpetueli tendure.

Cherubim and Seraphim and the Nine Orders.

Suffrau*n*ce of paynemys hath but a*n* appare*n*ce,
Doon for vey*n*glorie,* hangyng in ballau*n*ce;
But Cristis martirs, in verray existence
List ageyn tirau*n*t*es* make repugnau*n*ce;
Rather deie than doon God displesau*n*ce,
Shewed in no mero*ur* liknesse nor picture,
Take full pocessiou*n* for euere wi*th* Crist te*n*dure.

The constancy of pagans is but appearance done for vainglory; but Christ's martyrs are faithful unto death.

Suffrau*n*ce for vertu hath the premyne*n*ce
Of them that sette in God ther affiau*n*ce;
Record on Steuene, Vincent and Laurence;
Blissid Edmond bi long perseuerau*n*ce
Suffred for our feith victorious gr*e*uau*n*ce,

Record on Stephen, Vincent, Laurence, blessed Edmund, who suffered victorious pain for our faith,

2390. thi] bi R — tassure B, R. 2407. vey*n*gloire B.
2408. But] Bi R.
2412. te*n*dure] endure R.
2415. on] off R, of H, R 3, P, H 5.

Kyng, maide and martir, a palme to recure,
In the heuenli court perpetuelli tendure.

as have many other saints,

And for to sette a maner difference,
In Bochas book told eueri circumstaunce,
How for our feith be ful gret violence
Dyuers seyntis haue suffrid gret penaunce,
Stable of ther cheer, visage and contenaunce,
Neuer to varye for non auenture;
Lik Cristis championns perpetueli tendure.

who loved and feared God and lived and died in the hope of enduring forever with Patience.

Whos fundacioun bi notable prouidence,
Groundid on Crist ther soulis for tauaunce,
Graue in ther hertis & in ther conscience,
Voidyng al trouble of worldli perturbaunce,
Chaungis of Fortune with hir double chaunce;
Loued God & dradde, aboff ech creature,
In hope with hir perpetueli tendure.

[How Philip la Bele kyng of Fraunce was slayn with a wilde boor and of his thre sones and theire weddyng.] [1]

Philip the Fair then came to Bochas to complain his unhappy fate; for he

WHAN Bochas hadde write of pacience
And comendid the vertu of suffraunce,
Phelipp la Bele cam to his presence,
Fiffte of that name crownid kyng of France,
Gan compleyne his vnhappi chaunce
And on Fortune, of custum þat kan varie,
Which was to hym cruel aduersarie.

was slain by a wild boar in the Forest of Compiègne, after he had been vanquished and put to shame in Flanders.

Woundid he was, [&] with a greuous soor
Gan his compleynt to Bochas determyne,
How he was slay[e]n of a wilde boor
In a forest which callid is Compigne;
Tolde how he was disclaundrid [&] al his lyne;
Onis in Flaundris, with many a worþi kniht,
Venquisshed of Flemmynges & felli put to fliht.

He had four sons and a daughter Isabell,

Proceedyng ferther gan touche of his lynage,
How in his tyme he hadde sonys thre:
Lowis, Phelipp & Charlis yong of age,
The fourte Robert; a douhtir also had he

2436. la Bele] le bele H. 2437. 2nd of] in H, R, R 3, H 5. 2445. &] *om.* R, R 3, H 5. 2446. worþi] wery H.

[1] MS. J. leaf 179 recto.

Callid Isabell, riht excellent of beute.
Seide Robert, the stori is weel kouth,
Which that deide in his tendre youth.

To this stori who list haue good reward,
The circu*m*stau*n*ce wisli to discerne,
His douhtir Isabell was weddid to Edward
Carnervan, the book so doth vs lerene.
This yonger Phelipp weddid in Nau*er*ne
The kynges douhtir, a statli mariage,
Callid Iane, whil she was tendre of age.

who became the wife of Edward Carnarvon, and his son Philip married Jane, daughter of the king of Navarre, and

The same Phelipp aftir crownyd kyng
Of Nauerne, his fadir of assent,
Fyue sonis he hadde in his lyuy*n*g;
Of which[e] fyue, as in sentement,
Thre in nou*m*bre be riht pertynent
To the mateer, who-so list to look,
And the processe of this same book.

afterwards became king of France and had five sons.

The eldest sone callid was Lowis, [p. 437]
To whom his fadir gaf pocessiou*n*
Of Nauerne, because that he was wis
For to gouerne that noble regiou*n*.
Phelipp his brothir for his hih renou*n*
Was aftirward be iust enheritau*n*ce
And rihtful title crownid ky*n*g of F*r*ance.

Philip le Bel's eldest son was afterwards Louis X., and the second son, Philip V. the Tall.

The thridde brothir was be title of riht
Maad Erl of March, and namyd was Charlis.
Euerich of hem in the peeplis siht
Wer famous holde & passy*n*g of gret prys.
And for thei wern riht ma*n*li and riht wis
Phelipp and Charlis took in tendre age
The erlis douhtren of Burgoyne in mariage.

The third son, Charles IV., was made Earl of March, and all three were famous, manly and wise. Philip and Charles married daughters of the Earl of Burgundy,

But as the stori reme*m*breth in certeyne,
To ther noblesse Fortune had envie;
And bi a maner of malis and disdeyne
Brouht in be processe vpon the partie
Of ther too wyues froward auoutrie,
Causyng the deth of alle thes p*r*incis thre,
Wha*n* thei most floured in ther felicite.

but they were froward and adulterous and caused the death of all three princes.

2456. discerne] concerne H. 2459. This] The H.
2483. the] ther R.
2486. in be] into R. 2488. thes] the R.

Charles of Tarentum, who tried to make peace between the Guelphs and Ghibellines,

¶ Aftir thes thre princis glorious,
Tofor Bochas to shewen his entent,
A mihti duk, notable and riht famo*us*,
Ca*m* to co*m*pleyne, Charlis of Tharente,
Which in his tyme to Florence wente
To make pes in his roial estat
Tween Guerff and Gemeli*us* stondi*ng* at debat.

was born of the blood of France: but he was slain by an arrow in the wars between Florence and Pisa.

The saide Charlis, born of the blood of F*r*ance,
A ma*n*li kniht, the stori doth deuise,
Bi whos v*n*happi froward fatal chau*n*ce
In the werris atween Florence & Pise,
On hors[e]bak sitty*ng* in* knihtli wise,
Hurt with an arwe, fill lowe dou*n* to grou*n*de,
Wherbi he kauhte his laste fatal wou*n*de.

A Pisan soldier who trod on his body as it lay on the ground was made knight by the Ghibelline captain.

A man of armys beyng a soudio*ur*
W*ith* the Pisau*n*s, wer it wrong or riht,
Of fals disdeyn that day did his labo*ur*
To trede on Charlis in the peeplis siht,
Wha*n* he lay gruff; wherfor he was maad kniht
Be ther capteyn for a maner pride,
Which gouerned the Gibelynes side.

While Bochas sat still in his seat with a heavy cheer, Dante of Florence, the laureate poet, appeared to him with impressive countenance.

AND in his studie with ful heuy cheer
Whil Iohn Bochas abood still in his seete,
To hy*m* appeered & ga*n* approche neer
Dau*n*te of Florence, the laureat poete,
W*ith* his ditees and rethoriques sueete,
Demure of look, fulfilled w*ith* pacience,
W*ith* a visage notable of reuerence.

Bochas arose and met him with great reverence, saying, "O brightest sun, daystar of our city,

Wha*n* Boch*as* sauh hym, vpon his feet he stood,
And to meete hym he took his pas ful riht,
W*ith* gret reuerence aualed capp and hood,
And to hy*m* seide w*ith* humble cheer & siht:
" O cleerest son*n*e, daysterre and souereyn liht*
Of our cite, which callid is Florence,
Laude onto the, hono*ur* and reuerence!

Thou hast enlumyned Itaile & Lu*m*bardie
W*ith* laureat dites in thi floury*ng* daies,

2496. Guerff] Guelphes P — Gemelius] Gemellyns J, Gamelyns R 3, Gibellines P, Gemelyus H, Genelius R.
2501. in] on B. 2505. wher it wer wro*n*g or riht H, R 3.
2522. daysterre and souereyn liht] O verray sothfast liht B, R, J, H 5.

Ground and gynner of prudent policie,
Mong Florentynes suffredist gret affraies;
As gold purid, preeued at al assaies,
In trouthe madest meekli thi-silue strong
For comoun proffit to suffre peyne & wrong.

thou hast illumined Italy and Lombardy with thy works and suffered pain and wrong for the common weal.

O noble poete, touching this mateer,
How Florentynes wer to the vnkynde,
I wil remembre and write with good cheer
Thi pitous exil and put heer in mynde."
"Nay," quod Daunte, "but heer stant oon
behynde,
Duk of Athenis; turne toward hym þi stile,
His vnkouth stori breefli to compile.

"O noble poet, I will write with good cheer thy sad exile." "Nay," said Dante, "turn thy pen to the Duke of Athens, who stands behind me.

And yif thou list to do me this plesaunce,
To descryue his knihtli excellence,
I wil thou putte his lyff in remembrance,
How he oppressid be myhti violence
This famous cite [which] callid [is] Florence;
Be which[e] stori ful pleynli thou shalt see,
Which wer freendis & foon to that* cite,

"Do me this pleasure and describe his knightly excellence and tell how he oppressed the city of Florence,

And which wer hable for to been excusid,
Yif the trouthe be cleerli apparceyued;
And which wer worthi for to be refusid,
Be whom the cite ful falsli was deceyued,
The circumstaunces notabli conceyued,
To rekne in ordre upon eueri side,
Which sholde be chacid & which shold abide."

so that thou shalt know which were friends and which were foes to the town."

[How Duk Gaultere of Florence for his tyrannye Lecherye and couetise ended in mischef.] [1]

AND whan Bochas knew al thentencioun [p. 438]
Of seide Daunte, he cast hym anon riht
Tobeie* his maister, as it was resoun;
Took his penne; and as he cast his siht
A lite a-side, he sauh no maner wiht
Sauf Duk Gaulteer, of al that longe day;
For Daunt vnwarli vanshed was a-way.

And when Bochas took up his pen to obey his master he saw no one but Duke Gaultier; for Dante had vanished.

2533. How] How the R. 2536. but] *om.* H, P.
2539. thou] ye H. 2545. that] the B, J, this H.
2549. was] wer H — deceyued] *om.* R.
2555. To obeie B.

[1] MS. J. leaf 180 recto.

This said Gaultier was of the blood of France; and his father, lord of Athens,

This saide Gaulteer, breeffli to proceede,
Lik as it is Iput in reme*m*brau*n*ce,
Touchyng his lyne an[d] his roial ky*n*reede,
He was discendid of the blood of France.
Bi long processe and knihtli purueyau*n*ce
His fadir first, be dilligent labo*u*r,
Of Athenys was lord and gou*er*no*u*r.

was put down by the Greeks and his head smitten off.

Stood but a while in cleer pocessiou*n*,
Grekis to hym hadde ful gret envie,
Caste of assent[e] for to putte hy*m* dou*n*
And depryve hym of his famo*us* duchie;
To ther entent a leiseer did espie,
Took hy*m* at myscheef, &, quaki*n*g in his dreed,
Of hih despiht in hast smet of his hed.

To avenge his death Gaultier resolved to besiege the city, but was unsuccessful, and at that time two Pisan princes began to lay siege to Lucca.

Vpon whos deth auengid for to bee
The saide Gaulteer with myhti apparaille
Caste he wolde asege that cite;
But of his purpos longe he dide faille.
And in this while, *with* many gret* bataile,
Too myhti p*r*incis wer come dou*n* of Pise,
Leid a siege to Luk in knihtli wise.

The Florentines came down to help the Luccans, but were defeated;

Florentynes to Luk wer fauourable;
And to delyuere the siege fro the tou*n*,
With multitude almost in*n*umerable
Made ordynau*n*ce; & knihtli thei ca*m* dou*n*,
Which turned aftir to ther destrucciou*n*:
For it fill so of mortal auenture,
On Florentynes fill the disconfiture.

and at this Gaultier went to Florence from Naples

The noise and fame of this gr*e*t bataile
Gan spreede ferr bi report of langage
In Lombardie and thoruh[out] al Itaile
Mong soudio*u*r[e]s lusti of corage;
And among othir, feyny*n*g a pilg*r*image,
The saide Gaulteer be vnwar violence
Ca*m* fro Naplis dou*n* into Florence.

and was chosen governor by a parliament of magnates,

The Florentynes heeld first a parleme*n*t
For the sauaciou*n* and garde of her cite,
Be gret prudence and gret auiseme*n*t

2570. his] that R, H, R 3, P, H 5.
2578. gret] strong B, J, P.
2579. Pise] Parise H.
2589. report] recorde H.

Of suich as wer[e]n hiest of degre;
Bi oon assent thei gaff the souereynte
Them to gouerne, hoping to ther encres,
With statutis made bothe for werre & pes.

whose intention was to plunder the merchants and rob the town of its liberties.

The gret estatis, reulers of the toun,
Callid magnates tho daies in sothnesse,
To Gaulteer gaff this domynacioun,
Of entent the comouns to oppresse
And marchauntes to spoille of ther richesse,
Streyne men of crafft be froward violence
Ageyn the libertes vsid in Florence.

The people were discontented, but the notables preferred to let Gaultier reign rather than modify their exactions.

The peeple alway in a-wait liggyng
To be restorid onto ther liberte,
Gan gruchche sore, among hemsilf pleynyng
For gret extorsiouns doon to ther cite;
The grete also, of most auctorite,
Hadde leuere to suffre Gaulteer regne,
Than ther exacciouns to modefie or restreyne.

Gaultier feigned friendship for both parties,

The saide Gaulteer in ful sotil wise,
Be a fals maner of symulacioun,—
Enmy in herte vnto ther fraunchise;
Al that he wrouhte, for short conclusioun,
Was doon oonli to ther destruccioun,
With a pretence feyned of freendliheed,
To his promys ay contrarie was the deed,—

and climbed up by degrees to such power that all Florence carried out his desires.

Clamb up be processe to ful hih estat
Be feyned speche and sotil flaterie;
In his herte wex pompous & elat,
His werking outward no man koude espie;
Lite and litil drouh to his partie,
That to conclude, shortli for to seie,
Al Florence his lustis did obeie.

He made himself popular with the commons by promising to increase their franchises,

Gan sotilli plese the comounte,
For to acomplissh falsli his desirs,
Made promys tencrece ther liberte
To suich as wer[e]n froward of maneeres;
Made an oth to stroie ther officeeres,
But thei wolde of ther fre volunte
Graunte onto hym larger liberte,

2599 *is repeated* H. 2608. the] theire J, theyr P.
2624 *is misplaced at end of stanza* H. 2627. litil] lite H, R 3.

and finally became so powerful and tyrannous as to menace the very greatest of the town.

Gretter poweer and domynaciou*n* [p. 439]
Tenercee his miht upon eueri side.
Gan manace the grettest of the tou*n*
And day be day encresen in his p*r*ide;
Felli began, felli [he] did abide;
Wherupon,* kept cloos in ther ent*r*aille,
The Florentynes gretli ga*n* m*er*uaille.

At this time one Reynier, a high officer in Florence, supported Gaultier in order to share in his tyranny.

In this while was ther oon Reyneer,*
Of gret auctorite and of gret reuere*n*ce,
A mihti seruau*n*t and a gret officeer,
To whos biddyng obeied al Florence,
Which with Gaulteer acorded i*n* sente*n*ce,
With soudio*u*rs hadde stuffid ech hostrye
For to susteene of Gaulteer the partie.

And traito*u*rli for to fortefie
Thentent of Gaulteer, fel & a*m*bicious,
To haue thestat onli be tira*n*nye,
As ther cheeff lord, froward & surquedous,
To regne in Florence; the cas was pereilous,
Wha*n* too tirau*n*tis be bothe of oon assent
With multitude taco*m*plisshe ther entent.

The magnates could do nothing but acquiesce,

Which thyng considred bi ther gou*er*no*u*rs
And magnates callid in the cite,
Wha*n* that thei fond amo*n*g he*m* no soco*u*rs
To remedien ther gret aduersite;
Fill to accord[e] of necessite,
Gaff ther assent withoute variau*n*ce,
That Gaulter sholde haue al the gou*er*nau*n*ce.

and agreed that Gaultier should swear on the body of Christ to restore them their old franchises.

And co*n*descendid thei wer to this issu,
That Gaulteer sholde in al his beste wise
Vpon the bodi be sworn of Crist I*es*u,
Them to restore onto ther frau*n*chise
Vsid of old, and for no couetise
From ther promys, for lyff nor deth declyne,
As be co*n*uenciou*n* [the court] list determyne.

A trumpet was blown and a parliament held. Gaultier made his promise

Heerupon was blowen a trompet
For tassemble thestatis of the tou*n*;
A parleme*n*t holde, Gaulter first was set;

2642. Therupon B, P.
2644. R *omits lines* 2644 *to* 3588—ther was oon J, P—Reyneer]Reymeer B. 2648. acorded] accord H.
2671] As the conuenciou*n* list to determyne J.

And to pronounce the conuencioun,
With euery parcel entitle[d] be resoun,
Lik ther accord declaryng anon riht,
Stood up a vocat in the peeplis siht.

With men of armys in steel armid briht
Vnto ther paleis cheef and princepall
The saide Gaulteer conveied anon riht,
Set in a seete most statli and roiall.
And the peeple with vois memoriall
Gan crye loude, concluding this sentence:
Gaulteer for euere, cheef* lord of Florence —

and, conveyed by men-at-arms, was set on his throne, while the people cried loudly, "Gaultier forever!"

So to perseuere duryng al his lyff.
Took in the paleis ful pocessioun;
Ther durste non ageyn it make striff;
Graunted to hym the domynacioun
Of alle the castellis aboute environ, —
Tuscan, Areche and castel Florentyn,
With alle lordshipis to Mount Appenyn.

He took possession of the palace and all the neighbouring castles and lordships.

As ye haue herd[e], Gaulteer thus began.
Bi his owne furious dyuynaille,
Saide he was born to be lord of Tuscan,
With a gret parti also of Itaille;
Tolde he was lad, conueied be a quaile,
Saide ouermor[e], wer it riht or wronge,
That was the sentence of the birdis songe.

Thus he began; and he said overmore that he was born to be lord of Tuscany, for a quail had told him so

The same brid first brouht hym* to Florence,
Al the weie afforn hym took his fliht;
With soote syngyng did hym reuerence,
Hih in the hair of corage glad and liht;
Wolde neuer parte out of his siht;
Gaff hym tokenes to sette his herte affire,
That of Florence he shold be lord & sire.

and led him to Florence and done him reverence with its sweet singing.

The same bird he bar in his deuises
Ful richeli enbroudid with perre;
Took upon hym many gret emprises
As cheef lord of Florence the cite;
Sat in iugement; gouernid the contre;

He bore this same bird richly embroidered in his devices, and taking up the reins of government

2684. this] in J.
2685. cheef] was cheef B, P, R 3.
2686. al] *om.* H.
2691. Areche] Areth J, Auretium P.
2700. first brouht hym] brouht hym first B, J.

surrounded himself with people of ill fame.

Drouh to hym flaterers & folk þ*at* koude lie,
Baudis, ribaudis wher he myht he*m* espie.

He was so covetous, lecherous and quarrelsome and lacking in all mercy and grace, that it is abominable to tell about him.

Of that cite took merueillous truages;
Crocheth to hym richessis of the tou*n*;
Of lecherye vsid gret outrages,
Of maidnes, wyues maad non excepciou*n*.
Voide of mercy, grace and remyssiou*n*,
Fond quarelis for to be vengable,
That to reherse it is abhomynable.

He slew those whom he hated and destroyed franchises and old liberties.

Wher he hateth* merciles he sleth; [p. 440]
Brak frau*n*chises and old libertes.
The peeple pleynid, desiryng sore his deth,
Cried vengau*n*ce aboute in ther citees
For tiranye doon in the contrees,
Which was cause of gret discenciou*n*
And of ther cite almost subuersiou*n*.

The people desired his death and cried vengeance. They had lacked foresight to see the troubles that would follow,

Thus thei wern among he*m*silff deuided
For ther sodeyn gr*e*uous oppressioun;*
Lak of forsiht, that thei wer nat prouided
To seen myscheeuys that sholde falle i*n* þe tou*n*.
This verray soth: wher is dyuysiou*n*,
Be witnesse and record of scripture,
May no kyngdam nor cite long endure.

for which they now complained; and finally they began to conspire his destruction.

For which thei ga*n* co*m*pleyne oon & all,
Bothe the grete and al the comou*n*te;
And of accord amo*n*g the*m*silff thei fall
To refourme the hurt of ther cite.
And fynalli the[i] condescendid bee
Bi a maner fell coniuraciou*n*
To proceede to his destrucciou*n*.

One day they armed themselves and cried, "Let us slay this tyrant," and laid siege to his palace.

Vpon a day, thei armed in steel briht,
Magnates first, with comou*n*s of the tou*n*,
Alle of assent thei roos up ano*n* riht,
Gan to crie & make an hidous sou*n*:
"Lat sle this tirau*n*t! lat vs pulle hy*m* dou*n*!"
Leide a siege be myhti violence
Afforn his paleis, wher he was i*n* Florence.

2715. accrochith H, Acrochith R 3, Accrocheth P.
2721. hateth] hated B. 2724. ther] othir H, R 3.
2725. the] theire J, their P.
2729. oppressioun] oppressiou*n*s B — greuous sodeyn J, P.
2736. 1st the] o fthe J — 2nd the] of the J.

Swich as wern enclyned to Gaulteer,
Amyd the paleis, the stori doth vs lerne,
Teschewe the seege, w*ith* ful heuy cheere
Ordeyned hemsilf to fleen awey ful yerne
Out of the strengthe bi a smal posterne,
Wha*n* Florentynes dide ther labo*u*r
To vndermyne rou*n*d aboute the to*u*r.

His friends were glad to flee by a small postern;

Of which[e] thi*n*g wha*n* Gaulteer ga*n* take heed,
This massage he sente onto the tou*n*,
Nat of trouthe, but feyny*n*gli for dreed,
Made promys be fals collusiou*n*
For to make ful restituciou*n*
Of ther fredamys, as thei list deuise;
Sent hem out [oon] Guyllamy*n* Dassise,

but Gautier promised to restore the liberties of the town and sent out one William d'Assise,

Which to the cite was preeuid vttir foo;
Hadde afforn[e] doon hem gret damage.
With Guillamy*n* to them he sent also
His sone and heir to stynte al ther rage, —
Wers than his fadir of wil and of corage.
Bothe attonis wer hangid ano*n* riht
Tofor the paleis in Gaulteres siht.

an enemy of the city, and his own son, who was even worse than his father. Both were immediately hanged before the palace.

Another also, that callid was Herry,
Which hadde afforn[e] youe instrucciou*n*
Vnto Gaulteer and was eek gret enmy
To steren hy*m* ageyn that noble tou*n*,
Gyn*n*er and grou*n*d of ther dyuisiou*n*, —
Which tofor Gaulteer, his iugeme*n*t to shewe,
W*ith* sharp[e] suerdis he was al to-hewe.

Another enemy of the town, called Herry, who had incited Gaultier to new outrages, was cut in pieces with swords.

Thexecuciou*n* doon upon thes thre
In Tuscan born, the ranco*u*r did appese*
Of Florentynes, to stau*n*che the[r] cruelte
Ageyn Gaulteer, and to his lyff gret ese.
He glad tescape out of his disese,
Fledde away in ful secre wise,
The tou*n* restorid ageyn to þ*er* franchise.

After these three were executed the anger of the Florentines lessened, and Gaultier managed to escape.

Thus he loste be his insolence
Al his poweer and domynaciou*n*
Bothe of Tuscan and also of Florence;

Thus by his insolence he lost all his power.

2762. oon] *om.* J.
2763. vttir] a gret H, R 3, a great P.
2765. With] off H — he sent to them J. 2767. 2nd of] or H.
2773. steren] restoren H. 2778. appese] espie B, J.

He went to King John of France,

And as myn auctour maketh mencioun,
Fro Lumbardie he is descendid doun,
Drouh to kyng Iohn regnyng tho in France,
And of berthe ful nih of alliaunce.

and was at the battle of Poitiers when John was taken prisoner. He fled like a coward

As I fynde he was on that partie
With kyng Iohn, this Gaulteer, lik a kniht;
Whan that the kyng with al his cheualrie
Was take hymsilf, his lordis put to fliht,
Into Inglond lad aftir anon riht, —
The saide Gaulteer, hauyng no reward
To his disworshep,* fledde lik a coward.

and, falling into the hands of some Lombard soldiers, was slain by a certain Florentine.

Mette in his fliht with dyuers soudiours
Of Lumbardie abidyng with kyng Iohn,
Which that tyme as brigavntis & pillours
Took this Gaulteer, ledde hym foorth anon, —
His force, his corage, his herte was agon:
Of auenture a certeyn Florentyn
Smet of his hed; this was his fatal fyn.

[Off Philip Cathenoise born of lowe birthe cam to grete estat /& aftir she hir son & doughtir were brent.] [1]

Next in order, weeping and trembling, came Philipot Cathenoise.

BESPREYNT with teres, & [with] a woful noise, [p. 441]
Tofor Bochas quakyng in sorwe & dred,
Next in ordre cam Phelipp Cathenoise,
Poore of degre, born of louh kynreede,
Which roos aftir to gret estat in deede.
Gan with gret sorwe a compleynt ful mortall,
Ceriousli to telle hir* woful fall.

Although she rose to high estate, she was born of low bed, and Bochas was unwilling to spend much time on her story.

Touchyng hir berthe, dirk was hir lynage,
Of poore bed[de] born on outher side;
Bochas was loth to spende gret langage
On hir historie, long theron tabide,
Purposed hym nothyng for to hide
Of the substaunce, but telle al the grete,
And superfluite of the remnant lete.

2797. disworshep] worshep B, J — lik] as H.
2807. Philip J, R 3, P.
2811. hir] the B, his J. 2818. remnant] tyraunt H.

[1] MS. J. leaf 181 recto.

Which was rehersed to hy*m* in his youthe
Whan he was toward Robert of Cicile,
Kyng of Iherusalem, the stori is nat kouth;
Yit in his book he list it to co*m*pile
And it reherse be ful souerey*n* stile,
Lik in that court as it was [to] hy*m* told
Bi oon Bulgar clad in a slauey*n* old.

However, he decided to tell it in outline as he had heard it in his youth from one Bulgar, a mariner, when he was at the court of King Robert of Sicily.

The saide Bulgar was a maryneer,
With whom also was a Calabrien
Callid Consta*n*tyn, which ful many a yeer
Trauailled hadde & sondry thy*n*ges seen
In dyuers contres ther he hadde been.
Mong other thi*n*ges seyn in ther daies olde,
This was a stori which[e] Bulgar tolde.

With the said Bulgar was a Calabrian called Constantine, who had travelled far. Bulgar's tale was as follows:

Duk of Calabre, Robert be his name,
Bi his fadir Charlis, the myhti kyng,
Hadde in comau*n*deme*n*t, his stori seith þe same,
Geyn Frederik to make a stro*n*g ridy*n*g;
Which be force proudli vsurpi*n*g,
Took upon hy*m* to be lord of that ile,
Which callid was the kyngdam of Cicile.

Robert, Duke of Calabria, was commanded by his father to make war on Frederick III. of Aragon, who had usurped the kingdom of Sicily;

Drepan*n*e in soth[e] callid was the tou*n*
Wher Duk Robert his pauylou*n*s pihte,
Redi armyd, thoruh his hih renou*n*
Gey*n* Frederik for that* lond to fihte
And withstonde hy*m* pleynli yif he myhte.
And so befill, the morwe tofor p*r*ime
The dukis wiff of childyng bood hir tyme.

and while Robert was encamped at Depranum the Duchess Violanta was delivered of a child,

Violau*n*t men dide that ladi call,
In hir tyme a famous gret duchesse;
Destitut of other wome*n* all,
Whan hir child was born in that distresse,
To yiue it souke, the stori doth expresse,
Saue fro* myscheeff Philipot was brouht neer,
Of Cathenoise, the dukis cheef lauendeer.

and having no other nurse, she employed Philipot, the Duke's chief laundress,

Bi a fisshere, which was hir husbonde,
A child she hadde, lyuyng be ther t*r*auaile,

whose husband was a fisherman.

2824. to] *om.* H, R 3. 2835. his] the J.
2840. Depranum P. 2841. Robert] Roger P.
2843. that] the B, J, P. 2845. befor H, before J.
2852. Saue] And H — fro] for B, J, H 5, P, R 3 — Philipot] Philip P.

Thus Philipot became nurse to the Duchess, and lived in luxury,

Which fro the se onto the court be londe
Day be day caried vitaile.
And in this caas, because it myhte auaile,
Philipot was brouht, in this gr*e*t streihtnesse,
To be norice onto the duchesse.

and accompanied her mistress to Naples, where the child died.

Wher she was cherisshed aftir hir desirs,
Ech thyng reedi wha*n* that euer she sente.
With the duchesse mong other chau*m*berers
Into Naples I fynde that she wente,
Til Antropos, froward of entente,
Made of this child, ther is no mor to seyne,
The lyues threed[e] for to breke i*n* tweyne.

One Raymond of Champagne, King Charles' chief cook, had once bought an Ethiopian child from a pirate and

With kyng Charlis, of whom I spak toforn,
As my*n* aucto*u*r reme*m*brith in his book,
Was oon Raymond of Chau*m*payne born,
Which with the kyng was callid maist*er* cook.
And on a day his iourne he took
Toward the se; a pirat, as I fynde,
Sold hy*m* a child which was born in Ynde.

made him a Christian and taught him to be a master cook.

Lik Ethiopiens was his colo*u*r;
For who*m* this cook Raymo*n*d hath deuysed,
Be his notable [&] dilligent labo*u*r,
Made hy*m* cristene; & so he was baptised;
Gaff hym his* name, & hath also practised
Hym to promoote, that he vpon hy*m* took
Bi his doctryne to be maister cook;

After Raymond became a knight, the Ethiopian was made lord of the king's wardrobe, and although he was black, Philipot, whose husband had died, married him.

For he soone afftir took the ordr*e* of kniht.
The Ethiopien wex a good officeer,
Gat suich grace in the kyngis siht,
To be aboute hy*m* [was brouht up] mor neer;
Be processe he was maad wardropeer;
And thouh he was blak of his visage,
To Cathenoise was ioyned in mariage.

He grew bold and asked the king to knight him, which the king did.

Wex malapert, and of presumpcio*u*n [p. 442]
To be maad kniht the kyng he ga*n* requeere,
Which of fredam and gret affecciou*n*
Is condescendid to grau*n*ten his praieere.
But to declare pleynli the maneere,

2859. Philip P. 2867. i*n*] on H, J, R 3, H 5.
2872. his] this J, P. 2875. Ethiopes H.
2877. &] *om.* J. 2878. cristened J. 2879. his] the B, J.
2885. was brouht up] *om.* P, J. 2887. blak] *om.* H.

In this tyme Violau*n*t the duchesse,
Affor reme*m*bred, deide of seeknesse.

Aftir whos deth, the book doth certefie,
How Duk Robert of Naples the cite
Weddid a ladi that callid was Sansie,
To whom Philipot, as fill to hir degre,
Wi*th* dilligence and gret humylite
To plesen hire did so hir deueer,
That of hir cou*n*sail ther was no*n* so neer.

At this time Violanta died, and Duke Robert married a lady called Sancia, with whom Philipot soon became very intimate.

Euere redi at hir comau*n*dement,
Wrouhte atires plesau*n*t of deliht,
Wi*th* holsum watres that wer redolent
To make hir skyn bi wasshyng soote & whiht,
Made confecciou*n*s to serue hir appetiht.
Bi hir husbonde, the stori who list see,
The same Philipot hadde childre thre.

Philipot had three children,

She was kun*n*yng & of hir port prudent;
Chose be fauour for to be maistresse
To faire Iane, yong and in*n*ocent,
Which douhtir was to the gret duchesse
Of Calabre; and ferthermor texpresse,
Hir husbonde Thethiopien with-al
Of Charlis houshold was maad senescall.

and as she was prudent and knowing she became governess of Jane, daughter of the Duchess of Calabria. The Ethiopian was made seneschal of Charles' household.

"O Lord!" quod Boch*as*, spak of hih disdeyn,
"What meueth this Fortune for to make cheer*e*,
Wi*th* hir fauo*u*r to reise up a foreyn
Vpon hir wheel, with brihte fethres cleer*e*;
But of custum it is ay hir maneer*e*
Fairest tappeer*e* wi*th* cheer and co*n*tenau*n*ce,
Whan she wil bry*n*ge a ma*n* vnto myschau*n*ce.

"O Lord," said Bochas, "why should Fortune so lift up an alien, especially an ugly,

For he that was a boy the laste day,
An Ethiopien brou*n* and horrible of siht,
And afor-tyme in the kechyn lay
Amo*n*g the pottis with baudi cote aniht,
Now [he] of neue hath* take the ordre of kniht,
Wi*th* kyng Charlis now is he senescall:
Swich sodey*n* clymbyng axeth a sodey*n* fall."

brown Ethiopian, who once lay among the pots in the kitchen! Such sudden climbing asks a sudden fall."

2894. this] his H. 2896. doth] *om.* H.
2897. Robert] Roger P.
2901. hir] *corrected from* his *to* hir B. 2906. wasshyn H.
2918. for] *om.* H, R 3. 2923. vnto] *in* to H.
2928. he] *om.* J — hath] haue B.

He and Philipot his wife rose to great wealth, and their sons made stately marriages and became knights. But their father died at the height of his prosperity and had a great funeral.

He and Philipot, his wiff, fro pouerte
Been enhau*n*sid and rise to gret richesse;
Tweyne of ther sonis statli maried bee;
And for fauo*u*r mor than worthynesse
Took ordre of kniht; & in his most hihnesse
Ther fader deide, whos feeste funerall
Was solempnised and holde ful roiall.

Thus Fortune can change. The eldest son also died, and the second son left his books to take his father's place.

Thus ca*n* Fortune chau*n*gen as the moone,
Hir brihte face dirked with a skie:
His eldest sone deide aftir soone;
The secou*n*de lefft up his clergie,
To be maad kniht ga*n* hy*m*silf applie,
Stede of his fader, pleynli as I reede,
In his offis be fauo*u*r to succeede.

Philipot's welfare was in part eclipsed; but as the sun shines brightest after a rain, she too rose to still greater glory.

Thus be processe fro Philipot ano*n* riht,
Deth of hir husbonde & [of] hir sonis tweyne,
Fortune in parti eclipsed hath the liht
Of hir weelfare & ga*n* at hir disdeyne.
Yit euene lik, as wha*n* that it doth reyne,
Phebus aftir sheweth mor cleernesse,
So she fro trouble roos to mor noblesse.

Jane, who was not above criticism, married king Andreas of Hungary,

I meene as thus, r*e*hersi*n*g no v*er*tu
In hir persone that me*n* koude espie,
But onli this, be title of this issu:
Wha*n* Charlis douhtir Iane on that partie
Was to the ky*n*g weddid of Hungrie,
Callid Andree, a ma*n* of gret corage,
His saide wiff but riht tendr*e* of age,

and for a large bribe and by great labour had Philipot's son Robert made governor of Sicily.

The same Iane, nat al wit*h*oute vice,
As is rehersed su*m*what be my*n* aucto*u*r,
To who*m* Philipot whilom was* norice,
As ye haue herd, and be ful gret labo*u*r
Of saide Iane, Robert made gou*er*no*u*r,
Sone of Philipot, for a gret reward,
Made of Scicile & of that lond stiward.

The Sicilians were indignant.

This fauour doon to Philipot Cathenoise
Caused in that lond gret indignaciou*n*,
Whos douhtres weddyng caused eek gr*e*t noise,

2934. than] þan for H. 2937. holde] kept H.
2945. Phillippe P. 2951. noblesse] gladnesse H.
2957. Andreas P. 2958. His saide] he seid his J.
2959. *Stanza repeated* H. 2961. was whilo*m* B.

Maried to Charlis the gret erl of Marchou*n*,
Which gaff to folk gret occasiou*n*
To deeme amys aboute in ech contre,
That al that lond was gou*er*ned be tho thre,

Philipot's daughter then married the earl of Marcon, which increased her power.

Be queen Iane and Philipot Cathenoise [p. 443]
A*n*d saide Robert, stiward of Cicile,
Sone to Philipot; this was the comou*n* voise: —
The queen and Robert be ther sotil wile
Hadde of assent vsed a long[e] while
The hatful syn*n*e of auout[e]rie,—
Roos in Cicile & went up to Hungrie.

It was common gossip that Robert and Queen Jane had long been committing adultery.

For queen Iane bega*n* no man*er* thi*n*g
But Cathenoise assentid wer therto;
Thexecuciou*n* and fulli the werki*n*g
Brouht to conclusiou*n*, be Robert al was do.
And in this title roos a stryf also,
A disclau*n*drous and a froward discord
Atween the queen & hy*m* that was hir lord.

The news reached Hungary, and there was strife between the king and queen.

Hard to proceede upon suspeciou*n*,
Sclau*n*dre is swifft, lihtli taketh his fliht;
For which men sholde eschewe thoccasiou*n*
Of fame and noise, & euery man*er* wiht
Bi prouidence reme*m*bre in his forsiht,
Wha*n* the report is thoruh a lond Iron*n*e,
Hard is to stynte it wha*n* it is begon*n*e.

Slander travels swiftly and, once begun, is hard to stop;

Withstonde p*r*inciples, occasiou*n*s to declyne,
List vnwarli ther folwe gret damage;
To late kometh the salue and medecyne
To festrid soris wha*n* thei be incurable.
And in caas verray resemblable,
Teschewe slau*n*dre list nat for to spare,
May nat faillen to fallen in the snare.

so it is better not to give occasion for it: salve comes too late when a sore is festered and incurable.

Thus for a tyme the sclau*n*dre was kept cloos,
Al-be-it so it did a while abide,
Another mischeef tha*n** pitousli aroos,
Which afftirward spradde abrood ful wide:
Auoutrye to moordre is a guide, —
Set at a preeff, my*n* aucto*ur* doth recorde,
The kyng Andree was stranglid wit*h* a corde.

For a time the scandal was suppressed; but soon another mischief arose: King Andreas was murdered.

2971. deeme] don H.
3003. than] ful B, J, P, H 5, *om.* R 3.

Hugh, Earl of Avellino, undertook to punish the crime; and

Out of his chaum*m*bre reised a gret heihte
Bi a coniected fals conspiracioun,
He was entreted, brouht dou*n* be a sleihte,
Afftir stranglid, as maad is me*n*cioun.
Whos deth to pun[i]she be com*m*yssiou*n*,
Huhe Erl of Auelyn be a patent large
To be iuge took on hym the charge.

Philipot, her son and her daughter, were found guilty and burnt at the stake.

Of this moordre roos up a gret noise,
Be euidencis ful abhomynable,
Philipot [I]callid Cathenoise,
Hir sone, hir douhtir, that thei wer coupable;
Doom was youe be iuges ful notable;
And to co*n*clude shortli ther iugement,
W*ith* cheynis bou*n*de to stakis thei wer brent.

[Lenvoye.]

This tragedy tells the evils of presumption: no one is more cruel than a beggar who rises to domination.

THIS tragedie afforn rehersed heer
Tellith the damages of p*re*sumpciou*n*,
Bexperience declaryng þe maneer,
Whan beggers rise to domynaciou*n*,
Is non so dreedful execuciou*n*
Of cruelte, yif it be weel souht,
Than of such oon that ca*m* up of nouht.

Philipot was at first a simple laundress; but when she came to estate she never considered her birth.

Record on Philipot, that w*ith* humble cheer
Bi sodeyn fauou*r* and supportaciou*n*,
Which was tofor a symple smal lauendeer
Of no valu nor reputaciou*n*,
Be Fortunys gery mutaciou*n*,
Shad out hir malis, testat whan she was brouht,
List nat co*n*sidre how she ca*m* up of nouht.

Where is there more scornful pride or seeking of evil company or intriguing than among people who rise out of nothing?

Wher mor disdeyn or wher is mor dau*n*geer,
Or mor froward comunycaciou*n*,
Mor vengable veny*m* doth appeere,
Nor mor sleihti fals supplantaciou*n*,
Nor mor conspired vnwar collusiou*n*,
Nor vndermyny*n*g doon couertli & wrouht,
Than of such folk that komen up of nouht?

3008. heihte] liht H. 3015. this] his H.
3017. Icallid] that called was P, callid H, J.
3027. souht] I sought J, out sought P.
3029. on] of H, R 3, H 5 — Philip P.

Fortunys chau*n*ges & meeuy*n*ges circuleer,
Wit*h* hir most stormy transmutacioun*n*,
Now oon set up ful hih in hir chaieer,
Enhau*n*ceth vicious, vertuous she put dou*n*;
Record on Philipot, whos venymous tresou*n*
Compassid afforn[e] in hir secre thouht,
The deede brak out, whan she ca*m* up of nouht.

Fortune often sets up the vicious and puts down the virtuous.

Noble P*r*incis, with yo*u*r briht eien cleer
Aduertiseth in your discreciou*n*,
That no flaterer com in yo*u*r court to neer
Be no fraude of fals decepciou*n*,
Alwey reme*m*bryng afforn in yo*u*r resou*n*
On this tragedie, and on the tresou*n* wrouht
Bi fals flaterers that ca*m* up of nouht.

Noble Princes, remember this tragedy and the treason done by false flatterers who came up of nought!

[How kyng Sausys was slayn by his Cosyn whiche was brothir to the kyng of Arrogon.] [1]

THE tyme kam that of his [gret] t*r*auaile [p. 444]
Boch*as* dempte, holdyng for þe beste,
This noble poete of Florence & Itaile,
To make his pen*n*e a while for to reste,
Closed his book &* shette it in his cheste;
But or he mihte spere it with the keie,
Kam thre p*r*incis and meekli ga*n* hy*m* preye,

Bochas now thought to rest a while from his labour, so he shut up his book in a chest; but before he could turn the key,

Amongis othre reme*m*brid in his book
Ther greuau*n*ces breeffli to declare.
Wherwith Boch*as* gan cast up his look,
And of compassiou*n* beheeld her pito*us* fare,
Thouhte he wolde for no slouthe spare
To ther requestis goodli co*n*descende,
And of his book so to make an eende.

three kings came and prayed him to remember their grievances. Of compassion he could not refuse, and with their stories he made an end of the Fall of Princes.

And he gan first reherse be writy*n*g,
And his co*m*pleynt ful pitousli he made,
Touchyng the fall[e] of the grete ky*n*g
Icallid Sause, which his soio*u*r hade,
The place namyd was Astrosiade;

The first was Sancho, who lived in the Balearic Isles.

3045. hir] his H, the J. 3047. on] of H, R 3.
3061. &] to B, R 3, H 5.
3074. Sause] Sautius P — hade] made H.
3075. was] *om.* H, R 3.

[1] MS. J. leaf 182 verso.

And, as he writ, a litil ther beside
Was a smal isle callid Gemaside.

His kingdom was called Majorca, and there he lived in peace.

Bothe thes isles togidre knet in oon,
Wher Sausis hadde his domynacioun,
Lyuyng in pes; enmy hadde he non;
In long quiete heeld pocessioun.
Whos kyngdam hool, as maad is mencioun,
In that vulgar, myn auctour writ þe same,
Of Malliogres pleynli bar þe name.

Ther is also another smaller isle*
Callid Maillorge; & of bothe tweyne
The seid[e] kyng was lord a gret[e] while,
Keeping his stat notable and souereyne.

until his cousin, brother of the king of Aragon, became his enemy.

Hauyng a cosyn, gan at hym disdeyne,
Which brother was, as maad is mencioun,
Vnto the kyng that tyme of Arragoun.

It is said that in these isles slings for casting stones in battle were first invented.

In thes isles, remembrid be writyngis,
Whan the peeple went into bataile,
Was the vsage founde up first of slyngis,
With cast of stoon ther enmyes to assaile;
Thei hadde of shot non othir apparaile
In that tyme; arblast nouther bowe
Parauenture was tho but litil knowe.

Finally Sancho's cousin came down from Spain with an army and took away his kingdom and

Alle thes contres wer callid but o lond,
Wher that Sausis heeld pocessioun,
Til his cosyn with strong & myhti hond
[And] with gret poweer sodenli cam doun;
Brouhte peeple out of Arragoun,
Fill on kyng Sausis, feeble in his diffence,
Gat that kyndam be knihtli violence.

smote off his head. Though they were nearly related, no courtesy was shewn that day.

The ballaunce was nat of euene peis
Atween thes cosyns, who that list take heed;
For in his conquest this Arogoneis
Of cruelte bad smyten of the hed
Of kyng Sausis, quakyng in his dreed.
Thouh it stood so thei wer nih of allie,
Ther was that day shewed no curteisie.

3077. was] *with* H — Emacide P. 3079. Sautius (*throughout*) P. 3085. isle] Islee B. 3086. Maiora P. 3098. was tho but] þat tyme was H. 3100. that] *om.* P. 3108. this] the J — Aragoneise H, Arageneys R 3, Arragoneys J, Arrogoneys P.

[How Lowes kyng of Jer*usal*em & Cecile was put doun.] [1]

AFFTIR this storie told in woordes fewe,
And of kyng Sausis slay*n* be tiran*n*ye,
P*er* ca*m* a prince, & ga*n* his face shewe,
Callid Lowis lord of Trynacrye,
The same isle [w]as in that partie
Callid Cicane, the stori tellith thus,
Aftir the name of kyng Siculus.

Louis, lord of Trinacria, or Sicania, which was named after King Siculus, a

Trynacrye, a contre merueillous,
Took first his name of famous hilles thre:
The cheeff of hem is callid Pellorus,
The next Pachinvs,* the thridde Lillibe,
Nat fer fro*m* Ethna the saide hille[s] be,
Beside a se ful pereilous and ille,
With too dau*n*geeris Karibdis and eek Scille.

wonderful country with three famous hills, Pelorum. Pachynum, and Lilybaeum, not far from Etna,

This saide Lowys, kyng of Iherusalem
And of Sicile, the book maketh menciou*n*,
Which was enchasid & put out of his rewm
Bi another Lowis and put dou*n*,
Eendid in pouert, for short co*n*clusiou*n*.
This laste Lowis of pite did hy*m* grace,
Til he deide to haue a duellyng place.

was chased out of his realm and put down by another Louis, who had at least the grace to give him a dwelling place till he died.

[How kyng John of frau*n*ce at Peyters was take prisoner*e* by Prynce Edward & brouȝt in to Englond.] [2]

NEXT of alle and laste of euerichon,
Cursyng Fortune with al hir variau*n*ce,
Makyng his co*m*pleynt to Boch*as*, ca*m* Ky*n*g Iohn:
Tolde his mischeeff, how he was take i*n* F*r*ance
Bi P*r*ince Edward, for al his gr*e*t puissau*n*ce;
And aftir that, with stro*n*g & myhti hond,
He was fro Peiteres brouht into Inglond.

Afforn destroied his castellis & his tou*n*s, [p. 445]
And ouerthrowen manli in bataile,

Last of all came King John of France, cursing Fortune and all her variance. He told Bochas how Prince Edward took him prisoner in France and sent him from Poitiers to England.

3117. was] as P, H 5, *om.* J. 3118. Sicania P.
3123. Pachinvs] Pathmvs B, J, Pachmus H, Pachinvs R 3, Pachinus P. 3126. eek] *om.* H.
3142. ouerthrowen] ovircomen H, ouercomen R 3, ovyrcome H 5.

[1] MS. J. leaf 182 verso. [2] MS. J. leaf 182 verso.

His princes were slain, and the heaps of dead were searched and spoiled of plate and mail.

His p*r*incis slayn, ther baneres nor penou*n*s
Nor brode standardis mihte he*m* nat auaile;
The tras out souht, spoilled of plate & maile.
Maugre his miht kyng Iohn was p*r*isoneer,
In Inglond aftir abood ful many a yeer,

John remained in England many a year.

Set aftirward onto ful gret rau*n*sou*n*;
The worthi slay[e]n on the Frenssh partie.

At that time Britain flowered in noblesse of chivalry.

The same tyme in Brutis* Albiou*n*
Ther floured in soth noblesse of cheualrie,
Hihe prowesse* and prudent pollicie;
Mars and Mercurie aboue ech naciou*n*
Gou*er*ned that tyme Brutis* Albiou*n*.

Mars, their patron in battle, and Minerva gave them influence to excel in prudence and learning.

Mars for knihthod, ther patrou*n* i*n* bataille,
And Mynerua gaff hem influence,
Meynt with the brihtnesse of shyni*n*g plate & maile,
To floure in clergie and in hih prudence,
That Prince Edward be marcial violence,
That day on lyue oon the beste kniht,
Brouht hom Ki*n*g Iohn, maugre al his miht.

Bochas favoured John and France, and striving to belittle the famous chivalry of Englishmen, he left spear and shield and fought with pen and ink.

Thouh Boch*as* yaff hym fauo*u*r bi langage,
His herte enclyned onto that partie,
Which onto hym was but smal auau*n*tage:
Woord is but wynd brouht in be envie.
For to hyndre the famous cheualrie
Of Inglissh-men, ful narwe he ga*n* hy*m* thi*n*ke,
Lefft spere and sheeld[e], fauht with pen*n*e & i*n*ke.

Although he was a great poet he gave no mortal wound: his partial writing rebounded to his shame — blaming King John because he was taken by English-men, whom he disparaged!

Thouh seide Boch*as* floured in poet*r*ie,
His parcial writyng gaf no mortal wou*n*de;
Kauht a quarel in his malencolie,
Which to his shame did aftirward rebou*n*de,
In co*n*clusiou*n*, lik as it was fou*n*de,
Agey*n* Ki*n*g Iohn a quarell ga*n* to make,
Cause that he wolde of Inglissh-me*n* be take.

Heeld hem but smal of reputaciou*n*
In his report, men may his writi*n*g see;

3145. tras] cas H. 3148. onto] to J.
3150. Brutis] Brutus B, Brutes J, P. 3151. of] and J.
3152. Hihe prowesse] W*ith* hih prudence B, J.
3154. Brutus B, J. 3155. ther] the H.
3157. Meynt with the brihtnesse] w*ith* þe brihtnesse meynt H — the] *om.* J, P.
3158. To] þe H. 3168. fauht] & faught H 5.
3175. Cause] by cause H, be cause R 3.

His fantasie nor his oppyniou*n*
Stood in that caas of non auctorite:
Ther kyng was take; ther knihtis dide flee;
Wher was Bochas to helpe at such a neede?
Sauff wit*h* his pen*ne* he made no ma*n* to bleede.

And where was Bochas then? Save with his pen he made no man bleed!

Of rihtwisnesse euery cronicleer
Sholde in his writyng make no*n* excepciou*n*;
Indifferentli conueie his mateere;
Nat be parcial of non affecciou*n*,
But yiue the thank of marcial guerdou*n*,
His stile in ordre so egali obserued,
To euery parti as thei haue disserued.

Chroniclers should always be impartial. King John deserved praise because he acquitted himself like a manly knight when his lords were slain or fled.

Laude of Kyng Iohn was that he abood,
In that he quit hym lik a ma*n*li kniht;
His lordes slay[e]n; som*me* awey thei rood;
Most of his meyne took hem to the fliht.
This iourne take for Kyng Edwardis riht;
The feeld I-won*ne*; hath this in memorie:
Treuthis title hath gladli the victorie.

The battle was fought for King Edward's rights, and King Edward won.

Of Kyng Iohn what sholde I write more?
Brouht to this lond with othir p*r*isoneeris,
Vpon which the rewm co*m*pleyned sore.
Bi rehersaile of old cronicleeris,
Deied in Inglond; withyn*ne* a fewe yeeris
Lad hom ageyn; afftir ther writyngis,
Lyþ at Seyn[t] Denys with othir worthi ki*n*gis.

Why should I write more of King John? He died afterwards in England and now lies at St. Denis.

¶ Lenvoye.

OFF Boch*as* book the laste t*r*agedie
Compendiousli put i*n* remem*br*ance,
How P*r*ince Edward wit*h* his cheualrie
Fauht at Peiteres with Ki*n*g Iohn of F*r*ance;
And thoruh his mihti marcial puissau*n*ce
Grou*n*ded his quarel upon his fadres riht,
Took hym p*r*isoneer ful lik a ma*n*li kniht.

This last tragedy of Bochas's book remembers how Prince Edward took King John of France prisoner.

Bi collusiou*n* Ki*n*g Iohn did occupie,
Set out of ordre the roial alliau*n*ce;
Sceptre, crowne, wit*h* al the regalie

John occupied Edward's inheritance

3180. 2nd ther] his H, R 3, hys H 5. 3195. hath] have H, P.
3200. Cronyculeres J.

conveyed down to him by lineal descent.

Was doun descendid to Edward in substaunce,
Conueied the branchis be lyneal concordaunce,
For which[e] title groundid upon riht,
Prince Edward fauht ful lik a manli kniht.

And in token that he was in the right God gave Edward victory.

His cleym, his quarel mor to fortefie,
In tokne that God his quarel wolde auaunce,
Disconfiture was maad on that partie,
Vpon King Iohn be violent vttraunce,
An heuenli signe be influent purueiaunce
Sent from aboue to shewe Edwardis riht,
For which the Prince fauht lik a manli kniht.

Noble Princes, weigh this matter justly in balance; there is no variance in honest judges:

Noble Princis, your hertis doth applie [p. 446]
Iustli to weie this mateer in ballaunce.
Alle thynges peised, ye may it nat denye,
Yiff ye considre euery circumstaunce,
In rihtful iuges may be no variaunce:
The feeld darreyned, deemeth who hath riht,
For which Prince Edward fauht lik a manli kniht.

a thing committed to God allows of no controversy; and this is the plight in which France stood: her king was finely taken at Poitiers by Prince Edward.

A thyng bassent[e] put in iupartie
And commytted to Goddis ordenaunce,
Ther may been afftir no contrauersie
Atween parties, quarelis nor distaunce,
Who shal reioisshe; and in this caas stood France:
Fyn* take at Peiteres, declaryng who hath riht;
For which Prince Edward fauht lik a manli kniht.

3218. H 5 *omits to* 3478 (*one leaf missing between* 180 *and* 181).
3232. iupartie] memorye H, memory R 3.
3234. Contravesye H.
3237. Fyn] Syn B, Sith P — take] *om.* P, J.
3238. *This line is followed in* H *by the 14th stanza of the Envoy, after which comes the Chapitle of Fortune.*

¶ Finis libri Bochasij.

A chapitle of Fortune compilid howe she hath hir quytt to al wordly pepill.[1]

LAT folk of wisda*m* co*n*sidre i*n* þ*er* wit,
Gadre up, a-som*me** & cou*n*te in þ*er* resou*n*,
To all estatis hou Fortune hath hir quit,
To popis, prelatis, gyn*ne* first in Roome tou*n*,
To cardynalis most souerey*n* of renou*n*, —
Wha*n* thei sat hiest, koude hem nat diffende
Ageyn Fortune bi no prouisiou*n*;
But with a tourn she made he*m* to descende.

Let folk consider how Fortune behaves toward all estates: when they sit highest, with a turn of her wheel she makes them descend.

Afftir in ordre cal to reme*m*b*r*ance
Thestat imperial of famous emp*er*ou*r*s,
Which as Appollo thoruh ther mihti puissau*n*ce
Ther fame up blowe to Iubiteris to*u*rs,
And forget nat thes olde co*n*querou*r*s
Aboue Mercurye cast hem to assende,
Til that Fortune with hir froward sho*u*rs
Most sodenli made hem to descende.

Popes, cardinals, emperors, old conquerors — all were made suddenly to fall.

Kynges, p*r*incis of dyuers regiou*n*s,
In Asie, Europe, Affrik & Cartage,
Of Ethiopie the marcial champiou*n*s,
Monstres of Ynde, hidous of visage,
Athlas, Hercules, in ther most furious rage,
Ageyn whos myht no ma*n* koude hy*m* diffende, —
What folwed aftir? Fro*m* ther hiest stage
Fortune vnwarli made hem to descende.

Kings, princes of many lands and martial champions cast down from their highest stage.

Preestis, prelatis and weel-fed fat p*ar*sownis,
Richeli auau*n*ced, and clerkis of degre, —
Rekne up religious, wi*th* al ther brode crownis,
And patriarkes that haue gret souerey*n*te, —
Bisshoppis, abbottis confermed in ther see,
Seculeer chanou*n*s, wi*th* many gret prebende;
Behold of Fortune the mutabilite,
How sodenli she made hem to descende.

Priests, prelates, and well-fed parsons, monks and patriarchs, bishops, abbots and canons, with many a fat prebend, have also fallen.

3239. considren of wisda*m* H.
3240. a-som*me*] a son*ne* B, a sonne R 3.
3241. Fortune] she H, R 3. 3242. gyn*ne*] gan H.
3258. Monstres] Monstrous R 3. 3263. fed] *om.* R 3.
3264. clerkis] cherlys H. 3265. al] *om.* H.

[1] "Here Bochas makith a rehersaile how fortune hath made high estat*es* vnwarly to descende." MS. J. leaf 183 verso. *This chapter is collated with* H, J, R 3 *and* H 5 (*from line* 3478).

There are many conditions of men, but Fortune causes them all to rise or descend at her will.

Al that is write, is write to our doct*r*ine:
Oon courbith lowe, another goth upriht;
Sum*me* be vicious, sum*me* in vertu shyne;
Pheb*us* now clipsid, so*m*tyme his bemys briht,
Su*m*tyme cloudi, su*m*tyme a sterry niht;
Sum folk appeire, sum*me* doon amende,
Shewe off Fortune the poweer & the myht:
Oon goth upward, another doth descende.

Some are virtuous, others perversely wilful, some evil, some stable in Christ; but in spite of the world Fortune rules them all —

Sum ma*n* hooly encreseth in vertu,
A-nother rekles, of froward wilfulnesse;
Oon is parfit and stable in Crist I*es*u,
A-nother braideth upon frowardnesse;
Oon encreseth with treso*ur* & richesse, —
Who list thryue, to labo*ur* must entende, —
Maugre the world, Fortunis doubilnesse
Doth oon arise, another to discende.

the industrious and the idle, the wasters and the thrifty.

Oon is besi and set al his labo*ur*
Erli tarise his good to multeplie;
Another spendeth, & is a gret wastour;
Sum tre is bareyn, sum doth fructefie;
Oon kan seyn soth, another ca*n* weel lie;
Oon kan gadre, another ka*n* dispende, —
Vnto Fortune this mateer doth applie:
She maketh oon rise, a-nother to dissende.

Avoid the weed, and take the corn of virtue, as reason teaches; and the lesson of this book is that all men rise or fall on Fortune's wheel.

Al thes mateeres rehersed here to forne,*
Of which this book maketh me*n*ciou*n*,
Voideth the weed, of vertu tak the corn,
As resou*n* techeth in yo*ur* discreciou*n*.
And for to sette a short conclusiou*n*,
In a breeff som*me* this book to co*m*prehende:
Fortunis wheel bi reuoluciou*n*
Doth oon clymbe up, another to discende.

3271. 1st write] writen H. 3273. vertu] vertues H.
3279. ma*n*] men H. 3286. arise] to rise R 3.
3290. sum] som frute H.
3295. rehersed here toforne] conbyned into oon B, J.
3297. taketh J, takith H. 3298. techeth] *om.* R 3.

[¶ A lenvoye co*m*pyled vpon the book wryte*n* by the translatour specially direct to hym that causyd the t*r*anslaciou*n* & secundely to alle othir it shal seen.] [1]

RYGHT reu*er*ent Prynce, wi*th* support of your grace,
By your comaundement as I vndirtook
With dredful herte, pale of cheer and face,
I haue a-co*m*plysshed translaciou*n* of your book;
In which labour myn hand ful offte quook,
My penne also troublyd with ygnorau*n*ce
Lyst myn empryse wer nat to your plesau*n*ce.

Right reverent Prince, I have finished translating your book. My hand often trembled, and my pen was troubled lest my work were not to your pleasure.

Off ryght considred, of trouthe and equite,
I nat expert nor stuffyd with language,
Seyn howh that Ynglyssh in ryme hath skarsete,
How I also was ronne ferre in age,
Nat quyk, but rude and dul of my corage,
Off no presumpciou*n*, but atwix hope and drede
To obeye your byddyng took on* me to p*r*ocede.

For I am not skilled in language, and there is a lack of rhyming words in English, and I was far run in age and dull of heart when I began.

Hope with glad chere gaff me greet cou*n*fort,
Off trust I shulde agreen your noblesse;
But tho cam dreed, contraryous of repoort,
Gan manace and frowardly expresse,
Geyn me alleggyng vnkonnyng and dulnesse, —
Seyde for his part, by argumentys stronge,
I was not able for to vndirfonge

Hope gave me comfort that I should please your noblesse, and then came Dread alleging ignorance and dulness against me.

This seid empryse to p*er*forme & contvne;
The p*r*ofunde p*r*ocesse was so poetical,
Entirmedlyd with chau*n*ges of fortune
And strau*n*ge mat*er*ys that were hystoryal,
Towchyng estatys that hadde a sodeyn fal;
The Frenssh vnkouth co*m*pendyously co*m*pyled,
To which language my tou*n*ge was nat affyled.

The matter was inter-mingled of changes of Fortune and strange historical things, and the French difficult; and for French my tongue was not polished.

Dreed and vnkonnyng beeyng of assent
Made ageyn me a dau*n*gerous obstacle,
For tacomplysshe your comaundement,
Stondyng fer of fro Tullyvs habitacle:

Dread and lack of skill were dangerous obstacles to my fulfilling your commandment,

3303. Prynce] princes R 3. 3316. on] vpon H 1766.

[1] *The Envoy, together with the heading, is supplied from* MS. Harley 1766, leaf 260 verso, *collated with* R 3 *and* P.

until Hope again began to support me.

Myn eyen mystyd, and dirked my spectacle,
Tyl hope ageyn gan make[n] his repeyr;
Me to supporte he putte away dyspeyr.

The vines of Bacchus were sered, and Midas' aureate liquor and Juno's well dried up. I found no favour there. My heart was heavy, my purse light.

Yit of Bachus seryd wer the vynes,
Off Mygdas touch the aureat lycour,
And of Iuno wellys crystallynes
Wer dryed vp; ther fond I no favour:
A thrustlewh accesse cause of my langour,
Noon egal peys, herte hevy and purs lyght,
Which causith poetys syhen at mydnyght.

But I trust your liberality will relieve me of this quotidian, and that a spring tide of gracious plenty will follow.

Trustyng ageynward your liberal largesse,
Off this cotidien shal* relevyn me,
Hope hath brought tydyng to recure myn accesse;
Afftir this ebbe of froward skarsete
Shal folwe a spryng flood of gracious plente,
To wasshe a-way be plentevous inffluence
Al ground ebbys of constreyned indigence.

With Hope came Humble Affection, who said, you, my lord, would have compassion on my old age; and

With hope also cam humble affecciou*n*,
Made a p*ro*mys vn-to my dul corage,
Seyde, ye, my lord, shulde haue compassyou*n*,
Off royal pite supporte me in myn age;
Wherof I caught a man*er* avau*n*tage,
Thoughte I wolde rather condyscende
To your desir than your byddyng offende.

I plucked up my heart to obey your command, knowing that although skill were wanting, good will might prevail; for will has more might than force in battle.

Tobeye* your precept I plukkyd vp myn herte,
Caste in my conceyt though konnyng did[e] faylle;
By good avys I did also adverte,
How in suych caas good wyl myghte moost p*re*vaylle:
Wyl hath more myght than force hath in bataylle;
And with that thought inwardly supprysed,
For to p*ro*cede I was fully avysed.

And in excuse of my rudeness I ask mercy for my poor heart's ease, that this book may please you — to me the best reward.

But for exskus first of my rudnesse,
To suych as lyst haue of this book dissdeyn,
That ye, my lord, of mercyful goodnesse,
Whan this translaciou*n* ye haue rad and seyn,
Though it be spoke in wordys bare and pleyn,
I axe mercy for my poore hertys ese,
To me best guerdou*n*, so that it may yow plese.

3346. cotidian R 3, quotidian P — shal] that H 1766, R 3.
3359. Tobeye] Two obeye H 1766.
3362. p*re*vaylle] avail R 3. 3372. me] be R 3.

Yiff ought be wryte or seid to your plesau*n*ce,
The thank be yove to your royal noblesse;
And wher I faylle, atwyteth ygnorau*n*ce,
Al the diffautys aret to my rudnesse,
With this annexyd, requeryng of humblesse,
That alle thoo which shal this makyng rede,
For to correcte wher-as they se nede.

If aught be said to your pleasure, let the thanks be given to your royal noblesse, and all the faults laid to my lack of skill.

So it be doon with supportaciou*n*
Off ther goodnesse to be favourable,
Nat to pynche of indignaciou*n*,
Which wer to me verray importable.
And ye, my lord, for to be mercyable,
Off your hyh grace my good wyl to considre,
An hors with foure feet may stou*m*ble among* and slydre.

Let all correct where they see need, and be favourable to me of their goodness. Even with four feet a horse sometimes slips and stumbles.

And semblably though I goo nat vp-ryght,
But stowpe and halte for lak of elloquence,
Though Omerus hold nat the torche lyght
To forthre my penne with colours of cadence,
Nor moral Senek, moost sad of his sentence,
Gaff me no part of his moralytees,
Therfore I seye, thus knelyng on my knees:

And although I go stooping and halting along, Homer did not hold the torch to further my pen, nor did moral Senek lend me his moralities.

To alle thoo that shal this book be-holde,
I them be-seke to haue compassyou*n*,
And ther-with-al I prey hem that they wolde
Favoure the metre and do correccyou*n*;
Off gold nor asewr I hadde no foysou*n*,
Nor othir colours this p*ro*cesse tenlvmyne,
Sauff whyte and blak; and they but dully shyne.

Therefore I say to all who read this book, have compassion, pass lightly over the metre, and correct where you find need. I had no colours, but only white and black, and they shine but dully.

I nevir was aqueynted with Virgyle,
Nor with [the] sugryd dytees of Omer,
Nor Dares Frygius with his goldene style,
Nor with Ovyde, in poetrye moost entieer,
Nor with the sou*er*eyn balladys of Chauceer,*
Which among alle that eu*er*e wer rad or songe,
Excellyd al othir in our Englyssh tou*n*ge.

I never had acquaintance with Virgil nor Homer nor Dares nor Ovid, nor with the sovereign ballads of Chaucer, who excelled all other poets of our tongue.

I can nat been a iuge in this mateer,
As I conceyve folwyng my fantasye,
In moral mateer ful notable was Goweer,

I am no judge, but Gower and Strode were notable in their philosophy

3386. among] anoon H 1766, R 3. 3389. hold] heeld R 3.
3405. Chauuceer H 1766. 3409. my] in R 3.

and Richard Hermit, who wrote the Prick of Conscience;

And so was Stroode in his philosophye,
In parfyt* lyvyng, which passith poysye,
Richard Hermyte, contemplatyff of sentence,
Drowh in Ynglyssh the Prykke of Conscience.

yet as the summer sun surpasses all other stars and as Lucina chases away the dark clouds, so my master Chaucer, who also wrote tragedies, had no peer.

As the gold-tressyd bryght[e] somyr sonne
Passith othir sterrys with his beemys clere,
And as Lvcyna chaseth skyes donne,
The frosty nyghtes whan Esp*er*us doth appere,
Ryght* so my mayst*er* had[de] nevir pere, —
I mene Chauceer* — in stooryes that he tolde;
And he also wrot tragedyes olde.

Petrarch and John Bochas complained the Fall of Princes, how they were cast down for their sins, and so did Chaucer in the Monk's Tale.

The Fal of Prynces gan pitously co*m*pleyne,
As Petrark did, and also Iohn Bochas;
Laureat Fraunceys, poetys bothe tweyne,
Toold how prynces for ther greet trespace
Wer ovirthrowe, rehersyng al the caas,
As Chauceer* did[e] in the Monkys Tale.
But I that stonde lowe dou*n* in the vale,

But I, who stand low in the vale, made this book by constraint and not presumption — born in a village called Lydgate, where was once a castle beaten down in the time of the Danes.

So greet a book in Ynglyssh to translate,
Did it be constreynt and no presumpciou*n*.
Born in a vyllage which callyd is Lydgate,
Be old[e] tyme a famous castel tou*n*;
In Danys tyme it was bete dou*n*,
Tyme whan Seynt Edmond, martir, mayde and kyng,
Was slayn at Oxne, be recoord of wrytyng.

I was never yet at Cithæron nor on Mt. Parnassus, where the nine Muses dwell; and where I fail let Lydgate bear the blame.

I me excuse, now this book is I-doo,
How I was nevir yit at Cytherou*n*,
Nor on the mou*n*teyn callyd Pernaso,
Wheer nyne musys haue ther mansyou*n*.
But to* conclude myn entenciou*n*,
I wyl p*ro*cede forth with whyte and blak;
And where I faylle let Lydgate ber the lak.

The subject matter of this translation is in part sad and needs no flourishings or flowers of rhetoric.

Off this translacyou*n* considred the mat*er*e,
The p*ro*cesse is in party lamentable;
Wooful clausys of custom they requere,
No rethoryques nor florysshynges delyctable:
Lettrys of compleynt requere colour sable,

3412. parfight H 1766. 3419. Rygtht H 1766.
3420, 27. Chauuceer H 1766.
3432. Be] In R 3. 3435. be] *om.* P.
3440. to] two H 1766.
3446. delitable R 3.

And tragedyes in especial
Be rad and songe at feestys fun*er*al.

This book remembryng of the sodeyn fallys
Off famous prynces and surquedous pryncessys,
That wer vnwarly cast from ther royal stallys,
Which wer in erthe worshepyd as goddessys,
Ynde stonys vpon ther goldene tressys, —
What was ther ende? Rede Bochas, ye shal se,
By fatal spynnyng of Parchas sustryn thre.

The book remembers the sudden falls of famous princes and proud princesses, who were worshipped as goddesses on earth. What was their end? Read Bochas and you shall see.

Off this mat*er*e ther be bookys nyne,
Alle of Fortunys transmutaciou*n*s;
This blynde lady, how she made hem declyne
From ther moost famous exaltaciou*n*s:
Somme plou*n*gyd dou*n* to the infernal dongou*n*s,
With cruel Pluto depe dou*n* in helle,
With P*ro*serpyna perpetuelly to dwelle.

There are nine books, and all tell of the transmutations of Fortuna,

For* ther demerytes and lakkyng of vertu,
That they lyst nat ther Sou*er*eyn Lord to knowe:
For whoo is rekkeles to serve our Lord I*es*u,
Fortvnys wheel shal soone hym ovir-throwe,
Though Famys trompet of gold [a]lowde blowe
His victoryes, his marcial renou*n*s,
Rad and remembryd in dyvers regiou*n*s.

and of those who fell for their faults, who did not care to know the Sovereign Lord.

Whoo knoweth nat God is falle fer in slouthe;
Be-war ye Prynces eu*er*e of thynges tweyne:
In eu*er*y quarel that your grou*n*d be trouthe;
Next in ordre, doth your besy peyne
To love I*es*u, your Lord moost sovereyne,
Truste hym of herte, and he shal nat faylle
To be your socour in pees and in bataylle.

Beware, Princes, that in every quarrel your ground is truth; and do not fail to love and trust Jesus, who will be your succour.

For lak of trust twyes I sey, allas,
And make her-oon an exclamaciou*n*:
Alle the myschevys remembryd in Bochas,
Fro tyme of Crystes in-carnaciou*n*,
Haue been for lakkyng of devociou*n*,
That ye Prynces, of wylful necligence,
Lyst nat to God do dewe reu*er*ence.

Princes, you are no gods,

3464. For] Two H 1766.
3467. soone hym] hym sone R 3.
3468. alowde R 3. *Space of one stanza left here in* R 3 (214d) *but no omission of text.*
3478. H 5 *begins again with this line,* leaf 181.

but mortal men, more likely to fall than a beggar; and the most grievous fall is of those who sit highest.

Dysdeyneth nat to haue in remembrau*n*ce,
Ye be no goddys, ye be but men mortal;
Stonde vndir dau*n*geer of Fortunys chau*n*ce,
More lyk to towmble and more neer to* fal,
Than doth a beggere in this lyff mortal:
Off vertuous poore the fal is nat vnsoffte;
Moost grevous fal, of them that sitte aloffte.

Princes, do not stand in such case; for when Death comes you know no better help than the poor, no more than did rich Cyrus or Sardanapalus.

Ye Prynces quake, stond not in suych[e] caas;
Yit whan deth comyth, ye can no bet socour
Than can* the pore, record of Iohn Bochas;
Hath myndc heron and make yow a merour
Off suych as regnyd in glorye and [gret] honour,
As ryche Cyrus and Sardanapalle,
How fro the wheel of Fortune they wer falle.

Set not your trust on false Fortune: all this book treats of such as did so from Adam, who was expelled from Paradise,

Set nat your trust, beth war of fals Fortune;
For al this book tretith of suych mat*er*e,
Gynneth his p*ro*cesse, and so forth doth contvne
Lamentable and doolful for to here,
How Adam first, with a ful hevy chere,
From a place moost sou*er*eyn of delys
Whylom departyd, out of Paradys,

down to King John, who reigned in France and was taken prisoner at Poitiers

Cherubyn kepyng* the gate of Paradys
With brennyng swerd that ther shulde entre noon.
This book conveyed by ful greet avys,
Ceryously from Adam to Kyng Iohn,
Regnyng in Frau*n*ce; of whoom nat yoore agoon
I sawh remembryd the date of thylk[e] yeerys,
Whan he was take prysowneer at Peyterys,

in 1356, the last of all in this book.

A thousand toold by computaciou*n*,
Thre hundryd ovir, fyffty and sex yeer,
Trewly reknyd fro the Incarnaciou*n*,
Whan seid[e] Iohn was take prysowneer,
Toold and remembryd by the cronycleer.
As Adam was first that did[e] falle,
So in this book Kyng Iohn was last of alle.

We had never stood in such peril nor dread

We hadde nevir stondyn in dau*n*geer
Off worldly stryff nor p*er*ellys ful mortal,

3488. to] a H 1766, P, H 5. 3489. mortal] morall R 3.
3490. poore] power P. 3492. suyche] no such P.
3493. can] cam H 1766.
3506. kepyng] abydyng kepyng H 1766, H, R 3, P — gate] gatis H, gatys H 5.

Nor dreed of deth, nat in a thousand yeer,
Nor of Fortune that tournyth as a bal,
Yiff Adam hadde in Paradys had no* fal;
Touch of an appyl and inobedyence, —
Cause that Fortune is had in suych reu*er*ence.

of death nor of Fortune had it not been for Adam's fall in Paradise;

But for to telle and speke in wordys pleyn,
How Fortune kaught first an interesse
To be callyd, nat trewly but in veyn,
Off worldly peple a fals froward goddesse, —
This errour gan of bestial rudnesse,
Demyng them-sylff they wern assuryd wel,
Whan they sat hyh on hire vntrusty wheel.

and for that reason Fortune first came to be called a false goddess by worldly people, an error that began of brutish ignorance.

Rekne vp alle thoo that* haue doon hire seruice
And folwyd on in ther oppynyou*n*,
Lyk as this book in ordre doth devyse;
Peyse in ballau*n*ce: what was ther guerdou*n*?
A sodeyn reys, an vnwar tou*m*blyng dou*n*;
Yit, for al this, thorugh hire flaterye,
Al worldly peple doth hire magneffye!

Reckon up all who did her service — what was their reward? A sudden rise, an unexpected tumbling down. Yet all worldly people worship her.

[¶ The laste lenvoye direct vn to my lord.] [1]

NOBLE Prynce, remembreth al this thynges,
Peyseth* of resou*n*, lefft vp your eye and se,
As your lyne conveyed is fro kynges,
How vertu longeth vn-to dignyte.*
[What folwith afftyr? grace & prosperite.]
Hath this in mynde and theron doth attende,
Mawgre Fortvnys mutabilite,*
Ye shal to-Godward encresyn and ascende.

Noble Prince, remember that virtue belongs to dignity: have this in mind, and in spite of Fortune's mutability you shall prosper and ascend to God.

Off humble entent, with herte & hand quakyng,
Directe this book vn-to your mageste;
In which ye may, at good leyseer redyng,
Seen dyvers chau*n*ges of worldly vanyte, —
Prynces cast dou*n* from ther imp*er*yal se,

This book, in which you may see many changes of worldly vanity, is humbly addressed to your majesty.

3524. no] a H 1766. 3534. that] than H 1766.
3542. Peyseth] Peysed H 1766.
3544. vn-to dignyte] afftir grace and p*ro*sp*er*ite H 1766.
3546. theron] þ*er* of R 3 — attende] attende p*ar*de H 1766.
3547. mutabilite] whan she wyl pretende H 1766. *After* 3547 H 1766 *inserts:* "Whyl ye in vertu regne & dygnite."

[1] *The heading and following six stanzas are supplied from* MS. Harley 1766, leaf 264 verso, *collated with* R3, H5 *and* P.

For they wer froward, lyst nat condiscende
Vertu to sewe and vices [for] to fle,
So to-Godward tencresen and ascende.

Let the chastising by Providence of men for vicious living and lack of grace be a mirror to you! Where virtue reigns there is felicity. Although your estate shine like Phœbus, there is no certainty how long you may abide here; age and her cousin infirmity claim their right; death will take no bribe: provide yourself daily to increase in virtue while you are still free.

Fal of othir thorugh vicious lyvyng,
So*mm*e dysgradyd vn-to ful lowh degre,
Off p*ro*vidence lat ther chastysyng
For lak of g*ra*ce, to yow a merour be.
Wher vertu regnyth, ther is felycite
In suych as lyst ther froward lyff tamende;
Whoo lovith that Lord which hath the sou*er*eynte
Shal ay be grace encresyn and ascende.

Though your estat lyk Pheb*us* wer shynyng,
Yit, for al that, ye haue no sewerte,
How long[e] tyme is here your abydyng;
Age, wit*h* hire cosyn callyd Infirmyte,
Wyl cleyme hire ryght of verry dewete;
Deth takith no mede; afforn he wyl not sende.
Provide your-sylff whyl ye haue liberte,
Dayly in vertu tencresyn and ascende.

As men deserve shall they be punished or rewarded. Beware in time, for tongues are free and your story shall read according to your merit.

As men dysserve, be record of wrytyng,
An exp*er*t thyng by old auctoryte,
Ye shal receyve your mede or your punysshyng,
By egal peys of trouthe and equite.
Beth war afforn, folk haue ther tou*n*ges fre,
Lyk your dyscert shal rede your legende;
This verray soth, voyde of duplycite,
Yevith hem cause to preye ye may ascende.

If virtue guide you, then good report shall follow your parting from this world.

Off hyh prudence aforn ymagynyng,
Yiff vertu guye your magnanymyte,
Than good[e] repoort afftir your partyng
Shal floure and shyne in eu*ery* comou*n*te.
Almesse partyd to folk in poverte,
And compassyou*n* the poraylle to amende,
Is beest[e] mene toward the hevenly se
By vertuous lyff tencresyn and ascende.

3558. dysgrated H 5. 3563. that] ye P.
3571. your-sylff] your lyfe P.
3575. 1st your] to your R 3, P — 2nd your] *om.* H 5.
3578. shal] to R 3. 3579. soth] trouthe H 5.

¶ Woordis of the translatur vn to his book atte ende.[1]

WITH lettre* & leuys go litil book trembling, [p. 447]
Pray to þe Prince to haue on the pite,
Voide of picture & enlumyny[n]g,
Which hast of Cithero no corious dite,
Nor of his gardyn no flour[e]s of beute;
God graunt[e] grace thi reudnesse nat offende
The hih noblesse, the magnanymyte
Of his presence, whan thou shalt up ascende.

Go, little book, pray to the prince for pity. Thou hast no bright colours, no curious songs of Cithæron, no flowers of beauty: God grant that thy rudeness offend not his presence.

And, for my part, of oon hert abidyng,
Void of chaung and mutabilite,
I do presente this book with hand shaking,
Of hool affeccioun knelyng on my kne,
Praying the Lord, the Lord oon, too & thre,
Whos magnificence no clerk can comprehende,
To sende you miht, grace and prosperite
Euer in vertu tencresen & ascende.

And I, kneeling on my knee, with shaking hand do present this book of whole affection, praying the Lord to send you might, grace, and prosperity.

Finis libri Amen.

¶ Go kis the steppis of them that wer forthring,
Laureat poetes, which hadde souereynte
Of elloquence to supporte thy makyng,
And pray all tho that shal this processe see,
In thyn excus[e], that thei list to bee
Fauourable to lakke or to comende;
Set thi ground upon humylite,
Vnto ther grace that thou maist up ascende.

Go kiss the steps of those laureate poets who supported thy making, and be humble that thou mayst ascend unto the grace of men.

In a short clause thi content rehersing,
As oon up clymbeth to gret prosperite,
So another, bi expert knowleching,
Fro gret richesse is brouht to pouerte.
Alas, O book, what shal I seyn of the?
Thi tragedies thoruh al the world to sende,

Since one man climbs up to prosperity and another falls from wealth to poverty, alas, O book, what shall I say of thee?

3589. lettre] lettres B, letter P, lettir H, lettyr H 5.
3596. his] their H. 3599. shaking] quakyng H.
3601. 2nd Lord] *om.* P. 3602. can] may P.

[1] "The wordys of the translatour." MS. J. leaf 183d.

Go foorth, I pray; excuse thi-silf & me;
Who loueth most vertu hiest shal ascende.

Thou art clad in the black of complaint and mourning, thou art called the Fall of Princes, intermingled with adversity and joy; and those who will prosper must ascend by virtue.

Blak be thi weede of co*m*pleynt & moornyng,
Callid Fall of P*r*incis from ther felicite,
Lik chau*n*teplure, now si*n*gyng now weepi*ng*,
Wo afftir merthe, next ioie aduersite,
So entermedlid ther is no seurete,
Lik as this book doth preise and rep*re*hende, —
Now on the wheel, now set in louh degre;
Who wil encrece bi vertu must ascende.

Finis totius libri.

[Explicit John Bochas.] [1]

[1] MS. J. leaf 184 recto.

[Greneacres A Lenvoye vpon John Bochas.] [1]

Blake be thy bondes and thy wede alsoo,
Thou sorowfull book of matier disespeired,
In tokne of thyn inward mortal woo,
Which is so badde it may not be enpeired.
Thou owest nat outward to be feired,
That inward hast so many a rufull clause;
Such be thyn habite of colo*ur* as thi cause.

No cloth of tyssewe ne veluet crymesyne,
But lik thi monke, moorny*ng* vnder his hood,
Go weile and wepe *with* wofull Proserpyne,
And lat thi teeres multeplie the flood
Of blak Lythey vnder the bareyn wood,
Where-as goddesse hath hir hermytage,—
Helpe hir to wepe, and she wyll geve the wage.

Noblesse of Ioye sith thou maist nat approche,
This blak goddesse I councell the tobeie.
Compleyne *with* hir vnder the craggy roche,
With wepyng soules vpon the said Lythey,
Sith thou of sorowe art instrument and keye,—
So harpe and synge there, as thou may be herde;
For euery Ioie is of thi name afferd.

Pryncesse of woo and wepyng, Proserpyne,
Whiche herborowest sorow euen at thyn hert[e] roote,
Admytte this Bochas for a man of thyne;
And though his habite blakker be than soote,
Yitt was it maked of thi monkes boote,
That him translated in Englissh of Latyne:
Therfore now take him for a man of thyne.

1. bondes] hondes P, P 1.
4. impeyred P.
5. feared P.
6. Ruffull J.
8. cremesyne P 1, P.
20. mayst P.
21. euery] euer P, P 1.
26. boote] hode P, P 1.

[1] *The Envoy by Greneacres is supplied from* MS. J. leaf 184 recto, *collated with* P 1 *and* P.

APPENDIX.

¶ The Daunce of Machabree[1]

wherin is liuely expressed and shewed the state of manne, and howe he is called at vncertaine tymes by death, and when he thinketh least thereon: made by thaforesayde Dan John Lydgate Monke of Burye.

¶ The Prologe

O YE folkes hard hearted as a stone,
Whiche to this worlde geue* al your aduertence,
Lyke as it should euer lasten in one, —
Where is your wit, where is your prouidence
To seen aforne the sodayn violence
Of cruel death, that be so wyse and sage,
Which slayeth, alas, by stroke or pestilence
Both yong & olde of lowe and high parage?

Death spareth nought low ne high degre,
Popes, kynges, ne worthye Emperours;
Whan they shine most in felicite,
He can abate the freshnes of her flours,
Her bright[e] sunne clipsen with his shours,
Make them plunge fro her sees lowe; —
Mauger the might of al these conquerours,
Fortune hath them from her whele ythrow.

1. folkes] folkes that bene, Harley 116 = H.
2. this world geue] the worlde haue, Tottel = T.
3. laste eu*er* H. 6. be] dethe *corrected to* slethe H.
7.] *om.* H. 8. high and loue H. 9. hight ne law H.
10. in thaire felicite H. 15. Maugre H.

[1] The text, here printed because of its interest in connexion with the "Fall of Princes," is based on Tottel's edition (fol. ccxx to end of fol. ccxxiiii), collated with MS. Harley 116 and in part with MS. Lansdowne 669. The punctuation and use of capital letters have been modernized, and *th* substituted for *y* (þ). A superior text will be included by Miss Hammond in her forthcoming "Fifteenth Century Anthology." The two anonymous woodcuts (size of originals 160 x 110 and 158 x 110) are reproduced from Tottel. They are in both drawing and composition very superior to the average English woodcut of the period and of considerable interest as the work of an unknown designer of great talent.

Considereth this, ye folkes that been wyse,
And it emprinteth in your memoriall,
Like thensample which that at Parise
I fonde depict ones vppon* a wal
Full notably, as I rehearse shall.
Of a Frenche clarke takyng acquaintau*n*ce,
I toke on me to translaten all
Out of the Frenche Machabrees daunce.

By whose aduise and counsayle at the lest,
Through her stieryng and her mocion,
I obeyed vnto her request,
Therof to make a playn translacion
In English tonge, of entencion
That proud[e] folkes that bene stout and bolde,
As in a mirrour toforne in her reason
Her vgly fine there clearely may beholde.

By [this] ensample, that thei in her ententes
Amend her life in euery maner age.
The which[e] daunce at Sainct Innocentes
Portrayed is, with all the surplusage,
Youen vnto vs our liues to correct
And to declare the fine of our passage, —
Right anone my stile I wil direct
To shewe this worlde is but a pilgrimage.

¶ The ende of the Prologe.

¶ The Wordes of the Translatour.

O CREATURES ye th*a*t bene reasonable,
The life desiring which is eternall,
Ye may se*n* here doctrine ful notable
Your life to lead[e], which th*a*t is mortall,
Thereby to learne in especiall,
How ye shal trace the daunce of Machabree,
To man and woman ylike naturall;
For death ne spareth high ne lowe degree.

In this myrour euery wight may fynde,
That him behoueth to gone vpon this dau*n*ce.
Who goeth toforne or who shall go behynde,
All dependeth in Goddes ordinaunce.
Wherfore eche man lowly take* his chaunce;
Death spareth nouther poore ne* bloud royall:
Eche* ma*n* therfore haue this in reme*m*brau*n*ce,
Of oo matter God hath yforged all.

¶ The Daunce of Machabree.

20. vppon] in T. 30. that] whiche H.
32. may clerly ther H. *Line* 40 *is misplaced after line* 36 H.
41. ye] *om.* Lansdowne 699 = L. 42. which] þat H.
46. of Machabree] which that ye see L. 47. ylike] that be L.
49. wight] man L. 51. toforne] before L — shall go] goth L.
53. eche man lowly take] lowly euery man T.
54. nouther poore ne] not poore ne yet T. 55. Eche] euery T.

Cunctis mortalibus mors debetur.

¶ Death fyrst speaketh vnto the Pope, and after to euery degree as foloweth.

YE that been set most high in* dignitie
Of al estates in earth spirituall,
And like to* Peter hath the souerayntee
Ouer the church and states temporall,
Vpon this daunce ye first begin[ne] shall,
As most worthy lord and gouernour;
For al the worship of your estate papall,
And of [al] lordship to God is the honour.

The Pope maketh aunswere.

FYRST me behoueth this daunce for to lede,
Which sat in earth[e] highest in my see,
The state ful perilous, whoso taketh hede,
To occupie Seynt Petris* dignitee;
But for al that [fro] Death I may not flee,
Vpon* this daunce with other for to trace;
For which al honor, who prudently can see,
Is litle worth that doth so soone passe.

57. most] *om.* L — high in] in high T.
59. to] as T, H — hath] have L, hadde H.
60. chirche most in especiall L. 61. ye] *om.* H.
64. of] *om.* H. 65. for] with deth L. 67. ful] *om.* L.
68. Seynt Petris] Peters T, H. 69. fro] *om.* H.
70. Vpon] On T, H — this] his H. 71. which al] sich L.

Death speaketh to the Emperour.

SYR Emperour, lord of al the grounde,
[Most] souereine prince, surmountyng* of noblesse,
Ye mot forsake of gold your apple round,
Scepter and swerde, & al your high prowesse;
Behind you leue* your treasour and* riches,
And with other to my daunce obey:
Against my might is worth none hardines,
Adams children al they must[e] deye.

The Emperour maketh aunswer.

I NOTE to whom that I may [me] appeale
Touching death, which doth me so co*n*strein;
There is no gin to helpen my querel,
But spade and pickoys my graue to atteyne, —
A simple shete, there is nomore to seyn,
To wrappen in my body and visage:
And therupon I may me sore* compleyne,
That lordes great haue litle auauntage.

Death speaketh to the Cardinal.

YE been abashed, it semeth, and in drede,
Syr Cardinal, it sheweth by your chere;
But yet for-thy ye folowe shall in dede,
With other folke my daunce for to lere.
Your great aray, al shal [ye] leauen here, —
Your hat of red, your vesture of great coste;
All these thynges reckoned well in fere,*
In great[e] honour good auyse is loste.

The Cardinall maketh aunswere.

I HAUE great cause, certes this is no faile
To be abashed and greatly dread[e] me,
Sith Death is come me sodainly tassaile,*
That I shall neuer hereafter clothed be
In grise nor ermine like vnto my degree,
Mine hat of red leuen eke in distresse, —
By which I haue conceyued* wel and see
That worldly* ioye endeth in heauines.

Death speaketh to the Kyng.

O NOBLE Kyng, most worthy of renoun,
Come foorth anone, for al your worthines
That whylom had about you enuiron
Great royaltie and passing hye noblesse.

74. Most] *om.* H — surmountyng] & highest T, H.
75. mot] muste L, moste H.
77. you leue] leten T, L — and] and your T, L.
79. ' is worth] worthe is H. 81. me] *om.* L. 83. gin] bote H.
87. And theruppon I may me sore] wherupon sore I me T, L.
88. litle auauntage] so lytell vayntage H.
93. ye] *om.* L — leve H. 95. fere] feare T, L.
99. tassaile] to assaile T. 100 *and* 101 *are transposed in* H.
103. conceyued] learned T, L.
104. That] How that T, L — worldly] al T, L.

But right anon [for] al your great highnes,
Sole from your men in hast ye shall it lete,
Who most aboundeth here in great riches,
Shall beare with hym but a [single] shete.

The Kyng maketh aunswere.

I HAUE nought learned here-toforn to dau*n*ce
No daunce in sooth of footyng so sauage,
Where-through I se by clere demonstraunce,
What pride is worth or force of high linage!
Death all fordo[e]th, this is his vsage,
Great and smal that in this world soiourne:
Who is most meke, I hold[e] hym most sage;
For we shall all to dede* ashes tourne.

Death speaketh to the Patriarche.

SYR Patriarche, al your hu*m*ble chere
Ne quiteth you nought nor your humilitie;
Your double crosse of gold and stones clere,
Your power whole and al your dignitie
Some other shall of very equitie
Possede anon, as I rehearse can:
Trusteth neuer that ye shall Pope be;
For foly* hope deceiueth many a man!

The Patriarche maketh aunswere.

WORLDLY honour, gret treasour & riches
Haue me deceiued soothfastly in dede;
Mine old[e] ioyes been turned to* tristesse!
What auayleth such treasours to possede?
Hie clymbyng* vp a fall hath for his mede.
Great estates folke wasten out of number;
Who mounteth high, it is sure and no drede,
Great[e] burden doth hym oft encomber.

Death speaketh to the Cunstable.

IT is my ryght to arest you and constreyne
With vs to daunce, my mayster Sir Cunstable!
For more stro*n*ger tha*n* euer was Charlemain,
Death hath afforced, and more worshipable;
For hardines ne knighthode, this no* fable,
Nor stro*n*g armure of plates ne* of maile, —
What gayneth armes of folkes most notable,
Whan cruell death list hem* to assayle?

The Cunstable maketh aunswere.

MY purpose was and whole entencio*n*
To assail castel[le]s & mighty fortresses,
And bryng[e] folke vnto subieccion,
To seke honour, fame, and great richesses;

109. for] *om.* L. 112. single] *om.* L.
119. I holde hym] holde he is H. 120. dede] the dead T, L.
121. al] *with* all H. 128. foly] holy T, L. 131. to] into T, L.
133. Hie clymbyng] It climbeth T, L.
140. afforced] enforcede H.
141. this] *om.* H — no] is no T, L, H. 142. ne] nother T, L.
144. hem] him T. 146. fortresse H. 148. richesse H.

But I see that al worldly prowesse
Death can abate, which is a great despite;
To him alone, sorow and eke swetenes:
For agaynst death is found[e] no respite. 152

Death speaketh to the Archebishop.

SYR Archebishop, why do ye you withdrawe
So frowardly, as it wer by disdayne?
Ye must approche [vn] to my mortall lawe;
It to contrary it wer but* in vayne: 156
For day by day there is none other gayne,
Death at the hand pursueth euery coast;
Prest and debte mot bee yelde againe,
And at a daye men counten with her host. 160

The Archebishop maketh aunswere.

ALAS, I wote not what* partie for to flee,
For drede of death I haue so gret distres!
Tescape* his might I can no refute see;
That who-so knew his co*n*streint and duresse, 164
He would[e] take reason to maistresse.
Adue my treasour, my pompe & pride also,
My painted cha*m*bers, my port & my freshnes, —
Thyng that behoueth nedes mot be do. 168

Death speaketh to the Barone.

YE that among[es] Lordes and Barons
Haue had so long[e] worship and renoun,
Foryet your trumpetes and your clarions;
This is no dreame nor simulacion. 172
Whylom your custom and entencion
Was with ladies to daunsen in the shade;
But oft it happeth, in conclusion,
One man breaketh that another made. 176

The Baron maketh aunswere.

FULL oft[e] sith I haue been auctorised
To high e*m*prises & thi*n*ges of gret fame.
Of high & low my thanke also deuised,
Cherished *with* ladies & women high of name; 180
Ne neuer on me was put no defame,
In lordes courte,* which that was notable;
But deathes stroke hath made me [so] lame:
Under heauen in earth is nothyng stable. 184

Death speaketh to the Princesse.

COME forth anon, my Lady good Princesse,
Ye must also gon vpon this daunce.
Nought may auayle your great strau*n*genesse,
Nether your beauty nor your gret pleasau*n*ce, 188

153. you] so H. 155. vnto] to L.
156. but] nought but T, L. 158. the] *om.* H.
159. debte] death L. 160. a] oo H. 161. what] to what T, L.
163. Tescape] To escape T. 166. &] my H.
182. courte] of court T, L. 183. so] *om.* L.

Your riche aray, nother your daliaunce,
That whylom couth so many holde in hond
In loue, for al your double variaunce.
Ye mot as nowe this footyng vnderstonde.

The Princesse maketh aunswere.

ALAS, I see there is none other boote,
Deth hath in earth no lady nor maistres,
And* on this daunce yet mot I nedes fote:
For there nis quene, countesse ne dutchesse,
Flouring in bountie nor in her fayrenes,
That shode of Death mot passe the passage,
When our beautie and counterfeit fairnes
Dieth, adue then our rimpled age!

Death speaketh to the Bishop.

MY Lord Sir Bishop, with miter & crosse,
For al your riches, soothlye I ensure,
For all your treasour [so longe] kept in closse,
Your worldly goodes and goodes of nature,
[And] of your shepe the ghostly dredeful* cure,
With charge committed to your prelacie,
For to accoumpt ye shal be brought to lure, —
No wight is sure that climbeth ouer hye.

The Bishop maketh aunswere.

MINE heart truely is nother glad ne mery,
Of sodein tidinges which that ye [me] bring;
My feast is turned vnto a simple ferye,*
That for discomfort me list nothyng [to] syng.
The world contrarie now to my* werking,
Which al estates* can so disherite;
He al with-halt, alas, at our partyng,
And al* shall passe saue onely our merite.

Death speaketh to the Squyer.

COMMETH forth Syr Squyer, right fresh of your araye,
That conne of daunces al the new[e] guise,
Thoghe ye bare armes, fresshe horsed yesterday,*
With spere & shielde at your vncouth deuise,

195. And] & T — this] his H. 197. bountie] beaute H.
198.] That she of right most nedys the trace sew H — shode] shooe T. 199. When] For to H.
200.] Our Reueled age saith farwell adiev H.
201. with] your H. 203. For] *om.* H — so longe] *om.* L.
205. And] *om.* L — ghostly dredeful] dredeful ghostly T, L.
210. me] *om.* L.
211. vnto a simple ferye] into simple terie T, L.
212. to] *om.* L.
213. contrarie now to my] contrarieth to me now in T — world] word L — now] *om.* L — my] me in L.
214. Which al estatis] That al folkes T, H.
215.] And needis we must on to our departyng L.
216. And al] Al thyng T, H.
217. *This stanza is omitted in* L — Commeth] Come H — of] in H. 218. davnce H.
219.] If ye bare harnes freshly horsed yesterday T.

And toke on you so many high emprise,
Daunseth with vs; it wyl no better be;
There is no succour in no maner wyse:
For no man may fro Deathes stroke flee.

The Squyer maketh aunswere.

SITHENS that Death me holdeth in his lase,
Yet shal I speake oo worde or that* I passe:
Adue al myrth, adue now al solace,
Adue my ladies whilom so freshe of face,
Adue beautie, pleasaunce, and al solace!
Of Deathes chaunge euery day is prime,
Thinke on your soules or* that Death manace;
For all shal rot, and no man wot what time.

Death speaketh to the Abbot.

COMMETH forth Syr Abbot, with your brode hatte,
Beeth nought abashed thogh* ye hauen ryght;
Great is your head, your belly rounde* and fat,
Ye mot come daunce, thogh* ye be nothyng light.
Leaueth your abbey to some other wight,
Your heyre is of age your state to occupie;
Who that is fattest, I haue hym behyght,
[Shall] in his graue* soonest putrifie.

The Abbot maketh aunswere.

OF thy manace I hauen o gret* enuy,
That I shall now leaue al* gouernau*n*ce,
But that I shal as a cloystrer dye;
This Death is to me passing great greuaunce.
My libertie nor my great habundaunce,
What may they vayle* in any maner wyse?
Yet aske I mercy with devoute* repentau*n*ce,
Thogh* in dying to late men them auise.

Death speaketh to the Abbesse.

AND ye my lady, gentle dame Abbesse,
With your mantel[le]s furred large and wyde,
Your veile, your wi*m*ple, your ryng* of gret riches,
And bedes, sister, ye mot now leyn a-syde;*
For to this daunce I must be* your guide,
Thogh* ye be tender borne of gentle bloode,
While that ye* liue for your selfe prouide;
For after death[e] no man hath no good.

222. no] not H.
225. lace H. 226. or that] ere T, L. 231. or] ere T, L.
233. Come H. 234. abashed thogh] abasht if T, L.
235. rounde] large T, H. 236. if] thogh H.
239. fattest] most fatte H. 240. Shall in his graue] In his graue shall T, L. 241. thy] these T.
241. thy manace I haue no gret] these threts haue I none T — thi tretyse L — no gret] noon L.
242. al] al the T, L. 246. vayle] auayle T, H, L.
247. devoute] heartely T, L. 248. Thogh] If T, L.
250. mantel L. 251. your ryng] passing T, H.
252. a-syde] on syde T, H. 253. must be] shalbe T.
254. Thogh] If T — borne] and borne H.
255. While that ye] Whiles that you T, L. 256. man] wyght H.

The Abbesse maketh aunswere.

ALAS that Death hath thus for me ordeined,
That in no wise I maye it nought declyne,
If it so be ful oft I am* constreined,
Brest and throte my notes out to twyne,
My chekes round vernyshed* for to shine,
Ungird ful oft to walken at the large, —
Thus cruel Death with al estates fine,
Who hath no shippe must* rowe in bote or barge.

Death speaketh to the Bayly.

COME forth, Sir Bayly, that knowen all the guise,
By your office of trouth & rightwisnes,
Ye must come to a newe assyse,
Extorcions and wronges to redresse;
Ye be somned, as lawe biddeth expresse,
To yeue accomptes the* Iudge wil you charge,
Which hath ordeined to excluden al falsnes,
That euery man shal beare his own[e] charge.

The Bayly maketh aunswere.

O THOU Lord God this is a hard iourney,
To which aforne I toke but litle hede;
My chaunce is turned, & that forthinketh me,
Whilom with iudges what me list to spede
Lay in my might, by labour oft for mede.
But sith there is no rescus by battayle,
I hold him wise that couth wel seen in dede,
Again[es] Death that none apel may vayle.

Death speaketh to the Astronomer.

COME foorth, Maister, that lookest vp so farre,
With instrumentes of Astronomie
To take the grees and hyght of euery starre;
What may auaile all your astrologie? —
Sith of Adam all the genealogie,
Made first of God to walke vpon the ground,
Death aresteth;* thus sayth theologie:
And all shall dye for an apple rounde.

The Astronomer maketh aunswere.

FOR all my craft, cunnyng and* science,
I can nought find[e] no prouision,
Ne* in the starres seke* no difference
By domifying nor calculacion,

257. thus for me] for me so L.
258. it nought declyne] nat hym eschewe L.
259. am] haue T, L. 261. vernyshed] garnished T, L.
262. Vngirt H. 264. must] he must T, L.
268. Extorcioun H. 270. the] that T, L. 274. To] To the H.
277. by] for H. 278. sith] sethyn H — by] ne H.
279. couth wel seen] cowde see H.
285. of] that of H.
287. aresteth] with arest T, L. 289. and] or T, L.
291. Ne] Nother T, L — seke] search out T, L.
292. domifying] demonstrynge H — nor] ne H.

Saue finally, in conclusion,
For to descriue our cunnyng euery dele:
There is no more by sentence of reason,
Who liueth aryght mot nedes dye well.

Death speaketh to the Burgis.

SYR Burgis, what doe ye lenger* tarye?
For all your auoyre and youre great riches,
Thoghe* ye be strong, deinous and contrary,
Toward this daunce ye mot you nedes dresse;
For your* treasour, plentie and largesse,
From other it came and shall vnto strangers.
He is a foole that in such busines,
Wot nought for whom he stuffeth his garners!

The Burgis maketh aunswere.

CERTES to me it is great displeasaunce,
To leaue al this & mai it nought assure:
Howses,* rentes, treasor & substaunce, —
Death al fordoth, suche is his nature.
Therfore wise is no creature,
That set his heart on good that moste* disseuer;
The world it lent, the worlde wil it recure;
And who most hath, lothest dyeth euer.

Death speaketh to the Chanon Seculer.

AND ye, Syr Chanon, with many great prebende,
Ye may no lenger haue distribucion
Of golde [and] siluer, largelye to dispende;
For there is nowe no consolacion
But daunce with vs, for al your high renoun.
For ye of death[e] stonde* vpon the brinke,
Ye may therof haue no delacion;
Death commeth ay when men least on him thinke.

The Chanon maketh aunswere.

MY benefice with mony personage,
God wot ful lite may me now comfort.
Death hath of me so great auauntage,
That al my riches may me nought disport, —
Amisse of gris, they wyl ayein resorte,
Vnto the world a surples and prebende.
Al is vainglory, truely to reporte,
To dyen well eche man should entende.

297. lenger] long T, L. 298. auoyre] haueur H.
299. Thoghe] Yf T, L.
300. Toward] To H — mot you] muste now H.
301. your] of al T, L. 307. Howses] How these T, L.
308. fordoth] destroieth H.
310. on] of H — moste] may T, L. 311. Ist it] is H.
318. For ye of death stonde] For if death stode T, R.
320. ay] euer H.
321. benefice] benefices H. 322. lytell H. 323. of] ouer H.
324. That] *om.* H — me nought disport] be me not support H.
325. Amys H.

Death speaketh to the Marchaunte.

YE rich Marchant, ye mot looke hitherwarde,
That passed haue ful many diuers lond
On horse, on foote, hauing most regard
To lucre & winnyng, as I vnderstond.
But now to dau*n*ce ye mot geue me your ho*n*d;
For al your labour ful litle auayleth nowe.
Adue vaynglory, both of free and bonde,
None more coueit the*n* thei that haue ynow.

The Marchaunt maketh aunswere.

BY many an hyll and many a strong[e] vale
I haue trauailed with many marcha*n*dise;
Ouer the sea downe cary many a bale
To sondrye Iles, more than I can deuyse,
Mine heart inward ay fret* with couetise,
But al for nought, now Deth me doth* co*n*strein:
For which I se, by record of the wyse,
Who al embraceth litle shall restrayne.*

Death speaketh to the Chartreux.

YEUE me your honde, with chekes dead and pale,
Caused of watche & long abstine*n*ce,
Sir Chart[e]reux, and your self auale
Vnto this daunce with humble pacience.
To striue ayein may be no resistence,
Lenger to liue set nought your memorye;
Thogh* I be lothsome as in apparence,
Aboue[n] al men Death [hath] the victorie.

The Chartreux maketh aunswere.

VNTO this* world I was dead long agon
By mine order and my profession;
And eueryman, be he neuer so strong,
Dreadeth to dye by kindly mocion
After his fleshly inclinacion.
But please to God my soule [for] to borowe
Fro Fiendes myght and fro damnacion:
Some arne to-day th*a*t shal nought be to-morow.

Death speaketh to the Sargeaunte.

COME foorth Sir Sargeaunt, with your stately mase,
Make no defence nor rebellion,
Nought may* auaile to grutche*n* in this case,
Thogh* ye be deyners of condicion:

339. downe] do H.
341. fret] fretteth T. 342. me doth T. 343. For] By H.
344. restrayne] constrein T.
351. Thogh] If T — as] *om.* H. 353. this] the T.
355. And] Thoghe H. 358. to] it to H. 359. 2nd fro] *om.* H.
362. nor] ne no H. 363. Nought may] It may nought T.
364. Thogh] If T — deynous H.

For neyther [ap]pele nor proteccion
May you fraunchise to doe nature wrong;
For there is none so sturdy chaumpion,
Thogh* he be mightie, another is also strong.

The Sargeaunt maketh aunswere.

HOWE durste thou* Death set on me arest,
That am the kynges chosen officer,
Which yesterday, both[en] east and west,
Mine office dyd, ful surquedous of chere;
But now this day I am arested here,
And can nought flee, thoh* I had it sworne.
Eche* man is loth to die, both farre & nere,
Th*a*t hath nought learned for to dye* aforne.

Death speaketh to the Monke.

SYR Monke, also with your blacke habite,
Ye may no le*n*ger hold[e] here soioure;
There is nothyng that may you here respite
Agein my might you for to doe succour;
Ye mot accompt[e] touchyng your labour,
How ye haue spe*n*d it, in dede, word & thought.
To earth and ashes turneth euery floure;
The life of man is but a thyng of nought.

The Monke maketh aunswere.

I HAD leauer in the cloyster be,
At my booke and study my seruice,
Which is a place contemplatife to see;
But I haue spent my life in mony wyse,
Like as a foole dissolute and nice.
God of his mercy graunt me repentaunce.
By chere outward hard is to deuise,
Al be not merye which that me*n* seen dau*n*ce.

Death speaketh to the Usurer.

THOU Vsurer, looke vp and beholde,
Unto wynnyng that settest al* thy payne,
Whose couetise waxeth neuer colde,
Thy gredy thrust so sore the doth constraine.
But thou shalt neuer to thy desyre attayne,
Suche an etike thyne heart[e] freten shall,
But that of pitie God his honde refraine,
One perilous stroke shal make thee losen al.

367. a champyou*n* H.
368. Thogh] If T — another is] Deth is H.
369. durste thou] dare this T.
374. can] may H — thogh] if T. 375. Eche] Euery T, H.
376. dye] be ded T. 379.] P*er* may no thinge her you respite H. 380. for] *om.* H. 381. muste H.
382. spend it in dede word] spendid worde dede H.
385. the] my H — be] to be H. 391. is] *om.* H.
392. not] no H.
394. wynnyng that settest al] thy wynnyng thou settest aye T.
397. to] *om.* H. 399. But that] That but H.
400. loosen] lese H.

The Usurer maketh aunswere.

NOW [me] behoueth sodeinly to dye,
Which is to me great paine & eke greuance.
Succour to fynde I see no maner way
Of golde nor siluer by none cheuisance;
Death through his hast abideth no puruseia*n*ce
Of folkes blynde that can nought loke wel:
Full oft happeth by kynde of fatall chaunce,
Some haue fayre eyen that seen neuer adel.

The Poore Man boroweth of the Usurer.

VSURER to God is full great offence,
And in his syght a great abusion;
The poore boroweth percase for indige*n*ce,
The riche lent by false collusion,
Onely for lucre in his entencion.
Death shal both[e] to accoumptes fette,
To make reconing by computacion:
No man is quit that is behynd of dette.

Death speaketh to the Phisicien.

MAISTER of Phisike, which on your vryne
So looke and gase and stare agaynst the sunne,
For al your craft and study of medicine,
[And] all the practike and science that ye cunne,
Your lyues* course so farre forth is yrunne,
Ayein my might your craft may not endure,
For al the gold that ye thereby* haue wunne:
Good leche is he that can himself* recure.

The Phisicien maketh aunswer.

FULL long agon that I vnto Phisike
Set my wit and eke my diligence,
In speculatife and also in practike,*
To geat a name through mine excellence,
To fynd out agaynes* pestilence
Preseruatifes to staunche it and to fine:
But I dare [say] shortly in sentence,
Againes* Death is worth no medicine.

Death speaketh to the Amerous Squyre.

YE that be ge*n*tle, so fresh & amerous,
Of yeres yo*n*g flouring in your grene age,
Lusty [and] fre, of hert eke* desirous,
Ful of deuises & chaunge in your courage,

402. eke] *om.* H.
406. loke] se H. 407. chaunce] chaunge H.
409. *This stanza is omitted in* H.
416. No *is repeated in* T.
417. on] in H. 421. lyues] life T.
423. ye thereby] thereby ye T — haue] hath H.
424. can himself] himself can T. 426. eke] *om.* H.
427. practike] pracktife T.
429. agaynes] agaynst T.
432. Againes] Say that against T.
435. eke] & eke T, and (*the rest erased*) H.

Pleasaunt of port, of loke and of visage:
But al shal turne into ashes dead;
For al beautie is but a faynt ymage,
Which stealeth away or folkes can take hede.

The Squyer maketh aunswer.

ALAS, alas, I can nowe no succour
Agaynes* Death[e] for myselfe prouide!
A-due of youth the lusty fresh[e] flower,
Adue vainglory of beautie and of pride,*
Adue all seruice of the god Cupide,
Adue my Ladies, so fresh so wel beseyn:
For agayn[s] Death nothyng may abyde,
And windes great gon doun with litle rein.

Death speaketh to the Gentlewoman.

COME forth Maistresse, of yeres yonge and grene,
Which hold your selfe of beautie souereyn,
As fayre as ye was whilom Pollixene,
Penelope and the quene Helein.
Yet on this daunce thei went[e] both[e] tweyne,
And so shall ye, for al your straungenesse;
Thogh* daunger long in loue hath lad your rein,
Arested is your chaunge of doublenes.

The Gentlewoman maketh aunswer.

O CRUEL Death, that spareth none estate,
To old and yong thou art indifferent;
To my beautie thou hast said checkmate,
So hasty is thy mortail iudgement.
For in my youth[e] this was mine entent,
To my seruice many man to haue lured;
But she is a foole, shortly in sent[e]ment,
That in her beautie is to muche assured.

Death speaketh to the Man of Law.

SYR Aduocate, short proces for to make,
Ye mot come plete afore the* high[e] iudge.
Many a quarel* ye haue vndertake
And for lucre done to folke refuge;
But my fraunchise is so large and huge
That counsayle none auaile may but trouth:
He scapeth wisely of death the great deluge,
Tofore the dome who is nought teint wit*h* slouth.

The Man of Law maketh aunswer.

OF right & reaso*n* by Natures law,
I ca*n* nought putte against Deth no defe*n*ce,
Ne by my* sleight me kepen or withdraw,
For al my wit and al* my gret prude*n*ce,*

439. al] al yo*ur* H.
442. Against T. 444. of pride] the prouide T.
455. Thogh] Yf T — hath] haue H. 462. lured] alle*u*rede H.
462. sentement] sentence H. 466. the] that H.
467. a quarel] quarels T. 468. done to] to do H.
474. nought] *om.* H — putte] putte*n* T. 475 *is transposed after* 477 T. 475. Ne by my] Nother by no T — or] ne H.
476. and al] and H, for al T.

To [make] appeale from his dredful sentence;
Nor nothyng in earth may a man preserue,
Agayn his might to make resistence:
God quiteth all men like as they deserue.

Death speaketh to Maister John Rikil Tregetour.

MASTER John Rikil, whilom Tregetour
Of noble Henry king of Eng[e]lond,
And of Fraunce the mightie conquerour, —
For al the sleightes and turning of thine hond,
Thou must come nere my daunce to vnderstond.
Nought may auayle al thy conclusions;
For Death, shortly, nother on sea ne lond,
Is not deceiued by none illusions.

The Tregetour maketh aunswer.

WHAT may auayle magike naturall
Or any craft shewed by apparence,
Or course of starres aboue celestiall,
Or of the heauens al the influence
Ageynes* Death to stonde at defence?
Legerdmain now helpeth me right nought.
Fare wel my craft and [al] such sapience;
For Death hath mo maistries than I haue wrought.*

Death speaketh to the Person.

O SIR Curate, that been now here present,
That had your worldly inclinacion,
Your heart entere, your study & entent,
Most of your tithes and* oblacion,
Which should haue be of conuersacion
Mirrour to other, light and examplarie, —
Like your desert[e] shalbe your guerdon,
And to eche* labour due is the salarye.

The Person maketh aunswere.

MAUGER my wil I must[e] condescende;
For death assaileth euery liuely thing
Here in this world[e], who can comprehend
His sodein stroke and his vnware commyng.*
Fare wel [my] tithes, and fare wel mine offring, —
I mot go coumpten in* order by and by,
And for my shepe make a iust reckonyng:
Whom he acquiteth* I hold he is happye.

479. make] make no H.
481. *This stanza is transposed in* H, *following the Minstral.*
485. my] this H. 487. ne] and H.
492. the heauens] heuen H. 493. Ageynes] Against T.
496.] For Death mo maistries hath ywrought T — wrought] wronge H. 500. and] and your T. 504. eche] euery T.
508. commyng] turnyng T.
510. in] by T.
512. Whom he acquiteth] & who that so him quiteth T.

Death speaketh to the Iurrour.

MAISTER Iurrour, which that at assises
And at sheres questes dydst embrace,
Departist* lond like to thy deuises,
And who most gaue most stode in thy grace:
The poore man lost both[e] land and place;
For golde thou couldest folke disherite.
But now let se, with thy teynt[e] face
Tofore the Iudge how [thou] canst thee quite!

The Iurrour maketh aunswere.

WHILOM I was cleped in my countrey
The belweather, and that was not alite.
Nought loued but drad of high & low degree;
For whom me list by craft I could endite, —
Hongen the true and the thefe respite:
Al the countrey by my worde was lad.
But I dare sein, shortly for to write,
Of my death many a man is glad.

Death speaketh to the Minstral.

O THOU Minstrall, that can so note and pipe
Unto folke[s] for to done pleasaunce,
By thi* ryght honde anone I shall the gripe,
With these other to gone vpon my daunce;
There is no scape nother auoydaunce,
On no syde to contraire* my sentence:
For in musike by craft and accordaunce
Who maister is [shal] shewen his science.*

The Minstrall maketh aunswere.

THIS new[e] daunce is to me so straunge,
Wonder diuers and passingly contrarye;
The dredefull footyng doth so oft[e] chaunge
And the measures so oft[e] tymes* varye,
Which now to me is nothyng* necessarye.
If it wer so that I might asterte!
But many a man, if I shal nought tary,
Oft [tyme] daunseth, but nothyng of hert.

Death speaketh to the Labourer.

THOU Labourer, which in sorowe and peyn
Hast lad thy life in [ful] great trauayle,
Ye must eke daunce and therfore nought disdein;
For if thou do, it may the nought auayle.
And cause why that I thee assayle
Is onely this: from thee to disceuer
The false world that can so folkes fayle;
He is a foole that weneth to liuen euer.

513. at] is at H.
515. Departest] Deper didst T — deuises] devise H.
529. can] canst H. 531. thi] the T.
534. contraire] contune T. 536. science] sentence T.
540. tymes] sith T. 541. now to me is] vnto me is now T.
545. Thou] O thou H. 548. if] thoghe H.
552. liuen] liue H.

The Labourer maketh aunswere.

I HAUE wished after Death ful oft,
Albe that I would haue fled him nowe.
I had leauer to haue lyen vnsoft,
In wind & rain to haue gon at the plowe,
With spade & pikoys labored for my prowe,
Doluen and ditched and at the cart[e] gone:
For I may say and tell[e] platlye howe,
In this worlde there is rest[e] none.

Death speaketh to the Frere Menour.

SYR Cordelere, to you mine hande is raught,
To* this daunce [you] to conuay & leade,
Which in your preaching han ful oft ytaught
How that I am most gastful for to drede,
Albe that folke take thereto none hede.
Yet is there none so strong ne so hardye,
But Death dare hym rest and let for no mede;
For Death yche* houre is present and ready.

The Frere maketh aunswere.

WHAT may this be, that in this world no man
Here to abide may haue no suretie?
Strength, riches, nor what so that he can
Of worldly wisedom; all is but vanitie!
In great estate nor in pouertie
Is nothing founde that may from* death defend;
For which I saye to high and low degree,
Wise is the* sinner that doth his lyfe amend.

Death speaketh to the Chylde.

LITLE Faunte, that were but late borne,
Shape in this worlde to haue no pleasaunce,
Ye must with other, that gone here beforne,
Be lad in hast by fatall ordinaunce.
Learne ouer* new to gone [up]on my daunce:
There may none age escape in soth therefro.
Let euery wight haue this in remembraunce,
Who lengest liueth most shal suffer woe.

The Yong Childe maketh aunswer.

A A a, a woorde I cannot speake;
I am so yonge; I was borne yesterday.
Death is so hasty on me to be wreake,
And list no lenger to make no delaie.
I come but now,* and now I go my way;
Of me no more tale* shall [ye] be told.
The wyll of God no man withstonde maye;
As soone dyeth a yong [man] as an olde.

555. haue] haue had H. 557. labored] haue labored H.
558. ditched] dyke H. 560. there] here there H.
562. To] You to H. 563. oft taught H.
567. dare hym rest] dar arest him H. 568. yche] euery T.
574. from] his T. 576. the] that T. 577. Enfante H.
579. Ye] thou H. 581. ouer] of T. 585. A a a a] A A a H.
589. I come but now] I am but now borne T.
590. tale] to tale T.

Death speaketh to the Yong Clerke.

O YE, Syr Clerke, suppose ye to be free
Fro my daunce or your selfe defende,
That wend haue risen vnto high degree
Of benefice or some great prebende?
Who climbeth highest sometime shal desce*n*d.
Let no man grutche ayeines* his fortune,
But take at gree what-euer God him sende,
Which punisheth al when time is oportune.

The Clerke maketh aunswere.

SHALL [I] that am so yong a clerke now die,
Fro* my seruice & haue no bet guerdon?
Is there no gayn[e] ne no better way,
No seurer* fraunchise nor proteccion?
Death maketh alway a short conclusion;
To late ware, when me*n* been on the brynke:
The world shall fayle and all possession;
For much faileth of thing that foles* thinke.

Death speaketh to the Hermite.

YE that haue liued long in wildernes
And there continued long in abstinence,
At the last[e] yet ye mot you dresse,
Of my daunce to haue experience;
For there against may be* no resistence.
Take now leaue of thyne hermitage:
W[h]erfore yche* man aduert to this sentence,
That [in] this life is* no sure heritage.

The Hermite maketh aunswere.

TO liue in desert called solitarie
May again Death haue respite none nor space;
At vnset houre his commyng doth not tary,
And for my part welcom by Goddes grace,
Thankyng hym with humble chere & face
Of al his giftes and great haboundaunce,
Finally affirmyng in this place,
No man is riche that lacketh suffraunce.

Death speaketh agayn to the Hermite.

THAT is wel sayd, and thus should euery wight
Thanken his God & al his wittes dresse
To loue & dread him wit*h* all his heart & might,
Sith Death to escape maye be no sikernes.
As men deserue, God quiteth of rightwisnes
To riche and poore vpon euery syde:
A better lesson there can no clerke expresse,
Than til to-morow is no man sure to abide.

597. highest] hie H. 598. ayeines] ayeinst T.
599. in gree H. 602. Fro] Of T — bet] better T.
604. seurer] better T — nor] ne H. 608. foles] folkes T.
613. may be] is T. 615. yche] euery T — to] *om.* H.
616. is] here is T. 617. To liue] Lyff H.
619. hour] stewyne H. 624. suffraunce] suffisaunce T.
629. quiteth] quite H. 630. To] The H.

Nil ita sublime est, supraq; pericula tendit;
Non sit vt inferius, suppositumq; deo.

¶ The King ligging eaten of Wormes.

YE folke th*a*t loke vpo*n* this portrature,
Beholding here all estates daunce,
Seeth what ye been & what is your nature:
Meat vnto wormes; nought els in substaunce.
And haueth this mirrour aye in reme*m*brau*n*ce,
Howe I lye here whylom crouned [a] kyng,
To al estates a true resemblaunce,
That wormes foode is* fine of our* liuyng.

¶ Machabree the Doctoure.

MANS lyfe* is nought els, platly for to thinke,
But as [a] wi*n*d[e] which is tra*n*sitory,
Passing ay forth, whether he wake or winke,
Toward this dau*n*ce, haueth this in memorye,
Remembryng aye there is no better victory
In this life here than fle syn at the least;
Than shal ye reygne in paradise with glorye.
Happy is he that maketh in heauen his feast!

Yet been there folkemo than sixe or seuen,
Recheles of life in many maner wyse,
Like as there were hell[e] none nor heauen.
Such false errour let euery man despise;

633. folken*e* H.
634. Beholdithe H. 637. haue H — aye] eu*er* H.
640. is] is the T — our] your T.
641. Mans lyfe] Man is T, Man is life H — els] *om.* H.
648. in heuen that maketh H. 652. errours H.

For holy saynctes and olde clerkes wyse
Written contrary, her falsenes to deface:*
To liuen wel, take* for the best emprise,
Is much[e] worth whe*n* men shall* hence passe.

¶ Lenuoye of the Translatoure.

O YE my lordes & maisters all in fere,*
Of auenture th*a*t shal this daunce reade,
Lowely I pray with all myne heart entere
To correct[e] where-as ye se nede;
For nought elles I aske for my mede
But goodly support of this translacion,
And with fauour to suppowaile drede,
Bening[e]lye in your correccioun.

Out of the French I drough it of entent,
Not word by word but folowing in substau*n*ce,
And from Paris to Eng[e]land it sent,
Only of purpose you to do plesaunce.
Rude of langage, I was not borne in Fra*n*ce, —
Haue me excused, my name is Iohn Lidgate;*
Of ther tong I haue no suffisance,
Her curious miters in Englishe to tra*n*slate.

¶ Here endeth the Daunce of Machabree.

654. deface] defame T.
655. lyue H — take] take thys T.
656. shall] should T.
657. my lordes & maisters] maistres and folkes H — fere] feare T.
667 *and* 668 *are transposed in* T.
669 *and* 670 *are transposed in* T. 669. ther] other T.

Emily's Adventures
in Wonderland

Ryan & Julia

CPSIA information can be obtained
at www.ICGtesting.com
Printed in the USA
LVOW13s0337160917
548937LV00024B/1789/P